House Home Family

HOUSE HOME FAMILY

Living and Being Chinese

Edited by

RONALD G. KNAPP

and **KAI-YIN LO**

University of Hawai'i Press, Honolulu
China Institute in America, New York

spatial habitus

© 2005 University of Hawai'i Press
All rights reserved
Printed in China
10 09 08 07 06 05   6 5 4 3 2 1

Library of Congress Cataloging-in-Publication Data
House, home, family : living and being Chinese / edited by Ronald G. Knapp and Kai-Yin Lo.
    p. cm.—(Spatial habitus (Series))
Includes bibliographical references and index.
ISBN-13: 978-0-8248-2858-5 (hardcover : alk. paper)—
ISBN-10: 0-8248-2858-5 (hardcover : alk. paper)
ISBN-13: 978-0-8248-2953-7 (pbk. : alk. paper)—
ISBN-10: 0-8248-2953-0 (pbk. : alk. paper)
1. Architecture, Domestic—China.   2. Vernacular architecture—China.   3. Architecture and
society—China.   4. Architecture—Human factors—China.   5. Symbolism in architecture—
China.   I. Title: Living and being Chinese.   II. Knapp, Ronald G.   III. Lo, Kai-Yin.
IV. China Institute in America.   V. Series.
NA7448.H68 2005
728'.0951—dc22   2004025303

University of Hawai'i Press books are printed on acid-free
paper and meet the guidelines for permanence and durability
of the Council on Library Resources.

Designed by Barbara Pope Book Design

Printed by SNP Leefung Printers Ltd.

Publication of this book was made possible by the generous support of

Ruth and Bruce Dayton

Jack and Suzy Wadsworth

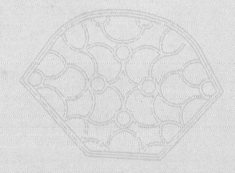

CONTENTS

WEN FONG

Foreword

Looking Back on Chinese Art, Architecture, and History

Fig. F.1. *Chinese vernacular architecture as viewed in Hongcun, Yixian, Anhui.* Source: Photograph by Ronald G. Knapp 2003.

This volume on *House Home Family: Living and Being Chinese,* as well as the preceding symposium (held at China Institute in New York in April 2001), gives us the chance to reflect on issues of identity in traditional and contemporary Chinese culture, as well as to consider the meaning of "living and being Chinese." It is clear that there is a wide range of compelling new interests in traditional Chinese domestic architecture—as evidence of China's rich and complex material culture and social life; as a part of Chinese cultural heritage in urgent need of preservation; and, finally, as a source of what Kai-Yin Lo calls "the chic of Chinese taste."

According to the anthropologist Pierre Bourdieu quoting Friedrich Nietzsche, all scholarly discourse on art suffers from "unconsciously introduc[ing] the 'spectator' into the concept 'beautiful.'" For Bourdieu, works of art become "beautiful" to us spectators only after they are "dead" (1990, 34). In China today, where economic development leads to wholesale displacement of traditional-style dwellings by modern brick and concrete constructions, beautiful structures and furnishings—such as were seen in the China Institute's exhibition "Living Heritage: Vernacular Environment in China" (January–June 2001), and presented throughout this book—are fast disappearing but are, in fact, *not* "dead" (Figure F.1). This is true even as the Chinese people, according to one observation, "seem to be unsentimental about the loss of traditional architecture, viewing demolition—perhaps even the disintegration of traditional culture in general—as the necessary, if unfortunate, accompaniment of modernization" (Knapp 2000, 332). The issue, of course, is to what degree such statements are relevant to China's reality.

Indeed, this is the topic that concerns most of the authors of the essays that follow in *House Home Family.* The destruction of artworks and monuments vital to human history, unfortunately, has gone on continuously throughout the ages in many parts of the world. Some of the most recent shocking reminders of this are the loss of the colossal Buddha statues at Bamiyan in Afghanistan, one 175 feet in height and another 120 feet, as well as the widespread depredation of material culture that has accompanied warfare in Iraq. Bernard Lewis (1996), the leading historian of the Middle East, has written about how the ancient Middle Eastern civilizations were "lost, forgotten and literally buried" as their lands underwent a series of cataclysmic changes from Hellenization, Romanization, and Christianization to Islamization. By contrast, it is said, Far Eastern civilizations have maintained a cultural self-awareness throughout the millennia of their existence. Over the broad sweep of Chinese history and especially over the past two hundred years, however, overlapping cycles of war and national turbulence have brought with them the devastation of China's architectural heritage, including the destruction of grand as well as common residences, temples, ancestral halls, city walls, and pagodas, among many other buildings. Losses during the scorched earth campaigns of the Taiping Rebellion in the middle of the nineteenth century and the more recent senseless depredation during the Great Proletarian Cultural Revolution between 1966 and 1976 are but two major and prolonged examples of such destruction of China's material culture.

When we consider the colossal Buddha statues of North China at Yungang (Figure F.2, second half of fifth century) or Longmen, which stylistically recall the Bamiyan colossi, we know that they are more than just relics of a lost civilization. The carved inscriptions at Longmen of the sixth century (Figure F.3), for example, are models of the epigraphic style of calligraphy that became the basis of an artistic renaissance in modern China. The story of this artistic revival, which began in the nineteenth century and continues today, has to do with "living and being Chinese." It also raises the question of Which Chinese?

In the late nineteenth century, the decline of the empire under the Qing dynasty in the face of the advancing Western military and industrial powers finally alerted the Chinese to the need for modernization. It was the southern Chinese, especially those whose mental horizons had been broadened by their introduction to Western learning in Treaty Ports in South China, who found in the monumental inscriptions of the Longmen cave temples the source for journeying back to the roots of ancient Chinese civilization in the Yellow River basin. Kang Youwei (1858–1927), a native of Canton and leading adviser to the reform emperor Guangxu, for example, concluded that the unification of ancient Chinese scripts was central to the creation of a cultural identity and the stabilization of political institutions (Kang 1936, 1–4). He noted, in particular, the art-historical importance of the monumental epigraphic inscriptions of the Northern Wei period during the sixth century in the development of Chinese calligraphy from the ancient clerical script to the modern standard script. For Kang, who saw modern China's malaise as a spiritual and cultural crisis as well as a political one, the reform of calligraphy was as crucial as governmental and social reforms.

As a youngster growing up in Shanghai in the 1940s, I studied under Master Li Jian (1881–1956), the leading epigraphic-style calligrapher at that time. I came to the United States as a student in 1948 and returned to China for the first time twenty-nine years later in 1977 as a member of the U.S. delegation on Chinese painting under the auspices of the Committee on Scholarly Communication with the People's Republic of China. My life during the intervening years had totally separated me from my ancestral land, which, as a youth growing up in wartime Shanghai, I had never really known or seen. I shall never forget my first, thrilling view of the Forbidden City from the Taihemen. The Imperial City (Figure F.4) is laid out along strict north-south and east-west axes, symbolic of the universe and a pattern that is mirrored in the layout of many Chinese dwellings, as can be noted throughout this book. Looking out on this grand architectural space, I recalled the image of a Han brick design (Figure F.5) from about 200 B.C. that appears in Professor Nelson Wu's book, *Chinese and Indian Architecture*. I realized that here, at last, I had returned to the heart of imperial China, which represented a cyclical worldview in which time and space fed a totally different dimension and meaning from those in our modern way of life. To quote Professor Wu:

> In the Han image, the world of man is a clearing marked off from the unknown on all four sides by symbols in animal forms [the Blue Dragon in the East, Red Phoenix in the South, White Tiger in the West, and Black

Fig. F.2. *Yungang, colossal Buddha at Cave 20.* Source: China Architecture and Building Press.

Fig. F.3. *Epigraphic inscription in a cave at Longmen.* Source: Fong 2001, 22, Fig. 16.

Tortoise in the North]. [Here], time is immeasurable and elastic. . . . Facing south, [with] his feet firmly on the fifth element, the earth, is man. Via a negative approach—not knowing how high is up, how deep is down, and how far away is the end of the earth in each direction—man fixes his position as equidistant from the end of the universe on all sides, and places himself squarely in the middle. He is not represented by any picture, but his desire is expressed clearly in the abstract form of writing. Scattered inside the square world of man are these words: "One thousand autumns and ten thousand years, enduring happiness, never to end!" (1968, 11-12)

Standing in front of Taihemen on that morning in 1977, I understood instantly what it meant for Kang Youwei—and for a part of me—to be "living and being Chinese." Here was the China admired by Voltaire, one of the enlightened thinkers of eighteenth-century Europe. Voltaire thought of China as the model state, led by scholarly mandarins and based on Confucian virtue ethics, bound by reason, not religious dogmas. Only today can we understand how the concept of virtue-ethic can tread a thin line between controlled thought or dogma and spontaneous fanaticism and how it can stand in the way of a modern, pluralistic society in which different ways of thought can coexist.

After coming to this country in 1948, I received an education that prepared me to work on classical Chinese art and art history. My most recent book, a study of modern Chinese painting entitled *Between Two Cultures* (2002), is written with the knowledge that the story of Chinese painting, unlike that of the Egyptian pyramids or the now lost Bamiyan statues, is not over. To be sure, China's struggle for modernization under the impact of Western culture has threatened the very continuity of traditional Chinese culture. Modern Chinese artists, who inherited the traditional Chinese art historiography shaped by a cyclical worldview and based on the rise and fall of dynastic histories, seem to have difficulty in finding meaning and inspiration in traditional art forms. In other words, the traditional representational system does not appear to fit modern Chinese discourse, which sees Western history as a universal model. If they have lost their traditional narrative, how are modern Chinese artists to express themselves?

I believe that Chinese art and architecture, as the China Institute's exhibition called them, are "a living heritage," and it is fair to ask, "Why do we study Chinese art and architectural history?" The lasting achievement of the great Renaissance art historian Erwin Panofsky was his ability to link art with ideas, specifically the

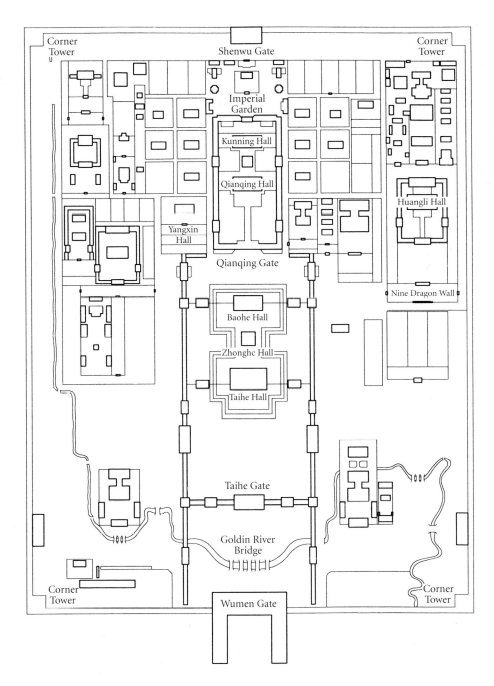

Fig. F.4. *The plan of the Imperial City is laid out along strict north-south and east-west axes, symbolic of the universe.* Source: China Architecture and Building Press.

Fig. F.5. *A Han brick design from about 200 B.C. that shows the* si shen, *or "four deities," representing the four directions.* Source: Wu 1967, Plate 1.

Renaissance belief that man is at the center of the universe (Panofsky 1962). By advancing our knowledge of Renaissance art, Panofsky's interpretive strategy also opens up a whole way of thinking about Western art and history. What can Chinese art and architecture tell us about Chinese history? If European Renaissance art shows that man is the measure of all things, Chinese art, architecture, and related social developments epitomize the equivocal relationship between man and the state. The underpinnings of Chinese art and architectural history—the cyclical rise and fall of dynasties, the polarities between political legitimacy and individual expression, loyalty and dissent, and conservatism and innovation—project a larger pattern of meaning: man's struggle to integrate himself with the ideals of a moral and ethical universe while maintaining a deep respect for history.

I am fully aware of the limitations of my own chosen profession—art history—which Pierre Bourdieu (1990) considers as merely a "pretext for a hagiographic hermeneutics." But I am also a firm believer in the proposition that art comes from art, and I support Kai-Yin Lo's dedication to reviving Chinese decorative arts and Ronald G. Knapp's appreciation of China's traditional domestic buildings and way of life. I have no doubt that the richness of classical Chinese art and architecture over the broad sweep of history is a profound cultural legacy worth exploring and reintegrating into modern Chinese life and culture.

Preface

House Home Family: Living and Being Chinese is the outcome of a multifaceted effort to expand the view of China's domestic architecture by going beyond the buildings themselves to include the families who live within the walls and who infuse their courtyards with life. In early 2001, an exhibition entitled *Living Heritage—Vernacular Environment in China,* which was guest curated by Kai-Yin Lo—brought to New York City's China Institute a rich collection of photographs and objects on this underappreciated and not very well known subject. Inspired by the exhibition's novel approach to the subject matter, the China Institute, in collaboration with the Asia Society, organized the "House Home Family: Living and Being" symposium to complement the exhibition. The symposium brought together scholars and experts in the fields of art, architecture, anthropology, cultural geography, and history to discuss the concept of the house and home, as well as issues of identity in traditional and contemporary Chinese culture. These scholars then transformed their contributions into the rich collection comprising this book. While Tu Wei-ming and Klaas Ruitenbeek participated in the symposium, their schedules did not permit them to contribute to the book. David Faure, James Flath, and Puay-peng Ho were invited to contribute new chapters that fill gaps and make as comprehensive as possible this multidisciplinary book on a range of subjects so far not addressed under one framework. The contributing authors share the editors' belief that a multidisciplinary approach not only elucidates but also stimulates multidimensional explorations and exchanges.

From a layman's enthusiasm derived from collecting Chinese furniture, Kai-Yin Lo's interest has moved beyond the functional, aesthetic, and structural aspects of furniture to its spiritual and symbolic value, its interrelatedness and synergies with the house, architecture, and people in the scheme of the living environment. This book represents another phase in her journey of understanding her heritage and identity.

After documenting China's traditional houses for forty years, Ronald G. Knapp similarly has moved toward explorations of the extraordinarily complex interrelationships of structures and space, the families who create and live in them, and the meaning of related symbols and folklore.

As editors, it is our joint hope that this volume, which offers a macro view of a dynamic and important topic that hitherto has not been addressed, yields a deeper and wider understanding of how Chinese families are organized and why the Chinese construct their living spaces the way they do—what "living and being Chinese" means. It is our intent that by advancing an understanding and appreciation of the vernacular heritage of China, this volume will promote a greater awareness of the need to conserve the buildings and environments that embody the essence and culture of Chinese life. This effort should lead us all to think differently about the complex subject of the "architecture of Chineseness" and provoke a cascade of further questions for future cooperative interdisciplinary exchanges.

Acknowledgments

For support of the January–June 2001 *Living Heritage—Vernacular Environment in China* exhibition, guest curated by Kai-Yin Lo, and the June 2001 "House Home Family: Living and Being Chinese" symposium, held at China Institute in collaboration with the Asia Society, we wish to thank the Wood-Rill Foundation; Fidelity Foundation; Lee Foundation, Singapore; Esquel Enterprises; WLS Spencer Foundation; the Shui On Group; Robert Ellsworth; Friends of the Gallery, and Cathay Pacific Airways. Special thanks for support of the production of this book are offered to Ruth and Bruce Dayton's Wood-Rill Foundation and Jack and Suzy Wadsworth's WLS Spencer Foundation.

The leadership of John R. Curtis, Chair of China Institute Gallery Committee, is gratefully acknowledged, as is the support of other committee members: Maggie Bickford, Claudia G. Brown, Maxwell K. Hearn, Wu Hung, Annette Juliano, H. Christopher Luce, Robert D. Mowry, and Marie-Hélène Weill. At China Institute, the cooperation and organizational support of Willow Hai Chang, Gallery Director; France Pepper, Associate Director of Public Programs; and Nancy Jervis, Vice President and Director of Programs; as well as Torrey Whitman, president at the time of the exhibition/symposium; and Jack Maisano, the current president, have been critical in sustaining the several facets of this project.

The *House Home Family: Living and Being Chinese* manuscript has benefited from the assistance of many scholars, institutions, and individuals, whose encouragement and financial support have made possible a richly produced volume at a modest price. Although the authors themselves took most of the photographs and prepared most of the drawings appearing in this volume, others have been generous in granting us permission to use their previously published illustrations. In addition to the authors, special thanks are offered to Chiu Kwong-chiu, Ivan Chi Ching Ho, Li Yuxiang, Huang Hanmin, Olivier Laude, Jerry Azevedo, LinHui-cheng, and Elizabeth J. Leppman for granting permission to use their illustrations. Permission to use images from their collections was also granted by the Freer Gallery of Art/Arthur M. Sackler Gallery of the Smithsonian Institution; the Nelson-Atkins Museum of Art; the Minneapolis Institute of Arts; the National Palace Museum,

Taibei; the Academia Sinica, Taibei; the Palace Museum, Beijing; the Museum of Chinese History, Beijing; the Asian Civilization Museum, Singapore, the East Asian Library, University of California, Berkeley; and the Morrison Collection, Harvard University. Individual authors in the volume also credit a large number of galleries, private collectors, and published books for the many types of illustrations they have used. To all of these, we offer grateful thanks since the visual dimension of *House Home Family* is equal to the text itself.

Special thanks are offered Yi-fu Tuan, member of the Editorial Advisory Board of the *Spatial Habitus: Making and Meaning in Asia's Vernacular Architecture* series, whose careful reading of the draft manuscript helped the editors to make several critical adjustments in organization. In addition, two anonymous peer reviewers offered abundant comments and insights for each chapter, as well as the book as a whole, that have helped improve it.

At the University of Hawai'i Press, we acknowledge the continuing support of executive editor Patricia Crosby, whose enthusiasm for Asian architecture has brought many titles to Hawai'i's outstanding catalog of books on Asia. Pat's willingness to explore an arrangement with China Architecture and Building Press (CABP), Beijing, led to negotiations with Huang Juzheng and Zhang Huizhen, senior editors at CABP, and the publication of this book in separate English and Chinese editions. Qi Linlin and Dong Suhua of CABP have played key roles in transforming an English manuscript, in the process bringing new insights to a Chinese readership. We are grateful for the assistance of Cheri Dunn, who served ably as managing editor for this project, and Bojana Ristich, who capably copyedited a complicated manuscript.

Special thanks to David Lie for contributing funds in support of another of Kai-Yin Lo's cultural projects; Chiu Kwong-chiu for his customary stimulating views; Yeung Chun-tong and Anita Wong of the University of Hong Kong Museum for their readiness in assisting to locate reference materials; Professor Cheng Pei-kai, Director, Chinese Civilisation Centre, and Professor Zhang Longxi, Director, Centre for Cross-Cultural Studies, both of City University, Hong Kong, for their willingness to share scholarly insights; Professor Leo Ou-fan Lee of Harvard University for his interest in the project; Professor Lu Yuanding for his encouragement; and Nancy Steinhardt for her generosity with time and constructive advice.

Corinne Nyquist and Russell Howitt of the Interlibrary Loan department of the Sojourner Truth Library at State University of New York (SUNY) at New Paltz are commended for their unflagging responsiveness to requests for difficult-to-obtain materials. Emily Trapp, director of the Instructional Media Services department at SUNY New Paltz, was generous in accommodating our need to use equipment and in offering the advice necessary to scan countless slides.

It is important to acknowledge the anonymous craftsmen whose skill and talent created the residences seen throughout this book. The carpenters who fashioned the furniture and the artisans who ornamented the dwellings transformed buildings of many types into objects of beauty as well as meaning. Much appreciation also must be offered to the countless families who opened their homes to our inquiry and permitted the photographing of their daily lives.

Both Xing Ruan and Ronald G. Knapp, the editors of *Spatial Habitus: Making and Meaning in Asia's Vernacular Architecture,* are pleased that *House Home Family: Living and Being Chinese* is the inaugural volume in what we hope will become an important window into the sociocultural, historical, and environmental factors that influence the structure and meaning of vernacular architecture—buildings, settlements, and landscapes—for more than half the world's population.

RONALD G. KNAPP   *1   China's Houses, Homes, and Families*

In China, as elsewhere in the world, it is generally within a house that a family creates its home. However, the term "house" alone is insufficient to encompass the full range of structures and inhabited places within which Chinese families live their lives. Dwellings in China embrace not only houses of many types at fixed locations—rudimentary huts, ordinary rectangular cottages, compact quadrangular courtyard residences, extensive manor complexes, even sumptuous palaces—but also include tents and boats of extraordinary variety that are certainly not "houses" or "buildings" as places of habitation for significant populations who live on the move. "All houses," of course, as Paul Oliver reminds us, "are dwellings, but all dwellings are not houses. To dwell is to make one's abode: to live in, or at, or on, or about a place" (2003, 15). It is important to keep in mind this broader noun and its associated verb—"dwelling" and "to dwell"—even as most of the focus of this book is on "houses," since the terms together suggest the remarkable diversity of habitats and, by extension, variations in the relationships of the people living within them.

Today, as in the past, most of China's population continues to live in relatively simple dwellings that—while they may not be "old dwellings"—are largely rural and the product of building practices and forms rooted in earlier times. Most of these dwellings are nondescript, rather unexceptional, and commonplace in that they are built of seemingly impermanent materials such as friable earth and perishable plant material that are readily accessible. Many, however, are well built, durable, grand in scale, and sometimes even exquisite in terms of their proportions, building materials, and delicately ornamented detail work in stone, wood, and clay. One is tempted to assert that families in China also vary in similar ways in terms of their simplicity or complexity.

Any dwelling reflects some of the countless ways in which available local building materials and building practices can be employed to compose and give shape to both internal and external spaces. Many common Chinese dwellings indeed are quite transitory in terms of their material aspects, and the household must expend substantial time and resources in simply maintaining the roof, walls, and floors against the onslaught of unceasing natural forces. However, a dwelling is more than a mere object that results from the series of practical tasks employed by craftsmen as they add value to raw materials by transforming them into something useful in order to meet a basic need—shelter. Over time, dwellings usually come to transcend the material structures and the defined spaces that give them shape, as the inhabited built form becomes a home, the theater for the lives of those living within it.

In attempting to capture the totality and the interrelatedness of both the artifactual and experiential elements of any dwelling—construction materials, building structure, spatial layout, orientation and siting, ornamentation, furniture and furnishings, calendrical rituals, beliefs and values, cosmo-magical symbolism, gender relations, residential hierarchies, economic status, age rankings, life cycle events (including births, weddings, and deaths), generations living and dead, wear and tear, daily and seasonal activities, and changing patterns of use, among many others, all viewed across the sweep of time—one realizes that there is indeed an *"archiCulture"* manifested in the full range of elusive interrelationships linking house, home, and family.[1] Through conscious as well as subconscious decisions relating to these elements, patterns are situated and life is animated in ways that then transcend even the temporal world of those living within at any given time. There indeed is an "architecture of Chineseness" that links many realms.

There are both commonalities and differences, some obvious and others subtle, through time as well as across space in what are generalized as "Chinese houses, homes, and families." There is, however, insufficient textual, archaeological, or visual evidence to speak confidently about how houses and families have varied over the full sweep of China's history. It is not possible to see clearly, for example, how a particular building form, floor plan, or structural element evolved historically. Major migrations of soldiers and peasants no doubt brought with them building norms that were adapted to new physical and social environments, but evidence is not at hand to understand the process of diffusion of a housing type, ornamental pattern, building ritual, or even family organizational form across China's vast landscape. Yet there is good evidence that many fundamental patterns were in fact set at an early date, with only minor modifications taking place subsequently. Moreover, unlike in the West, where simple houses and churches, for example, are radically different in terms of form and structure, each with unique characteristics that in fact differ over time and vary geographically, in China there is a remarkable consonance among various built forms. It can be stated with some confidence that a "Chinese building has a refreshing directness and functional clarity. . . . The greatest palace hall has a look of being a glorified farm building, and between the painted

Ronald G. Knapp

pavilion on the marble terrace and the humblest thatched hut there was real harmony" (Boyd 1962, 48). The weight of precedence and practical experience, as well as conventionalized building elements, all have contributed to what is admittedly a conservative building tradition in China.

On the other hand, there is significant visual evidence, observable even today, of striking variations in architectural style that are geographical—that is, varying over space—rather than the more elusive historical, varying over time. These variations reflect also the adaptability of conventionalized forms and practices as often practical responses to differing regional conditions. Similarities and differences in what constitutes a family form are not as readily apparent either historically or geographically, and thus it should not be surprising that much of what is "known" about family structure—even families today in China—is based less on actual information and analysis than ideals, myth, and lore.

Strong local or regional idioms indeed characterize dwelling forms throughout China to the degree that it is proper to view Chinese dwellings as "vernacular architecture," common forms whose variations are as diverse as vernacular languages and other aspects of everyday culture. Houses are among the most lasting of all cultural artifacts, even though the materials of which they are made may decay or disintegrate and the circumstances leading to their creation have passed. Like families, which also have local forms, dwellings take shape over time, sometimes growing and at others retrenching, but at all times suggestive of the internal as well as external dynamics giving them shape. Often occupied by successive generations, each house is a "living" entity in the broadest sense in that the household's daily life and cyclical rituals provide the structure for the family's identity. In the past, generation after generation often occupied the same house or adjacent ones at a particular site, showing a remarkable responsiveness to changing needs via ongoing accommodation even within very simple inherited structures.

Up to this point, careful readers will note that the term "Chinese" has been used as if it were a proper ethnonym that describes a relatively homogeneous people living within China. To be more precise, of course, one must recognize that within the geographical and political space known as China, "the Chinese" can be used in only a loose sense. Issues of ethnic identity are strikingly complex in China, reflected certainly by the fact that the People's Republic of China claims to be a "unitary multinational state" comprised of fifty-six recognized nationalities. The distinctive buildings, costumes, languages, and cultural patterns generally, including family structures, are sometimes celebrated and often, but not always, clearly distinguishable.

The majority ethnicity in China is that of the Han, who are sometimes referred to as Han Chinese and who represent some 92 percent of the country's total population. The Han today number nearly 1.2 billion people. In China, there is increasing knowledge of distinctive family structures within some ethnic minority groups, such as the Mongol, Hui, and Uyghur, but for many minorities their families are now mere variants of local Han patterns. Ethnographic research among the Han throughout the country is remarkably limited in regional scope and by historical period.

While ethnicity, like class, gender, and age, is a variable that likely influences how families live and give shape to their buildings, this is a subject that must await further research and is not dealt with to any extent in this book. Moreover, it must also be acknowledged that even among the Han, who are spread across a territory as large as the United States, there is significant diversity in terms of spoken language and other specific cultural characteristics. It is all too often not acknowledged that these subethnic differences among those called Han are actually as great as those among European nationalities, who are usually readily differentiated. China indeed is not a discrete cultural entity with homogeneous patterns of culture within either its contemporary or past political boundaries. *Within* China, regional patterns are as distinctive and frequently as sharp as those among nations in Europe. In addition to their size and topographic complexity, eight Chinese provinces each have populations exceeding 50 million, while France, the United Kingdom, and Italy—well known for their own internal regional differences—each have only about 58 million. Germany, Western Europe's largest nation, has a population of 83 million, while Sichuan, Shandong, and Hebei provinces are even more populous. "China" and "Chinese" are indeed capacious umbrellas to wrap any generalization.

Orally and experientially, individuals, families, neighbors, merchants, artisans, and others pass on practices, forms, and behaviors as traditions. However, the houses and families seen in China today are not the products of a motionless traditional culture in which either "structures" were static or values stagnant. The terms "tradition" and "traditional" are sometimes used to describe inherited forms from the past and even those of recent times, but these terms have limitations in that they are loaded with the ambiguities of agelessness, monotony, and permanence, as well as that they set up a series of false dichotomies. Yi-Fu Tuan asks, "When we say of a building that it is traditional, do we intend approval or, on the contrary, criticism? Why is it that the word 'traditional' can evoke, on the one hand, a feeling of the real and the authentic and hence some quality to be desired, but, on the other hand, a sense of limitation—of a deficiency in boldness and originality?" (1989, 27). His

Ronald G. Knapp

comments are appropriate in considering the nature of "traditional" Chinese families over time. While "traditional" may suggest something that is age-old, customary, perhaps even ageless, in fact the notion of "tradition" is rooted in the literal meaning of "that which is handed down," often a robustly dynamic process whatever its pace.

The term "tradition" is not intrinsically an antonym for "unchanging" and "modern" inasmuch as "traditions" are recreated and remodified as time passes and as buildings and families undergo change. Amos Rapoport, in looking at houses, declares: "Tradition can be seen as a positive or a negative concept, the latter being more common. It can also be neutral. This is the position I adopt. Also, tradition does not need to be rejected or embraced in toto; it is possible to admire traditional artifacts while rejecting the tradition that produced them" (1989, 81). Over time, indeed, some aspects of a tradition may disappear while other aspects persist, revealing a dynamic that results from the practical experiences of people and accumulates as a treasure house of know-how. *House Home Family* demonstrates this in countless ways.

No single or simple explanation is sufficient to tell us how a dwelling space or house in China was or is conceptualized. Like any building, a house protects those inside from the vagaries of weather—heat and cold, rain and snow, humidity, and wind—yet sheltering is only one of the factors contributing to house form. Every dwelling is constructed within a broader environmental context—climate (that is, the long-term conditions of weather), as well as soil, rock, and vegetation that is usually understood to a remarkable degree by the pragmatic habits and sensibility of peoples inhabiting an area. People certainly build their dwellings in order to provide some level of physical comfort—a habitable internal microclimate—within a particular milieu. Moreover, in China the application of *fengshui* (wind and water), or geomancy, reveals not only a sensitivity to recurring patterns of nature and a high level of environmental awareness, but also the *self-conscious* ways in which people give shape to space.

As compelling as are the varying responses to environmental conditions, the complexity of Chinese housing forms arises from the fact that although dwellings may be "typologically similar . . . they are created and sustained through independent evolution and culturally accumulated wisdom" related to local cultural practices (Oliver 1997, xxii). Across what must be accepted as a vastness of time *and* space *and* status, there is indeed a degree of complexity that confounds understanding and generalizing about Chinese houses, homes, and families. Dwellings are the sites of reproduction, work, socialization, and leisure, which together animate the human relationships within a family and often reach beyond an individual house to others in the broader community. Many, indeed perhaps most, Chinese houses have always been mere rectangles of walled spaces, with only the most elemental levels of spatial demarcation. Yet the physical layout of many Chinese houses reveals somewhat complicated patterns of relationships that express age, gender, and generational status, as well as child rearing and care of the aged. All too often, it seems that Chinese houses are in a continuous state of alteration in order to meet the shifting requirements of a household as marriages occur, new members are born, and others die. As the locus of family life, rural and urban houses serve as the arena for a household's production and consumption activities and reflect elements of their religious and cosmological beliefs.

Spurred by accelerating economic development after decades of relative stagnation, Chinese homes and families are undergoing unforeseen and sometimes startling transformations. In many places, old dwellings, including entire villages and complete neighborhoods, have been unceremoniously destroyed. As this century begins, social, economic, and political forces—in the guise of modernization—continue to assail housing and family forms in China, leading to replacement buildings and new human relationships that echo often only in a muffled way the richness of inherited patterns. Chinese give the impression of being largely unsentimental about the loss of their old dwellings and their old family forms, all too ready to supplant them with "modern" forms thought to be more suitable in meeting the needs of daily life as Chinese "progress." Many are grateful that cumbersome and restrictive family and housing forms have been swept aside, unleashing in the process a range of unparalleled personal freedoms and lifestyles.

To some, it is somewhat paradoxical that the onslaught of modernization and globalization, as well as the utter destruction of old dwellings, has not utterly subverted all traditional family patterns and practices. Beginning in the late 1970s and accelerating over the following two decades, new-style housing has increased throughout rural China, first in the peri-urban areas of the country's coastal cities but inexorably appearing throughout the country. While the new style varies from place to place, the Chinese countryside is replete with hybrid dwellings, often multi-storied, boxlike "villas" that are amalgamations of old and new elements. Even in the countryside and in small towns, apartment-like residences for small families are increasingly the norm.

Farming families, once dependent upon the labor of nearby kin, now find non-

Ronald G. Knapp

agricultural family members scattered beyond old communities. Nontraditional building materials and innovations, especially cement and prestressed concrete slabs with tensioned metal rods within them—used instead of wood and earth—have impacted housing designs, just as new notions of privacy and independence threaten traditional family organization. Western, or at least non-Chinese, architectural motifs—including oversized windows, sweeping staircases, and glazed walls of tile—have brought about a proliferation of new housing types, just as media in their many forms have introduced elements of a globalized youth culture with its variant lifestyles to those forming new families and adjusting to those in which they were born. Private beds—that is, those not shared with siblings or parents—and private bathrooms have increased in popularity even as ritual spaces have shrunk in size and prominence. Spaces once focusing on venerating ancestors now serve as entertainment centers replete with the latest electronic gadgetry. Changing aesthetics and expectations, moreover, continue to be stimulated by global media that forthrightly challenge traditional housing designs as well as long-standing ways of living.

Common inherited house forms that well served the needs of generations are also undermined not only by structural changes in the composition of individual families, but also by the fundamental restructuring of work patterns of rural as well as urban residents. As real estate values have climbed in peri urban areas, it has become more difficult for farmers to compete with developers, who are more interested in acquiring land for various purposes than considering any of the old structures on the land. As in post–World War II America and later in Europe, Australia, and Japan, revolutionary trends such as changes in urban structure, rural decline, suburbanization, increasing mobility via personal vehicles, proliferating media messages, and rising incomes have brought about transformations in families and their homes throughout China.

Economic, social, and cultural factors—those that are local as well as those that are truly global—have both corroded and, it must be stated, sometimes enriched long-standing housing and family forms, with intended and unintended consequences. Over the past quarter century especially, demographic and economic developments, such as the somewhat misnamed "One Child Policy" in particular and declining birth rates in general, have greatly impacted family organization, as well as housing forms. Whether the result of state-imposed restrictions on the number of children allowed per family or free choices related to rapid modernization, Chinese families are becoming smaller, although this is not always reflected in the size of Chinese dwellings. As discussed in several chapters, joint families, once characterized by the pooling of income, common residence, and a shared kitchen, are increasingly being replaced by a pronounced conjugalism, in which a husband and wife, with their one or two children, live as an autonomous economic unit in an independent dwelling apart from their parents and married siblings. Yet to some degree, extended families continue to exist as corporate entities in which there are both significant financial cooperation and social linkages, even though the bonds of spatial propinquity have been broken by the demise of coresidential living arrangements.

Some perspective on the tangible and intangible relationships among house, home, and family—that is, the dialectical and mutually productive relationship between the family as a social unit and the house as a concrete artifact—can be gleaned from the twelfth-century observations of Yuan Cai, whose ideas continue to resonate with those living today:

> To build a house is a very difficult project for a family. Even those in their middle years and familiar with the ways of the world are not experts in construction. Naturally it is even worse with those of little experience! Very few of them escape ruining their families.
>
> When a man begins to build, he starts by discussing his plans with a master builder. The master builder's primary fear is that the man will decide not to build when he hears the price, so he keeps the scale small and the cost low. The owner considers the project within his means and decides to go ahead. The master builder then gradually enlarges the scale until the cost has increased several-fold before the house is half done. The owner cannot halt the project in the middle so he borrows money or sells land elsewhere. The master builder, delighted, goes on with more construction, increasing the charges for labor even higher.
>
> I have advised people to build houses gradually over a decade or longer. That way, when the house is done the family will still be as rich as before. First consider the foundation; level the high spots and build up the low ones. Perhaps build the walls and dig out the ponds. Do this in stages, planning to take over ten years. Next consider the scale and the quantity of the materials needed, down to details such as the number of logs for beams and bamboo for fences. Each year buy some according to the numbers needed and have them hewn right away. Plan to have them all ready in ten-odd years. Again, calculate how many tiles and stones you will need; plan to use whatever

Ronald G. Knapp

resources you have left to gradually store them up. Even the wages should not be handled on the spur of the moment. With this method the house can be finished with the family as rich as before. (Ebrey 1984, 320–321)

Throughout this book, each of the authors demonstrates the many bonds linking house, home, and family, sometimes echoing these comments by Yuan Cai. Two major section introductory essays help to guide readers to an understanding of important relationships, as well as the tensions between the past and present, continuity and change. Although there are different emphases from chapter to chapter, each author—whether anthropologist, cultural geographer, architect, architectural historian, art historian, or historian—attempts to focus her/his disciplinary perspective on a number of common objectives related to "living and being Chinese." Seemingly encyclopedic in terms of the range of topics covered, the complexity of the subject matter, and the novelty of the various approaches, this book is not the final word on any topic. Examining regional housing types, environmental adaptations, characteristic floor plans, conventional structural components, frequently used building materials, house-building rituals, and sociocultural elements (including domestic routines, social organization, and ritual spaces), as well as the use of characteristic ornamentation and symbols, the authors raise many topics that demand further study. Some authors are more descriptive than analytical; others indeed place their arguments within a theoretical framework.

NOTES —————

1. Nancy Berliner's use of the term "archiculture" has spurred my use of it here, although I have chosen to alter the spelling to "archiCulture" in order to sharpen its reading. For an examination of the archiCulture of a remarkable dwelling, see her Yin Yu Tang (2003).

Part One

The House

NANCY SHATZMAN
STEINHARDT

2   *The House*

An Introduction

Jia, the title of the first part of the famous autobiographical trilogy by Ba Jin (1905–), is usually translated *Family* in English-language versions, but in the minds of Chinese readers it is simultaneously the story of a multigenerational household, or home; the family members who are born, live, work, struggle, aspire, die, and will be venerated in it; and the architectural structure in which it all takes places. Implicit in the word *jia,* as well, are the ways in which societal, economic, and political events inside and outside the house, home, and family influence or affect one another (Figure 2.1). In traditional Chinese society, house, home, and family and all that they touch are seamlessly interwoven.

Although in the Chinese mind a house has neither purpose nor meaning without the family that makes it a home, it is nevertheless an architectural structure, no matter how simple or complex (Figures 2.2–2.3). That formal aspect of *jia,* the subject of several of the essays in the first section of this volume, allies it with the multimillennial Chinese architectural system. The house, moreover, is the oldest Chinese building form, for all indications are that evolving man built shelter before worship, group living, or kingship became parts of his life.

The House as Chinese Architecture

Not only because of age but structurally as well, the Chinese house has more in common with a Chinese temple or palace than with other architectural forms (Figure 2.4). All three are most often supported by a timber frame made of posts and lintels, or vertical and horizontal pieces of wood, and usually have a noticeably decorative roof (Figures 2.5–2.6). Sometimes the posts are implanted directly into the soil, and other times a stone platform into which the pillars or pillar bases are lodged elevates and separates the wood from the earth (Figure 2.7). In either case, like all wooden architecture, Chinese houses and related buildings are highly subject to fire and deterioration from natural forces. Still, from earliest times until today, houses and temples stand in every village and town of every county of every Chinese province, regardless of climate or terrain. Palaces are less common but may

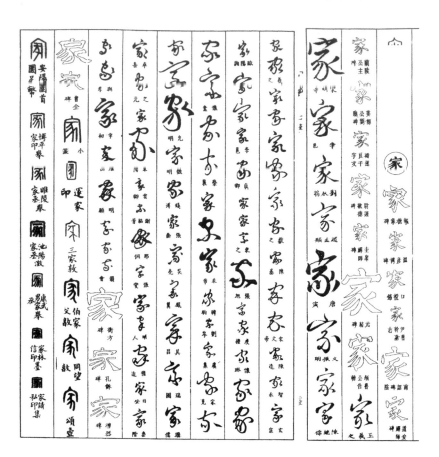

Fig. 2.1. *Just as with the more than one hundred different writing styles for the Chinese character jia—meaning house, home, and family—individual Chinese houses, homes, and families appear quite diverse even as they share common elements.* Source: Fujiwara 1961, 295–296.

be urban or rural, the latter usually "traveling palaces," or places the Chinese ruler stopped on journeys through his territory.

Urban environments, or cities, comprise the fourth Chinese structural type. Even they—especially the parts that were planned from the inception of a city—share a remarkable number of similarities with houses, temples, and palaces. Like individual buildings, planned Chinese cities conform to fundamental principles of orientation toward a cardinal direction, most often south; and expansion can occur in any direction but always horizontally and often symmetrically. As seen in the air view of the Forbidden City in Figure 2.8, principal buildings are arranged facing courtyards, and space is enclosed by both courtyard perimeters and walls beyond them. No building is independent. Rather, each is interrelated with other buildings. Orientation and symmetry dominate a Chinese house, palace, temple, and city by the placement of an ancestral shrine, throne, altar, or palace-city, respectively, in

Nancy Shatzman Steinhardt

Fig. 2.2. *Although limited in terms of scope, detail, and materials, Chinese paintings can serve as a partial record of rural and urban social life in the past. With myriad details that are skillfully depicted, the lives of individuals, groups, and families are sometimes shown. Built with fragile materials, this compact rural dwelling embodies structural principles and spatial forms characteristic of much grander residences.* Source: Qiao Zhongchang, *Su Shi's Second Poem on the Red Cliff.* Handscroll, ink on paper, 11.6 in. x 18 ft. 8 in. Northern Song dynasty, 1123. Used with the permission of the Nelson-Atkins Museum of Art, Kansas City, Missouri. (Purchase F80-5.) Photo credit: Robert Newcombe.

Fig. 2.3. *In this Cultural Revolution–era peasant painting, which highlights the varied sideline activities carried out by farming families in Huxian, Shaanxi, the external building elements of an unpretentious northern rural dwelling compound are quite clearly represented.* Source: Peasant Paintings 1974, 55.

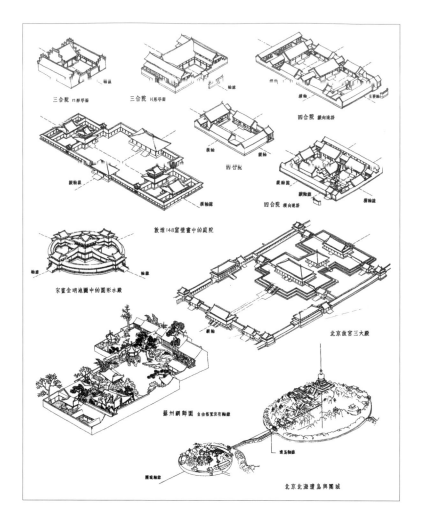

三合院 ∏形平面   三合院 H形平面   四合院 縱向連接

西營院

四合院 橫向連接

敦煌148窟壁畫中的庭院

宋畫金明池圖中的圓形水殿

北京故宮三大殿

蘇州網師園 自由佈置沒有軸線

北京北海瓊島與團城

2.5

2.6

Fig. 2.4. *Perspective drawings of homes, gardens, and palaces show similarities in terms of enclosure, axiality, symmetry, and hierarchy.* Source: Liu 1993, 12.

2.7

◄ **Fig. 2.5.** *Main Hall of Nanchan Monastery, Mount Wutai, Shanxi province, 782. This humble Buddhist hall on the sacred peak Wutaishan is supported by twelve vertical pillars joined by beams. The pillars provide the support for the beams and posts that frame its roof.* Source: After Chinese Academy of Architecture 1982, 65.

◄ **Fig. 2.6.** *Great Buddha Hall, Baoguo Monastery, Yuyao county, Zhejiang, 1013. Although its roof eaves slope more dramatically than those of Nanchan Monastery Main Hall (Fig. 2.5), the bracket sets and roof frame of the Great Buddha Hall are supported by the same kind of wooden system, vertical pillars connected by tiebeams, employed in the humbler hall of Nanchan Monastery.* Source: Photograph by Nancy Shatzman Steinhardt.

Fig. 2.8. *Overview of Forbidden City, Ming-Qing periods. The dominance of axiality, symmetry, and orientation to the four directions is especially evident when seen from the air. Although China's most perfectly planned city, most other capitals share these fundamental features of imperial planning. The interconnected courtyard residential compound of the imperial family was located in the northwest quadrant of this complex.* Source: China Architecture and Building Press.

◄ **Fig. 2.7.** *Hall of Pure Brightness, Daoist Monastery of Eternal Joy, Ruicheng, Shanxi, thirteenth century. The Hall of Pure Brightness does not boast the most complicated wooden structure or roof among the halls at this monastery. Still, it is important enough in the Chinese structural hierarchy to be elevated on a high platform, a feature rare in Chinese residential architecture.* Source: Photograph by Nancy Shatzman Steinhardt.

Fig. 2.10. *Interior of Hall of Great Harmony, Forbidden City, Beijing. Through the multi-millennial history of China, the emperor has sat on his throne in the Hall of Great Harmony or its predecessors in earlier Chinese imperial cities. This grandest and most elaborated space is nevertheless the equivalent of the table or altar for ancestral portraits in a Chinese house.* Source: China Architecture and Building Press.

Fig. 2.9. *Central ancestral room in house in Lugang, Taiwan. Whether the central room is of three or five bays, the focus of a traditional Chinese house is a ceremonial table on which are displayed pictures of a family's deceased ancestors or tablets with their names.* Source: Photograph by Nancy Shatzman Steinhardt.

the center or back-center, oriented toward the entryway (Figures 2.9–2.12). Houses, temples, and palaces are focal points in family compounds, monasteries, and imperial cities respectively, the building complexes spatially defined according to the same principles as the individual units. As shown in Figure 2.12, all the rules are prescriptive and idealized. Yet from smallest residence to greatest city, architecture is touched by man and nature, so that excess or lack of money, war, conquest, or change of ruler, for example, have led to houses, temples, palaces, and cities that respond to pragmatic or natural forces. An example of this response is that the southeastern and northeastern corners of the otherwise nearly perfectly planned Sui-Tang capital jutted beyond the outer wall to incorporate a pond and parkland (later a palace) respectively.

In addition to these four forms, the Chinese traditionally have viewed their architecture with between two and four more building types. Tombs are the fifth building type. Since ancient times, Chinese tombs have followed the structural and design patterns of residential architecture. The resemblances range from the arrange-

Nancy Shatzman Steinhardt

◄ **Fig. 2.11.** *Interior of Dragon King Temple, Guang-sheng Monastery, Hongdong county, Shanxi, ca. 1324. The highly polychromed statues and painted walls behind them are only a backdrop for the Dragon King, the focal point of worship in this Daoist temple. Whether painted in the central position on the back wall or elevated as a statue on the central altar, the main deity in a Chinese Buddhist or Daoist temple is equivalent in terms of status to the emperor on his throne in the Hall of Great Harmony or the deceased ancestors represented in the central room of a Chinese house.* Source: After pamphlet *Guangshengsi*, n.d.

Fig. 2.12. *Plan of Sui Tang capital Daxing-Chang'an, late sixth through early tenth centuries. In spite of the extensive scale of a city compared to a palace, temple, or house, the palace-city inside the urban walls is the equivalent of the emperor's throne, a deity's altar, or ancestor portraits in the smaller spatial environments. Also evident in a planned city such as Chang'an in Tang times (618–907) or its direct predecessor Daxing of the Sui dynasty (581–618) are the principles of four-sided enclosure, cardinal orientation, and axiality.* Source: Steinhardt 1990, 11.

West Inner Park

Daming Gong
大 明 宫

Palace-City
太 极 宫

Imperial-City

West Market

Xingqing Gong

East Market

Qujiang Pond

0   1000M

Fig. 2.13. *Interior of Tomb No. 61, Shaogou, Luoyang county, Henan, Western Han dynasty. The underground tomb, whose walls are made of hollow, patterned bricks or covered with paint, is an early surviving example of residential space transposed into an environment for the afterlife. Today the tomb can be seen in the Luoyang City Tomb Museum.* Source: After Huang and Guo 1996, 90.

Fig. 2.14. *Relief sculpture of tomb occupants and servants in Macun Tomb No. 4, Jishan, Shanxi, Jin dynasty. Carved into a wall niche, the seated tomb occupants, with servants on either side and decorative floral backdrop, are the focus of their burial chamber. They are posed and positioned in their house of the afterlife as they would be in the central ancestral room of their descendants' house.* Source: After Cui 1999, 85.

▼

ment of rooms in accordance with patterns of residential space above ground to depictions of the deceased as both ancestors in a focal point on a tomb wall and engaged in activities of daily life that occur inside rooms of the family house. Built for all eternity and thus of more permanent materials than architecture above ground—usually brick, sometimes stone, and sometimes with wooden parts—tombs provide some of our best evidence of residential architecture (Figures 2.13–2.15). Not only have tombs been built with the same attention to *fengshui* as houses (to be discussed in greater detail in Chapter 5), but through the imitation of wood they also share the fundamental support system of columns or posts and lintels and floorboards, as well as more decorative features, from bracket sets and vaulted ceilings (Figures 2.16–2.17) to screens and other furniture, decoration with symbolic

Nancy Shatzman Steinhardt

Fig. 2.16. *Ceiling of Tomb of Dong Ming, Houma, Shanxi, Jin dynasty. Some of the most lavish examples of carved-brick tomb interiors of the thirteenth century survive in ceilings. Like the exaggerated architectural decoration in Fig. 2.15, it is believed this ceiling is more typical of Chinese temple architecture of the period than of residential space. The ceiling thus provides excellent evidence of the desire of Chinese families to create more complex and dramatic spaces for the afterlife than for their residences.* Source: After Cui 1999, Plate 35.

▶

Fig. 2.15. *Wall of Macun Tomb No. 4, Jin dynasty. Covering the walls and ceiling of the tomb, in which the occupants are portrayed in a niche (Fig. 2.14), are detailed replicas of wooden architecture of a house. The highly elaborated bracketing, roof ornamentation, and sculptures of figures and animals were intended to provide comfort and entertainment for the tomb occupants in the afterlife. It is unlikely that interior residential space of thirteenth-century China was decorated to this extent.* Source: After Cui 1999, Plate 5.

Fig. 2.17. *Interior detail of tomb of Shi Zhe, Zhangzi county, Shanxi, Jin dynasty. The bracket sets in the tomb show correspondences to bracketing described in the twelfth-century Chinese architectural manual,* Yingzao fashi *[Building standards]. Decoration on the bracket members can be traced to patterns in the same book.* Source: After Su 1989, 174.

Fig. 2.18. *Interior of tomb in Dalicun, Houma county, Shanxi, Jin dynasty. The different floral types on the lattice window follow the forms of actual garden design seen in Fig. 2.19.* Source: After Cui 1999, Plate 31.

Fig. 2.19. *View of lattice windows in Liuyuan Garden, Suzhou, Ming dynasty. Not only is the Chinese garden, tandem to the Chinese house above ground, transferred to the funerary environment, but also the comparison between Figs. 2.18 and 2.19 shows that patterns of garden architecture are maintained over centuries.* Source: Cheng 1999, 266.

and aesthetic content, and garden design—even variety in flowering plants and lattices to mimic views (Figures 2.18–2.19).

Probably constructed by the same people who built houses, tombs are extensions of the house, home, and family and are occupied by the ancestors when the subsequent generation comes to occupy the house. It is not coincidence that the most common Chinese phrase for describing the architectural details of a tomb is *fang mu (jie)gou,* or "imitation of the timber (structural) skeleton." Yet although subject to some of the same terrestrial disasters as architecture above ground and never spared from destruction by underground water, one important difference between house and tomb cannot be denied: changes in family fortune, new or

Fig. 2.20. *Stone sarcophagus of member of Tang royal family, Tang dynasty. Shaanxi Provincial Museum, Xi'an. One of the closest correspondences between temple and funerary architecture is found in a comparison of the Main Hall of Nanchan Monastery (Fig. 2.5) and this sarcophagus.* Source: Shaanxi Provincial Museum, Xi'an.

▶
Fig. 2.21. *Wooden sarcophagus excavated in Tomb No. 7, Yemaotai, Faku county, Liaoning, Liao dynasty. Liaoning Provincial Museum. The similarities between architecture above and below ground are maintained through the course of tomb construction in China. When sarcophaguses are made of wood, such as the example here, more decorative roofs with more sharply sloping eaves than is possible in stone (Fig. 2.20) are achieved.* Source: Photograph by Nancy Shatzman Steinhardt.

Fig. 2.22. *Copper sarcophagus excavated in tomb in Xiangyun Dabona, Yunnan. This extraordinary sarcophagus from a province of China populated by so-called ethnic minorities may represent a regional style of house occupied by the tomb occupant. In every part of China from every time period, architecture and objects preserved in tombs continue to inform us about life above ground in instances (like this) when there are no known corresponding examples above ground. It is unlikely a house in any part of China was made of copper, but the solid walls and roof style may well have been built in Yunnan province.* Source: Unknown.

reduced status, and progeny—forces that cause alteration or augmentation of the Chinese house—do not affect tombs. A tomb is the embodiment of a family's prosperity and values at the time it is sealed. For this reason, it was sometimes common for a family to spend more time and money on a tomb than a house with the purpose of projecting a family's improved situation in the future. Finally, just as tombs follow patterns of residential complexes above ground, sarcophaguses appear to reproduce small dwellings and occasionally temples (Figures 2.20–2.22).

The sixth category of Chinese architecture is the garden, sometimes an extension of the house or the tomb, as seen above in Figures 2.19 and 2.20. Chinese gardens can also be repositories for rustic forms of house architecture, such as a teahouse that takes the form of a hut or pavilion with a thatched roof (Figure 2.23).

Rock-cut architecture may be a seventh category. Or cave temples may be considered monastery architecture, cave dwellings as residential architecture, and tombs carved into rock as funerary architecture. Similarly, pagodas, a uniquely Asian form, may be considered a structural type because they are easily distinguished from

Nancy Shatzman Steinhardt

Fig. 2.24. *Illustration of residential architecture from encyclopedia* Shilin guangji *[Compendium of a forest of affairs], issued at the Yuan court. With few examples of Chinese houses surviving from the fourteenth century, illustrated encyclopedias such as this one are invaluable sources of information about interior residential space at that time.* Source: Chen 1300s, n.p.

Fig. 2.25. *Illustration of residential architecture from* Shujing tushuo *[Illustrations and notes to the Classic of History], Qing dynasty, 1644–1911. Similar to Fig. 2.24, this illustration from a woodblock-printed text offers a glimpse of Chinese house style, in this case of a form that can be confirmed by extant buildings.*

larger, lower temples, or they may be viewed as part of the broader category of religious construction. No matter how these last two types are perceived by an individual Chinese or presented in scholarly literature, rock-carved architecture shares with other Chinese building complexes principles of orientation, quadrilateral ground plans, and sometimes enclosure; the pagoda or pavilion can be the focal point in a monastery whose other buildings are positioned symmetrically with respect to it, or it can be paired to create or enhance symmetry in a religious complex in the manner of side rooms with respect to the ancestral chamber of a Chinese house.

Finally, a nonstructural aspect of Chinese architecture, writings, is sometimes considered a category of Chinese building. Since the earliest investigations of Chinese architecture, researchers have turned to texts, some of them illustrated, to learn about rules and principles of Chinese construction and to see pictures of Chinese buildings (Figures 2.24–2.25). Since the 1950s, the written evidence has been studied together with excavated foundations and other remains to provide increasingly accurate knowledge about all forms of Chinese architecture. By now most building types can be documented through three or four thousand years of history.

In spite of the fact that a Chinese house adheres to the spatial and structural principles of this multimillennial, well-documented building tradition, visually

2.24

2.25

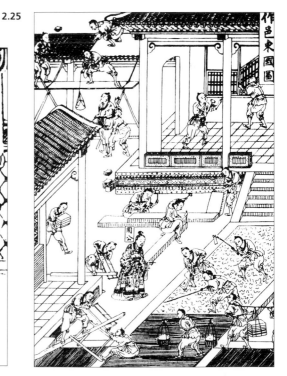

it is more diverse than any other Chinese architectural form. Several distinctions account for this. Houses, first of all, are more directly touched by nonimperial and nonaristocratic life than other architectural forms. Lower echelons of Chinese society have always worshiped in temples, but only infrequently have they played major roles in their design. Tomb construction might be abandoned or scaled down by economic or political necessity, even for a family member who lived in an aristocratic-style house. Chinese houses have been built with the greatest possible range of materials—not only wood, earth, stone, and ceramic tile, which dominate other architectural forms, but also metal, straw, animal skin, coral, and every possible decorative fabric. Often the choices are direct results of climate, topography, and family income, factors more likely to be overridden by ceremonial concerns in religious or palatial construction than in the building of a house. With their first allegiance to home and family rather than religion or statecraft, housing styles change more than other Chinese forms such as temples or palaces. Whereas a temple may gain aura and recognition through an archaic style and architectural details that recall the past and a palace may elicit respect through forms that have been symbolic of emperorship for ten generations, those who live in a house want the most modern conveniences they can afford. Historically, this has also meant that preservation is a much higher priority for religious architecture and a comparatively low priority for residential buildings. Old houses may be interesting to look at or study, but even preserved they have been much less desirable for daily living than newer versions.

Because of these factors, it is rare to find a Chinese house that is more than two hundred years old. Still, old-style houses remain in all parts of China. Sometimes they represent the most efficient architectural solutions for the family homes they are. Outside China's major cities in particular, the Chinese house is probably second only to costume in its visual declaration of geographic location and ethnicity. More than forty residential architectural styles that were present in Chinese vernacular architecture of the last dynasty, the Qing (1644–1911), remain today (Figure 2.26). Many are associated with specific ethnic groups sometimes known as "minorities," most of which populate China's autonomous regions but are scattered throughout the country as well.

Although it may not be surprising that the courtyard-style house, a type whose history can be traced to the last millennium B.C.E., is dominant among the broadest range of China's populations, it may be more impressive that more than twenty varieties of courtyard-style houses can be found, a subject discussed further in Chapter 3. The shapes of courtyards in central Shanxi, for example, have tended

Nancy Shatzman Steinhardt

to be rectangular as opposed to square; those in southeastern Shanxi have two- or even three-storied buildings on the sides of the courtyard; and in central Shaanxi the roofs of side rooms of courtyard-style houses slope only on one side. In Ningxia, courtyards of the Hui nationality tend not to be oriented toward the south, and in Jilin, courtyard houses used by people of Manchu descent are generally oriented westward and have heatable platforms on three sides that address the needs of Manchurian winters. Like much architecture in Qinghai, courtyard-style houses have been made of mud-earth and topped by flat roofs. Residences of the Bai in Yunnan have four courtyards enclosing a large, central one, all five with their own skywells. In Yunnan, courtyard-style residences of the Naxi people also often have five courtyards, with covered arcades in front. Houses whose dominant features are skywells remain in Jiangsu, Zhejiang, Anhui, Jiangxi, Hebei, Hunan, Fujian, and Guangdong—in other words, mainly in southeastern China. Among them, too, are variations and unique styles, such as *yikeyin,* or "one seal." A form of multistoried courtyard structure that houses multiple families within it and resembles a fortified compound may be circular or quadrilateral in plan. These odd shapes are found among the Hakka (Kejia) people in Fujian, Guangdong, and southern Jiangxi. In Yongding county of Fujian, another variety of grouped courtyard houses has hip-gable roofs of different heights.

In addition to courtyard-style houses, the Chinese countryside in particular is marked by subterranean houses and houses raised on stilts, both forms traceable to neolithic times, as well as tents and block houses. Among each of these, too, there is variety. Subterranean houses can be pit-style or excavated into caves, and inside they range from one room to courtyard-style with vaulted spaces. Most subterranean dwellings in China today are in Shanxi, Henan, Shaanxi, and Gansu. Houses elevated on stilts are in the subtropical southeastern and southwestern regions, particularly Guangxi, Guizhou, Yunnan, Hainan, and Taiwan. Eight nationalities—the Dai, Zhuang, Dong, Miao, Li, Jingpo, De'ang, and Buyi—build variants of houses raised on stilts. Some, such as the Dong, extend the architectural style to other building forms such as drum towers. Residential portable tents, often with wooden frames and felt exteriors, are found in Inner Mongolia, Xinjiang, Qinghai, and Gansu, today among Mongols, Khazaks, and Tajiks and for the last several millennia among their forebears. Multistory houses made of stone blocks are found in Tibet, Sichuan, and Yunnan, another example of a style used for both residential and religious construction. The Uyghur population of Xinjiang mainly builds mud dwellings with flat roofs.

Fig. 2.26. *Among the forty different housing styles found in China are significant regional variations of the dominant Han population, as well as distinctive dwelling types for many of the fifty-five designated national minorities, who largely populate the peripheral areas of the country.*

Fig. 2.26a–d.

a. *Citadel-like rammed-earth dwellings in southwestern Fujian include square, round, and a variety of other shapes. Taxia village, Shuyang township, Nanjing county, Fujian.* Source: Photograph by Ronald G. Knapp 1990.

b. *Model of a Beijing* siheyuan, *or quadrangular courtyard dwelling.* Source: Ma 1999, 9.

c. *Canalside residences similar to this one in Suzhou, Jiangsu, are common in the Jiangnan region of the lower Chang Jiang (Yangzi River).* Source: Photograph by Joseph C. Wang.

d. *Entry to a Bai nationality dwelling, Xizhou, Yunnan.* Source: Photograph by Olivier Laude.

a ▶

b ▶

◀ c

d ▶

f ►

e ▲ g ►

Fig. 2.26e–g.

e. *Courtyard dwellings excavated into the loessial soil in Qianxian, Shaanxi.* Source: Photograph by Ronald G. Knapp 1984.

f. *Even magnificent manor complexes were constructed to appear like cave dwellings. Wang family manor, Lingshi county, Shanxi.* Source: Photograph by Ronald G. Knapp 2003.

g. *Stone dwelling in Chamdo, Eastern Tibet, now Western Sichuan.* Source: Photograph by Olivier Laude.

Fig. 2.26h–i.

h. *Cottage-like structures with thatched roofs were once common in the rural areas of China. Jinjiawan, Dongling district, Shenyang, Liaoning.* Source: Photograph by Elizabeth Leppman 1994.

i. *Foreign influence in rural dwellings, northeastern Guangdong.* Source: Photograph by Ronald G. Knapp 2000.

h ▶

i ▼

Fig. 2.26j–k.

j. *Farmhouse set among the fields, Taoyuan, Taiwan.* Source: Photograph by Ronald G. Knapp 1994.

k. *High and wide verandas with deep, overhanging eaves are common in dwellings in southwest China. Birthplace of Deng Xiaoping. Paifang village, Guang'an township, Sichuan.* Source: Photograph by Ronald G. Knapp 1994.

k ▼

Fig. 2.26l. *This view from a side court shows the elevated veranda and main structure of a northern* siheyuan *courtyard house, the home of the famous opera singer Mei Lan-fang. Beijing.* Source: Photograph by Ronald G. Knapp 2003.

Fig. 2.26m. *A complex inverted horseshoe-shaped dwelling, this structure has multiple courtyards and a labyrinth of rooms. Meixian, Guangdong.* Source: Photograph by Ronald G. Knapp 2000.

Fig. 2.26n. *Reputedly a Yuan dynasty (1279–1368) structure, this impressive two-story residence— sadly unrestored—continues to be used as a barn for storage. Cheng-kan village, Shexian county, Anhui.* Source: Photograph by Ronald G. Knapp 2003.

The staggering variety, in contrast to palatial and religious architecture, is perhaps the greatest appeal of Chinese houses. It is also the reason Ronald G. Knapp titles his essay in Chapter 3 "In Search of the Elusive Chinese House." As Knapp explains, no single style defines the Chinese house, yet every spatial and structural aspect of the house is purely and usually uniquely Chinese, enough so that it is possible to define archetypes and through them better understand the range of variations.

Joseph C. Wang takes the reader outside the house and into its garden. Syntactically and semantically, he argues, the garden is as integral to the house as the writings that validate the house; the manuals, almanacs, and amulets that determine the house's potential as a home and the fortune of its family; and the furniture that completes its practical and philosophical purposes. Like aesthetics and furniture, discussed in essays by Cary Y. Liu and Kai-Yin Lo, the Chinese garden is the locus for individual creativity. All three are necessary and integrated aspects of the transformation of the physical structure of a house into a home. Although every Chinese has not been able to afford a plot of land; or to build a house, furnish the interior, and decorate the outside; or the extra land to build a garden, ideally a Chinese man aspires to all of these to ensure current and future success. All provide or enhance the setting for a good life. Thereby, all can be conceived of in idealized terms.

Ronald G. Knapp then elucidates the most intriguing body of writings about the Chinese house and Chinese architecture more generally, texts that deal with *fengshui* and truly deserve the description "elusive." The implications of *fengshui* texts, however, are more directed to a family's prosperity than the belles lettres, inscriptions on paintings, descriptions in Chinese novels, or even the Chinese classics, literary works that, according to Cary Liu, are interwoven in the aesthetic of the Chinese house. Chinese writings about siting are as familiar to those who build Chinese houses as are the construction tools: both determine the durability and longevity of the future and the family who reside in them. This is true even if the household is illiterate, for like the house amid the universe of Chinese forms, *fengshui* writings emerge from all other Chinese literature as the ones that inform us primarily about the nonelite human component in Chinese society. The *fengshui* system brings the builder and the site into the interactive dynamics of family and society implied by *jia*.

Cary Y. Liu builds on the formal features of the house described and explained in Knapp's essay on the elusive Chinese house to explore the aesthetic and philosophical aspects of Chinese vernacular architecture. He proposes that, like Chinese architecture, not only is the Chinese house intimately linked to writings, but also the uniqueness of this link allows us to understand both the philosophy behind and aesthetic results of Chinese house construction. He argues, in fact, that the literary association is crucial to successful completion of construction.

Kai-Yin Lo's essay takes the reader inside the house, examining furniture as a means of exploring the architectural aesthetics and their linkages with home and family investigated by Liu through writings. Lo explains how furniture embodies the visual and cultural aspects of the room and house that contain it.

Finally, as we learn from Nancy Berliner's essay, only recently has historic preservation been integrated into the vocabulary of Chinese vernacular architecture. Because of the primary practical function of a house, preservation has been slower to come to Chinese houses than to other architectural forms. Yet as Berliner demonstrates, it is the only hope of guaranteeing that old houses and all that they symbolize will continue to stand alongside those eternal features of the Chinese landscape that determined their placement in the first place.

The house, the garden, proper *fengshui,* aesthetics, furniture: is any of them a requirement for a good or successful or fulfilled Chinese life? Only the house itself. Wherever it stands, the house is the single most profound symbol of the Chinese family. It is a symbol as powerful as the Great Wall is for the country. It is thus fitting that its philosophical, textual, aesthetic, and symbolic aspects, interior and exterior, receive the kind of elucidation that follows.

3   In Search of the Elusive Chinese House

In spite of the seeming age—even agelessness—of countless buildings across the vastness of China, actual structures of great antiquity still standing are comparatively rare. While this statement is especially true of houses and other common buildings that are constructed principally of transitory materials such as wood and earth, there is nonetheless a timeless quality to the *idea* of what constitutes a Chinese dwelling—as is the case with other built forms such as palaces, temples, and even cities. Such notions are preserved in classical texts, substantiated in archaeological digs, replicated as pottery models and engraved on bricks in Han dynasty tombs, and detailed in novels, as well as portrayed in Song, Yuan, Ming, and Qing paintings. These words, depictions, and models offer suggestive evidence of the richness and diversity of ancient buildings presumably no longer in existence while also suggesting details about framing and wall systems, elevations and ground plans, roof and fenestration patterns, and ornamental motifs that enhanced living space, in addition to giving tantalizing clues to the ways of living in China in times past. To some observers, Chinese dwellings have an apparent ahistorical character, an obvious continuity, even a timelessness, in both form and structure that are in striking contrast to the progressively changing styles over time that are characteristic of European and American domestic architecture (Tuan 1969, 109). Yet it is a myth that Chinese architecture has not evolved over time and that it is relatively homogeneous in style from place to place, even though detailed studies have not provided specific evidence (Steinhardt et al. 2002, 3–4).[1]

It is nonetheless curious and intriguing that images of dwellings *appreciated as art* until rather recently were so strikingly different from what scholars and others actually saw in the parts of China in which they lived and worked. This is especially true for distinctive multistoried dwellings and fortresslike structures, which had been known from excavated tomb models as having existed two thousand years ago but whose form presumably vanished mysteriously at some time in the distant past (Figure 3.1). Moreover, it was not until the twentieth century that any of the thousands of surviving dwellings from the Ming (1368–1644) and Qing (1644–1912) periods—perhaps even some from the Yuan (1279–1368)—scattered throughout the country were even noticed. Precious few were recorded, and almost none were

Fig. 3.1a–d.
a–b. *The Han dynasty pottery* mingqi, *or funerary model of a fortress structure, found in an excavation in Guangdong province, echoes the substantial structure seen today in Hongkeng village, Yongding county, Fujian province.* Source: (a) Guangzhou 1983, 93; (b) photograph by Ronald G. Knapp 2000.

b ▶

a ▶

c ▲

c–d. *With its corner towers, this Han dynasty* mingqi *has some resemblance to the imposing fortress in Xinyou village, Longnan county, Jiangxi province.* Source: (c) Guangzhou 1983, n.p.; (d) photograph by Ronald G. Knapp 1993.

d ▲

heralded. As a result, it is only over the past quarter century that the diversity and distinctiveness of Chinese housing forms have begun to be realized. In recent decades, areas once considered remote and inaccessible to outsiders have become increasingly visited, sketched, photographed, and written about by researchers, as well as by even casual visitors. Dwelling types that were once thought to have vanished have reemerged from obscurity. This journey of discovery, the pursuit of once elusive Chinese houses, is the focus of this essay, as is a discussion of some of the common features of Chinese dwellings across space and through time. As the twenty-first century begins, it is important to realize that what is known about Chinese houses has only a very recent history, which has been complicated by the convoluted history of China during the twentieth century.

Until well into the first quarter of the twentieth century, only sporadic, disconnected, and tantalizing views and descriptions of "the homes of the Chinese" appeared in the writings of missionaries and adventurers who wrote about their travels and lives in rural and urban China. Chinese academics themselves first began to write about common Chinese houses only after 1937, as the extraordinary and intrepid migration of government, academic, and industrial personnel took place from the developed areas of northern and eastern China to the less developed mountain-ringed redoubts of China's southwest. "The difficult and exhausting conditions of travel from Peking to Kunming [in China's southwestern province of Yunnan] across fifteen hundred miles of back country, putting up at night in villages, had opened the eyes of [academics] to the special architectural significance of Chinese dwellings. The distinct features of such dwellings, their relationship to the lifestyles of the occupants, and their variations in different areas of the country were suddenly obvious and interesting" (Fairbank 1994, 110). Still, only a miniscule number of specific observations and survey reports was published over the next decade and a half, and it was not until the late 1950s that books, however slim, began to appear that called attention to extraordinary dwellings in once obscure areas.

First came architectural historian Liu Dunzhen's *Zhongguo zhuzhai gaishuo* in 1957 [Introduction to Chinese dwellings], followed in the same year by Zhang Zhongyi and others' *Huizhou Mingdai zhuzhai* [Ming dynasty houses of Huizhou], small volumes on large and important topics. These two books revealed cultural landscapes of heretofore unknown dwelling types that piqued the interest of some architectural cognoscenti but hardly caused a ripple in the thinking of others. Liu's book focused on dwellings he and others had visited that reached back to the Ming dynasty and included a very brief overview of houses from the neolithic period to

Fig. 3.2a–b.

a. *Among the first published glimpses of some of the unique dwelling forms in China was presented in Liu Dunzhen's book. The black-and-white photograph of a small, "round, earthen building" simply identified as being in Yongding county, Fujian province, was attributed to an unpublished research report by Zhang Buqian, Zhu Wuquan, and Hu Zhanlie and gives no sense as to when the village was visited.* Source: Liu 1957, 124.

b. *When we compare the color photograph of the same structure, taken in 1990, we see little change except for the cutting of additional openings through the solid walls.* Source: Photograph by Ronald G. Knapp 1990.

the Qing dynasty; his approach was morphological rather than historical. Very simple huts, elegant mansions, and, for readers at that time, several rather odd types—such as large, circular fortresses and underground structures—were depicted in drawings of perspective views and floor plans, as well as hazy photographs (Figure 3.2). In attempting to understand common characteristics, Liu cataloged dwellings into nine categories according to their plan and shape, offering brief glimpses of China's architectural heritage once believed no longer extant. *Huizhou Mingdai zhuzhai* focused on the dwellings of wealthy merchants of southern Anhui province, many of which had been standing for more than three hundred years but had been essentially unnoticed, let alone documented or celebrated as significant structures. Contrasting with the simplicity of folk architecture, the uncomplicated elegance of the merchants' mansions was revealed in Zhang's book (Figure 3.3). Flush with original drawings and photographs, this small book still stands as an outstanding source concerning these magnificent dwellings, many of which regrettably have disappeared over the past half century.

International events, Chinese politics, and the limited circulation of these two and a few other books—in China as well as abroad—clearly restricted their impact, and as a result, the richness of Chinese dwelling types remained largely obscure and unknown. In the West, R. T. F. Skinner offered a pithy, prescient, and hopeful note concerning Liu Dunzhen's book: "It is perhaps difficult for us in Europe, where at least all the main types of domestic architecture have been studied and presented

Ronald G. Knapp

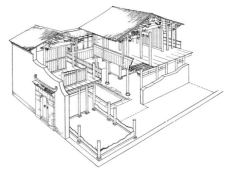

Fig. 3.3. *Zhang Zhongyi's book on Ming merchant dwellings in Anhui showed them to be ostensibly austere, boxy, and multistoried, with exquisite entryways and complex timber-framed structures.* Source: Zhang et al. 1957, 59, 63, 18.

in innumerable excellent publications, to realize how important it is that this research work has started in China, where the material is quite as rich as in Europe, and almost entirely unrecorded" (1958, 431). The British architect Andrew Boyd published *Chinese Architecture and Town Planning* in 1962—"a very small book on a very large subject"—that depended principally on Chinese materials published in the 1950s for its text, drawings, and photographs, but the materials carelessly were not clearly acknowledged as the work of specific Chinese architects and architectural historians. Further, many of the photographs and drawings subsequently were credited in other publications to Boyd rather than to the Chinese researchers who had produced them. In time in the West Boyd's generously illustrated volume became a standard, though brief and enticing, reference on the subject of Chinese architecture.

Fieldwork to survey, document, measure, and assess common dwellings, as well as the magnificent dwellings of gentry and merchants—many of which had historical significance—continued in China's countryside throughout the 1950s and to a lesser degree into the early 1960s. Unfortunately, as the 1960s began, the study of vernacular architecture began to enter a stage of relative dormancy, striking and sad inactivity, rather than the period of vigorous and healthy development hoped for by Liu Dunzhen and others just a short time before. As with other scholarship, that on dwellings was unappreciated, held hostage to the convulsions of the Cultural Revolution, which engulfed China between 1966 and 1976. The public humiliation of academics like the architectural historians Liu Dunzhen and the even better known Liang Sicheng tragically led to their untimely deaths, Liu in 1968 and Liang in 1972. Beyond the personal and professional adversities of individuals and their life work, the Cultural Revolution impacted the country's cultural landscape as historical monuments, as well as dwellings of all types, were destroyed. Just as in wartime, fragile photographs and drawings, which had been made under the most trying circumstances, were time and again lost.

In Search of the Elusive Chinese House

Fig. 3.4. *Variety of dwelling types.*

Fig. 3.4a–b.

a. *This quadrangular courtyard dwelling with multiple open spaces and interlinked and facing structures provides a template for organizing Chinese family life. Although varying in shape and complexity, other structures usually reveal similar hierarchical gradations.* Source: Adapted from a drawing by Pan An.

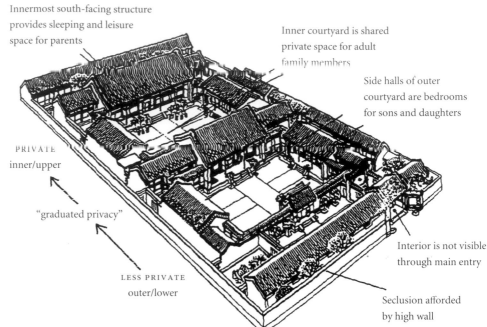

Innermost south-facing structure provides sleeping and leisure space for parents

Inner courtyard is shared private space for adult family members

Side halls of outer courtyard are bedrooms for sons and daughters

PRIVATE
inner/upper

"graduated privacy"

LESS PRIVATE
outer/lower

Interior is not visible through main entry

Seclusion afforded by high wall

b. *Set firmly on stone bases, these large fortresses have walls of thick tamped earth. Gaobei village, Guzhu township, Yongding county, Fujian.* Source: Photograph by Ronald G. Knapp 1990.

China's architectural studies, as other aspects of academic life, were invigorated by the political events of the late 1970s, leading eventually in the 1980s and 1990s to a resurgence of activity and an avalanche of publications relating to vernacular architecture. Over the past two decades, in addition to substantial increases in the quantity and quality of publications, there have been increasingly collegial and collaborative efforts at studying China's vernacular architectural traditions. During this period, a small number of Japanese, American, and European scholars began to visit China's countryside and write in greater detail about China's vernacular architecture. They tended to follow similar itineraries to those that had first been traced by Chinese scholars in the 1950s. It is remarkable that a full century separates the first detailed book in English on Japanese dwellings, published in 1885, from that on Chinese dwellings in 1986![2]

For the most part, Chinese and foreign researchers continued to look at Chinese dwellings as *objects*—mere structures–that were striking in terms of their aesthetics and often novel in terms of the organization of space and spatial structures. A great deal of effort was expended in identifying and then classifying what might be called representative types or models—standard patterns for relentless imitation—but such efforts increasingly were frustrated by growing awareness of a seemingly bewildering variety of structural categories, as well as perplexing questions concerning the social meanings of dwellings.

Ronald G. Knapp

c ▶

d ▼

e ▲

Fig. 3.4c–e.

c. This simple, dweller-built home, made of adobe, brick, stone, and thatch, serves as a nucleus of habitation, with essentially no functional division of space. Zhuangyuan village, near Langzhong, Sichuan. Source: Photograph by Ronald G. Knapp 1995.

d. Sunken courtyard dwelling excavated into the loessial soil in Houwang village, Pinglu county, Shanxi province. Source: Photograph by Ronald G. Knapp 2003.

e. These collapsible felt-tents are raised on cement foundations, indicating that the settlement site is perennial. Note the receding snow beneath the evergreens. Northern slopes of the Tianshan Mountains, Xinjiang. Source: Photograph by Ronald G. Knapp 1984.

China—with an area slightly larger than that of the United States and twice that of Europe, widely varying climatic conditions, fifty-six disparate nationalities, and a remarkable diversity even among the dominant Han majority—has dwellings that are at least as varied as those found in multinational Europe and certainly in the United States. Simple I-shaped rectangular dwellings are ubiquitous throughout China, but these are complemented by a number of conspicuously distinctive building types of great complexity. These include hierarchically organized quadrangular residences in the Beijing area; massive multistoried fortresses in the hilly south; unique below-ground cavelike dwellings in the north; and extraordinarily beautiful merchant dwelling complexes that are nearly four hundred years old, as well as tents and pile dwellings occupied by ethnic minority populations in remote areas of the country (Figure 3.4). Dwellings, of course, are more than mere structures. The remarks below focus largely on "the house" rather than "the home," ignoring for the most part the role of the latter in shaping and being shaped by family life.

In Search of the Elusive Chinese House

While there is no *single* style that can be called "a Chinese house" across time and space, it is possible to point to a set of remarkably similar elements shared by many—if not most—houses. Housing forms throughout China share a limited range of conventional spatial forms in terms of plan and general layout, although they vary in details. These fundamental building elements are rooted deeply in Chinese building traditions and have influenced the spatial conceptualization and building traditions found in Japan and Korea as well (Choi et al. 1999; Lee 2003; Matsuda 2003). In terms of how space is divided, as well as how materials are used to give shape to a structure, Chinese builders pay special attention to environmental conditions and have created at least six identifiable regional prototypes.

Division of Space

Chinese builders are attentive not only to structures—enclosures with a roof—but also are mindful of a need to create open spaces for living, work, and leisure. Whether in an opulent palace or a humble home, the common denominator of any Chinese building is a modular unit known as *jian*. A fundamental measure of width, *jian* is not only the span between two lateral columns that constitutes a bay, but also represents the two-dimensional floor space bounded by four columns, as well as the volumetric measure of the void defined by the floor and the walls (Figure 3.5). Sometimes *jian* form "a room," although often a room is made up of several structural *jian*. As a modular form, *jian* can be created and linked relatively easily to form ramified structures as a family's circumstances and resources change over several generations.

As noted, most Chinese dwellings are relatively simple I-shaped horizontal structures made up of at least three *jian* linked laterally along a transverse symmetrical line. As can be seen in Figure 3.6, facades of dwellings differ in appearance from one area of China to another because of variations in the height, width, and depth of the *jian* that make up the structure. In northern China, *jian* range in width between 3.3 and 3.6 meters, while they are typically between 3.6 and 3.9 meters in southern China. In southern China, the depth of a bay—often reaching as much as 6.6 meters—far exceeds the 4.8 meters that is common in the north (Figure 3.7). *Jian* are generally found in odd multiples, such as three, five, or seven, because odd-numbered units are believed by many Chinese to afford balance and symmetry. In

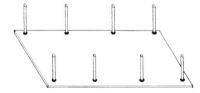

Fig. 3.5. *A* jian, *or bay, is the basic spatial module of most Chinese dwellings, constituting not only the area between four columns but also the three-dimensional volume.* Jian *is also commonly used to describe a "room," although several adjacent* jian *may actually constitute the space enclosed within walls.*

Ronald G. Knapp

Fig. 3.6. *Symmetrical facades are characteristic of dwellings throughout China, even as variations in height, width, and depth of the* jian, *or bays making up the I-shaped structure, allow for striking differences in the front elevation. Three-*jian *dwellings are common throughout the country and are often extended laterally before wings are added.*

a ▼   b ▶

◀ c

Fig. 3.6a–f.

a. *Chuandixia village, Zhaitang township, Mentougou district, in the mountains about ninety kilometers west of Beijing.* Source: Photograph by Ronald G. Knapp 2001.
b. *Wider, taller, and deeper, this dwelling in the Sichuan countryside also has a deep veranda along the front providing work space even during rainy periods. At the foot of Emei Mountain.* Source: Photograph by Ronald G. Knapp 1981.
c. *Two additional bays have been added at the ends of this three-bay structure. The central bay is open and deep, providing generous work space and fresh air. Shuitou, Cangnan county, Zhejiang.* Source: Photograph by Ronald G. Knapp 1988.

the past, sumptuary regulations contributed to standardization and modularization of Chinese houses by restricting the dimensions of timber, thus also constraining the relationship among *jian*. Moreover, sumptuary regulations also specified decorative details and colors, which served as clear indicators of social position, along the roof ridge, under the eaves, and on the gate. The central *jian* of a three- or five-bay rectangular dwelling—whether open or enclosed—typically was wider than flanking *jian* since it was usually the principal ceremonial or utility "room" in a dwelling. Symbolic of unity and continuity, this was a prominent and auspiciously located space in which standard furniture was symmetrically arranged. Facing the entryway and along the back wall was usually a long table to hold the ancestral tablets, images of gods and goddesses, family mementos, and ceremonial paraphernalia. Often termed a reception hall, it was here that a family gathered for ancestral rituals, enjoyed festive family meals (including those that were a part of weddings and funerals), entertained important guests, and even carried on day-to-day activities.

In Search of the Elusive Chinese House

d ▲   e ▲

Fig. 3.6d–f.

d. *This three-bay structure has essentially no eaves overhang or a veranda; it is tightly held within high walls that afford a second-floor living space. The dwelling was probably built during the early part of the nineteenth century and maintains the simplicity of earlier Ming houses. Maoping village, Luci township, Tonglu county, Zhejiang.* Source: Photograph by Ronald G. Knapp 1987.

e. *Five-bays in width and with a second story, this substantial home has an imposing entryway. The lower windows were not part of the original structure, which was built early in the twentieth century, but were added after 1949. Maoping village, Luci township, Tonglu county, Zhejiang.* Source: Photograph by Ronald G. Knapp 1987.

f. *Although apparently a narrow, three-jian structure with a simple facade, this dwelling actually is quite deep and has side single-story wings behind its high walls. Shaanxi.* Source: Photograph by Ronald G. Knapp 1990.

f ▶

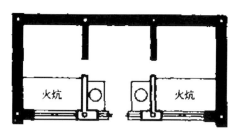

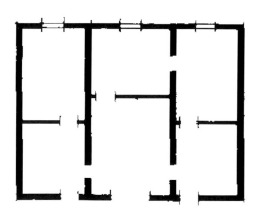

Fig. 3.7. *The frontal span of the simple three-jian northern dwelling on the left is similar to that for a southern dwelling, shown on the right. The depth of the structure on the right is accomplished by using a larger timber-frame structure.*

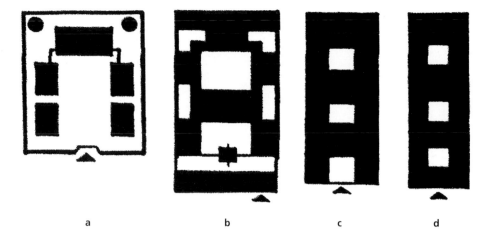

Fig. 3.8. *From* **(a)** *Jilin in the northeast to* **(b)** *Beijing and then* **(c)** *Zhejiang and* **(d)** *Guangdong in the southeast, the proportion of open space to enclosed space diminishes significantly.*

a   b   c   d

Uncovered open spaces—often loosely referred to as "courtyards"—are critical divisions in the spatial composition of any fully formed Chinese dwelling and exist in seemingly endless variations. Indeed, archaeological evidence reveals courtyard forms as early as three thousand years ago (see Knapp 2000, 30–33). In "composing a house," to use Nelson Wu's felicitous phrase, the student of Chinese architecture must recognize open spaces as part of a "house-yard" complex. Wu continues, "the student . . . will miss the point if he does not focus his attention on the space and the impalpable relationships between members of this complex, but, rather, fixes his eyes on the solids of the building alone" (1963, 32). Open spaces are axiomatic elements of Chinese domestic space and can be found throughout the country; however, such spaces differ to such a degree that the common English term "courtyard" or even its many Chinese-language equivalents are insufficient to differentiate them clearly. The proportion of open space to enclosed space diminishes significantly from northeast to southeast and southwest China (Figure 3.8). While courtyards are comparatively expansive in northeastern and northern China, they are usually condensed throughout southern China. In the south, the Chinese term *tianjing*, translated as "skywell," catches well the meaning of their form, especially in two-story dwellings, where their verticality accentuates their diminished horizontal dimensions.

The quintessential Chinese courtyard is found in north China: a quadrangle of low buildings enclosing a courtyard; its origins go back to the eleventh century B.C.E. (Figure 3.9 gives an example from Shanxi.) The back walls of each *siheyuan* lacked windows and doors, and there was clear orientation to the cardinal directions, axiality, balanced side-to-side symmetry, an implied hierarchical organization of space, and main halls generally facing south or southeast. Each *siheyuan*

Fig. 3.9. *In Dingcun village in central Shanxi are found a number of Ming and Qing dynasty* siheyuan, *which are elegant in proportions and simple in style and ornamentation and are precursor forms of those still found in Beijing and surrounding areas.* Source: Photograph by Ronald G. Knapp 2003.

Fig. 3.10a–c. *Surrounded by windowless walls, oriented toward the south, and with a single entrance at the southeastern corner, each of the* siheyuan *in this figure has a generous open space at its core* **(a)**, *while* **(b)** *also has a narrow forecourt and* **(c)** *has both a narrow forecourt and a slender backcourt.* Source: Chiu 2000, 142.

had at least one courtyard at its center, covering about 40 percent of the total area of the dwelling, while some had subsidiary courtyards to the front and/or rear (Figure 3.10). During the Ming and Qing dynasties in Beijing, rectangular *siheyuan*—jammed closely together along *hutong,* or narrow lanes, in well-defined neighborhoods—measured between 15 and 25 meters along their front and were about 25 and 50 meters in depth. Classic *siheyuan* are still seen today in remote villages in northern China, as shown in Figure 3.11, as well as in dwindling numbers in Beijing itself. After two decades of sweeping destruction of *hutong* neighborhoods, less than a thousand *siheyuan* have been designated for preservation and saved from summary destruction. Some *siheyuan* that otherwise would have been razed because of rising real estate values have been saved because they served as a residence at some time for a prominent person (Figure 3.12). The protection of

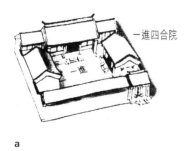

一進四合院

a

二進四合院

b

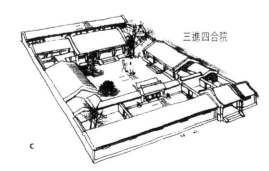

三進四合院

c

Ronald G. Knapp

Fig. 3.11a–b. *Small, tightly packed* siheyuan, *some of which may date to the Ming period, are found in Chuandixia, a small mountain village some ninety kilometers west of Beijing.* Source: Photographs by Ronald G. Knapp 2001.

3.11b ▶

Fig. 3.12a–b. *Used today as a commemorative museum for the Chinese opera star Mei Lanfang, who lived in the dwelling for only the last ten years of his life, this nineteenth-century Beijing* siheyuan *is stripped of its life even as it preserves its essential architectural elements.*

▲ **a.** *View across the larger courtyard from the "spirit wall" inside the second gate toward a side hall and the main hall.* Source: Photograph by Ronald G. Knapp 2003.

b. *The majestic main structure faces south and includes a sitting room, study, and bedroom.* Source: Photograph by Ronald G. Knapp 2003.

▶

Fig. 3.13a–b. *The centuries-old neighborhood of Nanchizi, which is just to the east of the Forbidden City, underwent radical changes in 2002–2003 with the destruction of countless older homes and the construction of two-story courtyard-style dwellings. Called* sihelou, *they are said by some to be in the traditional style, while others see them as an architectural affront to Beijing.*

a. *Two-story garden-style apartments are clustered around a common courtyard shared by a half-dozen families.* Source: Photograph by Ronald G. Knapp 2003.

b. *Workers put the finishing touches on reproductions of traditional features, which are now generally made of gray cement.* Source: Photograph by Ronald G. Knapp 2003.

siheyuan, which some see as an essential domestic architectural type, remains the focus of heated conflict concerning how to preserve the historical character of China's capital (Abramson 2001; Ma 1999). All too often, however, centuries-old neighborhoods—such as Nanchizi, which is just outside the crimson walls of the Forbidden City—have been utterly transformed by the demolition of old structures and "renovation" via the construction of new-style housing with only the flavor of a traditional *siheyuan* (Figure 3.13).

Even as some elements echo Beijing-type *siheyuan,* modularized quadrangular dwellings appear with striking regional differences that reveal the versatility and flexibility of the form. In the northeast region beyond the Great Wall, for example, courtyards are quite large; in Shanxi and Shaanxi provinces, courtyards are elongated and narrow; and in the loessial region, the courtyards are usually square but dug deep into the earth. Because of very hot summers and severe winters, buildings in central Shanxi are placed closer together than is the case in the Beijing area (Figure 3.14). As a result, direct and intense sunlight is blocked during the summer from entering rooms except in the early morning and late afternoon, while the structures mitigate the intrusion of cold winds in winter.

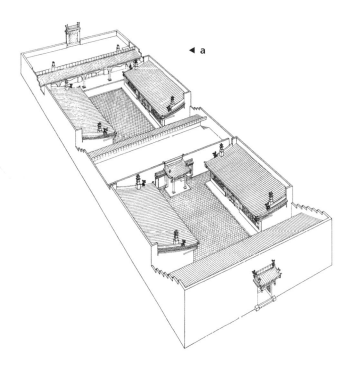

◀ a

b ▶

c ▶

d ▼

Fig. 3.14a–d.

a. *Wrapped with high walls, this elongated dwelling in central Shanxi has a pair of narrow rectangular courtyards.* Source: Song 2000, 68.

b. *Viewed across the rooftops, the narrow courtyards are hidden by the high outer walls. Pingyao, Shanxi.* Source: Photograph by Ronald G. Knapp 2001.

c. *Viewed from above the back structure, the inner courtyard is hidden and well contained. Pingyao, Shanxi.* Source: Photograph by Ronald G. Knapp 2003.

d. *At ground level in an elegant residence like that of the Qiao family manor, the adjacent tightly packed structures are enriched with see-through lattice panels, imposing entrances, colorful lanterns, and applied ornamentation. Qixian county, Shanxi.* Source: Photograph by Ronald G. Knapp 2003.

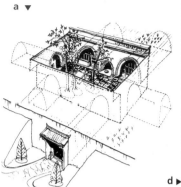

b ▼

c ▶

d ▶

Fig. 3.15a–d. *Four views of exca-vated courtyard dwellings.*

a. *This perspective drawing reveals not only the sunken void, but also the symmetrical layout of the cave-like rooms dug into the loessial soil.* Source: Hou et al. 1989, 30.

b. *Appearing as a pockmarked landscape, this is an aerial view of recessed courtyard cubes during winter in Henan.* Source: Graf zu Castell 1938, 86.

c. *Peering over a brick parapet and sloping tile roof, this young boy looks down into the excavated courtyard. Houwang village, Pinglu county, Shanxi.* Source: Photograph by Ronald G. Knapp 1996.

d. *In villages of excavated courtyard dwellings, villagers increasingly are building above-ground houses sometimes used only seasonally. In other cases, the below-ground residence is completely abandoned. Pinglu county, Shanxi.* Source: Photograph by Ronald G. Knapp 2003.

Clearly reminiscent of classic *siheyuan* courtyard houses are the sunken court-yards carved into the earth in Henan and Shanxi provinces (Figure 3.15). While the typical courtyard of a *siheyuan* emerges in the void formed by the buildings that enclose it, the courtyard of a subterranean dwelling is in fact formed first, the initial "constructed" component of the dwelling complex, whose "walls" provide the exposed surfaces for facades into which the flanking residential "structures" are then hewn. Excavated from the loessial soil, the sunken courtyard thus becomes a "walled" compound with significant outdoor living space open to the sky. Circular, trapezoidal, octagonal, semicircular, and rectangular courtyards are found at the core of massive earthen fortresses in Fujian and Guangdong, and there are less majestic, but still large, enclosures elsewhere in the country (Figure 3.16).

Throughout southern China, dwellings are often punctuated with skywells or *tianjing,* abbreviated rectangular open spaces or voids that do not qualify as true courtyards—even if local people may refer to them as "courtyards"—because they

Ronald G. Knapp

Fig. 3.16a–b.

a. *From above, the village plan reveals large-scale courtyards in various sizes and shapes, including round, oblong, and square.* Source: Photograph by Ronald G. Knapp 2000.

b. *Looking upslope, the individual structures, built upon stone bases, with tamped earth walls, high windows, and double-sloped wooden roofs covered with clay roof tiles, rhythmically rise up the terraced hillside. Tianluokeng village, Shuyang township, Nanjing county, Fujian.* Source: Photograph by Ronald G. Knapp 2000.

are so small and compact. As ingenious sunken interior cavities whose scale restricts the degree of openness to the broad sky above, skywells respond well to the hot and humid conditions characteristic of southern China by catching passing breezes, evacuating interior heat, and leading rainwater into dwellings (Figure 3.17). Perhaps the most distinctive *tianjing*-style dwellings are found in the multistoried merchant dwellings in Anhui, Jiangxi, and Zhejiang provinces, where some have survived from the Ming dynasty, but others are found throughout southern China. Unlike northern structures, which emphasize horizontality and openness to the sky above, many of these southern dwellings appear like squat boxes or elongated loaves with solid walls and limited windows. Most have multiple skywells, each an atrium-like enclosed vertical space whose size, shape, and number vary according to the scale of the residence. Exteriors often appear modest in terms of scale and building materials, but inside there is often a profuse use of expensive woods, as well as carved stone and brick, which are used structurally and ornamentally.

There are no sharp distinctions in terminology as these different forms of open spaces spread across great distances and accommodate local conditions. However, the Chinese language clearly differentiates the northern prototypical *yuanzi* court-yard-type open space from its condensed southern cousins, the *tianjing*, or "skywell type," as well as some variant types such as the compact *yikeyin*, or "seal style," in Yunnan province. While open spaces of many sorts can be designed into a dwelling's plan and "built" as part of it, many emerge rather from the expansion of common three-*jian* structures as a family becomes more prosperous over time. Figure 3.18 portrays conceptual progressions of building form and plan in northern and southern China, the first resulting from "enclosing" *[wei]* and the second "excavating" *[wa]*

◀ a

b ▶

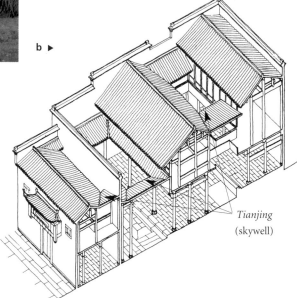

Tianjing
(skywell)

e ▶

Fig. 3.17a–e.

a. *The simple facade of this imposing, boxlike dwelling, built during the Ming dynasty, only suggests the complexity behind it. Ningyuantang, Zhanqi village, Shexian county, Anhui.* Source: Photograph by Ronald G. Knapp 1987.

b. *Beyond the adorned entryway, the dwelling is configured around three* tianjing, *or skywells, which vary in extent and height. The first* tianjing, *a mere sliver, is encountered after one enters the front gate; the second is larger but is confined by a low, sloping roof, while the third is extended upward by the higher roofs of the second-story structures.* Source: Gong 1996, 56.

c. *This* tianjing *provides an abbreviated open space within the core of* the dwelling. Surrounding the skywell is a generous gray space, neither indoors nor outdoors, which is shaded by an extension of the roof. The inward slopes of the adjacent roofs lead water into the tianjing. Langzhong, Sichuan. *Source: Photograph by Ronald G. Knapp 1994.*

d. *When viewed from inside a* tianjing, *the sky is often a mere patch, with the amount of light, wind, and rain able to penetrate dependent upon the time of day and season. Shexian county, Anhui.* Source: Photograph by Ronald G. Knapp 2003.

e. *Open spaces adjacent to a* tianjing *flow into it. Southern Jiangxi.* Source: Photograph by Ronald G. Knapp 1993.

◀ c d ▶

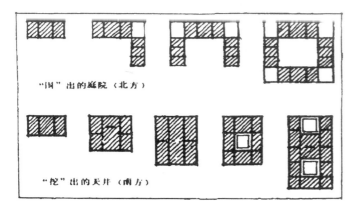

"间" 出的庭院（北方）

"挖" 出的天井（南方）

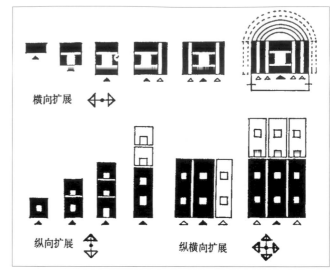

横向扩展

纵向扩展　　　　　纵横向扩展

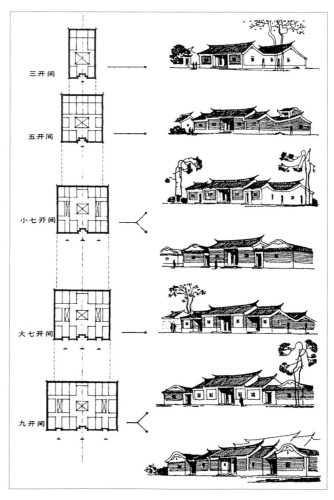

三开间

五开间

小七开间

大七开间

九开间

▲

Fig. 3.18. *Throughout rural China, dwellings frequently expand over time from a simple, three-jian form as a family becomes more prosperous and its needs change. The top series of drawings shows the evolution from an "I" to "L" to "U" shape to a culminating siheyuan type, with structures on four sides around a courtyard. This progression is called an "enclosing," or wei, type. In southern China, as seen in the bottom series, open spaces are "excavated," or wa, type as "wells" in various spaces throughout the interior of the structure.* Source: Huang et al. 1992, 5.

▶

Fig. 3.19a–b.

a. *Common patterns of side-to-side, front-to-back, and combination expansions of houses.* Source: Huang et al. 1992, 46.

b. *These floor plans and perspective views show a sequence of simple to more complex houses. North of Xiamen in Fujian. As the number of jian increases from three to nine—that is, the dwelling becomes broader— the number of tianjing multiplies. Jinjiang county, Fujian.* Source: Huang et al. 1992, 46.

Fig. 3.19c–d.

c. *A pair of adjacent, inverted U-shaped triple-jian houses, each with an additional inverted U. Quanzhou city, Fujian.* Source: Photograph by Ronald G. Knapp 2003.

d. *Linked by low side buildings, this horizontal pair of seven-*jian*-wide structures together forms an interior courtyard, a common rural dwelling type in Fujian, as well as across the straits in Taiwan. Wufeng village, Shishan township, Nan'an city, Fujian.* Source: Original photograph used with the permission of Huang Hanmin. In Huang 1994, 159.

open space. Adding one or (later) a second perpendicular wing creates first an L-shape, then a U-shape, which embraces an open courtyard. With the addition of a structure along the single exposed side, a complete quadrangular dwelling emerges. In southern China, three-*jian* longitudinal units are more likely to expand toward the front or the back as enclosed space is doubled. The opening of a well—a sky-well—in the interior of the building's mass may emerge as a true skywell and be duplicated as the dwelling grows (see Knapp 2000, 27–54, for details of these various configurations). The enclosing perimeter walls, as well as the structures themselves, effectively block the cacophony of sounds from the outside, assuring relative quiet in any of the open spaces.

In order to expand a dwelling by duplicating hall-courtyard modules, components can be placed front-to-back or side-to-side (Figure 3.19), with specific vertical or horizontal circulation paths designated in order to impose a clear spatial hierarchy. "Graduated privacy," a term coined by Nelson Wu, characterizes these spatial progressions: "the dual quality of the house, as a setting for ceremony and as a home, is a most important characteristic of the house as an image of human relationship" (1963, 32–34). Casual visitors are invited only into the entry vestibule near the front, while the first-level courtyard and adjacent halls are privileged spaces only for relatives and friends. Deeper in the dwelling is a realm of privacy for women in the family, as discussed in Chapter 11 by Francesca Bray. In some hall-courtyard complexes, there is a barely noticeable serial elevation of individual buildings as one passes from the exterior ones to the interior ones. Each structure is a few steps above the preceding courtyard, affording a vertical differentiation analogous to the gradations across horizontal space. As elaborated by Nelson Wu,

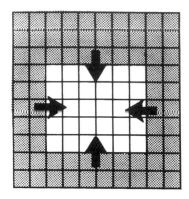

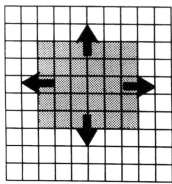

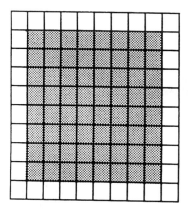

Fig. 3.20

"the raised terraces exercise yet another tyranny. They dictate the path for movement, and the statements of their inviting stairways and prohibitive corners are firm and final" (1963, 33–34). The spatial manifestations of open or closed, front or back, and above or below—all in series—not only echoed but also helped regulate traditional Chinese social relationships within the cellular form of a *siheyuan*.

Open and closed elements of this type express the complementary bipolarity of *yin* and *yang* cosmological thinking, as well as the aesthetic concepts of *xu* and *shi*. The significance of *yin* and *yang* within Chinese correlative thinking is well known, and thus the use of balanced paired concepts in expressing spatial relationships within residences is not surprising. While both *yin* and *yang* elements are essential and balancing, mutually dependent and producing harmony, *yang* is implicitly hierarchically dominant over *yin* as well as dynamically interrelated. *Xu* and *shi*, as expressions of Chinese aesthetics in art and buildings, convey the interdependence of the intangible and the tangible, in which both structures and voids have meaning in a spatial composition. Just as in a Chinese painting, where white areas without black brushstrokes are as much a part of the composition as the pigmented lines and dots, the spatial composition of a Chinese dwelling privileges open spaces as well as enclosed structures. Other correlative associations relating to domestic spatial compositions include interrelationships between interior and exterior, above and below, light and shade, and active and passive, as well as host and guest. One can observe an increasing proportion of transitional gray or shaded spaces that are neither interior nor exterior as one moves from northern to southern China.

Chinese architects have described northern *siheyuan*, with their large interior courtyards and adjacent side buildings, as well as compact southern multistoried dwellings, as "high-density" structures, even though traditionally the actual density of residents was low. Figure 3.20 compares the spatial relationships among three dwelling types and open space on building lots of the same size. The traditional *siheyuan* layout, as shown in the top drawing, has a ratio of 70 percent enclosed building space surrounding a central courtyard that represents 30 percent of the building lot. Even with substantial encircling structures, extensive open space remains, which of course is shared by all who live within the adjacent rooms. The middle figure illustrates a pattern typical of an American dwelling; the proportions of building and open space are reversed in comparison to those found in a classic Chinese *siheyuan*. This Western-style, single-family detached dwelling with a surrounding yard clearly serves a different social purpose. If Chinese architects were to abandon the courtyard as anachronistic and replicate the same amount of building space in a fashion that mimics Western residential layouts, the fringing yard would

Ronald G. Knapp

◀ **Fig. 3.20.** *These three figures show comparisons of open and built spaces on building lots of the same size in China and the United States. The top figure represents a traditional* siheyuan, *with a central courtyard occupying some 30 percent of the lot, which is shared by all residents, and 70 percent of the overall space given over to buildings. The middle figure shows a common house lot plan in the United States, with the structure placed near the center and surrounded by open space—front, back, and side yards. It is a mirror image of the* siheyuan *in terms of the ratio of built to unbuilt space. In the bottom figure open space is outside the structure and the buildings represent 70 percent of the lot; it clearly shows that the open space becomes essentially useless.* Source: After Shang and Yang 1982, 56.

become useless. Courtyards remain preferred spaces even today by Chinese living in rural as well as urban areas. Having evolved over several thousand years to meet changing environmental and social conditions, courtyards continue to be appropriate components in the spatial composition of Chinese residences.

Environmental Awareness _____

China is a vast country, similar in size to the United States and occupying similar latitudes. As a result, its inhabitants live in environments with quite different climates, ranging from the hot-humid subtropics to cold-dry temperate regions, and their dwellings differ in terms of fenestration, orientation, building materials, depth of caves overhang, and roof pitch. In North China, the orientation of many dwellings so that the facade faces south or southeast shows a clear awareness that heat can be gained from the low angles of winter sunshine even as the high sun angles of summer are restricted from penetrating the dwellings and warming them excessively (Figure 3.21). At the same time, the side and back walls are usually without windows or doors, so these walls provide important barriers against the intrusion of the predictably steady, relentless, and cold northwest winds in winter (Figure 3.22). Together with a thick roof—flat, concave, or pitched with a single or double slope—northern dwellings generally provide substantial protection for enduring the bitter cold and powerful winds of northern winters and early springs. As discussed above, the shape and size of courtyards differ from place to place in northern China as a response to local climatic conditions, with some being slender while others are broad. It is common for deciduous trees to be planted within courtyards in order to disperse heat in the summer and allow it to reach the ground in winter (Figure 3.23). Along the relatively open facade, sheets of paper traditionally were pasted on the inside of window frames and along cracks in the upper wall in order to lessen the seepage of cold air and contain some of the heat generated within. With the natural deterioration of the paper over the course of the year, it was renewed seasonally but only after the period during which the gaping holes welcomed the breezes of spring, summer, and fall. Because of the tightness of these paper linings, it was sometimes necessary during winter to poke a hole into one of those covering a window in order to vent poisonous gases, with the mouth of the vent hole usually reinforced with a decorative papercut (Figure 3.24). Houses built into hills or underground in the loessial region of China are particularly ingenious responses to climate in that the interior of such dwellings is cool during the day and warm at night. In arid regions, houses might be built with mud brick or pounded

In Search of the Elusive Chinese House

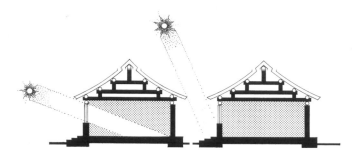

3.22 ▶

▲ **Fig. 3.21.** *By considering orientation, depth of the dwelling, and extent of the eaves overhang, villagers in North China continue to construct simple dwellings in which the low winter sun penetrates the interior while the more intense rays of summer are kept outside. The noon sun angles shown in this drawing represent the positions in Beijing during the December solstice and June solstice, when the sun is lowest and highest in the sky.*

Fig. 3.22. *These two south-facing dwellings have solid side and back walls that keep winter winds at bay. The darkened interior is quite apparent in this summer view, when the sun is high in the sky. Huairou county, Beijing.* Source: Photograph by Ronald G. Knapp 1987.

Fig. 3.23a–b.

a. *Workmen resting under the spreading branches of a pair of trees in a courtyard house undergoing renovation. Houhai area, Beijing.* Source: Photograph by Ronald G. Knapp 2000.

b. *This lone tree provides shade for the sunken courtyard of this subterranean dwelling. Qianxian, Shaanxi.* Source: Photograph by Ronald G. Knapp 1984.

Fig. 3.24a–c.

a. *Ready for winter, this south-facing facade of a northern dwelling has had paper added to the inside of its lattice windows. Chuandixia village, Zhaitang township, Beijing.* Source: Photograph by Ronald G. Knapp 2003.

b. *The papered lattice windows allow a diffused light to reach the interior of a dwelling. Pingyao, Shanxi.* Source: Photograph by Ronald G. Knapp 2003.

c. *Tattered paper allows air to enter the dwelling through the lattice. Chuandixia village, Zhaitang township, Beijing.* Source: Photograph by Ronald G. Knapp 2003.

a ▲

b ▶

Fig. 3.25a–d.

a. *This village in northern Zhejiang is arranged on the lower, south-facing slopes of a steep hill and adjacent to the rice fields. Mogan-shan area.* Source: Photograph by Ronald G. Knapp 1987.

b. *Positioned along a stream, this village in Anhui enjoys access to fresh water as well as an amelio-rated climate.* Source: Photograph by Ronald G. Knapp 1987.

c. *New brick houses are being built within the paddy fields. Guangxi Zhuang Autonomous Region.* Source: Photograph by Ronald G. Knapp 1985.

d. *This nucleated hamlet is wrapped within bamboo groves. Guang'an county, Sichuan.* Source: Photograph by Ronald G. Knapp 1994.

earth in order for the thermal properties of the earthen wall to help mediate the extreme diurnal changes in temperature in such a climate.

Modest single-story dwellings are still seen widely throughout southern China just as they are in northern China, but in the south multistoried dwellings are also common. Varying topographic conditions provided opportunities for villagers in the south to take advantage of sunny slopes, local microclimates, limited arable land, and available water as they built their dwellings (Figure 3.25). As discussed above, ingenious interior sunken spaces—the *tianjing* or skywells, which are open to the sky above—as well as shaded transitional arcades, formed by broad eaves overhangs and open rooms, respond well to the hot and humid conditions characteristic of the hotter areas of China. Ventilation and the prevention of intense sunlight from pene-trating the interior are critical coping elements in the design of southern dwellings. Ventilation not only removes heat, but it also plays a significant role in reducing humidity levels by flushing out moist air before it can condense on interior surfaces.

The selection of building sites that optimize the capturing of steady winds—characteristic of the southeast coast—is critical in this regard, as is the creation of channels that lead prevailing winds directly and indirectly through even a complex building. This effect is accomplished not only by the placement of openings, but

Ronald G. Knapp

d ▲

◄ c

also by taking advantage of differential pressures within a building that are due to even slight differences in temperatures and that result in a pumping effect. Rooftop transom windows, openings placed high on gable walls, lattice windows, and the careful placement of doors—some of which have ingenious designs that allow the door to be open yet secure—all facilitate the thorough ventilation of residences, cooling ambient air while helping reduce humidity by moving the moist air (Figure 3.26). Environmental awareness includes as well overall village siting, thermal insulation by massing structures, and the utilization of reflective surfaces for countering the intense rays of the sun, long periods of daylight, heavy precipitation, and sultry humidities (Figure 3.27).

Comfort at Home

Environmental awareness does not necessarily lead to comfort. Whether a dwelling is comfortable or not is as much a matter of fact as it is a matter of perception. Comfort has both measurable and nonmeasurable characteristics, and indeed any dwelling raised to the level of *home* is much more than a mere refuge or shelter from the vagaries of weather and the limits of climate. Comfort in a home, according to

Fig. 3.26a–b.
a. *Ringing this small courtyard is a veranda that serves as a gray space between the interior and exterior. Sheltered by a projecting roof that is supported by posts, this linear space can be used by the family even if it rains. Zhejiang.* Source: Photograph by Ronald G. Knapp 1988.

b. *Close-up of intricate lattice windows that allow air and light into the interior rooms. Langzhong city, Sichuan.* Source: Photograph by Ronald G. Knapp 1994.

Fig. 3.27. *The compact arrangement of dwellings along twisted paths, coupled with reflective white walls, helps to reduce the accumulation of ambient heat within a settlement. Wuyuan county, Jiangxi.* Source: Photograph by Ronald G. Knapp 1999.

Witold Rybczynski (1986), is many-layered, elusive, and historically conditioned and includes aspects related to privacy or intimacy in addition to convenience and physical ease. Comfort is sometimes the consequence of conscious design and sometimes merely an accidental result of experimentation to enhance light and ventilation or reduce cold, heat, and dampness. In China, as is the case throughout the world, improvements in physical comfort have come about over a long period of time, during which an evolution of sorts has occurred. Moreover, it is indisputable that for most of times past people were forced to endure physical conditions thought today to be utterly unacceptable.

Western visitors to Chinese dwellings—even those of the rich—throughout the nineteenth and twentieth centuries harshly judged Chinese homes in terms of physical comfort, remarking that rooms were dimly lighted, even gloomy, as well as damp and chilly or humid and hot, depending upon the place and time of year, without any consideration of other "comfort" factors. Descriptions of dirty kitchens, malodorous privies, discolored walls, cluttered passageways, uncomfortable furniture, dilapidated furnishings, and poor maintenance abound in the writings of short-term visitors and even of those one would assume were reasonably acclimated to and accepting of Chinese customs and life. Arthur H. Smith, a missionary in China for more than twenty years, for example, wrote of an apparent Chinese "indifference to comfort and convenience" and the fact that "a Chinese dwelling . . . always appears to a Westerner as a thesaurus of discomfort" (1894, 125, 133). He lamented that the Chinese "do not care for the shade of trees about their houses"; "houses are nearly always ill-lighted at night"; furniture is "clumsy and uncomfortable"; damp floors are "extremely prejudicial to health"; "paper windows will not keep out wind, rain, sun, heat, or dust"; and "steam and often smoke fill the room [kitchen] to an extent adapted to blind and strangle"; he concluded, "it is no wonder that a certain Taotai [local magistrate] who had been abroad remarked that in the United States the prisoners in jail had quarters more comfortable than his yamên [combined official residence and office]" (1894, 130–134).

Edward Sylvester Morse visited China in the 1890s and wrote articles for the *American Architect* in which he reiterated the comments of others, emphasizing as well "the appalling character of the dirt, not ordinary clean dirt, but what appeared to be pathogenic dirt" (1902, 54). While Morse admitted that some Westerners leveled similar criticisms at Japanese houses, he himself wrote glowingly of Japanese homes and compared them favorably with dwellings in Germany and England while finding that Victorian homes in the United States were "in need of domestic reform" (1902, xxiv). Morse acknowledged that a traditional Japanese home at first appearance was "unsubstantial," but it had "marvels" within, and each "answer[ed] admirably for the purposes intended" (1885, 12). His disparagement of Chinese homes was tempered with the following statement: "I must admit, for fear of doing the Chinese an injustice, that the contrast was the more pronounced having just come from Japan, where the shoes are always removed before entering the house, the floors and mats are repeatedly swept, and the woodwork of the rooms and the floor of the veranda are often wiped with a damp cloth" (1885, 54). Morse's comments, while clearly excessively judgmental, were also influential in embedding notions of Chinese backwardness in the thoughts of the American public. It is unfortunate that he failed to either reflect upon the nearly universal depredation impacting the living patterns of all strata of Chinese as the imperial system unraveled during the nineteenth century or probe any of the elements of environmental awareness apparent even in common Chinese dwellings. Failing to view the endemic destitution characteristic of the declining Qing dynasty as only a narrow slice of Chinese history, he totally ignored the broader periods, such as during the Tang, Song, or Ming dynasties, when significant numbers of Chinese dwellings no doubt surpassed homes elsewhere in the world in terms of comfort and quality. Morse's brief excursions into homes in and about Shanghai and Guangzhou offered little opportunity to contextualize his observations temporally or spatially.

Several other authors, while also speaking of the Chinese "indifference to comfort," offered more enlightened views. Émile Bard, after a sojourn of four years, opined that "I have attempted to avoid within the limits of the possible, the exaggerated optimism of certain writers on this country—chiefly travellers and missionaries— and I also have been careful not to fall into the spirit of systematic depreciation common to most Europeans in referring to the Celestial Empire and its inhabitants" (1906, x). He then added, "a people can be civilized without being comfortable," noting that "no one who visits the palace of Versailles to-day will say that it is a comfortable habitation, in the modern sense of the word" (1906, 26). But he then continued: "The houses of the natives rest on the ground without cellars, and are cold and damp. The doors are always swinging and for this reason afford little protection from cold in winter. The windows, with their paper panes, keep out neither cold, rain, heat, nor dust. . . . Nowhere are openings numerous, and they are never so arranged as to permit the circulation of air. In summer it is quite impossible to remain inside of a native house" (1906, 31).

On the other hand, some inveterate travelers such as P. Du Halde, John Francis

Ronald G. Knapp

Davis, Edwin Joshua Dukes, and Isabella Bird offered more positive perspectives, perhaps because (in the case of the first three) they journeyed to China at an earlier time, went into inland areas that were more prosperous than the teeming coastal villages and towns, and visited the more extensive dwellings of the rich in addition to those of the poor. They chose to emphasize positive qualities rather than physical comfort per se, even though they were critical of spitting and general "superstitions." Du Halde, writing at a time when Europeans generally had positive Enlightenment views of China, wrote the following:

> The Chinese love to be clean and neat in their Houses, but they have nothing very magnificent; their Architecture is not at all elegant, and they have no regular Buildings but the Emperor's Palaces, publick Edifices, Towers, Triumphal Arches, the Gates and Walls of the great Cities, Piers, Causeways, Bridges, and Pagodas. . . . The Houses of private Persons are very plain, for they have no Regard to any things but Usefulness. . . . The Houses of the Nobility and rich People, if compared with others, do not deserve to be mentioned; it would be an Abuse of the Term to give them the Name of Palaces, they being nothing but a Ground-floor raised something higher than common Houses; the Roof is neat, and the Outside of it has several Ornaments; the great Number of Courts and Apartments, fit to ledge their Domesticks, make amends for their Meanness and want of Magnificence. (1741, 144, 146)

John Francis Davis, described as His Majesty's Chief Superintendent in China, wrote extensively about Chinese dwellings, and noted, "The magnificence of Chinese mansions is estimated in some measure by the ground which they cover, and by the number and size of the courts and buildings. The real space is often eked out by winding and complicated passages or galleries, decorated with carving and trellis-work in very good taste" (1836, 1:345). Edwin Joshua Dukes, a missionary writing about Fujian, states, "Even the mandarins and wealthy gentry live in a plain and frugal fashion, which would astonish our English housekeepers, who are so frequently in bondage to that worst of tyrants, 'what will people say?' The palace of a viceroy ruling twenty to fifty millions has a tiled floor, straight-backed flat-bottomed chairs, a lounge covered with nothing softer than a plantain-leaf mat, and windows of tissue-paper or split oyster shell. Even he dines with the aid of a bowl and chopsticks" (1885, 45).

In writing about Hangzhou, Isabella L. Bird, after three years and eight thousand miles of travel throughout China, states, "The mansion of the Ting family, in which I took 'afternoon tea,' with its lofty reception-rooms, piazzas, and courts, must cover two acres of ground. It is stately, but not comfortable, and the richly carved blackwood chairs with panels of clouded grey marble for backs and seats, and table centres of the same, seem only fitted for the noon of a midsummer's day" (1900, 1:58). As she traveled deeper into the interior, especially in Sichuan, her views changed somewhat: "Every day I dropped some preconceived ideas of what Chinese scenery and buildings must be like, and I hope that my readers will drop theirs, if they are of willow-plate origin, before they have finished this volume" (1900, 1:328). Here, she noted and photographed "some Chinese Chatsworths and Eatons, and large 'brick noggin' farmhouses," as well as "landowners' houses rivaling some of our renowned English homes in size and stateliness" (Figure 3.28). Her language becomes even more effusive—some dwellings are called "palatial"—as she encounters the prosperity of the broad plains of inland Sichuan, a province whose population at the time was several times greater than that of England. She argues that "China is not in decay" and is a "country of paradoxes and contradictions" (1900, 1:334).

Whether the occupants of the houses visited by Smith, Morse, Bard, Du Halde, Davis, Dukes, or Bird found their own dwellings uncomfortable and unsanitary, of course, is unknowable. Enlightened knowledge of environmental sanitation and standards of convenience and comfort, as they are known today, are far removed from those a century ago and continue even today to differ from one place to another. Today, as in the past, the Chinese continue to make judgments about whether something is *shufu,* or "comfortable," based upon a range of expectations,

Fig. 3.28. *Unlike so many others, who found Chinese dwellings unsatisfactory, Isabella Bird waxed effusive about the "stately proportions," expansive courtyards, lofty rooms, and "sumptuous decorations" of grand country houses she encountered in the Sichuan countryside as well as urban Hangzhou. She said that they reminded her of the great estates of Chatsworth and Eaton in England.* Source: Bird 1900, 1:329.

Fig. 3.29. *Arthur H. Smith was astounded that the Chinese had "never learned to weave wool" for clothing and in order to endure winter's cold had to "wear an amount of wadded cotton clothing almost sufficient to double the bulk of their bodies. A child clad in this costume, if he happens to fall down, is often utterly unable to rise as if he had been strapped into a cask."* Source: Smith 1894, 126–127.

practical experiences, and a remarkable level of tolerance that sometimes differs from that in much of the West. A few examples suffice: The warmth of a brick bed, or *kang*, might be celebrated while its hardness is ignored. Moving a stool around the perimeter of a courtyard is used as a technique for following the passage of the sun in order to capture light and warmth from a predictable energy source, even as the effort expended to do so is disregarded. Voluminous layers of padded clothing, as seen in Figure 3.29, are worn in order to maintain body heat and render unnecessary the heating of rooms, even as the restrictions in one's movement are endured. Arthur H. Smith claimed, "Of the discomfort of such clumsy dress we never hear the Chinese complain," and even the lack of underclothing was noted: "Their burdensome wadded clothes hang around their bodies like so many bags, leaving yawning spaces through which the cold penetrates to the flesh, but they do not mind this circumstance, although ready to admit that it is not ideal" (1894, 127).

Throughout the first half of the twentieth century, the living situations for most Chinese in cities and in the countryside continued to deteriorate even from the generally unsatisfactory levels attested to by Smith and Morse. War, political movements, and natural disasters, as well as the overuse, abuse, and neglect of dwellings, all contributed to the worsening situation, and it is likely that these observers and others would have made similar judgments at midcentury as they had made many

In Search of the Elusive Chinese House

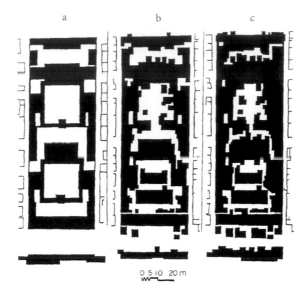

a   b   c

0 5 10 20 m

Fig. 3.30. *Transformation of a courtyard house in Beijing over the past half century, degraded by the infilling of the courtyard with "temporary" structures in order to accommodate multiple families.*

a. *Early 1950s. 2,440.5 square meters of enclosed floor space.*

b. *Late 1970s: 3,196.5 square meters of enclosed floor space—an increase of 31 percent.*

c. *1987: 3,786.5 square meters of enclosed floor space—an increase of 55 percent over early 1950s. By 1987, the open courtyard had ceased to exist.*
Source: Wu 1999, 59.

years before. In the decades after 1949, furthermore, China's population more than doubled so that urban and rural dwellings originally built for a household of one size were by necessity divided and then redivided to accommodate increasing numbers of residents, with destructive consequences. Courtyards that once served as outdoor spaces for family activities, circulation, ventilation, light, and drainage increasingly were degraded as overcrowding led to the proliferation of "temporary" structures that gobbled up open space (Figure 3.30). What had once been spacious for one family became crowded with the bodies and needs of multiple families, a condition that continues into the present (Figure 3.31).

During the Patriotic Sanitation Movement in the 1950s and into the 1960s, significant attention was paid to improving overall environmental sanitation in China's villages, with the recognition that living conditions were often filthy and unhealthy. As part of the effort to improve health through the prevention of disease, a "Five Haves and Eight Cleans" campaign was instituted. The "Five Haves" referred to a family latrine, a covered latrine, a pigsty, a chicken coop, and a cover on the well, while the "Eight Cleans" focused on the house (inside and outside), courtyard, lane, bedclothes, garments, kitchen, bowls, and chopsticks. Positive changes, however, continued to be uneven due to income disparities and differences in attitude and expectations regarding household sanitation. Since the reforms of the late 1970s, greater attention has been paid to household sanitation as new homes were built in accelerating numbers. The people's dissatisfaction with lives of penury and an awareness of new ways of life have led to a greater attention to kitchens and, to

Ronald G. Knapp

Fig. 3.31. *Traditional Beijing sihe-yuan had become unrecognizable as "temporary" structures made of scavenged brick and corrugated sheets gradually filled the once spacious courtyards. The clutter of stored items and the needs of daily life further degraded these once stately courtyard houses. Nanchizi neighborhood, Beijing.* Source: Photographs by Ronald G. Knapp 2003.

some degree, toilet facilities. With larger windows, artificial lights, glazed tile, and better ventilation, once dark spaces have been brightened. However, visitors to China even at the dawn of the twenty-first century continue to comment on unsatisfactory levels of cleanliness and general sanitation, even as dramatic improvements are apparent to longtime visitors and residents themselves.

Over the millennia and varying according to local environmental conditions, Chinese dwellings and villages changed relatively slowly except during periods of economic efflorescence, when grand manors and stately mansions were expanded or built. Each generation more or less bequeathed cultural landscapes—including houses, bridges, pavilions, and ancestral halls—that were not too different from the ones it had inherited. The slow pace of technological change, as well as a tendency for cultural conservatism, no doubt contributed to the maintenance of old dwelling forms. New styles and patterns of vernacular architecture in rural, urban, and suburban areas have emerged in recent decades, using materials and plans that differ significantly from traditional ones, a subject broached in several of the chapters that follow.

NOTES _____

1. Comprehensive bibliographies concerning Chinese dwellings can be found in Knapp (1999, 2000).

2. Edward Sylvester Morse's *Japanese Homes and Their Surroundings* was published in 1885 and Knapp's *China's Traditional Rural Architecture* in 1986. Morse also published *Glimpses of China and Chinese Homes* in 1902, but it only hints at the richness of Chinese dwellings.

In Search of the Elusive Chinese House

4   *House and Garden*

Sanctuary for the Body and the Mind

Lin Yutang—prolific author, humorist, and celebrated interpreter of China to the West—once observed that we do not know a man well until we find out how he spends his leisure time. When "a man ceases to do the things he has to do, and does the things he likes to do . . . his character is revealed . . . and we see the inner man, his real self" (Lin 1935, 329). Making a garden was among the traditional activities that a Chinese did best in the pursuit of leisure and contentment, a garden being that place where life could be enjoyed freely, happily, and artistically. Indeed, in China in the past—especially when politics were corrupt, commerce was distasteful, society was disorderly, and life was harsh—some Chinese were able to seek sanctuary and solace in a garden, however small or large, formal or informal. In addition to the fabled gardens and parks that were associated with the extensive imperial palaces, more modest yet still exceptional gardens were embedded in the social and aesthetic life not only of China's elite, but others as well.

As a visitor to any Chinese home with a garden becomes quickly aware, it is more than a confined landscape with geometric beds of ornamental plants or shade trees beneath which to sit. Before we proceed to a discussion of the larger, "designed" gardens of scholars and wealthy merchants, it is important to note that even in modest households efforts are often made to manipulate earth, stones, plants, and water in order to stimulate the senses, give pleasure, and create out of ordinary materials an enjoyable place for solitude. Even in the constricted spaces of skywells in southern China, the more expansive courtyards in northern China, near the ubiquitous and humble triple-*jian* dwellings found throughout the countryside, and even the balconies of modern apartment houses, attention is commonly paid to the placement of relatively simple natural compositions within a rectangular or circular pot or perhaps even planted within a patch of earth if it is available. In these spaces, vines are trained to grow on bamboo trellises, flowering plants are set to perfume the air, and an occassional tree is placed to bring forth a small seasonal harvest of colorful and tasty fruit.

Where space is limited, *penjing*—precursors of the better-known Japanese *bonsai,* literally "tree in a pot," which is essentially a cultivated dwarfed tree—provide a

vehicle for evoking nature in a miniature composition within a tray (Figure 4.1). While there are similarities between them, *penjing* are usually more complex in that they are literally "potted landscapes" with a structural unity of plants, including moss, rocks, earth, and water, as well as even miniature pavilions, bridges, and human figures (Stein 1990). Whether a mere clustering of cultivated plants or an artistic *penjing* creation, such a representation of nature becomes a personal element in one's home, a focus for family enjoyment, as well as an object to be manipulated during periods of leisure. Even utilitarian inkwells may be composed in a way to suggest a complex landscape sitting on a scholar's desk (Stein 1990, 37–38).

Fig. 4.1a–b. *While* penjing *may be as simple as a tree in a shallow pot, many are exquisite miniature landscapes with a structural unity that replicates the elements found in an extensive Chinese garden, even as each evokes the imagery of paintings and poetry.* Source: (a) Cao and Wu 1986, 158; (b) original *penjing* design by Zhao Qingquan; see Zhao 1997.

During the Ming dynasty, miniature landscapes were treated as surrogate gardens, sites of symbolic meaning for aesthetic appreciation (Ryor 2002). Utilizing simple elements generally found at hand, common folk in urban and rural areas throughout China continue to engage their imaginations, heighten their senses, and appreciate the material and philosophical complementarities of nature in gardens small and large (Figure 4.2).

The best-known Chinese gardens nonetheless exist beyond their physical expression in that they are vividly represented in texts, in calligraphy, and in paintings, where their meanings resonate at many levels beyond that of the artifactual. In China, a house and garden, however unsophisticated or intricate, together form elements of an organic whole in accordance with the principle of harmony with nature. The architect Tong Jun was the first scholar to probe into the essence of

Joseph C. Wang

Fig. 4.2. *Side corridor in a small courtyard of the Qiuxia Garden, Jiading.* Source: Cheng 1999, 215.

Fig. 4.3a–b.

▼ **a.** *The Chinese character* yuan 園, *or "garden," is dissected into meaningful parts symbolizing the components of a garden: architectural elements, a pond, strokes suggesting a rockery or plants, and an encircling wall.* Source: Original calligraphy by Wong Young-tsu.

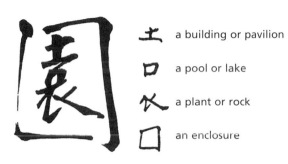

土 a building or pavilion

口 a pool or lake

仐 a plant or rock

口 an enclosure

▼ **b.** *Thirty different ways of writing the character* yuan 園, *by celebrated calligraphers in Chinese history.* Source: Adapted from Xia 1995.

Chinese gardens by dissecting the character *yuan* 園 [garden] into its meaningful parts (Figure 4.3). Referring to *Shuowen jiezi,* a Han dynasty dictionary compiled about A.D. 100, Tong Jun (1984, 7) demonstrated that the character *yuan* is made up of constituent elements—namely, 冂, an encircling wall; 土, architectural elements; ㅂ, a pond; and the remaining strokes suggesting a rockery and plants—to the degree that the remaining anatomy of the character *yuan* corresponds well to the assemblage of physical elements constituting a Chinese garden. In larger Chinese gardens, moreover, the prominence of architectural elements, which provide significant stages for the domestic life of a family, help distinguish Chinese gardens from garden counterparts in other cultures in which vegetation dominates.

The garden a man built was always an integral part of his house, and the Chinese concept of a home is explicitly included in the term *yuanzhai,* or "garden-house." Larger gardens usually contain a number of *ting* [open courts in front of halls and lounges], as well as *yuan* [inner courts or courtyards formed by adjacent buildings and walls], which interweave with the house and garden into a harmonious whole (Figure 4.4). A home, or *jia,* is also popularly referred to as *jiating* [home-court] or *jiayuan* [home-garden] in order to reflect the intimate relationship between a home and its gardens. A commonly used term for a garden is *huayuan,* or "flower garden," a term that demands literally that flowers be planted, but a Chinese *huayuan*

House and Garden

Fig. 4.4. *The simplicity and elegance of this courtyard* [ting *or* yuan] *in Wangshi Yuan, Suzhou, typifies the taste and aesthetic standard of the Chinese literati of the time.* Source: Photograph by Joseph C. Wang 1985.

usually contains much more than just ornamental displays of flowering plants. Traditionally, a *huayuan* was composed of trees, rockeries, a pond or lake, zigzagging footpaths, winding corridors, bridges, and other garden structures for habitation, quiet viewing, and merrymaking in which the elements were arranged in such a way that they were often more artistically designed than nature itself.

A fully developed garden, such as any of the literati gardens discussed below, is indeed an artistic recreation of nature and a landscape "painting" in three dimensions. For the Chinese, it may be said, a garden is an outdoor "living room," designed not only for the necessities of life, but for the art of living as well.

Life in a Garden

Gardens of many types have played an integral part in the lives of Chinese, and they were found in many parts of the country (Clunas 1996; Keswick and Hardie 2003; Valder 2003). In this chapter, only the private gardens of Jiangnan, the region that lies to the south of the Changjiang River in southeastern China, will be highlighted. Here, in the well-watered and prosperous "land of fish and rice," private gardens, also called literati gardens, were designed by or built for scholars who demanded simplicity, elegance, and poetic meaning in their personal worlds. Many of these exquisite gardens in Suzhou, Yangzhou, and Hangzhou have disappeared because of neglect and the ravages of time, but still other classical gardens continue to offer pleasure to countless visitors even as they no longer offer enjoyment exclusively to an individual family.

Perhaps mirroring the real life experiences of their authors, many famous Chinese novels have used gardens as metaphorical barometers for the vicissitudes of the households who populate the stories, in which, for example, a flourishing garden reflects the prosperity of its household whereas its desolation indicates a family's decline. This can be seen clearly in the lavish eighteenth-century novel *Hong lou meng,* known in English as *The Dream of the Red Chamber* or *The Story of the Stone,* in which the rise and decline of a powerful family is narrated; and the Ming novel *Jin ping mei,* known in English as *The Golden Lotus.* In the Daguan Yuan, or "Grand View Garden," which is depicted in *Hong lou meng,* the buildings (large and small), myriad pathways, pools and streams, and rockery, as well as the plants, all are symbolic elements in the privileged life of a gentry family. On the state of the nation, the Song dynasty scholar Li Gefei similarly observed that the rise of a garden culture mirrored a thriving empire, while its deterioration signaled the

Joseph C. Wang

decline of a kingdom (Wong 2001). In this regard, the rise and fall of the extensive imperial garden complex called Yuanming Yuan in Beijing during the Qing dynasty (1644–1911) was among the most vivid testimonies of such a phenomenon in China's long history.

Going back in time, literary accounts of the carefree lives of the hermits of the Wei (220–265) and Jin (265–420) dynasties not only affirm their contribution to landscape painting and poetry, but also shed light on the formulation of the literati gardens as breeding grounds for creativity and accomplishment. Seeking a good life in the company of their own kind, scholar-hermits regularly met in gardens and indulged in activities that may have included quietly meditating, philosophizing,

Fig. 4.5. *A scene from* Huan cui tang yuan jing tu *depicting the "floating cup" game of drinking and poetry making, a popular literary event that started with Wang Xizhi's gathering at the Orchid Pavilion in 353 during the Eastern Jin dynasty.* Source: *Huan cui tang yuan jing tu* [Garden scenes of the encircled Emerald Hall], a woodblock print produced between 1602 and 1605. From the author's collection.

composing and reading poetry, painting, playing the zither, concentrating on games of chess, sampling tea, drinking wine, fishing, boating, picking herbs for medicine, and making pills in pursuit of immortality, following Daoist practices. Solitude and cultivated socializing set precedents for later scholars and artists, as many of these fashionable and respected pastimes continued to be in vogue in garden culture well into Song, Ming, and Qing times (Figure 4.5).

The Song dynasty painter and scholar Guo Xi summarized the requirements for a garden particularly well. In a garden, he stipulated, there must be scenery to be viewed, circuits to be followed, pleasure to be enjoyed, and residential spaces to be available. What follows is that to view the scenery, pavilions and terraces must be

Fig. 4.6. *The covered pathway, or* lang, *in the western section of Zhuozheng Yuan, Suzhou, provides views of the garden in motion.* Source: Photograph by Joseph C. Wang 1985.

built; to allow circulation, trails and paths must be built; to enjoy the garden, places must be created to facilitate poetry reading, fishing, boating, dancing, and feasting; and rooms and halls must be provided to accommodate literary friends for overnight stays. For the last, the *ting* or *tang,* both translated as "halls," *xuan* [lounges], *guan* [guest houses], *lou* [two-story buildings], and *ge* [two-story pavilions] were built to contain the library, entertainment, and sleeping quarters. Also, *xie* [waterside pavilions], *fang* [land boats], *ting* [pavilions], and *lang* [covered pathways] were constructed for viewing scenery and merrymaking (Figure 4.6).

In addition to the above requirements, the Ming author and garden connoisseur Wen Zhenheng (1585–1645) set a high goal for the design of gardens. In his *Changwuzhi, or Treatise of Superfluous Things,* Wen demanded that the design should reach such a state of perfection that the experience of roaming in one would cause the roamer "to forget his age, forget to go home, and forget his fatigue." One such experience was recorded by the Ming scholar Qi Biaojia (1602–1645), who confessed, "I would go to the garden early in the morning and come back late at night and leave any domestic business to be attended to under the lamplight" (cited in Lin 1935, 334).

Among the materials used for the enjoyment of a garden, wine appears to have been indispensable. In the celebration of a scene of unusual beauty in a garden, drink seemed to provide added incentive for writing poetry and playing music. The great Song poet Ouyang Xiu (1007–1072) found happiness in his garden, as he often got drunk there while celebrating with his friends. He named the garden Zuiweng

Joseph C. Wang

Ting, or "Old Drunkard's Pavilion," after himself, but he insisted that his real inter-est was not the wine but the mountains and streams. Intoxicated by the seasonal changes of the garden scenes, he recorded his pleasure in these words: "When the sun rises, the forest mists vanish, and when the clouds return, the crags and grottos fall into shadows; these alternations of light and darkness mark the mountain's dawns and dusks. As the wild flowers blossom, they send forth a subtle fragrance; as tall trees bloom, they yield deep shade; then the winds and frost are lofty and pure, the rivers dry up and their stones are exposed; these are the four seasons in the mountains" (cited in Egan 1984, 216). In such an earthly paradise Ouyang shared his leisurely life with occasional visits from his closest friends. "They may freely fish in the brook, which is deep and filled with meaty fish, or brew wine from the brook, whose water is fragrant and whose wine is clear. To have, in addition, mountain fruits and wild herbs arrayed before one; this is a feast" (cited in Egan 1984, 216). What a garden—and what a life!

Literary accounts of the joys and pleasures of life in the Chinese garden are abundant, but Chen Fuyao, a Qing scholar, produced by far the most memorable narratives in his *Huajing,* or *Flower Mirror,* which was first published about 1688. His accounts, which read like an autobiography of a leisurely life, register the full extent of his seasonal itinerary in the setting of his naturalistic house garden. On a typical spring day, he notes the following:

> After getting up in the morning and drinking a cup of juice made from plum-flower petals, I went on to supervise the servants cleaning the garden paths and the house. Afterward, I read some books on seasonal planting and did maintenance work on the moss on the steps. Near noontime, I washed my hands with rose-scented cologne before lighting the delicate *yu rui* incense to refresh the house and also read some passages from the popular literature *Chiwen liuzi.*
>
> At noon, I went out in the garden and picked bamboo shoots and bracken as fuel to heat the springwater for the new tea leaves. In the afternoon, with a jug of wine and two oranges in hand, I rode my old horse to the bird sanctuary to hear orioles singing. Later in the afternoon, I sat under the willow tree and enjoyed the breeze while casually composing a few lines of poetry on my color-ful personal stationery. My favorite pastimes in the evening were taking a walk along the garden path, supervising the gardeners' work on the flowerbeds, and feeding the storks and fish. (Cited in Yang 1988, 71–72; my translation)

Fig. 4.7. *The "landscape window" by Li Liweng.* Source: Adapted from an illustration by Li Liweng.

Although no family participation is mentioned and no delineation of physical features or scenes is offered, the natural beauty and the many accommodations in Chen's garden are implicit in these accounts. Nature was abundant and the owner content. Chen must have been blessed with the good fortune of having a spacious garden at his disposal all year round.

Others may not have enjoyed such a luxury, but they led a good life in nature and with art in their own ways. One such person was Li Liweng (1611–1680), a dramatist, designer, epicure, musician, artist, and inventor. Li reported in *Xianqing ouji,* or *A Temporary Lodge for My Leisure Thoughts,* that he had invented a picture window that he had named "landscape window" and had had one installed in his small garden, Jiezi Yuan, or "Mustard Seed Garden" (Figure 4.7). Behind his garden studio, Fubai Xuan, or "Studio of Frothy White" (a name that itself signified drinking), there stood a miniature landscape Li had designed for himself. The assemblage had "a hill about ten feet high and seven feet wide, decorated with miniature scenery of red cliffs and blue water, thick forests and tall bamboo, singing birds and falling cataracts, thatched huts and wooden bridges, complete in all the things that we see in a mountain village." Li made a window in the studio wall to accommodate the view and "sat there the whole day looking at it, and could not bear to close the window." What followed was a sudden inspiration that led to his fuller enjoyment of the garden, art, and indeed life itself. His words record the serendipitous discovery of an "unintentional painting" and epitomize the art of living in a traditional Chinese garden:

> And one day inspired I said to myself, "This hill can be made into a painting, and this painting can be made into a window. All it will cost me will be just one day's drink money to provide the 'mounting' for this painting." I therefore asked a boy servant to cut out several pieces of paper, and pasted them above and below the window and at the sides, to serve as the mounting for a real picture. Thus the mounting was complete, and only the space usually occupied by the painting itself was left vacant, with the hill behind my house to take its place. Thus when one sits and looks at it, the window is no more a window, but a piece of painting, and the hill is no longer the hill behind my house but a hill in the painting. I could not help laughing out loud, and my wife and children, hearing my laughter, came to see it and joined in laughing at what I had been laughing at. This is the origin of the "unintentional painting," and the "landscape window." (Cited in Lin 1935, 272–273)

Joseph C. Wang

In the world of Chinese gardens, no coherent theory of design was available until 1634, when Ji Cheng (1582–?) published his *Yuan ye,* or *Manual of Garden Design.*[1] Ji, a painter and garden builder, was among a small number of first-generation professional gardeners who practiced their craft in the southeastern provinces of China during the late Ming dynasty. *Yuan ye* was in essence a summation of Ji's lifelong gardening practices and is the only early monograph on Chinese garden design and construction to have survived to the present. A collection of experiences rather than a system of theory and methods, *Yuan ye* is a reaffirmation of long-held conventions instead of a proposal for innovation and revolution:

- Ji advocates a natural look in the designed scenery, the creation of what might be called "land art" or "scenic art," so that "though man-made, it will look like something created naturally" (Ji 1932, vol. 1, *On Gardens:* 43). "Skill in landscape design is shown in the ability to 'follow' the lie of the land and 'borrow from' the existing scenery; artistic excellence is shown in the 'suitability' and 'appropriateness' created" in the garden's overall look (vol. 1, A Theory of Construction: 39).
- The notion of "borrowed" scenery—from the surrounding and often distant environment beyond the confines of the garden's walls—in the design of a garden is perhaps Ji's single most important contribution. He encourages "borrowing scenery from the distance, near at hand, above you, below you, and at certain times of the year." Scenes in a garden also borrow from one another and are linked in a sequence or progression. In addition, the sounds, colors, and smells from a larger environment could be borrowed to enhance the enjoyment of a particular garden (vol. 3, ch. 6, On Borrowing Scenery: 121).
- Ji's treatise offers clear and precise instructions on the importance of rockeries or hillocks, the piling up of "artificial hills": "If a single rock is set upright in the center as the 'chief stone' and two more rocks, known as 'split peaks,' are inserted on each side, the single one will stand in solitary magnificence and the lesser ones will act as supporters" (vol. 3, ch. 4, On Mountain-Building: 106).
- It is significant, however, that the book makes no mention of plants as garden elements.
- In the design process, *Yuan ye* underscores that the presentation of the garden's scenes should be given the greatest emphasis. In this regard, "The most important element in the layout of gardens is the siting of the principal buildings. The

Fig. 4.8a–b.

a. *Neither inlet nor outlet for the water can be seen along the main circulation route in Zhan Yuan, Nanjing.* Source: Photograph by Joseph C. Wang 1985.

b. *Ji Cheng's advice on the management of water in a Chinese garden: create an illusion to suggest that water comes from nowhere and that it is endless.* Source: Original drawing by Gan Yuhui.

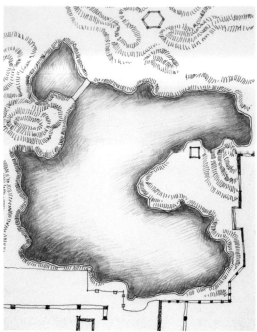

primary consideration is the view, and it is all the better if the buildings can face south" (vol. 1, ch. 2, Layout: 54).

- Rocks and water are considered by many Chinese gardeners, both before and after Ji's time, as the two most important elements in a garden. Ji counsels the garden designer to "build up mountains from the excavated soil and form embankments along the edges of the ponds," as well as that "high mounds can be further heightened and low-lying places should be dug deeper still." His advice on the management of water is most intriguing: "Water should be allowed to flow freely as if it had no end, and when it blocks your path, build a bridge across it." This statement can be interpreted to suggest that the shape of a pond should be such that neither inlet nor outlet for the water can be seen along the main circulation route (Figure 4.8). Where the source of the water must reveal itself, one should build a bridge to cover it. An illusion is thus created to suggest that water comes from nowhere and that it is endless (vol. 1, ch. 2, Layout: 55).

As outlined above, *Yuan ye* is intended to provide a general impression of how the Chinese garden is composed. While Ji's book contains design ideas and general guidelines, it fails to offer clearly defined methods and rules for creating a garden.

Joseph C. Wang

However, suggestions of practical value and artistic interest to garden designers are readily available from an array of classical literature. One such useful source is a simple genre called *xiaopinwen,* essays by scholar-gardeners such as Wen Zhenheng, Chen Fuyao, and Li Liweng. Their casual yet enlightening writings (those quoted above among them) offer useful information on the conception and techniques of design, as well as on the creative ways in which gardens were appreciated.

A little memoir by Shen Fu (1763–?), *Fusheng liuji,* or *Six Chapters of a Floating Life,* incorporates a discussion of what can be called the "art of deception" in scenery design for the Chinese garden. Shen suggests a bipolar formula—"showing the large in the small and the small in the large, providing for the real in the unreal and for the unreal in the real"—in which the beholder is simultaneously deceived and delighted as views are alternately revealed and concealed, making them sometimes apparent and sometimes hidden. In the chapter "The Little Pleasures of Life," Shen elaborates:

> In the big open spaces, plant bamboos that grow quickly and train plum trees with thick branches to cover them. This is to show the small in the large. When the courtyard is small, the wall should be a combination of convex and concave shapes, decorated with green, covered with ivy, and inlaid with big slabs of stone with inscriptions on them. Thus when you open your window, you seem to face a rocky hillside, alive with rugged beauty. This is to show the large in the small. Contrive so that an apparently blind alley leads suddenly into an open space and the kitchen leads through a back door into an unexpected courtyard. This is to provide for the real in the unreal. Let a door lead into a blind courtyard and conceal the view by placing a few bamboo trees and a few rocks. Thus you suggest something which is not there. Place low balustrades along the top of a wall so as to suggest a roof garden which does not exist. This is to provide for the unreal in the real. (Cited in Lin 1935, 331)

An anonymous writer offered an explicit prescription for the design of an approach to a common house garden that draws inspiration from Shen's concerns with viewing scenery and experiencing spaces:

> Inside the gate there is a footpath and the footpath must be winding. At the turning of the footpath there is an outdoor screen and the screen must be small. Behind the screen there is a terrace and the terrace must be level. On the banks of the terrace there are flowers and the flowers must be fresh. Beyond the flowers is a wall and the wall must be low. By the side of the wall,

there is a pine tree and the pine tree must be old. At the foot of the pine tree there are rocks and the rocks must be quaint. Over the rocks there is a pavilion and the pavilion must be simple. Behind the pavilion are bamboos and the bamboos must be thin and sparse. At the end of the bamboos there is a house and the house must be secluded. (Cited in Lin 1937, 267)

The early seventeenth-century writer Qi Biaojia characterized the process of garden design as one that was reiterative and accomplished by trial and error:

In general, where there is too much space I put in a thing; where it is too crowded I take away a thing; where things cluster together I spread them out; where the arrangement is too diffuse I tighten it a bit; where it is difficult to walk upon I level it; and where it is level I introduce a little unevenness. It is like a good doctor curing a patient, using both nourishing and excitative medicines, or like a good general in the field, using both normal and surprise tactics. Again, it is like a master painter at his work, not allowing a single dead stroke. (Cited in Lin 1935, 335)

The design approaches of all three of these writers seem to fall within the framework of Ji's conceptualization and manipulation of space. In particular, Shen understood perfectly the principle of visual perception and had mastered the art of contrast, concealment, and suggestion in the design of his humble garden. Like many scholar-gardeners before him, the unnamed author demonstrated his expertise in luring the visitor through a maze of vistas embedded with optical temptations and surprises. Qi spoke of the true nature of the creative endeavor, which, much like producing a painting, used no formula or logic but was rooted in subjective and personal judgment, as well as feelings and vision.

Whereas explicit statements concerning the methods of garden design are relatively rare in Chinese literature, theories of landscape painting abound and have guided garden design through the crucial stages of its long development. Landscape painting indeed was given the title "Mother of Garden Art" in recognition of the fact that the gardens and parks of ancient China were designed almost exclusively by painters. Records show that great painters such as Wang Wei (699–759) of the Tang dynasty, the Song emperor Huizhong, Ni Zan (1301–1374) of the Yuan dynasty, Wen Zhengming (1470–1559) of the Ming dynasty, and Shi Tao (Dao Ji or Tao-chi, 1641–ca. 1717) of the Qing dynasty left behind masterpieces that capture the moods and structures of famous gardens of their times. While their paintings served as the

Fig. 4.9. *A reconstructed sketch showing a bird's-eye view of the southern section of Pianshi Mountain House.* Source: Wu 1992. Redrawn by Wang Gang.

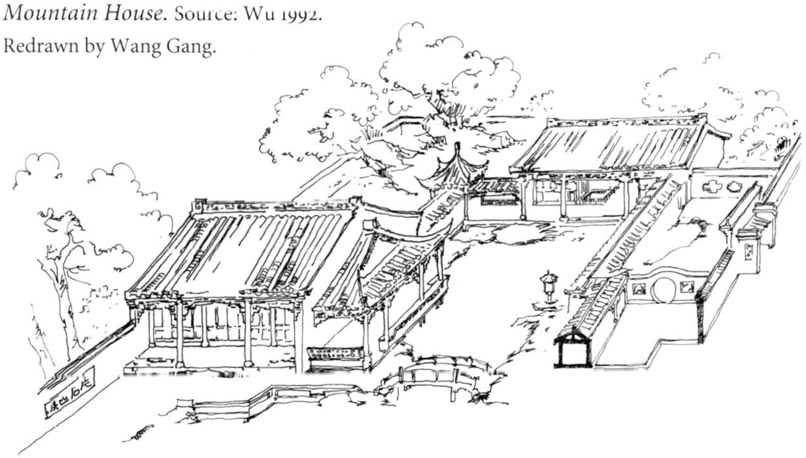

Fig. 4.10. *The whitewashed wall serves as a canvas, with the bamboo and rocks representing painting on it.* Source: Ji Cheng 1988, 26.

inspiration for garden designers, the artists themselves also participated in the design and construction of landscape gardens. Wang Wei's villa at Wangchuan, a hermitage designed for his use, is recorded in a twenty-one scene horizontal scroll, while the ruins of a rockery peak in Yangzhou's Pianshi Shanfang, or "Pianshi Mountain House," which was designed by Shi Tao, are still visible today (Figure 4.9).

A landscape artist approached garden design the same way he would execute a piece of landscape painting in that both a garden and a painting were inspired by the beauty of nature and circumstantial sentimentality. The interplay between painting and the garden arts was best described by Ji in *Yuan ye:* "Treat the whitewashed wall as if it were paper, and the rocks as painting upon it" (Ji 1988, 109) (Figure 4.10). The formation of rockery, in particular, was significantly influenced by and benefited from painting. Kan Duo, a modern-day scholar, commented on this relationship in his foreword to the 1932 edition of *Yuan ye:* "Mountain-building in a garden derived its art from painting in that the painter uses brushes and ink, while the rockery artist employs rocks and earth as design media. Whereas the media they use are different, the principle of design is the same" (Ji 1932, 18). As Ji advises, among other things, a garden designer could learn from painters to "study

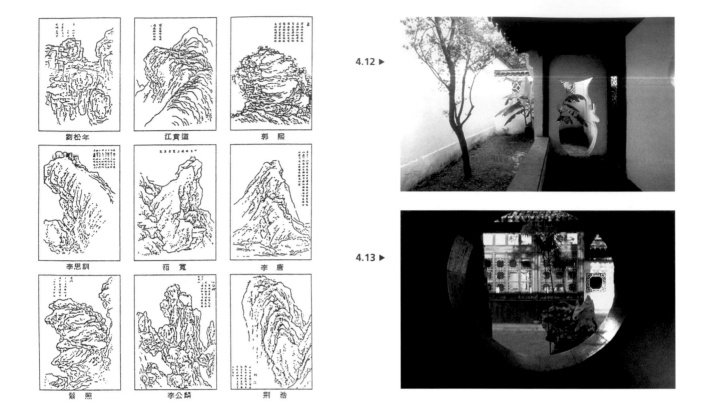

劉松年　　　　　江貫道　　　　　郭　熙

李思訓　　　　　范　寛　　　　　李　唐

郭　熙　　　　　李公麟　　　　　荊　浩

4.12 ▶

4.13 ▶

▲ **Fig. 4.11.** *The textured strokes of rocks and mountains by various painters were used as models for building artificial hills in gardens.* Source: Huang 1986.

Fig. 4.12. *A geometric opening in Cuilinglong, or "Delicate Emerald Hall," in Canglangting, Suzhou.* Source: Photograph by Joseph C. Wang 1985.

Fig. 4.13. *A circular window in Tuisi Yuan, Suzhou.* Source: Photograph by Joseph C. Wang 1985.

the natural cracks in the stone, and imitate the brushwork of the old masters" (Figure 4.11). In fact, at the height of garden art during the late Ming and early Qing dynasties, the most popular mountain-building approach used modeling after the texture strokes *(cun fa)* and pictorial compositions of the master painters of the Yuan dynasty, which immediately preceded. In the works of the Four Great Literati Painters of the Yuan dynasty, the mountains of Huang Gongwang (1269–1354), composed of small pieces of crystal, appear grandiose and heavy; the innumerable mountains and valleys by Wang Meng (ca. 1308–1385) are misty and finely crafted. Ni Zan was famous for his depiction of withered trees in combination with bamboo and rocks. His composition was simple and sparse, yet it projected a strong sentiment of loneliness and sadness. The broad, misty, and remote mountain views by Wu Zhen (1285–1354) added to the rich palette of ideas and patterns from which garden makers freely drew in their work.

The principles of painting—specifically the syntax of painting composition—have been directly and successfully applied to garden design. In Chinese painting, conventional formats include the vertical and horizontal, the handscroll, and the juxtaposition of individual frames, in addition to fan-shaped, circular, octagonal,

Fig. 4.14. *A framed view from Wuzhuyouju, or "The Secluded Pavilion amid Wutong and Bamboo," in Zhuozheng Yuan, Suzhou.* Source: Photograph by Joseph C. Wang 1985.

Fig. 4.15. *A moon gate framing the view beyond.* Source: Photograph by Joseph C. Wang 1985.

and other geometrical formats. Deliberately and thoughtfully, these geometrical forms are employed in the window-like openings that are part of the architectural elements of the garden in order to frame scenes (Figures 4.12–4.15). Thus a garden can be experienced as a three-dimensional painting in which pictures—mini-composed scenes—are framed by a variety of devices, including windows (as seen in Figure 4.16) and openings in the garden walls (Figure 4.17). As a visitor moves along a garden path, scenes will unfold in a progression of space and time much as if a handscroll were being unrolled for viewing (Figure 4.18).

As opposed to the Renaissance perspective technique, in which one, two, or three vanishing points are used in creating a picture, Chinese painters utilized scattered, or multiple, vanishing points in perspective drawing, a principle that was also employed in Chinese garden design. Utilizing this versatile technique of using as many vanishing points as deemed necessary to depict a particular scene, Chinese artists were able to enjoy complete freedom in content selection, sequencing, layout, and composition (Figure 4.19). Based on impressions and feelings about the task at hand, this freedom of movement, as well as the placement and sequencing of the "pictures," greatly benefited the design of gardens and parks. A cherished goal

House and Garden

Fig. 4.16. *Some of the tracery windows used in Chinese gardens.* Source: Liu 1993, 288.

▼

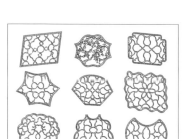

▲

Fig. 4.17. *Various shapes of gates, often generically referred to as "moon gates," are used in Chinese gardens.* Source: Liu 1993, 290.

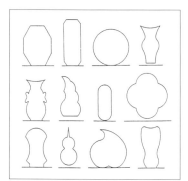

▶

Fig. 4.18. *The present-day entrance to Liu Yuan, Suzhou, with its 100-foot passage, embodies the essence of the design principles of a Chinese garden.* Source: Photographs by Joseph C. Wang 1985 and layout by Xu Jun.

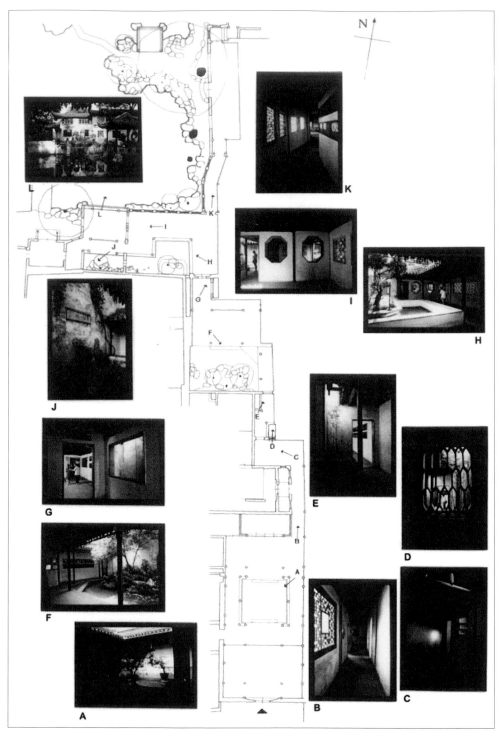

Fig. 4.19. *This imaginary panorama of Daguan Yuan, or "Grand View Garden," from* The Dream of the Red Chamber *provides a good example of the versatility of the scattered vanishing point technique in perspective drawing.* Source: *Shitou ji* [The story of the Stone]. Courtesy of Shanghai Tushu Guan Cang (Collection of the Shanghai Library).

of the scholar-gardener was to use his creation as a vehicle to embody and convey a specific set of *shi qing hua yi,* literally "poetic sentiments and artistic conceptions." While poetry and landscape painting were believed to be the most effective tools for achieving these goals, the *qing* [sentiment or feeling], best expressed in a poem, and the *yi* [conception or idea], best intimated in a landscape painting, helped guide the design objectives for garden schemes as well. As a result, the enormous wealth of *hua lun,* or "theories of painting," together with poems and prose from the past, became bounteous resources at the disposal of a garden designer.

Although there is no standardized process for the creation of a garden, an example of a design was developed from the southern courtyard of Zhan Yuan, an early Ming dynasty garden located in Nanjing (Figure 4.20). The procedure and sequence exhibited in this illustration do not necessarily reflect the actual process by which Zhan Yuan was designed and built since no such document ever existed in Chinese garden history. Yet as an academic exercise, it demonstrates reasonably well the genesis and evolution of a traditional Chinese garden design:

a. Once a site was selected, invariably the first decision was to establish the location and orientation of the main hall. Ideally, the hall was to be located in the northern section of the garden, facing south when possible, and overlooking the best scenes that the garden would provide.

House and Garden

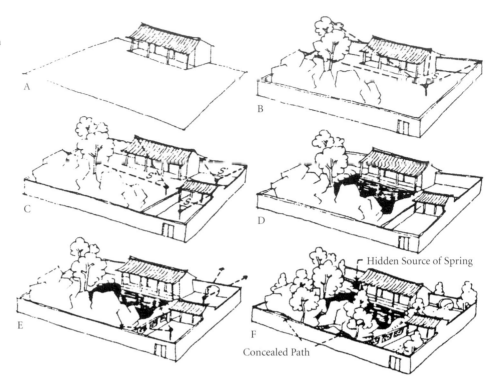

b. Next, high walls were laid up along the perimeter of the garden proper in order to enclose it. Critical elements, such as mature and old trees and rockery formations or artificial hills, were maintained and positioned. The heights of the main hall, trees, and rocks were decided to allow the proper "borrowing," in Ji Cheng's terms, of scenes from above and beyond the garden itself.

c. Spaces within the garden were skillfully subdivided to make a small garden appear large and multiply the variety of scenery found in it. Subdivision was the key to the creation of a sense of boundlessness within a limited site.

d. As a final touch for the composition, a body of water, usually a pond, was excavated and linked to channels of water coursing above and below ground. Pond water as well as circulating water was an indispensable element since it not only contrasted with the rockery and provided a mirrored image of scenic objects, but it also gave life to and mobilized the static artificial hills in a garden scene.

e. Latticed windows made of wood, stone, and brick were used to lure the visitor into the garden's space. A moon gate and other geometric openings were often employed to frame scenes within the garden and to create the illusion of depth. As a rule, no cul-de-sac or dead end was permitted in any garden space, so path-

Fig. 4.21. *A view of Gu Mu Jiao Ke, or "Intertwined Ancient Tree," in Liu Yuan, Suzhou. Here the garden spaces and pathways seem to continue in forward motion with no cul-de-sacs.* Source: Photograph by Joseph C. Wang 1985.

Fig. 4.22. *Simple techniques used in designing a sequence of garden scenes.* Source: Original drawing by Mac Mengzhou Liu.

ways always seemed to continue in forward motion (Figure 4.21). The visitor was never allowed to see the panoramic whole of the Chinese garden at the outset since it was only in a carefully designed sequence of the hidden, the peeking, and the revealed that scenes of enchantment would emerge along routes of movement and at observation spots (Figure 4.22).

f. To complete the design, the final step was to hide the source of the pond and to conceal the footpath amid the traces of imagined mountains and valleys.

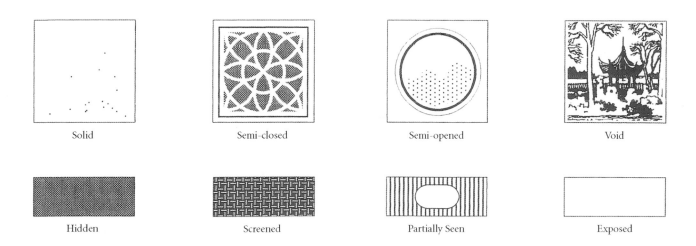

| Solid | Semi-closed | Semi-opened | Void |

| Hidden | Screened | Partially Seen | Exposed |

In a scholar's garden, literary inscriptions are integral components of its composition. Scenes and poetry are employed to complement each other in order to give the viewer the fullest possible appreciation of a landscape. Thus, poetry was traditionally incorporated into a garden scheme in order to invoke a semantic dimension, or meaning, in the garden's scenes. While complete calligraphic texts might be used, single Chinese characters and phrases were usually sufficient to evoke a more comprehensive meaning for the cognoscenti. For example, the name of the Yuanxiang Tang, or "Hall of Distant Fragrance," in Zhuozheng Yuan, "the Humble Administrator's Garden," in Suzhou, was taken from the verse "fragrance in the distance makes it even more pure and distinct," a reference from the popular treatise *Ailian shuo, The Love of Lotus,* by the Song dynasty philosopher Zhou Dunyi (Figure 4.23). A followup verse, "growing out of muddy waters yet remaining uncontaminated," was read with equal attention to its meaning. The association of Zhou's first verse with the building tells the visitor that there are fragrant flowers at a distance from the hall. Even though no specific plant is mentioned by name, the second verse hints that lotus blossoms give off the fragrance. Submerged in this mental context, any knowledgeable beholder with a highly refined taste would be all the more appreciative of the prominence of Yuanxiang Tang as one of the major scenic spots in the Zhuozheng Yuan. Already distinct due to its relative size and central location, its distinction was further enhanced by the presence of lotus blossoms and the recognition of their standing as central symbols of Buddhism.

Fig. 4.23. *A summer scene at Yuanxiang Tang, or "Hall of Distant Fragrance," in Zhuozheng Yuan, "the Humble Administrator's Garden," Suzhou.* Source: Photograph by Joseph C. Wang 1985.

In China, each garden bears a name, much like a painting has a distinctive title. The name was usually elegantly calligraphed and prominently inscribed on the garden gate, and it reflected the character of the garden, as well as the disposition of its owner-designer. The Ge Yuan in Yangzhou, for instance, has an apparently simple name, composed of a single character meaning "one" or "single," followed by the character for "garden." At the equally simple moon-shaped entrance, several shapely clumps of bamboo adorn the entryway against the white garden wall. The two Chinese characters "Ge Yuan," as seen in Figure 4.24, are inscribed horizontally in rectangular relief above the gate. At first glance, the pictorial composition appears plain and unpretentious, and few would be able to comprehend the subtlety behind this seemingly ordinary facade. The key rests with the character *ge* 个. The calligraphic shape of *ge* resembles one-half of the Chinese character *zhu* 竹, or bamboo, the symbol of unyielding integrity in the Chinese mind. By implication and thus indirectly, Huang Yingtai, who was the first owner of Ge Yuan, no doubt considered himself the single and only remaining bamboo branch left in a troubled world. Through the naming of his garden, he wanted others to appreciate his good character.

Assigning names to gardens, as well as to the buildings and scenery within them, began as early as the Qin and Han dynasties and has since become an integral part of garden design in China. Chinese characters are ubiquitous visual elements throughout gardens and function as much more than a mere ornamentation of line and texture. Brief names, antithetical couplets, poems, and chronicles about the garden were written in ink or carved on specially designed boards and tablets that were hung in either horizontal or vertical formats (Figure 4.25). In addition, literary expressions were added to upright stone tablets, steles, rocks, and cliffsides within

Fig. 4.24. *The entrance to Ge Yuan, Yangzhou, Jiangsu.* Source: Photograph by Xu Dejia 1976.

Fig. 4.25. *Couplets that adorn a translucent latticed window in Ou Yuan, Suzhou.* Source: Photograph by Joseph C. Wang 1985.

the garden and in nearby scenic spots. Aside from their ornamental value, these inscriptions served—and continue to serve—as a kind of guidebook for the garden visitor. Of course, and perhaps more important, they originally provided the owner-designer and his literary colleagues many opportunities to show off their erudition and skill in both calligraphy and poetry writing.

Literati gardens often held deeply rooted negative messages in that their owners frequently built them as expressions of denial, self-protection, and seclusion in response to the buffetings of the unstable and chaotic society in which they lived. Historical evidence has shown that most owner-designers of literati gardens were intellectuals who had experienced setbacks in their governmental careers. It is not surprising, then, that there is an overriding anti-establishment sentiment and a defensive mentality surrounding the art and craft of garden building. More often than not, the prevalent message was, "The court has wronged me." Gardens, there-fore, were not only retreats in the owners' exile, but also appropriate vehicles for members of the intelligentsia to tell stories that had not been told, air grievances that had not been disclosed, describe dreams that had not been fulfilled, and pro-pose visions that had not materialized. In other words, intellectuals used their pri-vate gardens as an art form to express their opinions about the affairs of the world, much as they used poetry to air their inner feelings. For fear of retaliation and pun-ishment by the imperial court, they used language that was negative yet subtle, sar-castic yet indirect, and melancholy yet proud. Although tinted with its owner's emotions, a private garden embodied universal ideals that strove for oneness with nature and transcended the confines of a small, enclosed microcosm. In this way, a literati garden was the antithesis of its imperial counterpart.

Aside from marital bliss, the Chinese also traditionally cherished lasting friend-ship as a form of romance. Tongyin Guan, or "Music from the Tong Tree Guest-house," in Nanjing's Xu Yuan, or "Warm Garden," has a moving story behind its name. The guesthouse was surrounded on all sides by *tong* trees—tall, soft-wooded, smooth-barked deciduous trees with leaves that are heart-shaped; these features together give clues to the significance of the story. According to the narratives in *Lushi chunqiu,* or *Lu's Annals of Spring and Autumn,* Yu Boya, a high-ranking official during the Spring and Autumn (770–476 B.C.), was an accomplished ama-teur zither player who regularly practiced his art in a secluded wilderness. His only admirer was a hermit named Zhong Ziqi, who lived in the mountains as a woods-man. Over the years, a deep friendship developed between the musician and his faithful audience, as Ziqi was able to appreciate fully the hidden messages in Boya's music. The "romance," however, abruptly ended when Ziqi suddenly died of

Joseph C. Wang

poverty. Out of profound sadness, Boya broke his instrument and never played again. Since the wood of the *tong* tree was known as one of the best materials for making Chinese string instruments, the Xu Yuan's owner planted *tong* trees around the guesthouse and named it Tongyin Guan in the absence of a faithful admirer and in honor of Ziqi. Did he also miss his sole admirer?

Members of the Chinese intelligentsia, both in the imperial service and in everyday life, passionately protected personal integrity as their most valued and cherished virtue. When the integrity of one of them was violated, he turned to poetry writing and garden building as suitable vehicles for airing grievances and clearing his name. Such instances are numerous and legendary. The building of the Ge Yuan, as mentioned above, is but one example. By naming his garden as he did, Huang Yingtai has come to be known in history as a man who cherished honesty and justice.

A similar story involving several of Suzhou's famous gardens and a wise angler of the Warring States period (475–221 B.C.) is equally revealing. After the great poet and statesman Qu Yuan (ca. 340–ca. 278 B.C.) was sent into exile by the king of Chu, he met a fisherman one day at the riverbank, and their discussion led to a conversation about the causes of Qu's apparent unhappiness. Describing his personal circumstances, Qu recited the famous verses from the *Chuci*, or *Songs of Chu*: "While the whole world is corrupt, I am the only one who is clean; while the whole world is drunk, I am the only one who is sober." Sympathetic and laughing, the fisherman responded, singing, "If the *cang lang* [blue waves] were clean, I would wash my tassel in them and join in to serve the King; if the *cang lang* were muddy, I would wash my feet in them and enjoy a carefree hermit life instead" (my translations). The term *cang lang*, taken from the fisherman's song, was later adopted for Canglangting Yuan, or "Surging-Wave Pavilion Garden," the oldest surviving garden in Suzhou. The story of Qu Yuan inspired the design of other gardens in Suzhou as well, including Xiaocanglang Ting, or "Little Canglang Pavilion," in Zhuozheng Yuan and in Yi Yuan, as well as the Zhuoying Shuige, or "Washing-Tassel Water Pavilion," in Wangshi Yuan. In memory of the fisherman, another garden in Suzhou was named Yuying Yuan, or "Fisherman Hermit Garden," whose name later was changed to Wangshi Yuan, or "Master of the Nets Garden," a clear reference to the fisherman.

Chinese scholar-painters—in contrast to the grandiose ambitions of the emperors—appeared to shun wealth and power, preaching instead a doctrine of simplicity and naturalness as the most meaningful lifestyle. Chuyue Xuan, "Hoe-Moon Lounge," in the Yi Yuan garden in Suzhou, suggested ridding the rice fields of

Fig. 4.26. *Illustration of a bucolic scene by Dao Ji (1641–ca. 1717) for an episode of* The Peach Blossom Spring, *by Tao Qian (also known as Tao Yuanming). Section of a handscroll, ink and color on paper, 9 7/8 in.* Source: Used with the permission of the Freer Gallery of Art, Smithsonian Institution, Washington, D.C. (Purchase F1957.4).

weeds, and the Huafeng Zhai, "Painted Pleasure boathouse," in many private gardens symbolized a safeguard against undesirable, usually political, storms, much like Noah's Ark in the biblical story. A simple life, good social relations, and clean politics were an integral part of the scholar's often unfulfilled lifelong ambitions and wishes.

Of all the poets mentioned so far in this discussion, Tao Qian of the Jin dynasty was perhaps the most influential in bringing visionary ideals to garden design. Living and working during one of the most troubled times in Chinese history, he became a symbol of hope and solace when he published a heart-throbbing and celebrated work entitled *Taohua yuan ji, The Peach Blossom Spring* (Figure 4.26). Using fablelike prose, Tao described how a fisherman accidentally discovered a happy land as he was rowing aimlessly one day along a stream:

> He suddenly came to a grove of peach trees in bloom. For several hundreds of paces on both banks of the stream there was no other kind of tree. The fragrant flowers were fresh and beautiful; fallen petals lay in rich profusion. . . . Where the [blossoming peach] grove ended at the stream's source there stood a hill, in which there was a small opening. . . . At first extremely narrow, . . . it opened out into a broad, level plain where houses and huts stood neatly, with rich fields and lovely ponds, mulberries, bamboos and the like. The field dikes crisscrossed; chickens and dogs could be heard from farm to farm. . . . White-haired elders and children with hair in flowing tufts were all happily enjoying themselves. When [the people] saw the fisherman, they were greatly surprised. . . . Then they invited him to their home, setting out wine and killing a chicken to prepare a meal. . . . They said their ancestors

fled from the troubles of Qin times . . . [and] asked what dynasty it was now; they knew nothing of the existence of the Han, let alone the Wei or the Jin. (Cited in Kwong 1994, 51)

The narrative of *The Peach Blossom Spring,* unlike pure fantasy, dwells on the description of a simple village community that is in appearance down to earth and familiar even to "outsiders." Poised between the poles of fact and fiction, Tao was able to stimulate the imaginations of centuries of poets and painters, as well as the designers of gardens, as they set out to create utopias according to their own emotions and agendas.

As the examples above clearly illustrate, a garden can be read as a metaphysical embodiment of an ideal romance (as in the story of Tongyin Guan in Nanjing), an ideal character (as in the cases of Ge Yuan, Canglangting Yuan, and Wangshi Yuan), an ideal ambition (as with Chuyue Xuan and Huafang Zhai), and an ideal world (as in the utopia in Tao Qian's *Taohua yuan ji*). In such displays of self-expression, the *qing,* or "feelings captured while 'flowing' from literature," and the *jing,* or "forms embodied in scenery 'projecting' out of visual images," are merged into one (Sun 1982, 46).

In the midst of urban chaos, a scholar-gardener was able to carve out for his family and himself an oasis in which he was able to indulge in sensual delight, artistic enrichment, and spiritual uplift. While gardens served in this way as sanctuaries for the bodies and minds of privileged dwellers, they also created an extended "living room," where fresh air and sunlight were abundant, guests were entertained, and children played. Often designed with the same careful thought given to the composition of a landscape painting, a Chinese garden took shape through the utilization of time-tested principles of spatial organization and visual perception. As with poetry and painting, scholarship and sophistication must be employed to fully appreciate these works of art. Nonetheless, the charm and natural beauty as well as the practical function of Chinese literati gardens can be readily enjoyed by everyone.

NOTES _____

This chapter is an abridged and rewritten version of *The Chinese Garden,* by Joseph C. Wang (1998). The author gratefully acknowledges the permission of Oxford University Press (China) to use the published material. This essay is dedicated to the happy memories of June Kuo-kiang Wang (1938–1999), who always shared my joy in writing about Chinese gardens and architecture.

1. *Yuan ye* was translated into English by Alison Hardie (1988) as *The Craft of Gardens.*

RONALD G. KNAPP

5   *Siting and Situating a Dwelling*

Fengshui, *House-Building Rituals, and Amulets*

Even as the popularity of *fengshui* in rural and urban China persists, the public at large and scholars elsewhere in the world have increased their interest in it. Countless *fengshui* guidebooks and manuals in Chinese as well as other languages— Bulgarian, Czech, Hebrew, Polish, Portuguese, Turkish (among others) in addition to abundant titles in English, Spanish, French, Japanese, Indonesian, Korean, Thai, and Vietnamese—attest not only to global awareness of a rather abstruse set of Chinese beliefs, but also to their enduring credibility. While much attention focuses on how *fengshui* can assist people in increasing their wealth, happiness, and longevity, there also is substantial concern for pursuing "a better life," "clearing your clutter," "love and romance," "well-being," "balance and harmony," "trouble-free remodeling," "helping children thrive," "improving relationships," "healing," "manipulating one's destiny," "and business success." Yet it is important to note that the precepts of *fengshui* are fundamentally rooted in the action of siting and situating a building—that is, choosing an auspicious location, a spatial setting— rather than the mere pursuit of bliss. A spatial setting involves two fundamental geographic attributes: a "site"—the actual space occupied by the structure—and its "situation"—the location of the site in relation to its broader surroundings. Traditionally, certain sites and situations for the structures of a particular family or lineage were viewed as more favorable than others, according to basic *fengshui* axioms, and a proper choice would then influence, perhaps even control, the fortunes and general benefits that would redound to those who occupied a structure built on the site. This *self-conscious* attention to siting and situating houses—as well as palaces, temples, and graves—manifests many aspects of traditional beliefs, including aspirations and fears. Some of these actions and efforts are conspicuously apparent in the character of individual dwellings, while many others are less obvious though no less significant.

The conceptual roots of *fengshui* are found in ancient classics such as the *Shijing* [Book of songs] and the *Shujing* [Book of documents], as well as other fragmentary texts, that reach back to the Zhou period (1100–770 B.C.). Taken together, they reveal some of the cosmo-symbolic conventions and practices for locating imperial

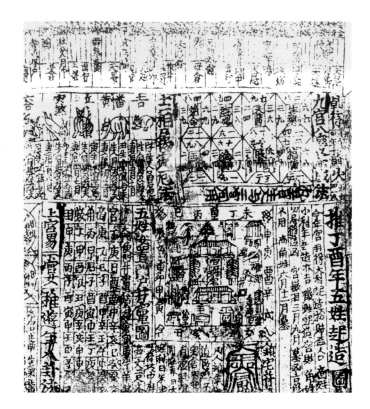

Fig. 5.1. *This page from a printed almanac dated 877 was found in a temple in Dunhuang in northwestern China. In addition to dos and don'ts in the vertical columns, the page includes a drawing of a quadrangular courtyard house, associating the main gate, well, latrine, storage, etc. to the twenty-four directions that are arrayed around it.* Source: By permission of the British Library, Or.8210/P.6.

capitals and palaces. *Fengshui*'s hold on the consciousness of common Chinese as they cope with decisions to modify the environments within which they live, however, is of more recent origin.[1] It is this powerful hold of *fengshui* practices on common people, who apply them at different scales in the search for auspicious sites for houses, graves, gardens, temples, and other buildings, as well as complete settlements, that is the focus of this chapter.

Throughout the Ming and Qing dynasties, popular almanacs provided points of access, a common lore, for the general public to the arcane features of divination, which was based upon correlative cosmology and of which *fengshui* was but one part (Figure 5.1). Although it is not easy to document the means by which Chinese villagers and townsfolk employed *fengshui* in the past, the results were subsequently readily observable in countless rural and urban landscapes. Traditional dwellings and villages throughout China today—in remote areas as well as in cosmopolitan centers—continue to be interpreted as having been sited via the elaborate application of *fengshui* esoterica, even if there is scant historical evidence of the actions themselves. In spite of the appealing and harmonious nature of many of these

Ronald G. Knapp

building sites and structures, as well as even the demonstrated good fortune of the inhabitants occupying them, it is nonetheless rarely clear that *fengshui* precepts were applied contemporaneously when the sites were selected. All too often, there is evidence of an after-the-fact application of *fengshui* ideas to structures already sited and built, thus leading to statements of lore based upon retrospective *fengshui* explanations that are "more convincing than [their] prospective counterpart," according to remarks by Freedman regarding burial sites (1966, 129). Moreover, it is important to recognize that Chinese elites and others who might have employed *fengshui*—whatever its ostensible authority over the ages—also have disdained it, even as they have used its explanatory metaphors (Xu 2000, 235). With the caveats that local practices diverge and that manuals and texts present often contradictory statements, it is still possible and useful to sketch out some of the core concepts and common applications regarding *fengshui*. With little thought to cosmological abstraction and theoretical constructs, even illiterate peasants, moreover, seem to have considered *fengshui* as they built their simple dwellings. Centuries ago, when the countryside was relatively unpopulated, the search for a suitable—even ideal— spatial setting for a house or grave often took a good deal of time. Today in China, while public interest in *fengshui* has increased significantly, even as the government has stigmatized it as "feudal superstition," the challenges of choosing auspicious sites in heavily built up and densely populated villages and towns are clearly easier to ponder than to carry out (Bruun 1996, 47–65, 2003; Knapp 1999b, 158–171).

Literally meaning "wind and water," *fengshui* is a modern colloquial expression of elaborated general ideas that encapsulates the more abstruse principles associated with earlier esoteric terms. *Buzhai* [divination of a house site], *kanyu* [cover and support *and* canopy of heaven and the chariot of earth], and *dili* [earth truth or land pattern, which is used today for the discipline of geography] are but three of a very large number of centuries-old terms employed as synonyms for *fengshui*. *Fengshui* is usually translated into English as "geomancy," but many specialists have found this term inadequate, offering some interesting alternatives—"topomancy" (Feuchtwang 1974, 2); "astro-ecology" and "topographical siting" (Bennett 1978, 2); "siting" (Smith 1991, 131); "ecomancy" (Rossides 1982); "mystical ecology" (Knapp 1986, 108–109); and "natural science of the landscape" (Berglund 1990, 240). Whatever the benefit of any of these terms, the Chinese term *fengshui* will be used in an untranslated form in this chapter.

The essence of *fengshui* is a universe animated by the interaction of *yin* and *yang*, in which an ethereal property known as *qi* [life breath or cosmic energy;

also called *shengqi*] gives character and meaning to a place at whatever the scale—city, town, village, residence, gravesite, etc. At an elementary level, each place exemplifies either *yin* or *yang* characteristics. Yet since sites usually exhibit both traits simultaneously and both *yin* and *yang* are intrinsically positive and beneficial, neither should be found in excess or in equilibrium. *Yin* sites, which are optimal for burial, frequently fall away from the sun to the north or northwest and render the female aspect, passivity and darkness, as well as the Earth and moon. The divination of a suitable grave site or *yinzhai* [an abode for the dead] using *fengshui* idioms has a long history of bringing good fortune to those continuing to live and "comfort" to those who occupy the *yinzhai* (Ahern 1973; Freedman 1966). In addition, locating a building site for a dwelling for the living, a *yangzhai,* as well as for a settlement such as a village—in a quest for benefits for those who are alive—similarly has been defined in both popular lore and written manuals.

Approaches to fengshui

By late imperial times, two basic approaches characterized *fengshui*, one stressing cosmic patterns and principles and the other their manifestations on the surface of the Earth: the former, the Compass School, also called the Analytical School [Liqi Zong or Fangwei Zong], depended upon complicated calculations; the latter, the somewhat older Configurations School, also called the Forms School [Xingshi Zong], was visually and intuitively based and emphasized topographical landscape features. Initially the schools may have been quite distinct, but over time and in practice their individual approaches came to be blurred as intuition and theory regarding celestial and terrestrial phenomena commingled with the realities of actual landscapes. Both schools are associated with traditions and practices that originated in southern China, especially Jiangxi, Fujian, and Zhejiang provinces. Emphasis in Jiangxi province was on the character of terrain, especially mountains and watercourses, while in Fujian and Zhejiang the use of a complicated *luopan,* or "compass," dominated. Whatever the school, the application of *fengshui* principles in very different geographic environments—the vast plains of North China, the restricted plots in the canal region of Jiangnan, the areas of rugged terrain throughout South China—led to a mélange of *fengshui* notions and conventions that sometimes defy any attempt to discern consistencies. Like various other forms of Chinese fate calculation, site selection is personalized by using eight Chinese characters, or *bazi,* consisting of one stem and one branch associated with an individ-

Ronald G. Knapp

ual's year, month, day, and hour of birth; these are then coordinated with a specific direction. *Fengshui* shares with traditional Chinese medicine a concern for equilibrium and harmony in order to obviate misfortune and offers as well prescriptions to "treat" perceived deficiencies. In addition to the determination of the optimal spatial aspects of a building site, attention traditionally was also paid to the temporal dimension—propitious timing—of building activities by consulting almanacs (Hwangbo 2002; Smith 1991, 131–171; 1992).

Compass School of fengshui. Utilizing his diagnostic as well as prognostic faculties, an "interpreter of wind and water" [*fengshui xiansheng,* among many other similar names]—sometimes simply called a geomancer in English and as often a professional as an amateur—provided access to this mystical ecology. As depicted in Figure 5.2, a *fengshui* practitioner in traditional China armed himself with a dishlike *luopan,* several manuals, and often a copy of the *Yijing* [Book of changes] in order to investigate the characteristics of a building site. Perambulating around the prospective building site, he approached the task with solemnity and mystery. "About all their movements there is an air of classic decorum," observed a Westerner at the end of the imperial period who disdained *fengshui* as mere superstition, "and it is no wonder, therefore, that the masses regard the geomancers as fountains of wisdom, marvels of learning, capable of fathoming all the mysteries of heaven and earth" (De Groot 1892–1910, 3:1010). Today, however, the practitioner "usually dresses in plain working clothes and lives in an unimpressive house which does not display his trade. He has the appearance of a craftsman . . . although his vocabulary contains a large number of terms that commoners do not understand" (Bruun 1996, 53). Today in China, one seeks recommendations from family and friends in order to locate suitable *fengshui xiansheng,* while in Taiwan and Hong Kong they can be found in Yellow Page telephone directories and via websites.

The *luopan,* also called *luojing,* is a saucerlike block of wood with a magnetized south-pointing needle at its center; hence the appellation "compass" (Figure 5.3). Yet the *luopan* is much more than a device for finding directions. Incorporated within it are not only the *yin-yang* symbol, but also at least a dozen—and ranging between three and nearly fifty—inscribed concentric rings, which in sum integrate the full scope of interrelating celestial and terrestrial relationships that comprise Chinese metaphysics. Among the multitude of cosmic variables embraced by the circular bands are the *taiji* symbol, the duality of *yin* and *yang,* the four seasons, the Five Phases, the Eight Trigrams [Bagua], the Nine Constellations, the Ten Heavenly

Fig. 5.3. *With a magnetized, south-pointing needle at its center, the saucerlike* luopan *has a series of inscribed concentric rings expressing the range of interrelated celestial and terrestrial relationships that comprise Chinese metaphysics.* Source: Collection of Ronald G. Knapp.

Fig. 5.2. *Utilizing a* luopan, *or geomancer's compass, a traditional* fengshui *practitioner and his assistants investigate the characteristics of a building site.* Source: Sun 1905, 32/2b.

Stems, the Twelve Earthly Branches, the Duodenary and Sexagenary Cycles, and the twenty-eight constellations. Manipulating the *luopan,* practitioners of the Compass School draw upon logical associations as well as intuition in making their decisions. They manipulate the cosmological correspondences among the ring complexes, especially numerical and correlative associations, in order to divine the potentialities of building sites and avoid the adversity arising from incorrect judgments.

Forms School of fengshui. In some respects, the Forms (or Configurations) School, with its emphasis on the lay of the land, is easier to comprehend than the abstruse correlations of the Compass School. For novices as well as the initiated, there often is an aesthetic logic to many of the landscape sites chosen by practitioners of this school, with both describing sites as "comfortable" and "suitable," in terms of the Chinese word *shufu,* and often enchantingly beautiful: "At a true site . . . there is a touch of magic light. . . . The hills are fair, the waters fine, the sun handsome, the breeze mild; and the sky has a new light: another world. Amid confusion, peace; amid peace, a festive air. Upon coming into its presence, one's eyes are opened; if one sits or lies, one's heart is joyful. Here the breath gathers, and the essence collects" (quoted in March 1968, 259).

Ronald G. Knapp

Metaphorical expressions and vivid imagery are abundant in the Forms School, with manuals that emphasize the shape of hills and diagrams of a multiplicity of terrain patterns. Basic hill and water configurations that are related to the Wuxing, or Five Agents (wood, fire, earth, metal, and water), are shown in Figure 5.4; by association they are related with the five planets so that "the terrestrial configurations are in agreement with the celestial order" *[xingfeng peitian]*. Because the transmutative Five Agents are capable of producing or destroying, any association is also assumed to have the same capacities, the effect of which is made complex by the fact that these capabilities wax and wane through a twelve-stage cycle, repeating itself five times, and thus resulting in an extraordinary number of permutations.

Mountains loom large in *fengshui* discourse, even when a landscape is in reality quite flat, perhaps because of an ancient veneration of mountains. *Fengshui* interpreters often begin at a macro-scale in which they attempt to link "dragon veins" *[longmai]* as they reach from the Kunlun Mountain through "grandparent" and "parent" mountains, diminishing in elevation and extent as they reach a specific local building site (Figures 5.5–5.7). Nearby topographical features, called "local eminences," or *sha*, include elevated ridges and watercourses, which are often painstakingly analyzed and distinguished. The use of the term *sha*, meaning "sand," is believed to stem from the fact that *fengshui* practitioners once shared ideas with their students by forming ridges and valleys of sand on the ground in order to model exemplary configurations. An optimal location was one in which *"yin* was at one's back and embraced by *yang*, with ridges to the back and facing water" *(fu yin bao yang, bei shan mian shui).*

Via correlative thinking, cardinal directions could be identified with one of the "four spiritual animals" *[si shen* or *si shou]* and then linked to terrain features: To the east is the azure dragon *[qinglong]* and the element wood, symbolizing spring, the rising sun, and the birth of *yang*. To the south is the vermilion phoenix *[zhuque],* representing the element fire, indicating summer and the period of maximum *yang*. To the west is the white tiger *[baihu],* associated with the element metal, symbolizing autumn and harvest and the birth of *yin*. Completing the cycle in the north is the black tortoise *[xuanwu],* representing the element water, winter, and maximum *yin*. Man was to be anchored in the soil or earth, the fifth agent/element in the center of the cosmic map. The center is considered a fifth "direction," thus resulting in the correlation of five directions with the Five Agents, which are sometimes called the Five Phases. In addition to the four cardinal directions and the center, four corner directions between sets of cardinal points are recognized and thus

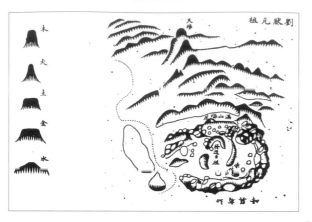

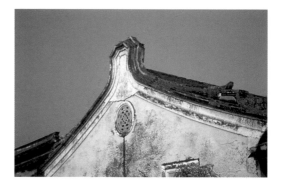

5.5a

5.5b

5.5c

Fig. 5.5a–c.

a. *Schematic drawings representing (from left to right) wood, fire, earth, water, and metal are sometimes given shape in the upper gable walls, called "mountain walls," or* shan qiang, *of houses in southern China.*

b. *This gable configuration represents wood. Shenzhen, Guangdong.* Source: Photograph by Ronald G. Knapp 2000.

c. *Metal is represented in this gable ornamentation. Taibei, Taiwan.* Source: Photograph by Ronald G. Knapp 1993.

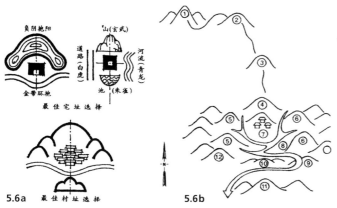

5.6a

5.6b

◀ **Fig. 5.6a–b.** *"*Yin *at one's back and embraced by* yang, *with ridges to the back and facing water" is a shorthand expression for optimal sites at different scales.*

a. *Optimal sites for dwellings. Bottom left: Optimal site for a village.* Source: Shang 1992, 27.

b. *An ideal building site with its constituent parts: (1) Kunlun Mountain; (2) grandparent mountain; (3) parent mountain; (4) master mountain; (5) Baihu, or White Tiger Mountain; (6) Qinglong, or Green Dragon Mountain; (7) settlement site; (8) watercourse; (9)* shuikou, *or water inlet; (10) Anshan; (11)* chaoshan; *(12)* luocheng. Source: Fan 1992, 40.

Fig. 5.7. *Schematic drawing of a Chinese village incorporates various* fengshui *terrain elements.* Source: Unknown.

define nine directions. The most prominent and immediate morphological markers associated with a building site are those on the left/east and right/west—that is, *qinglong* and *baihu*. Correlated with *yang* and *yin*, *qinglong* and *baihu* are not static but instead are vital, interacting, and intertwining, and they concentrate *qi* within a protected node. Naming landmarks in terms of the green dragon, vermilion phoenix, white tiger, and black tortoise creates a set of informal reference positions that have clear spatial implications. In describing bridges, gates, streets, pagodas, and temples, as well as ridges, watercourses, ponds, and groves, these terms are distinctive markers in the mental maps of many Chinese today.

Within such landscape configurations, the *fengshui* practitioner attempts to discover *xue,* a term meaning "lair," "cave," or "hole" and used also to describe critical acupuncture points. Usually shown on a *fengshui* schematic diagram as a small circle, the *xue* node is where *qi* concentrates. Buildings that are situated at a *xue* must be placed so as not to obstruct the movement of *qi*, since vital *qi* flows naturally from above and below. Yet a *xue* is more than a mere spot where *qi* concentrates; it is a converging point in an articulated horizontal, somewhat sloping, spatial composition that is wrapped by a serpentine chain of hills or mountains, embraced within the protective armchair-like set of lesser topographical features. At a different scale, this same armchair-like form is apparent in the shape of grave sites throughout southern China (Figures 5.8–5.9).

Siting and Situating a Dwelling

Fig. 5.8. *An embracing landscape configuration is apparent with armchair-like grave sites found throughout southern China.* Source: Photograph by Ronald G. Knapp 1966.

5.9 ▶

Fig. 5.9. *With a number of ridges to the back and a stream across the front, it is said that a village leans against the "dragon hills." "Hills bring sons, water brings prosperity" is how villagers across the suspicious character of a site. Shang Xiaoqi village, Jiangwan township, Wuyuan county, Jiangxi.* Source: Gong 2001, 3.

Sinuous mountains leading to a *xue* are metaphorically described as a "dragon," or *long,* whose body is an undulating yet interconnected organism that may be extensive and complex or rather simple. As characterized in a *fengshui* manual: "Mountain and water are male and female. . . . If the dragon curls left, the water has to curl right; if the dragon curls right, the water has to curl left; the two embrace each other, and only then does the site coalesce" (Ye 1696, *ce* 1.12b; quoted in March 1968, 258). In level areas without obvious ridgelike terrain features, a secluded location with only gentle breezes and slowly moving water must be identified in order to assure that *qi* is not dispersed. With a focus on affinities as well as oppositions, balanced and rather symmetrical sites are valued: "On a rock hill you must take an earthly site; on an earth hill you must take a rocky site. Where it is confined, take an open place; where it is open, take a confined space. On a prominence, take the flat; where it is flat, take the prominent. Where strong comes, take weak; where weak comes, take strong. Where there are many hills, emphasize water; where there is much water, emphasize hills" (*Shanghai xingxiang* 1957, 63; quoted in March 1968, 258).

Just as with ridges, hills, and mountains, meandering streams contributed to the spatial composition of a favorable site, and accumulated or ponded water was judged important. Indeed, an effort had to be made to bring the two categories into balance inasmuch as mountains were *yin* and watercourses *yang*. Phrases relating to

Ronald G. Knapp

water are reminiscent of the language invoked in the design of Chinese gardens, as sketched in the preceding chapter by Joseph C. Wang. Following the principles of *fengshui,* an individual dwelling, as well as an assemblage of dwellings in a village, often faces south or southeast throughout China, but proper siting goes well beyond mere compass readings. A good *fengshui* site is well drained, well watered, and reasonably sheltered from cold winds and intrusive heat. Throughout many areas of southern China, *fengshui* principles have helped limit building on cultivable land, led to construction on sites at which flooding and erosion are minimized, and restrained reckless decision making.

House-Building Rituals

Once a site was chosen for a dwelling, attention then turned to the erection of the structure. Like other construction in traditional China, building a house was an endeavor that went beyond the mere amassing of raw materials and their assembly by carpenters and masons. Just as with the initial selection of the home site, timing and ritual received careful attention throughout the construction process, continuing even later for details in and about the dwelling. Furthermore, because it was generally believed that there were intrinsic "antagonisms" among those involved in a building project—the household itself, the *fengshui* master, the tradesmen such as masons and carpenters—each addressed his suspicions in different ways. In some cases, written materials in almanacs available in the market or secret manuals passed down from generation to generation could be consulted. More generally, however, awareness came from orally conveyed lore or notions considered common knowledge in a community that—even if comprehended differently—essentially corroborated the more formalized ideas held in books.

A review of written records reveals that attention was paid to the dates and hours that trees could be felled, a building lot leveled, ground broken, and a stone foundation set. Careful thought was given to how the carpenter's trestle was placed, as well as to how wood was shaped within it. Special ritual attended several critical junctures in house building, each of which was judged especially consequential and demanding of attention as the dwelling took shape: raising the columns and beams; hoisting the ridgepole; determining the slope of the roof; laying the surrounding brick or tamped-earth wall; tiling the roof; paving the floors; plastering the walls; installing the door; building a kitchen stove; sweeping the floors; digging the well; creating a cowshed, stable, pigsty, or privy; and moving in. While nineteenth- and early-twentieth-century visitors to China observed and wrote of practices such as these and many practices seemed to have withered away over the past century, recent travelers—especially in remote areas in China's countryside, but also in its towns and thriving coastal areas—continue to encounter evidence of house-building rituals even as the twenty-first century begins.

For many Chinese, the building of a house was viewed as a lengthy project that took time to complete, a condition as true in the past as it is today. Rarely were—indeed, are—resources sufficient to construct a new house all at once; thus, building materials—wood, brick, roof tiles, stone—had to be acquired and stockpiled as money became available. Since household members, their kin, and even neighbors cooperated to make some of the building parts themselves, spare time during slack agricultural seasons provided opportunities to do the work. In some cases, timber was felled in nearby woods, then piled safely for later use, but large beams and the long ridgepole might have to be obtained from some distance away, with construction delayed until their arrival.[2] Where timber was especially scarce, such as in northern China, wood was scavenged from demolished buildings and made available in local markets, a practice that is still seen today (but perhaps less so than in the past).

Groundbreaking and Leveling. In many parts of central and southern China, groundbreaking *[dongtu]* and leveling the foundation *[pingji]* demanded caution since these actions had the potential of upsetting natural forces. Tutelary deities such as the Earth God Tudi Gong were offered incense and fruit with rituals accompanied by firecrackers. Chicken blood is often mentioned as being sprinkled on a new building site as a means of expelling malevolent forces stirred up by the breaking of the ground. Mysterious charms written on peachwood slips, as in Figure 5.10, are still seen in Zhejiang province, where they appeal to the guardians of each of the directions affected by the groundbreaking. Plumb lines and water levels continue to be used in order to level a foundation before rammers are employed to pound the earth until it is sufficiently firm to support columns and walls.

Raising the Ridgepole: **Shangliang.** While critical ritual steps in "assembling" a house include setting the foundation stones, erecting the columns, orienting the main doorframe, and shaping wooden building parts such as interior columns and beams, it was the hoisting of the ridgepole that normally received most attention. The ridgepole was not only likely to be the most costly building component, but its strength was also critical in supporting the weight of a massive roof, whether the latter was made of clay tile or thatch. The special significance of raising the ridgepole was acknowledged by an array of festivities on an auspicious date; these included not only programmed ritual, but also a bounteous meal shared with all of the craftsmen. For larger dwellings with multiple parallel buildings and thus multiple ridgepoles, attention was paid to identifying the "favorable" ridgepoles, which should be higher than others, and thus an ongoing series of different rituals was necessary.

Shangliang rituals and festivities have been recorded all over China, differing only in minor details, with only a small number that are as complex as those stipulated in the *Lu Ban jing* (Knapp 1999b, 41–51), the now classical carpenters' manual written by Lu Ban, the ingenious master craftsman of the fifth century B.C. and the patron of carpenters and masons. To the east of Xi'an in Shaanxi province, the raising of modern roof trusses and their securing with paired ridgepoles and associated purlins is still a community event with simplified ritual elements when compared to the more elaborate situation described above. As seen in Figure 5.11a, a *taiji* symbol and characters stating the time and date, as well as an auspicious phrase, are written directly on the interior underside of the rounded ridgepole so that they can be read from below once the pole is set in place. A relatively simple "solemn and reverential" ceremony accompanies the hoisting and setting of the main ridgepole above the inferior ones. The table of offerings, placed within the walls and beneath the roof trusses, contains only several carpenters' tools, incense, and two candles and is set before the ridgepole itself, which has a red cloth draping over each of its ends. After tribute is made to Lu Ban, accompanied by the sound of firecrackers, the ridgepole is hoisted atop the wooden framework (Figure 5.11b). As so often is the case throughout China today, younger villagers appear to have little understanding of the specific meaning of various amulets associated with buildings, seeing them instead only as "generalized emblem[s] of good luck" (Azevedo 1991, 78).

In rural Liaoning province, in an echo of more traditional rituals, each of the principal building actions preceding the raising of the ridgepole is accompanied by the chanting of rhymed, "luck-bringing" verses, or *da xi ge,* which praise the quality of the raw materials and the skill of the carpenters and summon good fortune (Jiang 1994). On the chosen day, the rough beam that will become the ridgepole is placed on a trestle and shaped according to specific measurements. Other rituals center on a square table set in the courtyard or in the middle of the dwelling, upon which a container is filled with "the five grains" (rice, wheat, beans, and two kinds of millet, which together are a propitious symbol for a good harvest) and three sticks of incense; nearby are steamed buns, food and wine, a wine pot, plates, and chopsticks,

Fig. 5.10. *Written on peachwood slips, these calligraphic charms appeal to the guardians of each of the five directions affected by a groundbreaking. Ruian county, Zhejiang.* Source: Photograph by Ronald G. Knapp 1988.

Fig. 5.11a–b.

a. *Villagers examine the ridgepole just before a raising ceremony begins, viewing the red Bagua with its* taiji *symbol. Lantian county, Shaanxi.* Source: Original photograph used with the permission of Azevedo 1990.

b. *To the sound of firecrackers and draped with auspicious red hangings, the ridgepole is hoisted. Lantian county, Shaanxi.* Source: Original photograph used with the permission of Azevedo 1990.

as well as a carpenter's square and an ink-line reel. Once the incense is lit, a set of rhymed verses is chanted to praise Lu Ban. The middle section of the ridgepole is ornamented with a combined *taiji* and Bagua, as antispectral charms, sometimes directly drawn on the pole but other times printed or drawn on a sheet of paper that is attached to the beam. A common pair of couplets can be observed hanging from the ridgepoles of new dwellings in many areas of China: "Jiang Taigong is here" *[Jiang Taigong zai ci]* and "All the spirits abdicate in his favor" *[Zhushen tuiwei].* (The former invokes the power of an eleventh-century B.C. martial minister and general.) Old copper octagonal coins, called *bagua qian,* are still sometimes nailed to the ridgepole as protective amulets and accompanied by chanting:

> First nail is for gold, the second for silver
> Third for the God of Wealth not leaving the gate
> Fourth for dependability in work
> Fifth for five sons passing the imperial examinations
> Sixth for matters to go smoothly
> Seventh for the seven stars to shine brightly and the family to have a
>   treasure bowl even after arranged marriages for sons and daughters;
> As I place the Bagua nail, high position and great wealth for ten
>   thousand springs.

Ronald G. Knapp

According to field observations in Liaoning, wine is then poured from a wine pot from one end of the ridgepole to the other as a set of rhymes calls for a noble position for the new residents. Once this is concluded, the owner shouts, "The auspicious time has come [Ji chen dao]!" while the carpenter follows with, "Raise the ridgepole [Shang liang]!" The ridgepole is then slowly hoisted with ropes, to the accompanying sounds of exploding firecrackers, until the massive timber is seated in place, where the carpenter taps it into a secure position. Strips of auspicious red cloth are then attached to the ridgepole, and money wrapped in red paper is handed over to the craftsmen. Near the ritual climax, the master carpenter then mounts the ridgepole and "runs along the beam" [pao liang], chanting as he checks that it is firmly seated:

> The phoenix does not light where there are no treasures.
> Today it perches at the end of the ridgepole.
> With one swing of my axe, the house will be solid forever.
> Ten thousand years solid, ten thousand years prosperous, riches,
>   and position, a number one family.

To complete the ritual, the master carpenter casts out the five grains, a handful at a time, hurling each handful toward the five directions as he alludes to each of the five elements, using a metered chant of subjugation that will "vanquish the demons" [da sha]. After verbally and symbolically neutralizing the demons, the master carpenter casts coins and steamed bread from atop the ridgepole toward each of the five directions. As he does so, he chants that riches of all types—gold and silver, a full treasure house, horses and mules—will arrive, in addition to a long life to the age of ninety-nine for the household head.

In many areas of coastal southern China even today, a bamboo lantern, bamboo sieve, grains of rice in small sacks, bundles of red chopsticks, or trousers are suspended from the ridgepole or from the eaves overhang of a dwelling in order to invoke hopes for fertility and prosperity. Some of the homophonous associations used are evident only in the local dialects of southeastern China and are not obvious in standard Chinese. As seen in Figure 5.12, for example, a hanging lantern invokes a desire for sons and grandsons, and this is underscored with multiple auspicious phrases. Lanterns traditionally were hung above a wedding bed for the same reason so that "adding a lantern" had the meaning "adding a son." A similar play on words exists with small silver nails, or *yinding*, which were pounded into the ridgepoles in the Ningbo area of eastern Zhejiang. The square openings in a red

bamboo sieve, as seen in Figure 5.13, are said to represent the "mouths," or *kou,* in a large family, while the attached chopsticks, pronounced *kuaizi,* have a punning relationship with "sons coming quickly" *[kuai zi].* Similarly, the word for men's trousers *[kuzi]* in some southern dialects sounds close to that of the auspicious Chinese character *fu,* meaning "riches." One late-twentieth-century observer noted: "Sometimes the trousers are merely passed around the beam during the ceremony, and I have once seen this happen with the trousers incongruously wrapped around a live chicken" (Baker 1979, 90).

According to news reports and field observations, there is an escalating popularity today of *shangliang* rituals, with their "luck-bringing songs," as the building of houses increases. In Liaoning, it has been noted that young carpenters apprentice themselves to ritual masters in order to learn the ceremonies that homeowners are demanding. Annual almanacs, which can still be bought in Hong Kong, Taiwan, and some areas of coastal China, specify the auspicious dates for the raising of a ridgepole, as they do for other building tasks such as breaking ground and digging a well, as well as installing a doorframe, stove, or bed (Figure 5.14).

Auspicious Measurements. Traditional carpenters paid special attention to fixing favorable measurements and avoiding unfavorable ones for the length, width, and height of a dwelling and the slope of the roof. Nonstructural carpentry for specific building parts, such as doors, windows, and interior partition walls, also was carried out with the same attention to appropriate measurements. Carpenters set their measurements using long as well as short rulers and a carpenter's square made of metal or wood, all of which varied in length from one area of China to another. Special rulers, called *menguang chi* and *Lu Ban chi,* were used in Taiwan and coastal

Ronald G. Knapp

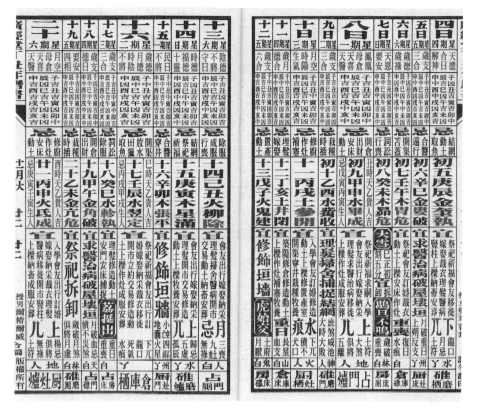

Fig. 5.14. *Two pages from a Hong Kong almanac that indicate the favorable and unfavorable times for a myriad of activities, including not only for cutting one's hair, but also for digging a foundation, sinking a well, and raising a ridgepole.*
Source: Collection of Ronald G. Knapp.

China to measure door and window openings as well as furniture. Rulers are divided into auspicious intervals or "inches" that are marked with the Chinese characters for wealth, righteousness, position, and good luck, as well as inauspicious intervals pointing to illness, separation, calamity, and harm (Figure 5.15). Ruitenbeek (1993, 81) calls this type of measurement device a "ritual object" rather than an article of "practical use," even though its use helped to standardize measurements. Verses that amplified the characteristics of the favorable and unfavorable intervals were well known by traditional carpenters. For example, the "Wealth" poem mused:

> When a door has been measured according to Wealth with due care,
> Then if it is the outer door, talents and good qualities from outside
>   are obtained.
> If it is an inner door, you will always be independent.
> To accumulate riches, the main gate must be designed accordingly.
> And if in the inner rooms you keep to this (character),

Then silver and silk will fill a thousand, nay ten thousand chests.
If the carpenter is able to understand this principle well,
Then happiness and riches will prosper in the house all by themselves.

Quoted in Ruitenbeek 1993, 170–171

Throughout China today, it is still possible to find rulers marked with auspicious and inauspicious intervals, including contemporary retractable metal tape measures for use by do-it-yourselfers.

Building Sorcery: The Use of Charms and Spells

Well before an auspicious day and hour are selected for a family to move into a new house, the head of the household must consider the possibility that carpenters and masons who built the dwelling might have employed sorcery that would bring harm to the family. It is still a well-known belief that Chinese craftsmen had the ability to secrete objects during the process of building in an attempt to exact vengeance over slights, stinginess, loss of face, and general mistreatment, but it is less well known that artisans also had the ability to "reward" a family for its generosity and kindnesses. Apprentices learned about charms and spells from their masters, but measures were recounted in manuals as well. In the *Lu Ban jing,* which details the various types of charm-based actions that craftsmen might take, three-quarters of the actions avenge slights while a far smaller number deal with recompense for worthy acts. Of the twelve charms to be concealed in various hiding places that are shown in Figure 5.16, five are positive, promising wealth, righteousness, long life, high position, and general happiness.[3] Among other hidden amulets, a cassia leaf—whose name in Chinese, *gui,* is synonymous with "honorable" and "of high rank"—was said to ensure a first degree in the civil service examination system when placed on top of a column, while a broken rice bowl with a single chopstick hidden in the doorframe was said to bring penury and hardship to both sons and grandsons.

Masons used similar curses to those of carpenters, but theirs often were made of clay. Eberhard (1965, 73–75) tells of "The Magic of the Mason," a tale in which unhappy workers molded a small clay boat with a boatman and hid it on top of a column and under the eaves. Facing outward rather than inward, the vessel, it was said, would carry away the wealth of the family, leaving it destitute. With quarrels plaguing the household and nothing to eat, the family became impoverished. Many years later, providentially and unexpectedly, the master mason passed the house

Ronald G. Knapp

Fig. 5.15. *The Lu Ban chi (with other rulers of its type) helped to establish proportions by governing critical measures, in the process helping to standardize sizes. The eight divisions in the central column of the rule are favorable and unfavorable dimensions. The first (wealth) and the last (luck) are most favorable; the fourth (justice) and fifth (office) are rather favorable, the remaining four (illness, separation, plunder, and harm) are unlucky.* Source: Collection of Ronald G. Knapp 2001.

Fig. 5.16. *This page from a carpenter's manual illustrates various amulets that could be used to bring fortune or misfortune to a household. Only five of the twelve shown (numbers 3, 7, 8, 9, and 11) are auspicious. Number 3 shows a gourd to be drawn at the top of a wall on a crossbeam, indicating that practitioners of every art will reside in the house. Number 7 tells that hiding two copper coins face down on the ends of the ridgepole, one to the left and one to the right, will ensure wealth and good fortune, with the husband winning fame, the son obtaining a noble rank, and titles of honor for the wife. Number 9 suggests concealing a brush and ink stick in a tie beam to guarantee wealth and high rank. Number 11 indicates that hiding a handful of rice grains in a block of the building's frame will ensure riches for the household. Number 1 shows an ox bone, which, if hidden in the principal bay of the house, will bring bitter hardship day after day.*

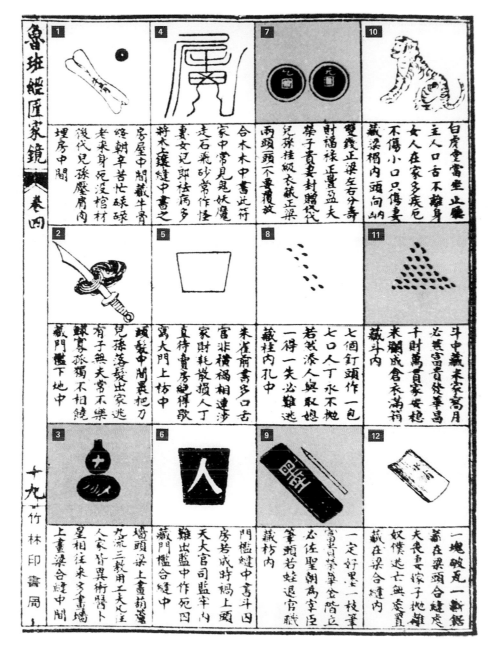

When one gets old and dies, there will be no coffin, and sons and grandsons will shoulder a heavy burden. Inauspicious amulets focus on sons leaving home (2); a bewitched home (4); frequent altercations and sudden calamities (5);

lawsuits and misery in prison (6); constant family quarreling and sickness for women (10); and death of the husband, remarriage of the wife, and departure of the sons (12). Source: *Huitu Lu Ban jing, juan 4.*

Fig. 5.17. *A charm featuring the "Heavenly Master," Zhang Tianshi, is coupled with calligraphy and serves to exorcise building curses, cleanse well water, and bring good luck. Guidelines for energizing the charm are presented on the left. The lower left all-purpose charm is titled "Charm for resolving a hundred different things."* Source: Collection of Ronald G. Knapp.

Fig. 5.18. *This all-purpose charm, with its arcane and sometimes illegible characters, is hung on a beam at the entry to a wing of a house. Shengxian, Zhejiang.* Source: Photograph by Ronald G. Knapp 1987.

and was touched by the sincerity of the penniless widow, whereupon he climbed a ladder, turned the bow of the boat inward, and reversed the misfortunes of the household by bringing riches back toward it.

Homeowners' suspicions of the possible tricks and curses of workers led naturally to the use of neutralizing amulets to protect the family and its new home by "stabilizing the dwelling" *[zhenzhai]*. *Fengshui* manuals usually list precautionary dos and don'ts, specifying the type, size, and color of a host of charms that could be affixed to or near a dwelling in order to shield it. Sometimes a Daoist priest or a *fengshui* master was necessary to energize or activate a charm made of paper, stone, or wood via a series of rituals, but often a household could simply make and place its own amulet to ward off misfortune. For paper charms, details included various paper shapes, as well as the kind of calligraphic ink that would be most efficacious. Sometimes the charm consisted of a number of twisted and irregularly formed Chinese characters that are difficult to decipher and that have written within them others that are readable. All-purpose calligraphic amulets are found in many *fengshui* manuals and some almanacs, and similar forms are still encountered in various parts of China. Written in cinnabar on yellow paper and attached to the ridgepole with a bit of paste, an all-purpose charm is said to be able to break a multitude of spells that might have been brought into play during house construction.[4] In some cases, bizarre Chinese characters merely had to be "written in the air" in a running style to be effective.[5] Annual almanacs also reproduce calligraphic charms "to stabilize," or *zhen*, the bed, stove, well, or chicken coop, among other parts of a dwelling. An image of the "Heavenly Master," Zhang Tianshi, seen in Figure 5.17, is coupled with calligraphy and serves to exorcise building curses, cleanse well water, and bring good luck.[6] Guidelines for energizing the charm are presented on the left. Clenching his teeth three times while holding water in his mouth, the exorcist is told to face east before spitting out the water and beginning the incantation to rid the house of evil and sickness. Calligraphic charms of this type usually have elongated lines of ink that denote lightning, which is said to disrupt negative forces and strike down malevolence. A calligraphic charm is shown in the lower right-hand section of the old almanac pictured in Figure 5.1. Some charms are hung, as seen in Figure 5.18, while others are burned, with the ashes mixed with water that is sprinkled in place.

Ronald G. Knapp

Overcoming Situational Deficiencies

In the search for an auspicious landscape configuration according to *fengshui*, it was expected that shortcomings, imperfections, and lacunae would be encountered—since few locations were considered universally ideal—and modifications would be necessary to rebalance a site. In order to mitigate the shortages of naturally flowing water or to dampen the potentially destructive peaks of "fire" visible from a village, for example, ponds and channels of water might be dug to offset incendiary dangers (Figure 5.19). The planting of a grove of trees, sometimes even a protective line of trees, as well as dense stands of bamboo, as seen in Figure 5.20, was judged helpful in overcoming terrain deficiencies, such as the absence of a needed ridgeline. In villages and towns throughout rural China, striking *fengshui* pagodas, or *fengshui ta,* were raised to counter unsatisfactory or ominous terrain characteristics, thus improving the propitious elements of a settlement's geomantic character (Figure 5.21). In southern China, special attention was paid to *shuikou,* the location of water inlets and outlets, as a stream coursed through a village. Associated with an outsized or odd-shaped rock, enormous camphor or banyan tree, or an extensive clump of bamboo, *shuikou* sites in many villages are viewed as numinous or sacred places. They often provide a location for a shrine to the Earth God or other local deity, as well as for ancestral halls, as seen in Figure 5.22.

Fig. 5.19. *The pointed peaks in the distance are viewed as incendiary elements that must be controlled by the introduction of water into a site. As shown here in Cangpo village, Zhejiang, a pond and numerous channels of water serve this function.* Source: Photograph by Ronald G. Knapp 1987.

Fig. 5.20. *Terrain deficiencies around this village in Longyan county, Fujian, are countered by the planting of groves of bamboo and trees on the north and west of the village.* Source: He 1990, 80.

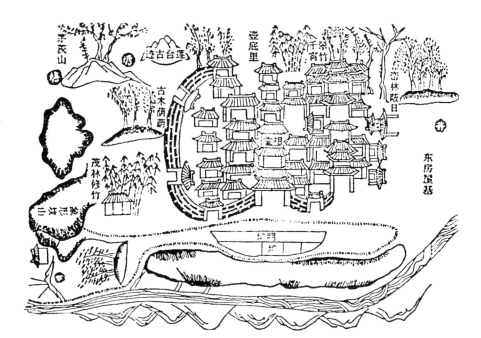

Fig. 5.21. *This* fengshui *pagoda was raised in order to overcome negative environmental circumstances. Wuyuan county, Jiangxi.* Source: Photograph by Ronald G. Knapp 1999.

Fig. 5.22. *Nestled beneath an imposing old tree, this Earth God shrine is also adjacent to the village* shuikou. *Hongkeng village, Hukeng township, Yongding county, Fujian.* Source: Photograph by Ronald G. Knapp 2001.

Once a location for a building was determined, the first-level responsibility of the *fengshui* practitioner was completed, but the tasks necessary for securing the dwelling itself continued, as decisions were made concerning the immediate environs and even the dwelling interior. The template for an auspicious and harmonious dwelling was the shape of a body with two outstretched or embracing arms, as with analogous and broader *fengshui* configurations (Figure 5.23), as are seen in the floor plans of courtyard-style houses. In Fujian and Guangdong in southern China, a semicircular pond, called *mingtang*, or "bright or cosmic court," sometimes was dug at the front of a village or an individual dwelling, and the dwelling was sited within the break in slope of a hill (Figures 5.24–5.25). Even a utilitarian, semicircular threshing ground-cum-courtyard might serve the same purpose as a pond. In order to compensate for deficiencies relating to directional orientation or configuration of the terrain, features of the dwelling could be manipulated. Both small and more extensive remedies might be strategically situated to "summon good fortune and keep misfortune at bay" *[qu ji bi xiong]*. Using diagrams and explanatory inscriptions, *fengshui* manuals, as well as carpenters' handbooks such as the *Lu Ban jing,* called attention to how surrounding trees, rocks, ditches, pools, wells, watercourses, roads, and other houses might individually and cumulatively augur good or bad fortune for a household. Much advice in these manuals and handbooks centered on the pathways leading to a dwelling, with admonitions that certain lines or curvatures would open the home to calamity while others would

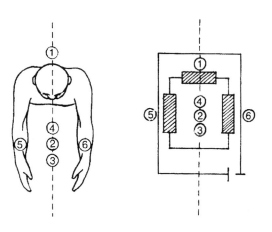

Fig. 5.23. Fengshui *texts sometimes draw analogies between a human figure with outstretched arms and a residential courtyard dwelling:* (1) yin *toward the back;* (2) yang *at the front;* (3) mingtang, *or open courtyard;* (4) xue, *or node;* (5) baihu, *or "white tiger," on the west side;* (6) qinglong, *or "green dragon," on the east side. Both the figure and the courtyard obviously are facing south.* Source: Fan 1992, 38.

Fig. 5.24. *The plan of this Kejia dwelling shows a hemispheric* mingtang, *while the elevation drawing calls attention to the armchair-like composition of the dwelling, with its wrapping upper wall. Nankou township, Meixian, Guangdong.* Source: Lu and Wei 1990, 342, 343.

▼

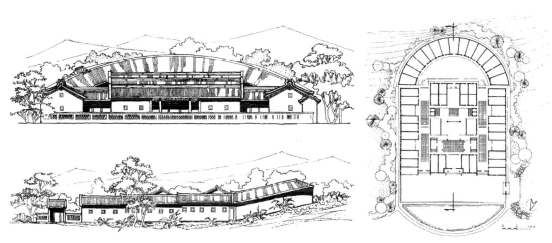

Fig. 5.25. *Glimpse of the hemispheric* mingtang *shown in Fig. 5.24. Nankou township, Meixian, Guangdong.* Source: Photograph by Ronald G. Knapp 2000.

protect it and ensure prosperity. A seventeenth-century edition of the *Lu Ban jing* included seventy-one illustrated sets of such admonitions in four-line rhymes, with fifty-two of them portraying unfavorable situations (Figure 5.26).[7] As a motivation to follow the prescriptions and thus avoid unsatisfactory layouts, the manuals promise male progeny and marital harmony and assure that wealth will increase. The alternative is to court financial disaster, with family members leaving home, escalating illness, growing strife, death of children, childless marriages, mounting bad luck, desperate poverty, quarrels between a father and his sons, and attendant family division and eventual decline. In some ways, such prescriptions heightened the awareness of cause and effect by affirming hopes, acknowledging fears, and providing simple procedures for coping with life.

Stabilizing the Dwelling. Just as with the use of amulets and charms to overcome possible curses invoked by the craftsmen and initial efforts at "stabilizing the dwelling," additional objects and rituals often needed to be employed because of changing circumstances in the environs of a dwelling (Figure 5.27). New buildings, realigned paths and lanes, and newly dug ditches may necessitate the use of protective objects to counteract, neutralize, or exorcise potentially malignant forces. Precisely positioned on the roof or ridgepole; in the courtyard; above, in front of, or on the door or gate; and even at some distance from the dwelling, these elements give form to a concentric spatial defense system. Called *yasheng* [dominating], *yaxie* [suppressing], and *bixie* [exorcising] objects, they are deployed at critical vulnerable points and junctures to forestall intrusions and to reduce misfortune.[8] Calligraphic or noncalligraphic charms, printed on paper, carved on tablets, or represented by actual objects, include cosmic symbols such as the Bagua, *taiji,* and *yin-yang,* as well as the Luoshu [Luo River writing] and Hetu [Yellow River chart] diagrams; weapons such as arrows, swords, axes, and mirrors; and images of ferocious animals and powerful people. Usually mounted to correct "mutually antagonistic" *[xiangchong]* situations that may arise and are considered disadvantageous, they sometimes are used well before any demonstrated need in order to provide a prophylactic defense.

Common mutually antagonistic circumstances, which emerge as new construction impinges upon older dwellings, include "a road against a house" *[luchong],* "a house against a house" *[zhaichong],* or "a pole against a house" *[zhuchong].* A sample survey carried out in rural and urban Taiwan in 1977–1978 revealed that some 71 percent of *yasheng* objects were placed to correct problems with nearby

Ronald G. Knapp

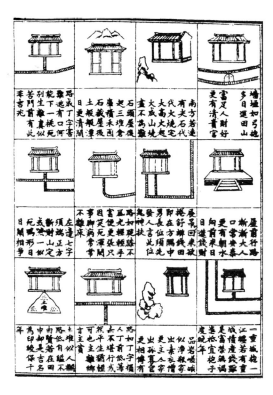

Fig. 5.26. *Each consisting of a drawing and a caption, here are twelve of the many examples of auspicious and inauspicious building situations, most of which point to inauspicious or unlucky configurations.*

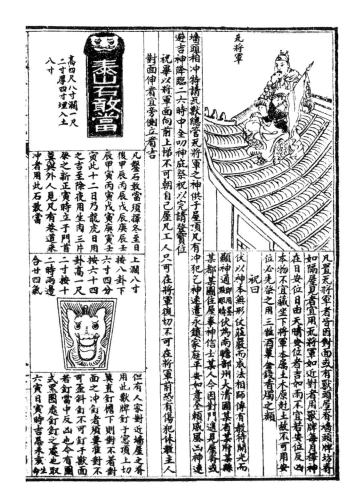

a ▶

Fig. 5.27a–b.

a. *Among some of the defensive measures spelled out in the* Lu Ban jing *are the following: right: the "Roof-Tile General" [Wa Jiangjun], said to be able to guard against antagonistic features along the ridge of a house or at the top of a wall; top left: "Taishan resisting stones," which are to be placed at vulnerable positions such as the corners of buildings or where a lane leads directly toward a doorway; and bottom left: the "head of a monster plaque," which is to be nailed under the eaves or above a window.* Source: *Huitu Lu Ban jing, juan 3.*

b. *Standing in a defensive position, the "Roof-Tile General" guards a village home.* Source: Photograph by Ronald G. Knapp 1985.

b ▶

houses, 17 percent to counter threatening lanes or roads, and 11 percent because of some intruding vertical element such as a chimney or pole (Dong 1988, 64–68). Whenever a new gate is installed, a building rises taller than its surrounding structures, or a lane or driveway leads directly to a doorway, vigilance must be heightened to counter the potentially antagonistic situations. Particularly significant is the main gate, which is considered critically important: "Just as the mouth and nostrils are the means by which the human body is able to live, so the main entrance is thought to be the channel through which happiness and good fortune can be absorbed" (Chen 1993, 8). Protective screens called *yingbi* or *zhaobi,* as seen in Figures 5.28 and 5.29, are used throughout China as barriers inside the gates of common as well as imperial dwellings in order to mask the view into a courtyard and effectively block any human or spectral intrusion. In some cases, as seen in Figure 5.30, large screens are positioned at the figurative entrance to a village, less to block a view than to serve a defensive *fengshui* purpose.

The *Lu Ban jing* recommends the installation of a unique type of mirror called an "inverting mirror" *[daojing]* or "tiger or white tiger mirror" *[hujing* or *baihujing],* in the shape of a concave plate with a higher rim and a depressed middle; it is said to be capable of overturning whatever antagonistic feature is reflected in it, just as the image itself is turned on its head.[9] Ordinary mirrors, said to radiate *yang,* are widely regarded as potent deflectors of malevolent influences and are still commonly hung above doorways in association with other amulets (Figure 5.31). Just as the Bagua sign (usually with the *taiji* and *yin-yang* symbols incorporated into it) is affixed to the ridgepole when it is raised, Bagua are commonly found attached above the lintel of the main gate or frequently placed directly on the leaves of the gate (Figure 5.32). Additional cryptic charms such as the *Yijing*-inspired knotted cord configurations of the Hetu, a numerical representation of the natural order embodying strength and stability, are sometimes added to Bagua plaques, as shown in Figure 5.33. In some cases, as is shown in Figure 5.34, a Chinese character such as *tun,* "to devour" or "gulp down," is written on the mirror as a further safeguarding agent. As a supplementary figurative defensive object, either a long, three-pronged trident or a pair of scissors is also hung to accompany a mirror or a Bagua plaque (Figure 5.35). A crimson rooster, or *gongji,* a propitious *yang* creature that crows as the sun rises and ascends and whose name, *daji,* is homophonous with "greatly auspicious," serves double duty as a protective amulet with a mirror around its neck (Figure 5.36).

The head of a wild animal, a ferocious beast growling viciously while baring its

Ronald G. Knapp

Fig. 5.30. *Villagers sometimes find it necessary to place a protecting* zhaobi, *or spirit wall, at the entry to their settlement. The spirit wall in Changle village is placed between a commemorative arch and the main village lane. The pond in front is the village's* mingtang, *reinforcing good fengshui while moderating temperatures and providing a place for water buffalo to cool off and women to do laundry. Lanxi city, Zhejiang.* Source: Photograph by Ronald G. Knapp 1987.

▲ **Fig. 5.28.** *Emblazoned with an auspicious* fu *character for good fortune, the screen wall effectively blocks the view into the courtyard from the open gate. Wangjia manor, Lingshi county, Shanxi.* Source: Photograph by Ronald G. Knapp 1996.

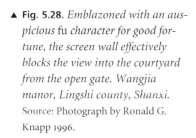

Fig. 5.29. *This* zhaobi, *or spirit screen, with ornamentation featuring a longevity character and five encircling bats, dominates the entry to the Hall of Crimson Snowflakes, one of the imperial courtyard residences within the Forbidden City in Beijing.* Source: Photograph by Ronald G. Knapp 1997.

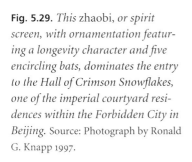

a ▼

b ▼

c ▲

Fig. 5.31a–c. *Radiating* yang, *common mirrors of many types are hung above doorways throughout China as effective deflectors of malevolent influences. Xiaoqi village, Wuyuan county, Jiangxi.* Source: Photographs by Ronald G. Knapp 1999.

Fig. 5.33. *This Bagua plaque is circled by cryptic charms related to the* Yijing-*inspired knotted cord configurations of the Hetu [Yellow River Chart], a numerical representation of the natural order embodying strength and stability. Zhanghua county, Taiwan.* Source: Collection of Ronald G. Knapp 1993.

▼

Fig. 5.32. *The Eight Trigrams, or Bagua, sign with the yin-yang symbol at its core is printed here on a mirror and hung above the entryway. Behind it is the auspicious invocation* hongxi, *or "grand blessings," written in gold on red cloth. Meixian, Guangdong.* Source: Photograph by Ronald G. Knapp 2000.

Fig. 5.34. *A reflecting mirror with the character* tun, *"to devour" or "gulp down," written on it proclaims that evil forces will be consumed. Shangchuan village, Wuyuan county, Jiangxi.* Source: Photograph by Ronald G. Knapp 1999.

▲
Fig. 5.36. *The rooster,* daji, *is homophonous with "greatly auspicious" and is a propitious* yang *creature. Here it serves double duty as a protective amulet with a mirror in front. Nanjing county, Fujian.* Source: Photograph by Ronald G. Knapp 2000.

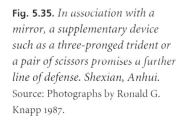

Fig. 5.35. *In association with a mirror, a supplementary device such as a three-pronged trident or a pair of scissors promises a further line of defense. Shexian, Anhui.* Source: Photographs by Ronald G. Knapp 1987.

Fig. 5.37. *Where it is not possible to hang a "head of a monster" because the occupants of the house opposite may be relatives or friends, the* Lu Ban jing *recommends nailing on the wall or under the eaves a "luck-bestowing" tablet that reads* Tianguan cifu, *"Tianguan [the heavenly official] grants good fortune." This vertical tablet is here supplemented with other auspicious emblems. Xinxing village, Zhanghua county, Taiwan.* Source: Photograph by Ronald G. Knapp 1991.

Fig. 5.38. *Poised above Chinese characters that request, "Bring riches to me" [Dui wo sheng cai], this threatening tiger amulet serves as a guardian at the front entry of a home. Shengxian, Zhejiang.* Source: Photograph by Ronald G. Knapp 1987.

teeth—sometimes strangely appearing to smile—is hung on a window, from the lintel of a door, or low beneath the eaves. As shown above in Figure 5.27, its stated size and trapezoidal shape are clearly correlated to other cosmographic elements:

> The width across the top is 8 *cun*,
>   corresponding to the Eight Trigrams.
> The width across the bottom is 6 *cun* and 4 *fen*,
>   corresponding to the Sixty-four Hexagrams.[10]
> The height is 12 *cun*,
>   corresponding to the Twelve Hours.
> The two sides together correspond with
>   the Twenty-four Solar Terms.

The ferocious animal is often a tiger, a *yang* creature, with a furrowed brow that can be read as wang 王, the Chinese character for "king," although sometimes the animal appears playful, with its purpose proclaimed with Chinese characters reading, "Evil is repelled and the gods return." According to the *Lu Ban jing*, it is sometimes not possible to hang the "head of a monster" amulet because the occupants of the house opposite may be relatives or friends, and therefore a "luck-bestowing" tablet should be hung instead (Figure 5.37). In other cases, as seen in Figure 5.38, characters with the request, "Bring riches to me," complement the threatening tiger

Fig. 5.39. *According to lore, villagers describe the imposing wooden Ximen, or West Gate, at the entrance into Cangpo village as the face of a ferocious tiger with its teeth bared. Yongjia county, Zhejiang.* Source: Photograph by Ronald G. Knapp 1990.

amulet. The imposing wooden gate at the entrance of Cangpo village in the Nanxijiang area of southeastern Zhejiang province is itself described in village lore as representing the face of a ferocious tiger with its teeth bared (Figure 5.39). Zoomorphic amulets of many types were used on the doors of tombs in the past. Even today, Chinese parents continue to purchase or ornament hats, shoes, bibs, and collars in the shape of tigers as protective amulets to be given to their baby sons on the one-month anniversary of their birth.[11]

"Resisting stones" with three or five Chinese characters inscribed on them are sometimes strategically placed at the foot of a wall, along a corner, beside a doorway, at the head of a bridge, or at a juncture as a type of defensive shield, as glimpsed above in Figure 5.27a. On the Penghu Islands between Taiwan and Fujian, there are at least 219 "resisting stones" of different shapes and configurations, about 1.7 per square kilometer. In their most basic form, each is a rectangular-shaped stele with only the three characters *shi gandang*, or "this stone dares to resist," etched into it. Two characters—*Taishan* [Mount Tai]—are commonly added atop *shi gandang* to form an idiom meaning "The stone of Taishan dares to resist evil/danger/catastrophe" (Figure 5.40). By invoking Mount Tai, this five-character phrase augments the power of an otherwise common stone slab. Mythical and historical associations celebrate Taishan as the easternmost and most important of China's Five Sacred Peaks, the birthplace of all creatures. Since Taishan is also the abode of

Fig. 5.41. *Even without the imputed power of an actual stone, the characters* Taishan shi gandang, *here written as a pair along the entry to a village dwelling, can be viewed as a potent charm. Zhiyan village, Zhiyan township, Lanxi city, Zhejiang.* Source: Photograph by Ronald G. Knapp 1987.

Fig. 5.42. Taishan zai ci, *or "Taishan is here," serves as an abbreviated amulet on stone that is conflated with another saying,* Taigong zai ci, *or "Jiang Taigong is here." Cangpo village, Gangtou township, Yongjia county, Zhejiang.* Source: Photograph by Ronald G. Knapp 1990.

the Emperor of the Eastern Peak (Dongyue Dadi), whose responsibilities were to detain errant souls and have them escorted to the halls of judgment, it was believed that he served as a bureaucratic mediator between the realms of *yin* and *yang*. In part, Taishan "resisting stones" might be explained as metonymic representations of the "legal" authority of heaven to repel, restrain, and dispatch errant ghosts who threaten the living.[12]

Ideally, Taishan stones should have been hewn from the rock face of the mountain itself in order to be potent, but it is clear that many of the reputed Taishan stones found in villages are probably bogus, spurious imitations whose calligraphic assertion alone is believed sufficiently powerful to provide adequate defense. As seen in Figure 5.41, the five-character phrase *Taishan shi gandang* itself can be written on a wall as a simple, nonmaterial yet efficacious warning amulet. It is not uncommon to see the simpler homophonous character *tai* 太, meaning "extremely" or "highly," incorrectly substituted for the relatively complicated accurate character. In other cases, one or another character is mistakenly left out or confused with another saying, such as when the amulet "Jiang Taigong is here"—or a variant, "Jiang Ziya is here" *[Jiang Ziya zai ci]*—is conflated so as to appear as "Taishan is here" *[Taishan zai ci]* (Figure 5.42). As can be seen in Figure 5.43, multiple amulets can appear on the same plaque, such as the image of a tiger, a Bagua, and characters invoking the protection of the Taishan stone. *Zhi sha!* "Resist all demons!" is sometimes also

Fig. 5.43. *With only four characters—Tai shi gandang, or "Tai stone dares to resist"—this entryway protective amulet also includes a complex Bagua diagram and a snarling tiger. The trapezoidal shape of the plaque conforms to the dimensions stated in the* Lu Ban jing *measures shown in Fig. 5.27. Qianlang village, Shengxian, Zhejiang.* Source: Photograph by Ronald G. Knapp 1987.

Fig. 5.44a–b.
a. *At the New Year, a gate is adorned with a vertical pair of couplets, a horizontal invocation above the lintel, hanging charms, and a pair of Menshen, Door Gods, in full regalia. Sheung Wo Hang, New Territories, Hong Kong.* Source: Photograph by Ronald G. Knapp 1998.
b. *Closeup of Door Gods. Ganzhou, Jiangxi.* Source: Photograph by Ronald G. Knapp 1995.

added. Carpenters' and general *fengshui* manuals generally prescribe clearly the size and form of Taishan "resisting stones," as well as particulars concerning when the stones should be selected and set up. A relatively massive size is specified for the Taishan "resisting stone" shown in Figure 5.27a—4 *chi* 8 *cun* high, 1 *chi* 2 *cun* wide, and 4 *cun* thick, *chi* being a Chinese "foot"—but most are much smaller, and it is recommended that the stone be carved twelve days after the winter solstice and set up in the early hours of New Year's Day.

Door Gods—Protective Guardians. Door Gods or Guardians of the Gate, known as Menshen in Chinese, are affixed to double-leaf entrance gates at city and country homes throughout China. In villages of North China even today, the mud and brick walls lining dusty lanes are punctuated by splashes of seemingly random color at each of the gates that lead into individual dwellings. The display of color, however, is no mere ornamentation, but instead (as discussed in more detail in Chapter 14 by James Flath) comprises significant ritual objects: a pair of paper likenesses of Menshen—foreboding enough to repel malevolence, yet benign enough to welcome visitors. In comparison to the equally ubiquitous oversized guardians painted on the doors of Chinese temples that loom larger than life, those found on the gates of dwellings are small (Figure 5.44). Usually multicolored in reds, greens, blues, and yellows but some simply outlined in black lines, these solemn guards are renewed at

Fig. 5.45. *Colored woodblock prints of Yu Lei, on the left, and Shen Tu, on the right, portray them in full battle gear.* Source: Dun 1906, frontispiece.

the New Year. Gate guardians are believed capable of banishing pestilential demons, punishing ghosts, slaying wild animals, and keeping generalized malevolent and demonic forces at bay. Most images are replete with auspicious symbolic motifs, in addition to ancillary defensive objects, such as a circular object on the chest that looks like a mirror that is believed capable of repelling evil. A panoply of variant guardians of secondary gates, back gates, and gates into wing rooms and adjacent courtyards traditionally were found at critical transition points inside the dwelling.

While intense and intimidating generals usually wear body armor and a helmet and bear a sword, spear, halberd, or bow, Menshen in fact vary significantly from place to place since they represent a variety of historical or mythical figures, some broadly known but others only local heroes. In full martial regalia, two brothers, Shen Tu and Yu Lei, as seen in Figures 5.45 and 5.46, have served as gate guardians since at least the fourth century B.C. In time, they were joined by a pair of brave generals of the Tang period, Qin Shubao and Yuchi Gong (also known as Yuchi Jingde or Hu Jingde), one with a white face and the other older and darker, as well as heroic and patriotic generals of different historical periods such as Guan Gong, Yue Fei, Wen Tianxiang, and Wei Zheng.

Ronald G. Knapp

Fig. 5.46. *Low-relief carved figures of Shen Tu and Yu Lei, here armed as usual with maces, are placed in a pair of guardhouses alongside an interior doorway. Kangbaiwan manor, Gongyi city, Henan.* Source: Photographs by Ronald G. Knapp 2003.

Only the wealthy could afford to engage artists to paint protective deities on their gates prior to the Song period (960–1279), while commoners used objects such as a light broom or a dark piece of coal to represent Menshen. During the Song dynasty, the popularization of woodblock printing facilitated the dissemination of cheap protective paper door prints, many of which were monochromatic and relatively crude. Advances in multiple-block color printing technology during the Ming dynasty made possible a richer artistic portrayal of figures that were accessible to most Chinese. While the poor, by necessity, obtained only rudimentary and inexpensive representations of Menshen produced by village artisans, it became customary in succeeding centuries for wealthy Chinese to invite a local artist to paint a pair of Menshen for each door in the house as the New Year approached.[13]

Lesser "soldiers," whose power comes from homophonous associations, reinforce the martial bearing of the gate gods in northern Shaanxi:

> In the Yan'an area on the last day of the year, the family elders also send children down to the river-bank to chip off lumps of ice and bring them home; the lumps of ice *(bing)* are then placed at the courtyard gate, behind the door, and in the animal pens, to serve sentry duty as troops *(bing)* in the household's garrison. And on the tablelands south of Yan'an—in Fuxian and Luochuan counties—people take blocks of coal or charcoal, tie them up

Fig. 5.47. *With a vertical row of characters proclaiming* zhen zhai, *"guarding the home," and* pingan, *"peace," this simple woodblock print shows Zhong Kui armed with a sword. Lingshan village, Zhouping township, Xihu district, Hangzhou city.* Source: Photograph by Ronald G. Knapp 1987.

with rope, and hang them from the door lintel and from the corners of the walls, these serve as "black tigers" (*heihu*) warding off noxious influences. (Holm 1991, 147)

While most martial Menshen are poised standing alert and vigilant, others ride tigers or horses. Many appear like human figures in Chinese operas, with their painted faces and trappings, such as flags attached to their backs and headdresses to indicate they are high-ranking generals.

An image of Zhong Kui, not a door god but a formidable demon queller and exorcist, sometimes accompanies Menshen on the front gate of a Chinese dwelling at the lunar New Year, as discussed in Chapter 14. Zhong Kui was a Tang dynasty scholar who committed suicide after not being recognized for his achievements in the imperial examinations. The addition of Chinese characters such as *zhen zhai,* "guarding the home"; *chiling,* "imperial edict"; and the characters for Zhong Kui's name underscores his protective function (Figure 5.47). However, unlike the prints of Menshen, which are placed only once each year and presumed to have a potency lasting until the next New Year, the image of Zhong Kui is replaced at least once in the following months, on the day of the summer solstice, which is considered especially inauspicious. Commemorated as Duanwu or Duanyang on the fifth day of the fifth month according to the lunar calendar, the summer solstice is the date when the noon sun reaches its zenith in the sky and then begins to decline day by day until six months later at the winter solstice, when its declining pattern is reversed and the days begin to lengthen. On the fifth day of the fifth month *yang* elements reach their peak, and negative *yin* elements, including "ghosts" that are responsible for disease, accidental death, and financial disaster, begin to emerge (Figure 5.48). This is a time also when the so-called five noxious or poisonous creatures, or *wudu*—the snake, centipede, scorpion, gecko, and toad or spider—are said to multiply. In fact, this time of year brings hot and wet weather, when mosquitoes, flies, poisonous spiders, and insects generally flourish. Thus, exposed to general danger, environmentally related health problems, and misfortune, villagers and townspeople alike took precautions. Since the young were especially vulnerable to disease, children received special care at Duanwu. Amulets, bracelets, and necklaces containing pungent herbs were presented to them, and children were bathed in water infused with herbal medicines in order to counter illness (Berliner 1986, 22, 77–78, 160–171).

Zhong Kui is an efficacious all-purpose expeller of malign influences and threats. Usually depicted with a martial bearing and in full combat dress, in one hand Zhong Kui waves a magical sword that is said to extinguish evil spirits, and in the

Ronald G. Knapp

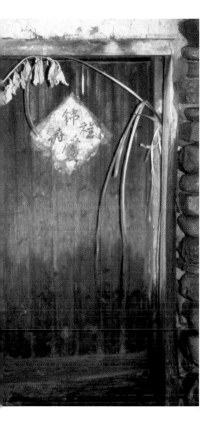

Fig. 5.48. *Said to be a precaution against misfortune, Artemisia and the herb sweetflag are sometimes hung on the door or stuck into crevices along the doorframe at the time of the summer solstice, the fifth day of the fifth lunar month. Lubu village, Shuidong township, Lishui county, Zhejiang.* Source: Photograph by Ronald G. Knapp 1988.

other he holds a fan-shaped tablet with a magical inscription. Bud-shaped objects on his hat are regarded as demon-seeking devices that point to unforeseen and lurking random dangers. The bats seen circling around his head, however, are not the sinister objects of his fury, as a Westerner might suspect. Instead, to Chinese, bats represent good fortune through a punning linguistic association. Zhong Kui's foot is usually raised, as if it is about to stamp out the poisonous creatures beneath. Regarded as ugly because of his bulging eyes and messy hair, Zhong Kui radiates a fearsome image that can be likened to the faces of lions and tigers in terms of their suitability as powerful demon quellers.[14] Zhong Kui has been absorbed into the Daoist pantheon, where he is viewed as a drawer of protective talismans.

Aromatic plant stalks—sweet flag *[changpucao, Acorus calamus],* a hardy aromatic perennial herb with sword-shaped leaves, and mugwort *[ai, Artemisia vulgaris],* with slender purplish leaves and said to have an offensive odor and even look like a protective tiger—are also hung on doorways to repel malignant forces on the fifth day of the fifth month. In the Minnan dialect spoken in Taiwan and Fujian, the homophonous relationship between sweet flag and *chang* [prosperous or flourishing] adds a layer of auspicious and salutary meaning. (Beyond the symbolic protection of pungent plants such as sweet flag and mugwort, they and others are decocted and drunk as folk remedies for various illnesses.) Willow and peachwood twigs also are considered capable of repelling demons. In Hunan and Hubei in central China, rattan is collected and attached to the gate for Zhong Kui to use in tying up spirits. Early in the twentieth century in Zhejiang province, Clarence Day (1940, 43–46) remarked that the peasant fear of demons was pervasive, including apprehensions concerning those believed lurking at the cornerstone of houses and capable of bruising shins and those who waited to harm women as they washed vegetables at the water's edge. Even as the entrance gate of a dwelling is protected with calligraphic and pictorial imagery, a range of other, clearly auspicious messages are also employed in order to summon good fortune to the family, a broad topic that is not covered in this chapter.[15]

Environmental Awareness

Chinese have a long history of manipulating landscape settings in order to occupy them successfully. Because they are attentive to both the site and the situation characteristics of a particular spatial setting, they consider and evaluate drainage, natural light, ventilation, sanitation, and access—all reasonable ingredients for a pleasant and healthful living space. This level of environmental awareness, as well as a propensity for pragmatism, laid a foundation for the aesthetic, psychological, and philosophical merits of employing *fengshui,* amulets, and ritual.

Chinese villagers and observers generally sometimes wax poetic about the *fengshui* characteristics of places, many of which are quite generic. Protected on the northern side by interlocking mountain ranges, a building site situated on a south-facing slope is open to the sun throughout the year and protected in winter from the cold winds characteristic of much of eastern Asia's climate. Care can be taken so that no part of a dwelling will be shaded by hills or trees on the east, south, or west, thus ensuring an early sunrise and a late sunset. A phrase describing a south-facing building—*zuobei chaonan,* or "sitting north and facing south"—is a well-understood instruction for an orientation that assures abundant sun and steady wind. This concern acknowledges an understanding of the critical relationship regarding the regularity of the sun as its path varies during the year and prevailing wind directions. In areas of southern China where the sun's rays are particularly intense, the majority of villages and houses deviate from a strict southern orientation and are situated facing a direction that reduces heat buildup. Working with nature, practical and aware peasants traditionally were able to avoid marshy areas and build their dwellings on well-drained sites even though water coursed across them. From the broader context of a village and its productive environs, it is possible to postulate a relationship between *fengshui* principles and the realities of lowland rice farming. Valley bottoms and adjacent hill slopes provide landscape elements that can be reasonably modified to control the flow as well as the storage of water via weirs, channeled streams, and ponds that are necessary for the cultivation of wet rice: "water moving through the rice fields should not become stagnant, or move too quickly. A steady, gentle flow is needed. The constant flow of water helps to ensure a continuous supply of nutrients which, paralleling the life-giving *hei [qi]* of fung shui [*fengshui*] should be allowed to penetrate the soil" (Webb 1995, 42).

Attention to the siting and situating of dwellings and villages no doubt prevented some risky and ill-advised environmental decisions, in the process nurturing a tradition of responsive and sustainable building practices. Yet one must be careful not to universalize these efforts or to romanticize them since there is substantial evidence that Chinese peasants all too often seriously damaged the environment in which they lived—draining wetlands, cutting woodlands for fuel, among many other activities—even while espousing a desire to live harmoniously in nature by appropriately siting their dwellings.

Ronald G. Knapp

1. Among the sources that focus on *fengshui* in the site selection for imperial capitals and other cities are Steinhardt (1990); Steinhardt et al. (2002, 206-207, 255-259); and Xu (2000, 208-236). Good surveys concerning the broader applications of *fengshui* to everyday decision making are Feuchtwang (1974); Huangbo (2002); March (1968); Smith (1991, 131-171); and Xu (1990, 1998).

2. The importation of wood from great distances is discussed in detail by Ruitenbeek (1993, 8-15).

3. Fifteen additional charms are illustrated in Knapp (1999b, 53; 1989, 147); a full set is in Ruitenbeek (1993, 298-305).

4. Potent antispectral charms made up of bizarre black or gold calligraphy on yellow paper were collected in the early 1900s, as seen in De Groot (1907, 1024-1061). For an all-purpose charm, see Knapp (1999b, 54).

5. Ruitenbeek (1993, 306-312) includes a selection of calligraphic amulets with details concerning their use.

6. Zhang Tianshi is described further in Chapter 14 as being employed during the fifth day of the fifth month in order to dispel the five poisons.

7. Facsimile reproductions of this and several other rare editions of the *Lu Ban jing,* as well as comparative translations, are found in Ruitenbeek (1993). A similar set of seventy-two admonitions appears in a reprint edition of the *Huitu Lu Ban jing,* published in Shanghai in the nineteenth century and reprinted regularly today in Taiwan.

8. An illustrated discussion of the full range of *yasheng* objects and rituals in Taiwan is found in Chen (1993, 5-26) and of those elsewhere in China in Knapp (1999b, 52-78).

9. An inverting mirror is illustrated in Knapp (1999b, 61).

10. A *cun* is a Chinese "inch" and equals one-third of a decimeter; a *fen* equals one-tenth of a *cun.*

11. For examples of Chinese handicrafts or folk art made to protect children, see Berliner (1986, 82-87).

12. I thank an anonymous peer reviewer for reminding me of these important associations.

13. For a representative selection of regional styles of Menshen over time, see Chen et al. (1992, 87-125); Po and Johnson (1992, 110-123); and Fong (1989, 6-24).

14. For various images of Zhong Kui, see Po and Johnson (1992, 106, 136-145); Rudova (1988, 18-19, 29).

15. While avoiding disaster and expelling evil were judged essential in pursuing a good life, Chinese traditionally believed it was equally necessary to pursue good fortune if well-being and happiness were to be assured. For a comprehensive examination of the iconographic elements involved in this activity, see Knapp (1999b, 81-157).

CARY Y. LIU

6 Chinese Architectural Aesthetics

Patterns of Living and Being between Past and Present

The functional, social, and symbolic meanings of Chinese vernacular architecture reflect the structural shape of the family and organization of society. The Chinese home also was a repository of heritage, a text or template that was imprinted with social, spiritual, and family patterns (Knapp 1999, 16–17; Lo and Ho 1999, 3). Among such imprints, one that has received little consideration is Chinese architectural aesthetics—as distinct from architectural theory. Architectural theory involves a range of spatial, visual, structural, and functional precepts that help guide building practice and methods, but it may play only an indirect role in determining the aesthetic judgment of a building's success or achievement.[1] The aesthetic judgment of successful building, such as in creating a dwelling, consequently, may rely only in some small way on a combination of visual and organizational factors, including the aptness of colors, textures, and detail; size relationships and proportions; the ordering of spatial elements related to hierarchy, axis/axes, and symmetry/asymmetry; and structural integrity, the suitability of materials, appropriate siting, context within the broader settlement landscape, recognition of climatic conditions, and functionality in terms of habitat. Many of these factors are explored throughout this book, yet rarely is there any recognition of the distinction between architectural theory as building practice and architectural aesthetics in terms of broader cultural assumptions relating to judgments of what determines successful architecture. As the discussion below reveals, architectural aesthetics is only partially a visual judgment and is not merely "beauty" per se.

In any inquiry into the relationship between architectural aesthetics and the house, home, and family, the term "vernacular" needs clarification. It can narrowly be understood in the Chinese context as referring to the domain of regional, domestic, and functional buildings of a nonimperial or nonmonumental nature. This common understanding of the term offers helpful insights; however, it also assumes a perspective of regional, chronological, and social isolation that downplays cultural interaction among geographic regions, the aspirations of social rank, and the imitation of past models. For example, it tends to deny the influence of imperial design on nonimperial building, as well as the appropriation of popular forms for imperial building. Moreover, such a narrow interpretation unconsciously relegates the "vernacular" into the arbitrary category of "low art" and is of limited use as a context within which to discuss the broader cultural phenomenon of Chinese architectural aesthetics. In a broader sense, because every person can be said to participate daily in the experience of architecture, all architecture can be seen as a vernacular art form (Scruton 1979, 16–17). John Summerson (1963, 212) notes with a complementary sentiment that the use of the term "vernacular" by historians is a "confession of ignorance" since any vernacular aesthetic or style can only be an unintended consequence that, if projected as contemporary objectives, becomes mere "chimera." With this in mind, one approach to exploring the principles of Chinese aesthetics in vernacular architecture has been to think about the history of building techniques and styles through isolated case-by-case studies for specific regions and peoples across China. Such a methodology promotes an autochthonous or anthropological particularization from which limited patterns of living and being can be grouped and examined through inductive reasoning. Conversely, architectural aesthetics can be viewed broadly as a confluence of diverse cultural factors across places, peoples, and periods that extend beyond just family homes and nonmonumental buildings to the fields of art, literature, music, philosophy, and politics, as well as into other architectural arenas including imperial, religious, public, and garden building. The aesthetic principles in each of these areas are different, yet together they contribute to a more comprehensive understanding of Chinese architectural aesthetics as part of a shared cultural heritage in ways that particularized studies may overlook. For this reason, it is important to approach architectural aesthetics as general patterns or vernacular imprints manifested throughout Chinese culture and then by deductive reasoning to discern what they reveal about house, home, and family in the Chinese context.

While the former approach involving particularized investigations ought properly be conducted within specific isolated regional and historical contexts, the latter approach calls for a widespread inspection across geographic and chronological boundaries. Providing a conceptual overview, the deductive methodology also enlarges the "vernacular" domain for the experience of living to include all China and broadens the human condition for being to become entangled with the issue of "Chineseness" (Mote 1989a, 5–11).[2] In crossing chronological boundaries, the patterns of house, home, and family as a living heritage cannot be separated from either past traditions or present changes, which unavoidably necessitates an attempt to define "modernism" in China. Explanations as to if, when, and how

Cary Y. Liu

Fig. 6.1. *Traditional courtyard houses and modern apartment complexes in Beijing.* Source: Photograph by Cary Y. Liu 2002.

Fig. 6.2. *The character* wen. *Detail from* Stele for Yi Ying *(Yi Ying Bei) 153, Temple of Confucius, Qufu, Shandong province. Rubbing.* Source: *Shoseki meihin sōkan* 1965.

modernism occurs in the Chinese intellectual, social, economic, and artistic contexts, however, remain controversial.[3] It is, of course, also questionable whether the term "modernism" can be applied to the public or participatory practice of architecture in the same way it is used for the more private or individual forms of art (Scruton 1979, 13–16). In addition, issues of nationalism, globalization, and transnationalism complicate the contemporary picture of architectural aesthetics in China.[4] The problems of defining "Chineseness" and "modernism" cannot be resolved in this preliminary investigation into Chinese architectural aesthetics. Nor is it possible to write definitively about the full range of domestic, religious, imperial, commercial, and civic buildings in China, especially since the study of Chinese architecture is still in its relative infancy (Knapp 2000, 7–18). Instead, an effort will be made to view vernacular architecture as both a living heritage balanced between past and present (Figure 6.1) and a phenomenon transgressing historical periodization as we "think with history" instead of think about history.[5]

In this conceptual overview of Chinese aesthetic principles, an attempt will be made to investigate architecture as a "manifestation of culture," or *wen* (Figure 6.2). Note, first, the meaning of *wen* as "writing" or "words" *(wenzi)* and, second, the legendary origins of *wen* as cosmic or exemplary patterns (*tian wen* or *di wen*,

Fig. 6.3. *Modern rebuilding of the Yellow Crane Tower, Wuhan, Hubei province.* Source: Photograph used with the permission of Jay Xu 1993.

literally "heavenly patterns" and "earthly patterns"); architecture can then be seen as manifesting imperishable words and potent patterns—*embodied images* (Liu 2000, 2–9). In architecture, embodiment can take the form of numerology, geomancy, cosmology, building rites and deities, sumptuary regulations, and symbology, but it is also important to take into consideration the way embodied words and patterns are transmitted. With the distance of geography or the passage of time, new meanings are often superimposed, dressed in new forms, functions, and materials, but the fundamental words and patterns persist as cultural imprints.

The aesthetic conception of architecture and its connection to the memory of the "word" in China (Kao 1991, 47–90; Mote 1976, 3–8) was expressed in the writings of the French archaeologist and littérateur Victor Segalen (1988, 1990, 1991) at the turn of the twentieth century and in Frederick Mote's (1973) seminal article on the city of Suzhou.[6] In China the imperishability *[buxiu]* of words predominates over physical durability.[7] An edifice's enduring name links it forever with persons, places, or events, whereas its built reality is only temporal. An example is the well-known Yellow Crane Tower (Huanghe Lou) at Wuchang (modern Wuhan in Hubei province), which is immortalized in poetry ("Noted Towers" 1943; Fan 1980, 147–163; Sun 1957, 49–51). Repeatedly rebuilt, the tower was destroyed during the Taiping Rebellion in the mid-nineteenth century during the Qing dynasty. Today, the tower is reincarnated in steel and concrete (Figure 6.3). Still, the present-day structure is perceived as original because the memory of its name substantiates its authenticity in words and writing—truly a building caught between its past and present. The building and rebuilding of even common homes, as well as the act of

Fig. 6.4. *Reconstruction of the fictional Hengzhi Qingfen Hall in the Daguan Yuan residential garden, Beijing.* Source: Photograph used with the permission of Melissa McCormick 1993.

naming them, with phrases painted or etched on placards above their entry, reflects this imperishability of home and house as well. This calls attention to the general observation that throughout China, one can discern architectural forms and practices that were shared in the residences of members of the imperial household, officials, scholars, merchants, shopkeepers, and other common people. It is too often generally assumed without conclusive evidence that such shared features originally must have been developed by the ruling and upper classes and subsequently deliberately appropriated and remolded by others of lower social standing, or vice versa. These scenarios set up convenient yet arbitrary dichotomies between upper and lower classes, high and low art, and imperial and nonimperial architecture; however, for the understanding of Chinese architectural aesthetics, it may be better to ignore such dichotomies and to view the situation as an unintended sharing of common cultural experiences.

Taken to extremes, the imperishable power of "words" is epitomized by the Daguan Yuan, or Prospect Garden, outlined in the eighteenth-century novel *Hong lou meng,* known in English as *The Story of the Stone* and *The Dream of the Red Chamber.* This fictional residential garden, discussed in Chapter 4 above, is arguably the most famous architectural structure in modern China and has even been given physical form in both Beijing and Shanghai (Figure 6.4). In the novel, the garden's construction is given only passing notice. Instead, attention focuses on the act of naming the scenic spots and buildings in the garden sanctuary (Cao 1973, Chapters 16–17). This bestowal of words embodies an aesthetic of spontaneity. As important as the first note in music or the first brush stroke in calligraphy and painting, in architecture the instant of naming confers to a building its imperishable mark of authenticity (Liu 1997, 269–281).

Nowhere can this relationship between China's architectural heritage and its strong connection to the imperishable word better be seen than in the Qing dynasty Wenyuan Ge, the imperial library hall, built in a residential garden setting in 1776 within the Palace City, or *gong cheng,* known as the Forbidden City in Beijing (Figure 6.5). This six-bay-wide library, a repository for words, was specially built to house the primary set of *The Comprehensive Library of the Four Treasuries (Siku quanshu),* an immense anthology of manuscript books that formed the core of the Qing imperial library collection. As such, it represented the sum of knowledge bestowed from heaven—a symbol of the dynasty's legitimacy and ability to rule. The design and name of the library hall, consequently, came to have special significance. Dedicatory records composed by the Qianlong emperor who reigned

Fig. 6.5. *Wenyuan Ge, Imperial Library Hall, 1776, Forbidden City, Beijing.* Source: Yu 1984, Fig. 224 (detail).

between 1736 and 1795 outlined the design symbology of the library that likened the collecting of knowledge to flowing water converging on a vast sea. The water imagery is echoed in the calligraphy composed and brushed by the Qianlong emperor inside the library hall. For example, the central placard, suspended over the imperial throne in the Wenyuan Ge, reads, "Converging Streams like a Pure Mirror" *[hui liu cheng jian].* The imagery likens water flowing to the sea with knowledge gathering in a reservoir that reflects cultural wisdom and societal harmony. Many other calligraphy placards and couplets in the library hall reinforced this symbology, helping to embody the library's design and significance. Here, words manifested in calligraphy provide a key to understanding the underlying pattern of the architecture (Liu 1997).

Cary Y. Liu

Fig. 6.6. *Tianyi Ge, private library hall, 1561, Ningbo, Zhejiang province.* Source: Photograph used with the permission of Virginia Bower 1993.

As a palace hall, the Wenyuan Ge reflects imperial aspirations, yet the design of this library, as well as that of the six sister halls also built to house sets of the *Four Treasuries,* was partly based on the imitation of patterns believed to be exemplified in the six-bay Tianyi Ge, a private library hall built in 1561 by the Ming dynasty official Fan Qin (1506–1585). Built within a family residential compound in Ningbo, Zhejiang, the Tianyi Ge was purportedly the oldest surviving library structure in the 1770s, so its design was considered the most efficacious against fire and damage (Figure 6.6). As a result, the Qianlong emperor ordered a survey team to produce sketches, draw blueprints, and prepare models of it.[8] The aim was to determine the apotropaic properties and patterns of longevity believed to be embodied in the design of the Tianyi Ge so that they could be duplicated in the building of the Wenyuan Ge. The mythic design of the Tianyi Ge was also manifested in words through its name. The characters *tian* [heaven] and *yi* [one] were associated with

Chinese Architectural Aesthetics

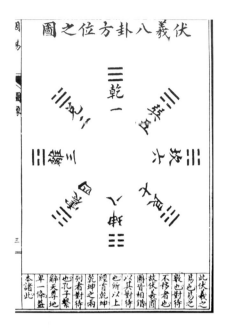

Fig. 6.7. *Diagram of the ancient sage Fu Xi's arrangement of the Eight Trigrams.* Source: Lai 1971, 3.

words connected to the late-third-century B.C. divinatory text, the *Book of Change* (*Yijing*): "Heaven and the number one give rise to water, and Earth and the number six complete them" [*tian yi cheng shui, di liu cheng zhi*].[9] In this particular case of architectural imitation, numerology based on the numbers one and six was appropriated from a residential prototype and applied to the design of the imperial palace library (Liu 1997, 134–154; 1999, 194–199).

This leads to the second understanding of *wen*—that is, as denoting patterns—which is closely tied to its meaning as "words" or "writing." Cosmic or exemplary patterns can be seen in architecture through the concept of *ti*, "embodiment," or *ti xiang*, "embodied image." The term "embodied image" is used in an architectural context in the *Western Capital Rhapsody,* written in the first century A.D. by Ban Gu (32–92):

> The palaces and halls:
> Their embodied images were patterned after heaven and earth;
> Their warp and weft conformed to *yin* and *yang*
> [*qi gong shi ye, ti xiang hu tian di, jing wei hu yin yang*].[10]

In this passage, architecture is praised for its ability to ritually embody and image the cosmos, the realm of heaven and earth, or *tian di*. Here, "embodied images" refers to the ability of visual, ritual, and physical patterns to recreate and duplicate the cosmos in a distilled form with greater potency. Seen in this way, architecture, calligraphy, and painting in China are more than a means of built, written, or visual communication; they are artistic duplications of cosmic patterns. They were believed not only to manifest the world of knowable things and ideas, but also to duplicate their unknowable cosmic patterns or divine configurations (Liu 2000, 2–9). Similarly, cosmic images are duplicated and embodied not only in the overall plans of palace halls, imperial libraries, temples, and individual houses throughout China, as shown in many examples in this book, but also in the rituals carried out within them by those inhabiting the structures.

How can we illustrate this concept of embodying cosmic patterns? The *Book of Change* notes that in antiquity the Eight Trigrams, or Bagua, were invented in order to comprehend the potency of the knowable and unknowable patterns of heaven and earth (Figure 6.7). The trigrams and their configurations not only represented or symbolized the patterns of things, ideas, and events, but they were also believed to embody, duplicate, or possess the powers and attributes of what they duplicated with distilled potency. The trigrams are duplicates and not mere copies or symbols, and according to legend, they are the precursors of words as

Cary Y. Liu

written patterns (Liu 2000, 2; Peterson 1982). In China, such patterns extend to all things and events (e.g., historical patterns) in the cosmos and form the basis for understanding art and literature as visual and verbal patterns and architecture—buildings—as embodying patterns for living and being.

It is this condensed potency through duplication that allowed the ruler as dynast and archon to embody the mandate of heaven. Translated into architectural pattern, the Qing dynasty Imperial Summer Villa, or Bishu Shanzhuang, at Rehe, modern Chengde, serves as an example at multiple scales of living and being (Figures 6.8–6.9). The overall site plan of this eighteenth-century imperial garden palace, a new Manchu architectural typology for living and governing, established a clear hierarchy with the residential and ceremonial palaces for the emperor at the center; scenic sites, duplicated from subordinate areas of the empire, around him like the spokes of a wheel; and an outlying ring of temple-residential compounds for allied and subjugated frontier peoples (Figure 6.9). Many of these perimeter compounds were built in the regional styles of the frontier peoples they were meant to house and represented an imitation or transplantation of local "vernacular" styles for imperial use. A synecdochical relationship was created, with the microcosm of the Summer Villa serving to duplicate on Earth a harmonious macrocosm of the nation and the heavenly cosmos. Conversely, the villa can be seen to be manifested in the body of the emperor at its center.[11] Here, the realms of heaven, man, and earth—the Three Powers, or *san cai*, as tendered in the *Book of Change*[12]—embody each other and are duplicated in architectural pattern.

Fig. 6.8. *Leng Mei*, Painting of the Imperial Summer Villa *(Bishu Shanzhuang Tu; ca. 1708–1711)*. Source: Tianjin daxue jianzhuxi 1982, Fig. 1.

Fig. 6.9. *Putuo Zongcheng Temple, 1771, Imperial Summer Villa, Chengde, Hebei province.* Source: Photograph by Cary Y. Liu 1984.

Fig. 6.10. *Painted and calligraphic manifestations of Door Gods. Kun Ting Study Hall, Ping Shan, Yuen Long, New Territories, Hong Kong.* Source: Photograph by Li Yuxiang.

Repeatedly we return to the *Book of Change* as the likely source, the *locus classicus*, for many of the terms and ideas later attached to aesthetic, theoretical, and critical views of both art and architecture. The *Book of Change* provides a datum for understanding the concept of the "embodied image," or *ti xiang*, in which a key term in this binome is the character *xiang*, meaning "image." In the *Book of Change*, "image" is associated with heavenly patterns *[tian wen]* and can be translated as "figures," the configurations of space and time in the heavens. These heavenly patterns find their complement in earthly patterns *[diwen* or *dili]*, the configurations of earthly bodies and energies that underlie the practice of geomantic prognostication, *kanyu*, or now more commonly *fengshui* (Bennett 1978). The ritual embodiment of such cosmic patterns in residential, palace, temple, commercial, and garden architecture is manifested through the practice of geomancy, building magic, numerology, cosmology, and symbology, only the general outlines of which were discussed in Chapter 4 above.

In China, the building and dwelling processes and progressions are accompanied at almost every step by ritual patterns, and sacrifices and ceremonies are offered to deities who are believed to inhabit various parts of a building (Figure 6.10). Too often dismissed as mere superstition along with geomancy and building magic, such practices should be reevaluated in relation to the embodiment of cosmic patterns in the very conception of architecture in China (Eberhard 1970; Liu 1994, 28, 34–36; Ruitenbeek 1993, 36–39, 45–115 passim). A general observation has been that traditional homes have deities and rituals assigned to their various parts, while modern constructions often appear empty of such traditions (Knapp 1999, 18). A logical question is, To what degree is this true? Furthermore, are basic patterns only clothed in new building forms with new, but shallow, layers of meaning? For example, while family ancestral altars were traditionally erected in the geomantic center, the *zhong tang* or *zhong gong*, of a traditional house, in modern housing structures, ranging from suburban villas to high-rise apartments, family altars are still present but in different spaces. Building practices such as geomantic divination, the selection of auspicious days, and rituals related to raising the ridgepole, or *shangliang*, are all still in evidence in many parts of China, as can be seen in Chapter 5 and as is discussed in detail in Ruitenbeek (1986, 1–23).

On the scale of individual behavior with a goal toward family and societal harmony, the embodiment of cosmic patterns is further mirrored in patterns of exemplary behavior (Nylan 1999, 16–77). Although any attempt to recreate the moral universe regulating correct behavior among members of a society in a particular place or time is difficult, one general guideline with major implications for residen-

Cary Y. Liu

tial, religious, and imperial architecture that must be noted is the Confucian notion of *zheng ming,* or "rectifying names" (Nylan 2001, 268–275). A "name" designates, and can be said to duplicate, the unique qualities that define a person's or a thing's substantive or real *[shi]* identity and establishes its relationship with other things. According to the "Zi Lu" section of the *Analects,* when Confucius was asked how to govern, he answered: "I would definitely start with Rectifying Names. . . . If names are not rectified, then words will not follow. If words do not follow, then affairs will not be completed. If affairs are not completed, then rites and music will not flourish" (in Nylan 2001, 269–270).

One aspect of rectifying names called for people to act in accordance with their proper or named societal roles. The result was a clear hierarchy that distinguished family and social relationships and that throughout history was embodied in architecture through hierarchic ordering and sumptuary laws governing building size and type, construction module and material, and building ritual and decoration. Sumptuary regulations are recorded in Zhou and Han dynasty texts describing funerary and shrine building and spelled out in detail in the early-twelfth-century Song dynasty *Yingzao fashi* imperial building manual, as well as in numerous later construction manuals and regulations. In fact, while many modern studies have tended to consider Chinese architecture—especially its bracket sets—as modular construction or mass production systems, they tend to overlook a primary function of these systems as manifestations of sumptuary laws. In this manner, the principle of rectifying names cannot be separated from the cultural notion of aesthetics in Chinese architecture, and it may be in the very duplication of an ideal hierarchic order or harmonious pattern that the notion of beauty is to be found in Chinese architecture.

Through this process, the embodying of cosmic or exemplary patterns by rectifying names, we return full circle to the importance of the word in Chinese architecture. Words give a building its proper name, identify its symbology and appropriate rank, and can be said to call out its authenticity, its substantive or real identity. When considering *wen* as meaning "words" or "patterns" in terms of Chinese architectural aesthetics, however, we must remember to think geographically from place to place and, as noted above, to "think with history" from ancient to modern times. While many words and patterns persist between past and present, as well as in various localities and in various historical periods, differing formal, functional, moral, political, or spiritual interpretations can be superimposed by the architect, historian, or viewer. Two examples are selected to make this point, one in the field of painting and the other in architecture.

Chinese Architectural Aesthetics

Fig. 6.11a–b.

a. *Li Gongnian (fl. ca. 1120),* Winter Night Landscape. *Hanging scroll, ink on silk, 129.6 x 48.3 cm.*

b. *Detail of the moon at upper right.*
Source: Princeton University Art Museum, DuBois Schanck Morris Collection.
Photograph by Bruce M. White.

First, we examine two paintings in the Princeton University Art Museum depicting images of the moon. An ink-on-silk hanging scroll, bearing the descriptive title *Winter Landscape,* as seen in Figure 6.11, is an early-twelfth-century late Northern Song painting signed by the artist Li Gongnian (fl. ca. 1120). In the painting's upper right corner, an image of the moon has recently been discovered, which suggests a new title, *Winter Night Landscape.*[13] In its imagery, with the Earth below as terra firma and the moon above as celestial orb, this landscape represents in visual terms man's traditional place in the universe; the celestial moon hangs high above and appears unreachable. In the late twentieth century, with the Apollo space flights to the moon, this relationship changed (Arendt 1958, 1–2). Inspired by photographs of Earthrise taken from orbits around the moon, in 1971 Liu Guosong (born 1932) painted a set of five hanging scrolls entitled *Full Moon.* As seen in Figure 6.12, man's viewing point has changed, and his place in the universe is freed from the confines of the Earth. In his related painting series, entitled *Which Is Earth?,* the artist even directly questions whether we are looking at the moon or Earth.[14] Yet despite these changes in interpretation, the basic pattern of placing a celestial orb—an ideal realm—in the far distance remains constant.

Second, similar transformations in meaning, as well as in form, materials, and function, can be observed in the development of architectural typologies in examples as diverse as courtyard houses, palace audience halls, libraries, and temples. The concept can be illustrated best in the evolution of the stupa-pagoda. After the

Chinese Architectural Aesthetics

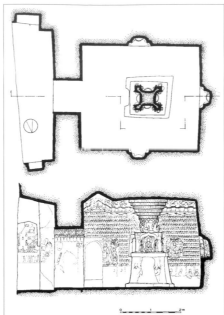

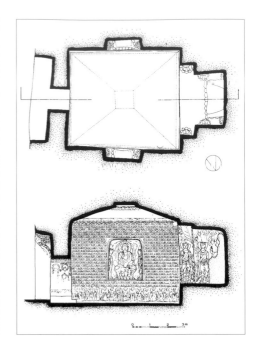

Fig. 6.13. *Pagoda at Songyue Si Temple 523, Dengfeng, Henan province.* Source: Chinese Academy of Architecture 1986, 53.

Fig. 6.14. *Cave 302, Sui dynasty (581–618), Dunhuang, Gansu province. Plan and section drawings.* Source: *Chūgoku sekkutsu Tonkō Bakukōkutsu* 1981, 2:266.

Fig. 6.15. *Cave 420, Sui dynasty (581–618), Dunhuang, Gansu province. Plan and section drawings.* Source: *Chūgoku sekkutsu Tonkō Bakukōkutsu* 1981, 2:267.

early introduction of the stupa into China as Buddhist reliquaries, Chinese pagodas first imitated the Indian prototypes. An example is the pagoda at the Songyue Si Temple in Henan province, seen in Figure 6.13. Built in 523 in the Northern Wei period, this twelve-sided pagoda has fifteen close-set eaves rising to a stone finial. In Sui dynasty cave temples at Dunhuang, Gansu province, the focus of the inner sanctum was often a stupa or cosmic pillar or a main Buddha group placed in a niche in the back wall, as seen in Figures 6.14 and 6.15. In the latter case, the cosmic pillar was replaced by a pyramidal ceiling topped by a heavenly-well caisson ceiling. Both the pillar and the caisson—positive and negative examples respectively—implied, in religious, imperial, and residential architecture, an *axis mundi* leading up into the celestial heavens and down into the realms of the earth (Liu 1994).

An adoption of native Chinese timber construction methods led to the development of wooden pagoda forms, as seen in the Sakyamuni Pagoda at Fogong Si Temple, Yingxian, Shanxi province, the oldest and tallest surviving wood pagoda in China (Figure 6.16) (Chen 1980; Steinhardt 1997, 103–121). Built in 1056 during the Liao dynasty, the pagoda has an octagonal plan and was positioned inside the temple gate on the central axis of the main courtyard. The exterior rises in six roof eaves leading to a central top finial, while the interior has five main floors plus four hidden mezzanine levels. Staircases connect the outer galleries on each floor, creating a circulation ring that also acts to brace and support the pagoda structure. In

Cary Y. Liu

Fig. 6.16a–b.

a. *Sakyamuni Pagoda, 1056, Fogong Si Temple, Ying county, Shanxi province.* Source: Chinese Academy of Architecture 1986, 94.

b. *Sakyamuni Pagoda. Section drawing.* Source: Liang 1984, Fig. 31d.

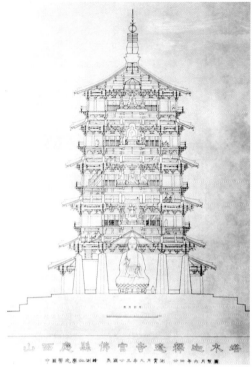

the center room or inner sanctum on each of the main floors are Buddhist sculpture groups, some with hidden sutras and other religious relics and artifacts (Shanxi sheng wenwuju 1991). This was more than a change of materials and architectural language; the very experience of the pagoda as a cosmic pillar had been transformed from its early function as reliquary and object of worship to a setting for a vertical pilgrimage through multiple Buddhist paradises. Believers who climb the Sakyamuni Pagoda not only pass through various paradises, but they also rise along the pillar of the cosmos, and the grand exterior vistas encountered along the way may have been calculated to inspire greater devotion.

In addition to such developments, the very function of a pagoda sometimes changed so that it became a channel for geomantic energy or provided a scenic accent in an inhabited landscape. To correct perceived geomantic deficiencies, so-called *fengshui* pagodas were built in the environs of many villages, towns, or cities. Often built as temple pagodas that also functioned as geomantic pillars, they some-

Fig. 6.17. *Often built as geomantic pillars, pagodas provided significant visual markers for localities throughout China. It is said that this Pagoda of Heavenly Investiture was first built in Ningbo, Zhejiang, in 696 in order to "repel evil,"* Source: Moule 1911, facing page 86.

times were erected solely to enhance geomantic qualities, to provide a visual landmark in a locality, or (only later) to take on the properties of a geomantic pillar (Figure 6.17).[15] Regardless of the changes in form, materials, or function or differences from place to place or time to time, the basic pattern of pagoda structures as cosmic pillars linking earth and heaven remained fundamentally unchanged.

This continuation of the tiered pagoda pattern is also true for the recently completed Jin Mao Tower in Shanghai's new business district, as seen in Figure 6.18 (Campanella 2000, 82–89). Rising 420.5 meters (1,380 feet) above the city and described in promotional publicity as a "super-tall structure exemplifying traditional Chinese style," the Jin Mao Tower is at present China's tallest building and one of the world's tallest, ranked after the Taipei 101 in Taibei, Taiwan; the Petronas Towers in Kuala Lumpur, Malaysia; and the Sears Tower in Chicago. Designed by a Chinese and American team led by the Chicago office of Skidmore, Owings and Merrill, this multi-use Chinese skyscraper deliberately imitates the form of ancient pagodas yet combines offices for commerce and hotel rooms for living. With its tapered shape, the tower rises in a series of thirteen setbacks leading up to a top finial. Because the number eight, or *ba,* is considered auspicious for its phonetic closeness to the word *fa,* meaning "acquiring wealth," the design for the tower

incorporates it as a numerological unit: the tower is eighty-eight stories tall, its height-to-width ratio is 8:1, and the height of each successive setback is diminished by a multiple of eight. Though the tower is new in its materials—steel, concrete, and glass—new in its size and height, and new also in its functions, its basic pattern as a pagoda persists. It can still be likened to a cosmic pillar soaring into the sky in the heart of Shanghai's financial district; it is a pillar to mammon, designed for Asia's new national, transnational, and global "masters of the universe."

In contemporary architecture, consequently, traditional patterns can still be understood to underlie the conception of buildings constructed with new materials, forms, and functions. Changes in modern housing include innovations in sanitation, convenience, and communication that affect the spatial arrangement of homes, as well as family and social relationships. Modern urbanization and commercialization have led to new housing forms, including apartment buildings, hotels, and suburban villas, as seen above in Figure 6.1 and in Figures 6.19 and 6.20. In some

Fig. 6.19. *New housing development next to the Tengzhou Han Dynasty Pictorial Stones Museum, Tengzhou, Shandong.* Source: Photograph by Cary Y. Liu 2002.

Fig. 6.20. *Model suburban villas located at the Fuwah Hotel, Weifang, Shandong.* Source: Photograph by Cary Y. Liu 2002.

cases, as seen in Figure 6.21 and in Figure 3.13 in Chapter 3, old, single-story *siheyuan* dwellings in Beijing have been demolished and replaced with new-style, two-story housing. In other cases, garage doors, which forcibly hint at greater transformations inside, have been set in the once stark walls of renovated older structures (Figure 6.22). Globalization and transnational competition have encouraged the introduction of foreign architectural styles and models. With all these changes, it may now be in the way new materials, forms, styles, and functions are expressed in relation to traditional patterns that a new aesthetic paradigm or vernacular style may begin to be perceived as part of "a global postmodernity mediated by the terrains and histories identifiable as Chinese" (Dirlik and Zhang 2000, 9).

In conclusion, it is also important to speculate about the cultural underpinnings of aesthetics in China. Whereas the Western study of aesthetics has primarily revolved around the notion of "beauty," Susan Bush and Shih Hsiao-yen have noted that "the concept of 'beauty' does not figure in Chinese aesthetic concerns" (1985, 2), and there may be no equivalent term in the Chinese language. In Chinese, for example, terms such as "lovely" *[mei* or *meili]*, "pretty" *[piaoliang]*, or "good" *[shan]* tend to relate more to outer appearance, taste, and goodness than any sense of an innate or divine "beauty." As a result, any consideration of Chinese aesthetics requires an understanding of beauty that significantly differs from Western artistic ideals based on mimesis and on an identification with godhead.[16] The Western ideal of an intrinsic divine beauty is foreign to Chinese aesthetic thought, and its conceptual absence may find parallels in the argument that has sometimes been

Fig. 6.21. *In the old Nanchizi neighborhood in Beijing, new, two-story courtyard-style apartment dwellings, called* sihelou, *are clustered around a common courtyard and have replaced countless* siheyuan *of the past.* Source: Photograph by Ronald G. Knapp 2003.

Fig. 6.22. *Along some of the narrow, centuries-old* hutong *lanes in Beijing, automatic garage doors have been fitted into the old walls, at once suggesting major transformations within while, as in the past, hiding the changes from passersby.* Source: Photograph by Ronald G. Knapp 2003.

made of a lack of an ubiquitous divine law in China (Bodde 1981, 238–245, 299–315; Mote 1989a, 12–25; Needham 1954, 2: 286–287).

To borrow a distinction by Thomas E. Jessop (1964, 531–532), the judgment of beauty varies with the artistic medium. Painting, music, architecture, and sculpture are capable of being judged according to their own particular natures. For example, a painted color, sculpted line, or proportioned building can be inherently beautiful by itself. In contrast, in the literary field, words are dependent on their relationship to signified ideas and meanings. There is little intrinsic beauty in a word apart from its meaning. In this way, Jessop distinguishes between "sensory" and "ideo-sensory" beauty. It should be added, however, that the two are not mutually exclusive, and both qualities interact in the judgment of art. Speculatively, it may be said that Western art tends toward sensory beauty, while Chinese art focuses more on the ideo-sensory. A Chinese calligraphic or painterly brush stroke can be beautiful in itself, but the stroke through its stylistic choice, connection with magico-efficacy, historic and poetic references, and configured pattern connotes a host of other artistic and cultural meanings (Harrist et al. 1999; Liu, Ching, and Smith 1999). Likewise, in Chinese architecture—palaces, pagodas, and even common dwellings—an edifice is judged beautiful not only by its outward form or visual appearance, but even more by its cultural symbology. This symbology is often focused on the word as a duplication of cosmic patterns and was embodied in the names of buildings, as well as through numerology, ornamentation, ordering of spatial elements, and choice of design prototypes (Liu 1997, 6–7; 2000, 2–9).

Chinese Architectural Aesthetics

1. On the distinction between architectural aesthetics and architectural theory, Roger Scruton notes the following: "It is essential to distinguish architectural aesthetics . . . from something else that sometimes goes by the same name, but which one might call . . . architectural theory. Architectural theory consists in the attempt to formulate the maxims, rules and precepts which govern, or ought to govern, the practice of the builder. . . . Such precepts assume that we already know what we are seeking to achieve. . . . The question is, rather, how best to achieve it" (1979, 4; see also 37–70). On the other hand, architectural aesthetics deals with the nature or judgment of architectural success or achievement.

2. The issue of "Chineseness" is also an attempt to identify or define "Chinese civilization," as seen in Bodde (1981).

3. According to Jonathan D. Spence (1990, xx), a "modern" nation is understood to be one that is confident in its own identity yet able to cooperate with other nations in economic, technological, and intellectual terms. Spence concludes that while the past sheds light on our understanding of the present, China has yet to satisfy the conditions of "modernism." Eight years later, Julia Andrews and Kuiyi Shen describe a pluralistic situation in the twentieth century where various forms of modernism, socialist realism, postmodernism, and traditionalism coexist, "competing and interacting in ways that may bear little relationship to the history of Western art" (1998, 9).

4. On the influence of globalization and transnationalism on contemporary residential and public architecture, see King and Kusno (2000, 41–67). My gratitude to Stephen J. Goldberg for bringing this essay to my attention.

5. On approaching the relationship between the past and the present, see Schorske (1998, 3–4) and Arendt (1961, 3–15). The problem of defining "Chineseness" parallels problems in trying to identify the subsets of "Chinese art" or "Chinese architecture." See Clunas (1997, 9–13).

6. For an interesting study that develops many of Mote's ideas and offers new insights, see Xu (2000).

7. The imperishable quality of words is maintained in the *Zuo zhuan,* where it is recorded that words or discourses *[yan]* are the third imperishable behind virtue *[de]* and merit *[gong].* See *Chun qiu Zuo zhuan zhengyi, Shisan jing zhushu* edition (1980, 35/1979); Legge (1985, 5: 505, 507). Also see Liu (1997, 2–3, 270–281).

8. Imperial orders to imitate the Tianyi Ge are recorded in various documents including, the 1774 "Wenyuan Ge ji" building record. Translated in Liu (1997, 284–287).

9. The wording here paraphrases Zheng Xuan's commentary in *Zhou yi Zheng Kangcheng zhu* (1983–1986, 7: *juan* 1, p. 26a). To my knowledge the earliest reproduction of the exact wording appears in Zhao (1970, 262).

10. Ban (1974, *juan* 1, p. 5). Translation modified from Xiao Tong (501–531) in Knechtges (1982, 1: 114–117).

Cary Y. Liu

11. My gratitude to Jack W. Chen for bringing this line of thinking to my attention in personal correspondence, November 11, 2000.

12. See *Zhou yi zhengyi, Shisan jing zhushu* edition (1980, 93–94).

13. Reproduced in Rowley (1947, pl. 24, pl. 19) and *Bunjinga* (1977, 219, pl. 34).

14. A painting in this series, *Which is Earth? No. 9* (1969), is reproduced in Sullivan (1996, 182, Figure 8.5).

15. Yinong Xu (2000, 208–218) demonstrates in his study of Suzhou that the symbolic attributes of geomantic elements, such as *fengshui* pagodas, were often retrospectively stated and interpreted, rather than having been part of an initial design.

16. Plato and Aristotle introduced "imitation" into the discussion of the arts. With Plotinus (1962, 422–433) and the concept of Pythagorean harmony, it was extended to ideal forms and divinity, and by the eighteenth century it came to be recognized as a common principle of all the arts. See also Batteux (1746, 9) and Wittkower (1971, 101–154). For a concise summary of "imitation" in aesthetic theory, see *New Encyclopedia Britannica*, 15th ed. (Chicago: Encyclopedia Britannica, 1974), s.v. "Aesthetics," by Roger Scruton, in vol. 13: 26–27 passim.

7   Traditional Chinese Architecture and Furniture

A Cultural Interpretation

Any cultural interpretation of traditional Chinese architecture and furniture must be based on a broad and interdisciplinary approach if it is to lead to an inclusive view of their basic interrelatedness and symbiotic development. New perspectives on the all-embracing subject of "house, home, and family" and related issues of "living and being Chinese" are also likely to emerge from a discourse focusing on the interdependence of furniture and architecture. The cultural interpreter must ask not only why and how the Chinese built in the way they did, but also why they lived and behaved in the manner they did through the ages, with few apparent changes, until recent times, when social and economic forces brought modernizing, even revolutionary, transformations in house forms, family size, living patterns, values, and customs.

Wang Shixiang, the connoisseur and foremost authority on Chinese furniture, endorsed such a broad, multidisciplinary approach when he wrote in 1998 in the foreword to *Classical and Vernacular Furniture in the Living Environment* that "the term 'living environment' is actually a framework encompassing furniture, architecture and gardens, long recognized to be interrelated and indivisible. Previously, studies have only focused on these aspects in isolation and have not examined the subject as an organic whole." The aim therefore is "to probe and examine their links and pattern to arrive at a new level of awareness of the living environment" (Lo 1998, 7).

Interest in Chinese Architecture and Furniture

The serious study of traditional Chinese domestic architecture has a history of only fifty years, as Ronald G. Knapp explains in Chapter 3. Similarly, the first book on traditional Chinese furniture to include technical drawings and descriptions appeared in 1944 with the publication of a limited Shanghai edition of Gustav Ecke's *Domestic Chinese Furniture*. This pioneering work, however, by concentrating solely on the simple lines and forms of hardwood furniture, started the trend of equating elevated Chinese taste with the "austere, dignified luxury" of the "amber and purple hues of rosewood pieces," showing "a respect for organic substance" as found in the "home of the ruling class" of the Ming dynasty (Ecke 1944, 1, 28–33).

Ecke excluded furniture with elaborate carving and also that in lacquer, a major furniture tradition in China that was *de rigueur* from Han to Ming and through Qing times. *Domestic Chinese Furniture,* which was the first book in any language on Chinese hardwood furniture, echoed the taste shared by a coterie of Westerners residing in China who equated Ming hardwood furniture with minimalist Bauhaus design. "We are not dealing with an ever-changing, inconstant fashion, but with discreet and intelligent variation upon a single noble theme," wrote the distinguished George Kates (1948: 3, 18–58), thus dismissing the development in furniture of the past millennium and enforcing the view that hardwood furniture *was* "Chinese furniture."

There were few Chinese collectors in the mid-twentieth century and no published material in Chinese on the subject. Robert Ellsworth, in his significant tome, *Chinese Furniture: Hardwood Examples of the Ming and Early Ch'ing Dynasties* (1970), further equated furniture made of hardwoods, which had been imported from Southeast Asia since Ming times, as the only worthwhile Chinese furniture. Wang Shixiang's seminal works—*Classic Chinese Furniture* (1986) and *Connoisseurship of Chinese Furniture* (1990), the fruits of forty years of collecting and research—were the first authoritative accounts written by a Chinese, with illustrations from Chinese collections (Handler 2001, 3–4; Lo and Ho 1999, 38–40). The appearance of Wang's work in French and German editions in addition to the English further helped to expand interest in Chinese furniture worldwide. "Ming" assumed a magical cachet, and the term "Ming-style classical Chinese furniture" was taken to represent exclusively the best Chinese furniture, usually made of precious hardwood and adhering to the famous definition by Lawrence Sickman (1978) of classic design as bearing the qualities of "restraint, balance and grandeur." In fact, Ming style did not end with the fall of that dynasty, and there is little difference technically or stylistically between furniture of the late Ming and early Qing eras.

In contrast, furniture made of softwoods indigenous to China, constructed in classic line and form yet expressing regional characteristics, often coated with a thin lacquer veneer for protection, and widely used in most provincial households in the countryside—hence the term "vernacular"—was hardly mentioned. By the early 1990s, furniture made of such precious woods—the yellow flower pear wood *[huanghuali]* and purple sandalwood *[zitan],* as well as even good quality chicken-wing wood *[jichimu]*—had become scarce and expensive. Dealers began to promote furniture in softwoods such as walnut *[hetaomu],* northern elm *[yumu]* and southern elm *[jumu],* cypress *[baimu],* longyan *[longyanmu],* camphor *[zhangmu]* and willow *[liumu],* to name a few. *Nanmu,* a type of cedar, was reserved for use by

Fig. 7.1. *A particular type of cedar called* nanmu *is a much-desired softwood for both furniture and building and was used by the court and the wealthy. The roof of the Hall of Awesome Grace, Ling'en Dian, in Changling, the mausoleum of Yongle (1403–1424), the third Ming emperor, is supported by 60* nanmu *columns; 32 of them are each 12.58 meters high, and the four in the middle of the hall are 1.12 meters in diameter. Each column is made out of a single tree trunk. The beams, pillars, brackets, and window frames in the hall are all made of precious* nanmu *and, unlike other imperial architecture, are unpainted.* Source: Photograph by Kai-Yin Lo 2002.

the elite in both furniture and architecture. In the afterlife, to be housed in a coffin made of *nanmu*, which purportedly exuded fragrance and prevented decay of the body, was the ultimate luxury. The sixty unpainted columns of immense proportion supporting the roof of the memorial Hall of Awesome Grace [Ling'en Dian], built in 1409 outside Beijing, are arguably the most magnificent manifestation of the use of *nanmu* in architecture (Figure 7.1). The hall lies within Changling, the mausoleum of Yongle, the third emperor of the Ming dynasty, who reigned from 1403 to 1424 (Wang Tianxing 1997, 35).

The increased interest in and support for both Chinese architecture and furniture in Asia and the West during the last twenty and particularly the last ten years have resulted in a steady stream of writing in books, journals, magazines, symposia, exhibitions, preservation projects, and a heightened prominence of Chinese furniture at international auctions and fairs and in the marketplace. Furniture dealers and collectors have been even more eager than scholars and connoisseurs to focus on the varied regional forms and construction of softwood furniture, and new information on regional vernacular furniture has emerged during the last decade as dealers have traveled to different parts of China.

It has come to light that there are four major regional furniture traditions in China: the tradition of the capital, Beijing, with imperial and court patronage and where the most skilled craftsmen were assembled; the Suzhou and Jiangnan tradition, which was directed by literati tastes; the tradition of the Shanxi area, whose highly recognizable style to a great extent was sustained by rich merchant-patrons; and the Lingnan tradition in present-day Guangdong, with ornately carved furniture made from ample supplies of imported hardwoods, such as *zitan* and *tielimu,* or *hongmu* [types of redwood or blackwood from Southeast Asia]. Until 1998, there were only two books on vernacular furniture (Berliner and Handler 1995; Lo 1998). These were followed by a noteworthy volume that shed new light on the Shanxi tradition (Evarts 1999). Debate, however, continues to dwell on aesthetic, decorative, structural, and preservation issues, and until the past five years, hardwood furniture remained the focus.

A probe of the linkages between architecture and furniture has also been limited and tentative, often restricted to discussions on isolated aspects of construction techniques and ornamentation. Basic questions on material and construction, such as why hardwood is so valued in Chinese furniture and design, have already been answered: the nature of the wood allows for the intricate construction of joinery supporting well-defined proportions, graceful curves, and a luminous surface, already perfected and stabilized in treatment and polish in Ming times. As Robert Ellsworth points out, "timber alone should not establish beauty or value. Far-sighted collectors buy furniture, not woods" (Ellsworth 1996, 20). Appreciation of the beauty and worth of softwood furniture is bound to grow with increasing knowledge and exposure, inviting further explorations, specifically those that address questions of "why" relating to the historical, social, and cultural aspects of furniture rather than merely issues of "how."

The difficulties of making great strides in research are obvious: there is a striking scarcity of excavated archaeological examples and only limited documentation for Chinese architecture and furniture prior to the sixteenth century. The oldest extant, although renovated, domestic dwelling, Laowu Ge in Huizhou, present-day southern Anhui, dates only to the last decade of the fifteenth century (Figure 7.2). The oldest timber structure in China, Nanchan Monastery in Wutaishan [Mount Wutai],

Shanxi, dates to 782, and the nearby Foguang Monastery was built in 857. These two religious edifices are isolated parts of larger architectural complexes and do not fully convey the highest achievements of the time (Figure 7.3). The earliest excavated chair that has been dated is a funerary piece in a form resembling the later yokeback model. Excavated in 1920 from a tomb of the Liao dynasty (916–1125) in Jiefang-yingzi, Inner Mongolia, it is low, has heavy members, and recalls chairs depicted in tomb paintings of the same period. A later version from the early twelfth century, found in Julu county, Hebei province, has splayed legs and a curved backsplat and yoke, heralding a Ming dynasty style (Figure 7.4).

Reliably dated materials, therefore, are limited, and while visual and literary references are important, as interpretive representations of reality, they are often not accurate. For example, furniture pieces excavated from tombs, whether full size or miniature, were mostly made for burial and were not intended for domestic use. Their construction and form often were of the wrong proportions and were not indicative of actual furniture. The Liao funeral chair mentioned above is a good example. In other examples, in Dunhuang murals and in paintings from the Song and Ming dynasties, couch-beds and principal seats often are depicted in enlarged or elevated proportions to accentuate status, with the result that the size and height of the furniture and its relation to space is misrepresented (Figure 7.5). Similarly, a fragment of a Han dynasty mural showing only two seated figures on platforms cannot be taken as evidence that there were no other pieces of furniture in the room, and it is therefore not useful for shedding light on the arrangement of furniture of the period (Figure 7.6).

Paintings attributed to one period were often copies executed at a later date. The celebrated handscroll *The Night Revels of Han Xizai* is attributed to Gu Hongzhong of the tenth century, but it should be treated as a Song copy (Figure 7.7). The painting is generally used as a key reference to illustrate the fledgling chair-level mode of living and interior decors of the period. However, there was also a later Ming version, with an interpretation of fifteenth-century interiors. Sources such as these, together with other visual materials (including stone engravings, woodblock prints, and even literary texts and excavated examples), need to be treated with caution when used for dating references. Instead, they should be considered in a broad historical context showing developments in style, form, relation to space, social role, and significance. In addition to its functional role, domestic furniture is a marker of the owner's taste, wealth, and status and shows the material culture of the time. In the end, the challenge lies not so much in the paucity of data, but in the way we interpret them.

Fig. 7.2a–d. *Laowu Ge, considered to be the oldest extant (albeit restored) vernacular dwelling in China, was built between 1495 and 1500 by the Wu family in Xixinan village, Huizhou, present-day southeast Anhui province. It is the best example of a large Huizhou merchant's house, showing representative as well as unique features in the construction and decoration of this region. Completely renovated between August 1999 and October 2001 (including a new construction of the second house of the complex), the dwelling offers a rare occasion to study the architectural details of an early Ming house.*

a. *The first courtyard, showing the skywell* [tianjing] *and the newly restored wooden facade.* Source: Photograph by Kai-Yin Lo 2002.

b. *The original apron* [lanban] *and lattice windows* [lingge chuang] *of the upper story remain in good condition. Note the double-tiered bracket sets* [dougong] *supporting the eaves.* Source: Photograph by Kai-Yin Lo 2001.

c. *Large timber members of the east wall of the main hall* [tingtang] *on the second floor of the first building.* Source: Photograph by Kai-Yin Lo 2002.

d. *When the outer walls of the original house were removed, the construction details of the framework could be seen.* Source: Photograph by Kai-Yin Lo 2001.

b

d ▼

c ▶

▶
Fig. 7.4a–c. *The earliest chair forms date to Song and Liao times. In addition to the officially excavated examples, Liao dynasty chairs (and tables) have recently surfaced to enter private and museum collections.*

a. *Liao dynasty funeral yokeback chair [guanmaoyi] in softwood with thick members; excavated from a tomb at Jiefangyingzi, Inner Mongolia. 50 cm x 40 cm x 41 cm.* Source: Used with the permission of the Chifeng Municipal Museum.

b. *Rendering of a softwood chair found in Julu county, Hebei, dated to 1108. Nanjing Museum. Note the form resembles the style of Ming dynasty chairs. 20.5 cm x 10.5 cm.* Source: Handler 2001, 48.

c. *Liao dynasty softwood funeral chair from a private collection. Note the* kunmen *[openings] on the apron. 57.5 cm x 47.5 cm.* Source: Used with the permission of Mr. Tsai Li-yin.

▶
Fig. 7.5a–b.
a. *A* luohan *seated on a meditation* chan *[chair] with a donor. Anonymous. Song dynasty (960–1279). It is in the Chinese visual tradition to depict the principle figure—in this case the* luohan—*in exaggeratedly large proportions to emphasize his importance and worthiness, while the donor is rendered in diminutive size.* Source: Used with the permission of the National Palace Museum, Taibei, Taiwan, Republic of China.

b. *This scene of Mount Wutai in Cave 61, Dunhuang, shows a monk seated in an open area with attendants, reflecting his senior position.* Source: Used with the permission of Cultural Relics Publishing House.

▲ **Fig. 7.3a–b.** *Two of the oldest wooden structures in China are religious edifices in Shanxi province.*

a. *Nanchan Monastery, Mount Wutai, built during the Tang dynasty in 782, is the earliest extant wooden structure in China. Part of a larger religious complex, this single hall contains seventeen exceptional freestanding statues on the large central platform—the prototype of the* ta, *which evolved into domestic furniture in the same period (see Fig. 7.10a).* Source: Photograph by Kai-Yin Lo 1998.

b. *The Great East Hall, the main building of Foguang Monastery, located near Mount Wutai, was built in 857 during the Tang dynasty, although it shows traces of its earlier founding under the reign of Emperor Xiaowen of the Northern Wei dynasty (471–499). The impressive proportions of the building, seven* jian *in width and four* jian *in depth, recall the grandeur of the great Tang building tradition in wood.* Source: Photograph by Kai-Yin Lo 1998.

7.4b ▼

7.4a ▲

7.4c ▲

Fig. 7.6a–b. *Often only significant elements are shown in murals and other visuals.*

a. *A fragment from an Eastern Han dynasty (25–220) mural showing two men, probably of high birth, seated on platforms, their shoes removed, and engaged in conversation. It is believed that drapery was a main divider of interior space. The emptiness does not preclude the existence of other furniture or decoration.* Source: Reproduced from *Ancient China: An Illustrated Guide,* published by Commercial Press (HK).

b. *A Northern Wei dynasty (386–534) stone slab depicting an official seated on a platform and flanked by attendants. The lack of other details suggests that the craftsman wanted to emphasize the sculpted figures.* Source: Used with the permission of Littleton and Hennessy Asian Art.

Queries and Thoughts _____

This essay presents some observations and ideas based on my experience as a collector of Chinese furniture and a student of the Chinese house. I believe that artifacts and articles used in daily life are key components of material culture, and examining them on a macro-scale beyond the focuses of scholastic disciplines can bring cross-fertilization and greater understanding. Therefore, in this essay there are few detailed descriptions of architectural structures and comparative styles of the Chinese house, and historical development is mentioned only to support a point of view, because elsewhere in this book leading scholars have written cogent and well-supported theses that explore these topics. Similarly, fine points in style and structure in furniture serve only to illustrate their spiritual and practical role in the scheme of the living environment.

An earlier essay of mine (in Lo and Ho 1999, 38–61) focused on the relationship between Chinese architecture and furniture, especially the technical and structural developments, as well as the decorative and material similarities and interconnections. Since then, scholarship has increasingly examined not only the physical, but also the social and historical significance of Chinese furniture—for example, Sarah Handler's impressive *Austere Luminosity of Chinese Classical Furniture* (2001) and Hu Wenyan and Yu Shuyan's *Zhongguo jiaju wenhua* (2002). To look at Chinese

Fig. 7.7a–b. *An important painting is likely to have copies made subsequently out of deference and respect. The Night Revels of Han Xizai, attributed to Gu Hongzhong of the tenth century, is frequently used as a key reference to illustrate the new chair-level mode of living and the interior decors of that period.*

a. *This version, much mentioned in academic references, is probably an early-twelfth-century copy. Note the small tables laid with food; their height is awkward for the men, who are seated on chairs with their legs pendant. The couch-bed, with a high back and sides, is a typical transitional shape that is used here as a seat. Chairs are covered with embroidered cloth.* Source: National Palace Museum, Beijing.

b. *The Ming rendering by Tang Yin shows a different style in textiles decoration and furniture forms, as well as a painting style representative of the period.* Source: Chongqing Museum.

architecture and furniture from a cultural vantage point—evaluating how and why the Chinese invented and developed such a unique framework for containing and supporting people and things—has led me to consider further the dynamics and interrelationships of history, art history, design and decoration, philosophy, and intellectual thought, as well as social and economic developments in China. This line of thought at the same time has led me to raise questions that no doubt have fascinated many for a long time—for example, why, in contrast to Western architecture, do Chinese buildings (including imperial, religious, and domestic structures) show so few ostensible physical and material changes through the ages?

As was suggested by Ronald Knapp in Chapter 1, variations in the style and form of Chinese houses are manifestations of regional differences rather than secular or historical developments. In other words, stylistic variations are clearly more apparent in the horizontal or geographic dimension than when viewed in terms of vertical or historical processes. Many share the opinion that Chinese civilization had reached early maturity by the Han dynasty (206–220), with a well-developed political and social organization, including building and living patterns. Thus, to some, subsequent changes are only modifications on fixed principles. Experts have acknowledged that noticeable innovations in Chinese architectural style and building technique were introduced during the Liao dynasty, ruled by semi-nomads occupying northeast China. The artistic and cultural achievements of these people are coming to light with recent archeological finds. It is equally significant to realize that in about 40 percent of China's recorded history since the Han era, large parts of the country were ruled by foreign, sometimes called "alien," dynasties, such as the Tuoba people of Northern Wei (386–534); the Khitans of the Liao dynasty; the Jurchen of Jin; the Dangxiang or Tanguts of Xixia; the Mongols, who ruled as the Yuan dynasty (1279–1368); and the Manchus, who reigned as the Qing dynasty (1644–1912). These "barbarians" brought into the Chinese body politic new energy, manners, and customs, while they themselves assimilated into mainstream Chinese culture. The vibrancy and multifaceted lifestyle of the great Tang dynasty (618–907) owed much to its tolerance and incorporation of ethnic cultures from outside its realm, notably from those along the Silk Road.

In a similar fashion, Buddhism, a well-developed system of spiritual values and beliefs originating from India about 500 B.C.E., soon became sinicized after its introduction into China in the first century. It encountered a culture of great self-confidence with an established temporal structure, thought pattern, and social order. Changes and transformation soon took place to accommodate the needs of an environment markedly different from India's, and the Chinese accepted Buddhist teachings, practices, and objects that they deemed useful and suitable. For all the importance of Buddhism in shaping Chinese conceptions of the afterlife, there is little trace of it in tombs or the artifacts placed in them (Kieschnick 2003, 293). This is because the Buddhist religion did not reconcile with the entrenched Chinese belief of ancestor worship or with the practical material provisions connected with burial and afterlife.

China's long history of building with wood—for both the frame or skeleton of buildings and the interior decor—remains a key point of reflection and curiosity. What is the reason for this faithful adherence to what appear to be unchanging practices? Could there be an interplay of external dynamics responsible for a grad-

Kai-Yin Lo

ual infiltration of ideas and internal dynamics responsible for assimilating them, operating under a seemingly unchanging facade that is often interpreted as timelessness or strong lingering tradition? Many other questions are similarly worth pondering. To what degree are Confucian precepts, which regulate social behavior throughout a lifetime, reflected in government edicts and laws? Are they at the root of this lack of change and hence, at the same time, a cause for the longevity of Chinese civilization as well as the slow pace of its material progress? In addition, does this apparent lack of change, prolonged and deep-rooted, finally and inexorably lead to China's tumultuous upheavals, which took place in the nineteenth and twentieth centuries? And how many of the traditions that have been handed down in spiritual and physical forms still remain in present-day China? These queries all involve weighty consideration and thoughtful debate and can only be partially answered within the limited space of this essay.

Furniture and the House

Chinese names and terms are not only descriptive, but they also embody essential meanings. The commonly used term for furniture, *jiaju,* means "implements of the house." In the Wu dialect, which is spoken in the region centering on Suzhou, Chinese furniture is still referred to by its old name, *jiasheng,* or "active objects in the house," a term commonly used in the twelfth-century Southern Song era (Meng and Li 2001). In other words, while furniture is an integral part of the house and garden, its usefulness and flexibility lie in its portability. Furniture, in fact, is *portable architecture* and serves as a vehicle for human contact and interaction in daily life. In the process, it enlivens the environment while giving it content and meaning. The compatibility and relationship between the articles in an internal space—furniture—and the environment are acknowledged in a passage from *Kaogong ji* (1996, *juan* 258), the oldest manual in China on production and crafts, which was incorporated into the *Book of Rites,* China's classic describing religious, cultural, and social practices, about the beginning of the Warring States period (475–221 B.C.). It notes the following: "The seasons have their timing, the earth has its crops, materials possess special usefulness, and the crafts display ingenuity" [*Tian you shi, di you qi, cai you mei, gong you qiao*]. Acknowledging the importance of the crafts in the scheme of things, it goes on to say that the measurement of large internal spaces is determined by the size of the mats and that of small spaces by units of *kang ji,* or small low tables, reckoned to be three Chinese feet long, according to the measurements of the time and equivalent to 59.1 cm, a "foot" being 19.7 cm. Hence portable furniture has been an integral part of living spaces since ancient times. The manual further states that craftsmen are important because they help to build and maintain the country, thereby fulfilling a spiritual and physical function. This same principle was recognized by the architect Frank Lloyd Wright when in 1940 he commented on a passage in the *Dao de jing,* by Laozi. Wright acknowledged the philosopher's prescience, which heralded Wright's own famous concept of organic architecture, stressing the importance of empty space as an essential part of architecture, fulfilling a key function in the house.

In Chinese, as was mentioned in earlier chapters, *jia* means both a dwelling and the family who lives in it. Thus, the house is the architectural frame that accommodates both the contents—furniture—and life of the family. The term *jiating,* denoting the domicile of a family, literally means "domestic household with a courtyard" or "the family in a house with a courtyard." The courtyard in varying sizes and forms—from the larger proportions it occupies in relation to the house in northern dwellings to the small *tianjing,* or "skywells," inside southern houses—is usually an integral part of domestic dwellings, whether simple or grand, small or large, urban or rural. The significance of the courtyard is recognized on all levels of Chinese life, even when it is not present. It is in such open spaces, however modest, that people are said to communicate and be in harmony with nature, an outlook that differs markedly from that in the West. The home of the emperor is called the *gongting* or "palace with a courtyard," and the place where he holds court is the *chaoting,* or "large open area with a courtyard for audiences with the ruler."

Confucian Order in Society

A two-word compound, *guojia*—country *[guo]* and family *[jia]*—means "country" in Chinese, whereas in the West this term encompasses three separate notions—country, state, and nation. The concept that the family is the basic unit of the country was established in pre-Confucian times, but it was Confucian philosophy and rites that transformed it into a system of stipulated social behavior that to some degree is still practiced today in China and in overseas Chinese communities. The phrase "to protect your home is to protect your country" *[bao jia wei guo]* expresses the concept that the country is an enlarged version of the family. "Think the right thoughts, look after your body, regulate your family, then you serve your country and will bring peace and harmony to the world" *[Zheng xin, xiu shen, ji jia, zhi guo ping tianxia]*

Kai-Yin Lo

(*Li chi* 1967, 411–412) as presented in the *Book of Rites,* is a set of maxims that can be applied equally to family and country (translation in Legge 1967, 411–412).

The father/son relationship in the family, moreover, has a parallel in the relationship of a ruler and his people: the emperor, a symbol of leadership and authority by right and by birth, was also seen as the "father" of an extended family. It was thus seen as "going against your father and your ruler" *[wu jun wu fu]* if one contradicted the emperor. By extension, then, it was natural to see the family as a microcosm of the country and society—indeed, its fundamental foundation. Rites prescribed by Confucius emanate from family ethics and were systemized into a code of behavior that then became the order of the country. Worshiping ancestors, teaching offspring to be obedient according to prescribed social stations, and maintaining a harmonious relationship within the family were extended to a national scale. Public ceremonies paid homage to the heavens as well as to ancestors, and a body of sumptuary laws governed the mode of living: house size, materials, type of construction, colors, and decoration, as well as dress and music codes, regulated even the minutiae of social behavior (Cheng 2002, 1–6, 21–30; Ge 2003, 47–58).

Ancestor worship is not a religion; it is a belief embedded in the Chinese intellectual and ethical system. Fortified by the Confucian canon, it served to perpetuate the family as the bedrock of the country's political and social makeup. Popular religion in China, whether Buddhist or Daoist, coexisted with the Confucian canon, but it never played as dominant a role as the veneration of the family, its members, and its deeds. Perhaps this is why, unlike architecture in the West, religious buildings—temples, monasteries, nunneries, and shrines—are not strikingly different in appearance, construction methods, or building materials from common houses and mansions. The modular construction of Chinese buildings allows them to easily adapt from small to large, secular to religious. Similarly, furniture, such as altar tables (Figure 7.8) and incense stands (Figure 7.9), whether found in temples or houses, shares the same structure and often the same form. This is also true in early furniture types, especially platforms, which in religious buildings form the base of altars and in houses are called *ta* and are used for sitting or reclining. In different versions, the chair becomes a throne for a Buddha or a bodhisattva statue (Figure 7.10). The sinicization of Buddhism in China meant that the religion in many ways became humanized. To venerate ancestors is to honor and nourish the family both in the home and in ancestral halls erected for broader worship (a subject discussed in Chapter 13 below).

a ▲   b ▼   c ▼

Fig. 7.8a–d. *The early altar table placed in a house bore a close resemblance to those in religious edifices.*

a. *Shanxi table of northern elm [yumu] with base; 57 cm x 198 cm x 89 cm; fifteenth century or earlier; it has precedents in two earlier extant examples, one found in the Liao Bhaga Repository (1038) at Datong and the other, as shown in* **(b),** *in the Wenshu Temple at Foguangsi near Mount Wutai.* Source: (a) Used with the permission of the C. L. Ma Collection; (b) Shanxi shent 1984, 34.

c. *In the house, any long table could be used as an offering altar table. This rare example, with a shape similar to the altar tables used in temples, is made of precious* huang-huali *and* nanmu *woods and bamboo.* Source: Used with the permission of the Mimi and Raymond Hung Collection.

d ▼

d. *Altar table in front of ancestral tablets at the Hu Ancestral Hall in Jixicun, Jixi county, Anhui. This ancestral hall of the family of Hu Jintao, Party Secretary and President of China since 2003, is one of the outstanding architectural examples of an ancestral hall in South China. The inscription by the famous Ming literatus Wen Zhenming (1470–1559) is evidence of the high position held by Hu Zhongxian, who erected this edifice during the reign of Ming emperor Jiajing (1522–1566).* Source: Photograph by Kai-Yin Lo.

Fig. 7.9a–c. *Whether for domestic or religious use, incense stands have the same shapes.*

a. *This Ming incense stand in red lacquer is elegantly shaped. 88 cm; diameter on top 38.5 cm.* Source: National Palace Museum, Beijing.

b. *An early Ming incense stand in brownish black lacquer, a coating common in vernacular furniture, recalls a Song dynasty shape. 83.5 cm x 58 cm.* Source: Used with the permission of the C. L. Ma Collection.

c. *The Song-style octagonal incense stand with six legs, railings, and lotus petal base complements the monk's chair. Painting attributed to Li Sung (1190–1264).* Source: Used with the permission of the National Palace Museum, Taibei, Taiwan, Republic of China.

a ▲

b ▲

c ▲

b. *This handscroll, ink and color on paper, shows a Yuan literati seated on his* ta *with cusped openings. As was the fashion of the time, archaistic objects were displayed on small tables.* Portrait of Ni Zan, *inscribed by Chang Yu. Yuan Dynasty (1279–1368).* Source: Used with the permission of the National Palace Museum, Taibei, Taiwan, Republic of China.

c. *The chair becomes a throne when Buddha or a bodhisattva sits in it. This statue of Yi Jiang in painted clay is at the Shengmudian, "Hall of the Holy Mother," Jinci, Taiyuan.* Source: Photograph by Kai-Yin Lo.

b ▼

c ▼

Fig. 7.10a–c. *The platform, or* ta, *that found its way into domestic furniture had its antecedents in religious quarters.*

▲ **a.** *After the Five Dynasties, furniture increased in variety. As seen here, a platform could be used as the center of gatherings in a variety of places, including studios, pavilions, and halls. The large, box-shaped platform shown in this painting,* Literary Gathering, *attributed to Qiu Wenbo (tenth century), has cusped openings that became wider as the corner posts were integrated with the stretcher below.* Source: Used with the permission of the National Palace Museum, Taibei, Taiwan, Republic of China.

Fig. 7.11. *In ancient Chinese cosmology, the heavens were considered as round, a notion that was given expression in a flat, round disc with a small hole in the middle. In both the Hongshan (3500–2500 B.C.E.) and Liangzhu cultures (3000–2000 B.C.E.), bi were used as talismans and placed on dead bodies at burial. This bi, measuring 33.4 cm in diameter, was found in Guangzhou in the tomb of the king of Nanyue* [Nanyue wang] *of the early Western Han (second century B.C.E.) and is the largest one excavated.* Source: Used with the permission of the Museum of the King of Nanyue, Guangzhou.

▼

Significance of the Center

The Confucian world centered on the Han people, inhabiting the region between the old capitals of Chang'an and Luoyang in northern China, which was regarded as the epicenter of the country. From the heart of the realm down to a small courtyard house, the principle of inner, *nei,* and outer, *wai,* was manifested. Enclosures defined space and separated what was inside from what was outside, whether in palaces, houses, gardens, villages, towns, or cities. The Great Wall protected China proper or, as it was viewed, the China of the civilized Han race from the barbarous nomads outside the wall. The cosmic view held by the Chinese from very early times, already established by the Warring States period, placed China firmly in the center of the civilized universe. Nine provinces, or *jiuzhou,* were viewed as radiating from the old capital of Luoyang in the middle reaches of the Yellow River; from Luoyang and its vicinity governance and power extended outward. The farther from this "chess board" domain, the less civilized and the more barbaric were those occupying distant regions. Such a concept is related to the belief that the universe is round and the earth square *[tian yuan di fang],* and it is evidenced (among other ways) in the sacrificial objects fashioned from jade, such as the round *bi,* [disc] (Figure 7.11) and the cylindrical *cong* (Figure 7.12), and in building plans

Fig. 7.12. *With a square outer section, a round inner part, and a circular hole, the* cong *symbolizes the earth. This piece, 31 cm tall, tapers from a diameter of 7.4 cm on top to 6.5 cm at the bottom. Liangzhu culture.* Source: National Palace Museum, Beijing.

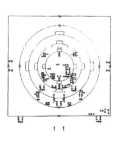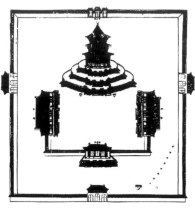

Fig. 7.13a–b. *The cosmic concept of* tian yuan di fang *governed the heavenly and earthly realms.*

a. *These two drawings display the spatial complex of a square, chessboard-like, earthly realm and a round or circular cosmic realm.* Source: Ge 2002, 7.

b. *The upper sides of these chairs are round, while the lower parts have square members. Together they symbolize the belief that "the heavens are round, the earth flat"* [tian yuan di fang]. *Chairs of* huanghuali, *60 cm x 47 cm x 105 cm.* Source: Used with the permission of the Take a Step Back Collection.

patterned on the square chessboard form of the earthly realm (Figure 7.13). Cities, palaces, and religious and dwelling complexes, large and small, have traditionally been modeled on this cosmic pattern, with a north to south orientation and a central axis (Figure 7.14). It is not coincidental that the same formal arrangement is observed with furniture in the principal room of the house, the main hall, or *tingtang*, which will be discussed below, and that the *tian yuan di fang* concept, unquestioned from very early times until the sixteenth century, is rendered in furniture forms (Figure 7.13b).

Despite military, trade, and cultural contacts with the Near East and Europe via the northern Silk Road; maritime expeditions from the Han to the Song dynasties; and the Mongol conquest that established the Yuan dynasty, this cosmic view of the Middle Kingdom ruled by Han Chinese has not fundamentally altered in the Chinese consciousness. The Mandate of Heaven, which gave the ruler legitimacy, resided in a power base called *zhongyang*, where the authority to rule and to give orders was legitimized. In a reinterpretation, the *zhongyang* represents the seat of legitimate power in the Communist regime in China today.

Ultimately, the Chinese considered that with their superior civilization they rightly ruled the world. The only challenge that could have altered this unquestioned view, which dismissed all other lands and influences as culturally inferior, was the infiltration of the Buddhist faith. However, as noted, Buddhism soon took on a Chinese guise by blending with Confucianism, Daoism, and other traditional beliefs. Since the emperor was the temporal as well as the spiritual head, the ultimate authority in the hierarchical society, with the family as the foundation stone of the social order, religion existed as an adjunct, subject to temporal power. This

Kai-Yin Lo

Fig. 7.14a–c. *Cities, palaces, and dwelling complexes, large and small, were modeled on the cosmic pattern, with an orientation along a central axis (termed axiality) from north to south, as well as side-to-side symmetry and balance.*

a. *Yonghe Palace, Beijing.* Source: Steinhardt et al. 2002, 327.

b. *Detail of a Ming dynasty painting showing the Palace City in Beijing, patterned on the principles of axiality and balance.* Source: Museum of Chinese History.

c. *The layout of a cave dwelling in Yanchun, Shaanxi province.* Source: Steinhardt el al. 2002, 311.

long-held cosmic concept of the Middle Kingdom met its first serious challenge in 1584, when the Jesuit Matteo Ricci presented Emperor Wanli with a map demonstrating that the world was round and that China occupied only a small portion of one continent. However, it was not until three centuries later, with the arrival of cannons and gunboats manned by "barbarians" from afar, that China painfully accepted the fact it was not the center of the world.

Traditional Chinese Architecture and Furniture

Fig. 7.15. *Furniture layout plan of a main hall: (1) front courtyard; (2) Eight Immortals table; (3) yoke-back armchair; (4) altar table; (5) low table; (6) divisible round table; (7) stool; (8) high standing table (or vase); (9) square table; (10) altar table; (11) side chair; (12) altar table; (13) clock; (14) vase; (15) screen panel (or mirror); (16) ancestral tablet; (17) candle; (18) censer; (19) rear courtyard.*

Fig. 7.16. *The altar table on the north wall of the house, often with everted flanges, serves as the surface for the placement of ancestral tablets. In an ordinary household, the altar table would more likely be made of softwood, such as this one in cypress* [baimu], *219 cm x 47 cm x 91.5 cm.* Source: Yungmingtang Collection.

Cosmic and Earthly Space

The long-held cosmic view of the Middle Kingdom is reflected in the spatial organization of buildings, which follows a central axis with symmetrical extensions on either side. Confucian thinking built on this concept of centrality to create a worldly order of balance, security, harmony, and, above all, control. The spatial layout of the archetypical courtyard house, the *siheyuan,* was derived from larger complexes, be they a mansion, palace, or city; in all cases the inner private life and outer public space are clearly separated and delineated. According to scholar-architect Liang Sicheng (1998), this evolution of spatial layouts was not the result of design but of natural development. In the same way, the arrangement of furniture, especially in the *tingtang*—the nucleus of the house and a symbol of its power and continuity— follows a formal and solemn pattern, based on a north/south orientation with east/west extensions. Symmetry and axial positioning also convey a formal aura of hierarchy.

The *tingtang,* however, was usually "a conference room, a court of judgment, and a miniature ancestral hall" at the same time (Chiu 2000, 145), so (as seen in Figure 7.15) furniture placement could be flexible, according to the needs of the occasion, especially in more modest households. Ancestral tablets would generally be placed along the north or back wall and, depending on how wealthy the household was, either on a prominent altar table *[shenlong anzhuo],* which varied in dimensions, style, and choice of wood, or in a case attached to the wall (Figure 7.16). The altar table was not adapted to the height of mere mortals, as the offerings, which were usually placed on another rectangular table in front of the altar table and forming a unit with it, were meant for spirits, gods, and deceased ancestors.

Below these was normally a square table, called from Ming times the "Eight Immortals table," or *baxian zhuo,* a highly versatile and necessary piece of furniture

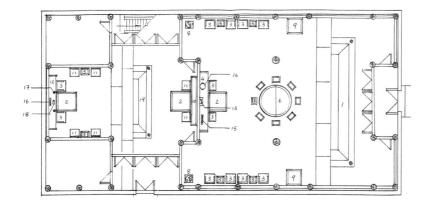

b, c ▶

a ▲   d ▶

Fig. 7.17a–d. *Each family has at least one* baxian *[Eight Immortals] table, which is highly versatile and portable and has multiple uses inside and outside the house.*

a. *The remarkably intricate "four dragon" square table in bronze, used for sacrificial purposes, was excavated in Pingshan, Hebei province. Warring States era (475–221 B.C.E.).* Source: Hu and Yu 2002, 2.

b. *The square table is used in the kitchen in this famous stone relief carving of the Northern Song era (960–1127).* Source: Yu 1997, 323.

c. *The square table is used for preparations before a feast, while in* **(d)** *tea is being brewed, testimony to the popular pastime of the period. Note the rich variety of vessels for wine and tea used at the time.* Source: Used with the permission of Cultural Relics Publishing House.

with multiple uses, including as a platform for ritual offerings ranging from food and wine to symbolic decorations; a surface for family meals, banquets, or games; a temporary desk for the young; and an occasional table for indoor or outdoor activities. Square tables of this type—used as prototypes for sacrificial ceremonies (Figure 7.17a), in different parts of the house (Figure 7.17b–d), in shops, and in

Fig. 7.18a–b. *The ubiquitous* baxian *table shares a similar style of construction with the waisted, unwaisted, or "one leg, three spandrels" [yituo sanya] types of side tables.*

a. *The highly portable square table is often put to good use in the courtyard. Here, a scene of tea preparation in the garden, from a painting attributed to the famous court painter Liu Songnian (1163–1190), shows a recessed-leg square table set for outdoor use.* Source: Used with the permission of the National Palace Museum, Taibei, Taiwan, Republic of China.

b. *This form of square table reflects the bracketed post-and-beam construction of ancient Chinese wood buildings. The architectural terminology "one bracket, three spandrels," or* yidou sansheng, *describes the cantilever system under the roof of a building and corresponds to the type of construction found in some square or side tables.* Source: Yungmingtang Collection.

gardens (Figure 7.18)—are the most prevalent form of Chinese furniture found in textual and pictorial illustrations. Even today, Eight Immortals tables are ubiquitous in households throughout China. It is not uncommon to find a hefty yet portable square table made of softwood along the north wall of the main room or outside in the courtyard of an old or remodeled dwelling.

The choice of furniture is determined by the family's budget, taste, and status, while the layout follows regional preferences. In Shanxi, where rooms are shallow in order to catch the southern light, there is only limited space for furniture. Houses in the Wannan area of southern Anhui, which are often of two or more stories, are compact and have beautifully carved wooden partitions, lattice window panels, and doors. The main hall, placed on the ground floor, opens onto a small courtyard without a wall to separate interior from exterior space (Figure 7.19). The long altar table and the square table placed against a timber "teacher," or *taishi* [northern wall], are usually flanked by a pair of principal chairs, which ideally are the imposing "lamphanger-style yokeback armchairs" *[sichutouguanmaoyi]*, named for the protruding ends of the crestrails, which resemble the wings of an official's cap (Figure 7.20a–c). They are seats of large proportions that denote high status and are to be occupied by the most senior members in the family hierarchy. In rare examples, carving and decoration on the back splats indicate hierarchical status or gender (Figure 7.20d). "Southern official's hat armchairs" *[nanguanmaoyi]*, a modern term applied to chairs of fluid lines and smaller size for easy mobility that are prevalent in literati households in the Jiangnan region, are grouped on either side of the hall in a formal symmetrical pattern (Figure 7.21). Such an arrangement,

Kai-Yin Lo

Fig. 7.19a–b.

a. *A ground floor main hall, with side chairs flanking both sides of the room. Fang Wentai House, Qiankou, Huizhou. Due to the general lack of furniture in this late Ming* minju *[vernacular house], however, a formal arrangement is not observed. Note the exquisite carving of the upper story.*
b. *The inner hall of the home of intellectual and diplomat Hu Shi (1891–1962), with furniture observing a formal placement (except for the bench inadvertently placed in the middle). Note the water drainage pipe on the left, extending from the roof to the courtyard. Metal replaced brick for drainage from the late eighteenth century in Anhui houses.* Source: Photographs by Kai-Yin Lo.

a, b ▶

Fig. 7.20a–d. *The qualities of "restraint, balance and grandeur" (Sickman 1978) apply to the classic Chinese yokeback armchair, the principal seat in the main hall.*

a. *Pair in* huanghuali *hardwood; each 59 cm x 47.8 cm x 115 cm.* Source: Yungmingtang Collection.

b. *This pair, in lacquered* yumu *[elm] softwood from Shanxi province, is a good representation of the better type of vernacular furniture found in some* minju *households. Each 59 cm x 48.5 cm x 94 cm.* Source: Private collection.

c. *A mural scene from the Yuan era, excavated in Pucheng county, Shaanxi province, reaffirms the importance of the yokeback armchair in a formal hierarchical and symmetrical seating arrangement.* Source: Hu and Yu 2002, 24.

c ▶

▶

d. *Seventeenth-century* huanghuali *chairs, each 64 cm x 42 cm x 119.4 cm. The open relief carved decoration in the shape of medallion badges, with open work on the back splats, is rare. It has been suggested that the motifs indicate hierarchical seating between man and wife, host and guest.* Source: Used with the permission of Christie's Images 2003.

Fig. 7.21a–b.

◄ *a. As seen in the Wanjuan Tang, or "Hall of 10,000 Volumes," in the Master of Nets Garden, Suzhou, furniture is arranged on a central axis, with an altar table on the north wall fronted by a* baxian *table. Crestrail and southern officials' armchairs flank both sides for a balanced setting.* Source: Photograph by Kai-Yin Lo.

b. *A unique pair of southern official's hat armchairs, or* nanguanmaoyi, *in* zhajinmu, *a wood indigenous to the eastern coast of China, especially in the Zhejiang and Jiangsu areas.* Source: Private collection.

Fig. 7.22. *Woodblock illustration showing the formality between host and guest, with both seated on yokeback armchairs.* Source: *Records of the Red Pear,* or *Hongli ji,* Wanli period (1573–1620), Ming dynasty.

of course, applies generally, but, as noted, the specific choice of wood and style is indicative of a family's economic position and taste. Even during the golden period of classical Chinese furniture, from 1550 to 1680, precious woods, such as *zitan* and *huanghuali,* were in short supply and were expensive, as they had to be imported from Southeast Asia and were in demand with the growing affluence of the middle class (Clunas 1988, 8–10). The average household thus would use portable stools or hire an itinerant carpenter to make simple bamboo or softwood chairs for daily and ceremonial use.

Symmetry and pair arrangement in a Chinese house are associated with the cosmological concept of balance and bipolarity characteristic of *yin* and *yang,* as well as the aesthetic principle of *xu* and *shi.* These principles govern furniture placement regarding various status relationships, such as senior/junior, host/guest, and male/female (Figure 7.22). This ingrained principle of affiliation and duality is

Traditional Chinese Architecture and Furniture

Fig. 7.23a–b. *The late Ming literati who wrote on the art of living treated it more as a moral and aesthetic rather than a lifestyle discourse. Furniture and its arrangement was part of the scheme of things, serving only as vehicles and not as works of special merit.*

a. *A seventeenth-century scholar's study is admirably recreated in the Ruth Ann Dayton rooms of the Minneapolis Institute of Arts, transposed from the Wu family house in Dongshan on Lake Tai.* Source: Used with the permission of the Minneapolis Institute of Arts.

b. *A scene in Liu Yuan, Suzhou. Full-length doors open onto the garden, integrating the interiors with nature outside. The patterns found in lattice doors and windows frequently resemble those in furniture.* Source: Photograph by Kai-Yin Lo.

embedded in scores of expressions in the Chinese language—height is denoted as high/low *[gao/di]*, quantity as more/less *[duo/shao]*, direction as left/right *[zuo/you]*, wealth as riches/rank *[fu/gui]*, and ideal relationships as ruler/official *[jun/chen]* and father/son *[fu/zi]*, to cite a few examples.

The arbiters of taste in the late Ming were notably Wen Zhenheng, Gao Lian, Li Yu. The latter's book, *Xianqing ouji* [Occasional records of leisurely sentiments], published in 1617, was a treatise on gardens and interiors that also described furniture as part of the scheme of good living. This literati attitude toward furniture and decoration was further expanded by Wen Zhenheng in his *The Treatise on Superfluous Things*, written from 1615 to 1620 in Suzhou. He defined his ideal of *ya*, "elegance," against *su*, "vulgarity," as part of an aesthetic and moral discourse Lacquer furniture was regarded as refined, and only in the use of calligraphy tables should an exception be permitted (Figure 7.23a). In the scheme of refined living, adhering to a long-held Chinese tradition, furniture was regarded merely as crafts or household objects and not as an example of an elevated art form.

Dwellings in the Jiangnan region of Jiangsu and Zhejiang reflect the prosperity and the more relaxed lifestyle of the area, due to the climate and also due to the refined lifestyles of retired scholar-officials of the Song and Ming eras. Houses here often have several main halls, and unlike elsewhere in China, these rooms are not

Kai-Yin Lo

designated as ancestral halls. The arrangement of furniture, moreover, is less structured. For example, it is not unusual to find a couch-bed placed in a public room for leisurely resting, and stools are interchangeably used indoors and outdoors. The gentler climate allows lattice doors to act as partitions as well as links between openings (Figure 7.23b). By not separating the interior from the exterior, the lattice doors invite nature inside in a full play of light and shade, and *xu* and *shi* become part of the decor.

Interrelations: Shared Craftsmen, Related Construction, Symbiotic Growth

Over a period of a thousand years, only two compendia were complied about building in China, the *Yingzao fashi* [Building standards] in 1103 and the *Gongbu Gongcheng zuofa celi* [Engineering manual of the Board of Works] in 1734. Both were designed to keep better records for the building ministries under the Song and Qing dynasties respectively (Glahn 1984, 48–57). The *Lu Ban jing,* an illustrated carpenter's manual published during the Ming emperor Wanli's reign (1573–1619), is an important document for building and furniture studies, specifying requirements and intermingling technical, social, and other information, including *fengshui.* Apart from these three texts, there are no manuals devoted to building specifications or methods. Nor were there any "architects" in the modern sense of the word. Echoing what has been discussed above, Nancy Steinhardt writes in the introduction to the admirable tome *A History of Chinese Architecture,* "for many thousands of years, architecture was not a specialty, but instead was a part of the overall religious and imperial culture of China" (Steinhardt et al. 2002, 3). Skills were not recorded but passed down from master to apprentice and father to son. All were anonymous craftsmen whose expertise and comprehensive knowledge maintained the building tradition of China. There were two types of specialists—those involved with major carpentry *[damuzuo],* who erected the frameworks of buildings and were also responsible for their maintenance, and those involved with minor carpentry *[xiaomuzuo],* who fashioned and decorated the interiors, including the lattice windows, doors, and partitions, and also furniture. The separation of their disciplines came to be acknowledged during the Song dynasty, about the time of the publication of *Yingzao fashi.* Because the two groups had a common background and their work overlapped, it is not surprising to find similarities and a relative unity in structure, construction methods, and ornamentation when comparing Chinese buildings and Chinese furniture (Figure 7.24). This interrelationship of

◀ b

◀ c

a ▲

Fig. 7.24. *Craftsmen who were engaged in major and minor carpentry often found their work overlapped; as a result, similarities in style and decoration are found when one compares houses and furniture.* Source: Photographs by Kai-Yin Lo unless otherwise specified.

Fig. 7.24a–f.

a. *Bench and lattice partitions are likely by the same hand. Yongjia, Zhejiang.*

b. *This couch-bed in* yumu *and pine bears typical traits of seventeenth- and eighteenth-century Shanxi furniture.* Source: Used with the permission of the C. L. Ma Collection.

c. *Similarities in style and motif abound: a wooden carving of the upper story of the Fang Wentai house, late Ming, in Qiankou, Huizhou, resembles* **(d).**

e ▼

▲

d. *Drawing of the panel in Fang Wentai's house, from Zhang Zhongyi, Huizhou Mingdai zhuzhai, 1990.*

e. *A window panel of the same house.*

f. *Window panels in a more modest mid-Qing house in the same region.*

f ▶

h ▲

i ▲

g ▲

j ▲

k ▲

Fig. 7.24g–l.

g. *Staircase in Luowu Ge, Xixinan, Anhui. Note that this scrolling pattern is found throughout the region in different media, from wood to stone.*

h. *The same motif seen in stone railings in a memorial hall in Huangcun, Shexian, Huizhou.*

i. *Seventeenth-century straightback* huanghuali *armchair with patterns that resemble motifs in window panels in the Huizhou region. Seventeenth–eighteenth centuries.* Source: Yungmingtang Collection.

j. *Ming dynasty couch-bed in* huanghuali *wood with panels similar to those in the house of Fang Wentai (shown in* **c***); 48.26 cm x 208.28 cm x 120.65 cm.* Source: Used with the permission of Ming Furniture.

k. *A side table of lacquered softwood at Fang Wentai house. Note the lyrical lines of the cusped apron.*

▲
l. *This long built-in bench [feileiyi], on the second floor main hall of the Hu Changfu house (mid-Ming), Xixinan, Huizhou, is distinguished by the cusped formation on the apron.*

◀ m

Fig. 7.24m–o.

m. *The front of the second hall of Baolun Ge, showing the carved* queti *brackets under the crescent beams.*

n. *The decorative braces and curved stretchers of this seventeenth-century* tielimu *table recall the curved beams of Baolun Ge.* Source: Used with the permission of the Asian Civilisations Museum, Singapore.

o. Queti *becomes decoration on the arms of chairs.* Source: Collection of the Academy of Arts and Design, Tsinghua University, Beijing.

o ▲

n ▲

architecture and furniture in an elite household is vividly illustrated in a passage from the celebrated eighteenth-century novel *The Story of the Stone,* or *Hong lou meng* (Cao 1973), which describes how the master of the House of Rong, while conducting a tour of his mansion to visiting relatives, comes upon a small pavilion with "couches, stands, chairs and tables, all fittingly installed" *[hezhe di bu da zuo chuang ji yi zhuo].* The pavilion and the furniture inside it complement each other to achieve a pleasing, harmonious whole that functions well.

Architecture and furniture share many similar construction methods. The post-and-beam *[tailiang]* and the post-and-tie-beam *[chuandou]* wooden structural frameworks for buildings recall the wooden structures employed in furniture construction: horizontal floating panels, stretchers, and four supporting leg formations of recessed-leg or waistless furniture; "waisted" shapes derived from the *xumizuo* [religious stone pedestal] imported from Greece via India and described in the *Yingzao fashi* as alternating rectangular blocks with recessed "waisted" sections marked with carved or open cusps *[kunmen].* These in turn developed into *ta,* platforms and beds, frequently depicted in Tang and Song paintings (Figure 7.24h–k). The *queti* [older term *chuomu*] are carved corner pieces positioned between the beam and column in buildings, resembling spandrels in many forms of furniture (Figure 7.24k–l), and these outwardly angled columns in architecture take the shape of splayed legs *[cijiao]* in furniture. The canopy bed is constructed like a house and is the most architectural representation in furniture (Figure 7.25).

The wooden interlocking framework of both architecture and furniture is held together by an ingenious and unique mortise and tenon joinery system without the use of adhesives or fasteners. This remarkable system was already in place seven thousand years ago in neolithic Hemudu society, found in today's Zhejiang province. Rightly recognized to be the single most distinguishing and distinguished development in Chinese architecture and furniture, this joinery system was well developed by the Warring States period, as seen in the sophisticated small lacquer table excavated from Xinyang, Henan province (Figure 7.26).

Another unique feature in Chinese architecture is the use of modular brackets, called *dougong,* which by the Tang dynasty had been developed into very large sizes. Together with beam trusses, modular brackets raised the height of a structure and enlarged the facade as well as the interior, thus not only creating more room for the arrangement of furniture, but also helping to develop a different style of furniture, such as the roundback armchair, stool, and long bench (at that time the last was only slightly lower than a banquet table and did not allow sufficient legroom for comfort) (Figure 7.27). This transitional stage from the mat-level mode of living

Fig. 7.25a–c. *The canopy bed and the more rare alcove bed most resemble the framework of a house.*

a. *The famous Ming dynasty alcove bed, which represents the woman's universe.* Source: The Nelson-Atkins Museum of Art, Kansas City, Missouri (Purchase: Nelson Trust) 64-4/4.

b. *The carved framework at the entrance of a house in Pingyao, Shanxi, recalls the structure of a canopy bed.* Source: Photograph by Kai-Yin Lo.

c. *A nineteenth-century softwood bed in a house in Wuyuan, Jiangxi province, has an enclosed framework to ensure privacy.* Source: Photograph by Puay-peng Ho.

◄ a

◄ b   ▲ c

to the fully developed chair-level mode that took place in the Song era showed that furniture had become an important component of dwelling interiors. While we have noted that paintings and other visual materials may not be faithful renditions of actual circumstances, the Song copy of the Five Dynasty painting *The Night Revels of Han Xizai* (Figure 7.7) nevertheless can be used as an indicator of interior decor of that period. Screens, which acted as partitions of space, had become taller and wider, reflecting the size of the room and the height of the seats. Tables and chairs were still about the same height. Food, wine, and tea were laid out on small tables, as had been the practice in earlier times.

It is generally believed that the seat in the form of a folding stool with matting, the *huchuang*, the prototype of later chair development, was first introduced into China from Central Asia at the time of the Han emperor Lingdi at the end of the second century; it soon proved its versatility by appearing in the palace, inside the home, and on the battlefield. It contributed toward the shift in posture from kneeling to sitting with legs pendant, as witnessed in the Maitreya Buddhas in Longmen, Yungang, and Dunhuang and in an early stele dated 543 (Figure 7.28). As described by the monk Ennin about an encounter with a visiting minister of state in his monas-

Fig. 7.26. *Small lacquer table excavated from Xinyang, Henan province, shows that joinery was already well developed.* Source: Hu and Yu 2002, 18.

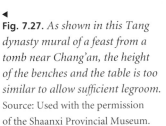

◀ **Fig. 7.27.** *As shown in this Tang dynasty mural of a feast from a tomb near Chang'an, the height of the benches and the table is too similar to allow sufficient legroom.* Source: Used with the permission of the Shaanxi Provincial Museum.

▲ **Fig. 7.28.** *The earliest depiction of a seat, a* huchuang, *in a rubbing of a Tang coffin stele dated 534.* Source: Used with the permission of the Fu Ssu-nien Library, Institute of History and Philology, Academia Sinica.

Fig. 7.29a–b. *Details of the ink and color on paper handscroll* Qingming Festival on the River *painted by Zhang Zeduan (1119– 1123), depicting daily activities of Northern Song times, including those with new forms of furniture.*

a. *People sitting on high chairs and using chopsticks to share food from common dishes, a newly introduced custom.* Source: National Palace Museum, Beijing.

b. *Goods arrive on camels, while men sitting on chairs at a shop are probably checking inventory.* Source: National Palace Museum, Beijing.

tery in 838, the chair came to China as monastic furniture and made inroads into secular life by the mid Tang era. The monk recalled, "They called out to us to sit down, and we all seated ourselves on the chairs and sipped tea" (Reischauer 1955, 52).

The economic and social forces that transformed society in the Song dynasty also brought significant changes in everyday living. They included the full adaptation of the chair, and a new mode of living accompanied this change. For example, close-up scenes in the painting *Qingming Festival on the River [Qingming shanghe tu]*, by Zhang Zeduan [in Figure 7.29], show a more relaxed eating style, using chopsticks to share a common dish from an increasing variety of ceramic containers (Lo 1998, 68). The new chair-level mode of living brought about a revolution

not only in building proportions and room configurations, but also in furniture design. New shapes and dimensions appeared in the *ta* platform, the canopy bed, the couch-bed (which served a dual function as seat and bed), variations of the yoke-back chair *[guanmaoyi]*, the rose chair *[meguiyi]*, the crestrail roundback chair *[chuanyi]*, the meditation chair *[chanyi]*, the horseshoe and yokeback armchair *[jiaoyi]*, stools, and benches—all of which reached their maturity in design, crafts-manship, structure, and form in the ensuing Ming dynasty (Figure 7.30). The vari-ety of furniture and implements, large and small, that came to be developed and refined—from wardrobes, cabinets, boxes, clothes hangers, and mirror stands to bookcases, curio stands, and scholars' articles—amply served the needs of daily life.

The raised-level mode of living also ushered in changes in psychological and cultural outlook, which dramatically influenced social behavior. No longer was the high seat reserved for the privileged few while others were placed in lower positions, according to the social code that had been observed since the mat-level mode of liv-ing. In marked contrast, the introduction of the chair about the same time in Japan did not have the same impact, and the mat-level posture remained there for several more centuries, affecting the nation in a different way aesthetically and physically. As one authority writes, "The decision to adopt the chair is a complicated cultural choice rather than a technological one" (Kieschnick 2003, 248). As wealth spread with economic growth in different strata of the Song society, the adoption of the chair level of living was both "a symbol and product of a new prosperity that entailed a new mode of living" (Handler 2001, 9).

Adherence to Wood

The preoccupation with wood in the life of the Chinese is demonstrated by the fact that there are 1,413 words with the "wood" 木 radical in the *Kangxi Dictionary*, which was complied during the great emperor's reign (1662–1722). Out of these, over 400 are related to architecture and the house. In addition, there are quite a few words denoting architectural parts written interchangeably with the "wood" and "stone" radicals, such as 柱/砫, meaning column; 櫍/礩, describing the column base, which can be made of wood or stone; and 棋/碁, describing chess-board-shaped configuration made of either material. In the course of a long build-ing history, with the exception of bridges, commemorative monuments, and tombs, the Chinese have used wood as the primary material for building, and it accounts for over 70 percent of a typical structure. While most neolithic communities in both the East and West originally erected timber structures, Westerners soon

Fig. 7.30. *The chair-level mode of living brought about a revolution in furniture design.*

Fig. 7.30a–c.

a. *The* ta *evolved into the portable day-bed for indoor and outdoor use. This example illustrates the grandeur of classical Ming furniture.* Source: Courtesy of the Minneapolis Institute of Arts Collection.

b. *This platform of* nanmu *in three sections is a variation of the* ta. *It can be used as a flexible series of tables. Seventeenth–eighteenth centuries, 62.5 cm x 156 cm x 43 cm.* Source: Yungmingtang Collection.

c. *Often placed in corridors and back chambers of a house, the rose chair, or* meguiyi, *is associated with female qualities. 86 cm x 59 cm x 45 cm.* Source: Yungmingtang Collection.

Fig. 7.30d–i.

d. *Rose chairs in the inner quarters of the house of Dai Jin (1388–1462). From woodblock* A Nocturnal Outing of the Demon Queller Zhong Kui, *ca. 1450.* Source: Handler 2001, 75; woodblock illustrations from *The Phoenix Seeks a Mate (Huang qiu feng),* early Qing edition.

e. *The crestrail roundback chair, or* chuanyi, *is ingeniously constructed, a graceful formation in Chinese furniture. Huanghuali, 99 cm x 66 cm x 45.7 cm.* Source: Yungmingtang Collection.

f. *The horseshoe armchair, or* jiaoyi, *is developed from the* hucheng. *Imported via India and the Middle East, it became an important multi-purpose chair. It is often treated as the principal chair in a room. This example, 94.8 cm x 69.5 cm x 53 cm, is of exceptional size.* Source: Wang 1986, 104.

g. *Yokeback folding chair made of softwood, with traces of lacquer, is from Shanxi. The folding chair was popular due to its size and the ease with which it could be moved. 60 cm x 58 cm x 102 cm.* Source: Used with the permission of the C. L. Ma Collection.

h. *Servants in* Returning from a Spring Outing *are carrying home both a portable folding stool and a low stool.* Source: National Palace Museum, Beijing.

i. *Folding chair, woodblock print illustration. Ming dynasty, Chongzhen period (1639).* Source: Jin and Che 1994.

d ▲

e ▲

f ▲

g ▲

h, i ▶

Fig. 7.30j–k.

j. *The most portable and versatile of furniture, stools find their way inside and outside the house. Antique stools are rare, as most of them are worn out with use. This pair of seventeenth-century* huanghuali *rectangular stools, with the unusual "wrapped bamboo" feature in the leg formation, shows the attributes of a refined style.* Source: Used with the permission of the Minneapolis Institute of Arts.

k. *A scene from the Tang dynasty painting* Palace Women Playing Double Sixes, *by Chou Fang (late eighth century), shows crescent-shaped decorated stools.* Source: Used with the permission of the National Palace Museum, Taibei, Taiwan, Republic of China.

concentrated on building with stone. An attempt to probe into the reasons for the faithful adherence of the Chinese to building with wood is as challenging as it is fascinating.

The Tang poet Du Mu's lines in "Ode to the Epang Palace" about the First Emperor's vast residence are celebrated: "Epang Palace rises from the woods of Shu Mountain." The poem dispels the premise that local materials were used. In fact, the timber used in the construction of the palace had to be transported to Shaanxi province from far away Sichuan province (whose forests were decimated as a result and did not revive until the Ming dynasty). Nor could it be said that Central China, the cradle of early civilization, did not have stones, boulders, or a labor force. The primary reason, as Joseph Needham points out (and most agree), is that by the end of the Warring States period, the basic character and principles of Chinese architecture—the flexible timber frame, the sturdy foundation platform built with a compound of stone and earth, and the decorative roof held together by the ingenious system of joinery—were firmly established. "The breakthrough with the most developed and appropriate structure and building technique [had] been achieved" (1971, 29–31).

Understanding this phenomenon involves many factors, including the climatic, geographical, technical, and economic, as well as the cultural and cosmic. In the cosmic scheme of the Five Agents, or *wuxing,* wood is associated with the left/east

Fig. 7.30l–n.

l. *Detail of a hanging scroll,* Children Playing in a Garden in Autumn, *by Song painter Su Hachen (1110–1165). Note that the stool is of lacquer.* Source: Used with the permission of the National Palace Museum, Taibei, Taiwan, Republic of China.

m. *Stone stools were placed in gardens so that indoor furniture would not have to be moved for outdoor activities. This stool, probably of late Ming date, imitates pressed rope. 47.5 cm x 30 cm x 30 cm.* Source: Private collection.

n. *First introduced for use in religious quarters, this seventeenth-century meditation chair* [chanyi] *in tieli wood is of larger proportions than a normal chair to allow for sitting cross-legged.* Source: Dr. S. Y. Yip Collection; courtesy of Grace Wu Bruce.

direction, correlating with the azure dragon of the east *[qinglong],* and is equated with the *qi,* or energy of spring, life, and growth. In an agricultural community, where dwellings house growing families, the regular growth of new trees is convenient. There are sayings such as "In three years you see a sprout; in five years you see a tree" (Jia 1996, 173), and "A ten-year plan yields good timber; a hundred-year plan yields a good person as solid as the tree" (Guanzi 1985, 96). Hence, timber is regarded not only as an essential commodity, but also as something solid, something to be aspired to in life. The modular system allows the Chinese to build quickly. (The greater part of the Forbidden City in Beijing was completed in less than five years, from 1412 to 1416). Tearing down, replacing, and rebuilding have been customary processes throughout history, and wood is a material that easily allows for these processes. In some rural areas, it is customary to plant trees with each newborn child, and timber forms part of the dowry. Wood therefore is linked with the beginning of life, and the wooden coffin is the ultimate shelter at the end of life. Tombs are erected with the support system and decorative details imitating wooden buildings, from *dougong* sets to vaulted ceilings. The flexibility of wood has facilitated the development of brackets and also the mortise and tenon joinery system, and its pliability has helped it to withstand earthquakes, contraction in the cold, and expansion in the heat.

Traditional Chinese Architecture and Furniture

It is remarkable to find that the building system in China attained a mature level of development two thousand years ago. In this vast expanse of time and space, there have been no major transformations in structure, building techniques, or materials. Changes that have occurred are mere modifications in style, size, and decoration. The continuation of a formula that has proved to be convenient and successful to a great extent accounts for the apparent unchanging nature and similar appearance of buildings of all types. Furniture, constructed on architectural principles, developed new forms, variations, and refinements in concert with the house. These physical aspects become resonant with meaning when placed in the cultural context of the symbiotic relationship of architecture and furniture. In the last fifty years, the traditional living patterns of the Chinese, in both urban and rural areas, have undergone significant changes, assuming seemingly cataclysmic proportions in recent decades. If the very qualities that Yan Yunxiang describes in his chapter, "Making Room for Intimacy," are becoming increasingly valued in China—awareness of the individual, privacy, freedom, and ease, or *ziyou*—then "the harmony and order maintained through discipline and hierarchy in the traditional household can only be seen as enforced, confining, and inconvenient." With the accepted ideology of the family unit as a husband, wife, and one child, physical space in a basic household is reconfigured to accommodate a kitchen, dining and drawing room for public interaction, and a bedroom for private life. Because the extended family members are now excluded—there is a "transformation of the family from a disciplined corporate group to a private haven"—exteriority and interiority are redefined in spatial and cultural terms.

Rural workers, envisaging opportunities for easy money in the city, need little encouragement to sell their land. The drift from rural to urban areas has led to the abandonment of family dwellings and the disintegration of the accepted social order, values, and customs, including the veneration of ancestors, as traditional settlements are abandoned for newer housing with modern amenities. The central government's ideal, a well-off "*xiao kang* family," lives in an apartment in town or in any one of the new faceless suburbs that have sprung up as a result of the redevelopment of rural areas. Such families' new homes are equipped with amenities, including a refrigerator, television set, efficient stove, and comfortable furniture, such as sofas and chairs, on which to relax. One hears tales from the countryside of the exchange of a finely made antique wooden chair for a new, upholstered sofa

Fig. 7.31. *One finds a mixture of traditional and modern furniture in the main room of a rural house. Here sofas add modern comfort to otherwise traditional furnishings.* Source: Photograph by Kai-Yin Lo.

Fig. 7.32. *A modern apartment in Shanghai.* Source: Used with the permission of Michael Freeman.

(Figure 7.31). This is a clear indication of the rejection of the old, as well as a lack of appreciation of cultural value and a slavish adoption of the new. In more affluent urban households, the trend is to follow Western decor and fashion, and some homes, more likely those in large cities like Beijing and Shanghai, are decorated tastefully (Figure 7.32). Businesses connected with household improvement and furnishings are thriving throughout China, as are the increasing number of interior decoration and lifestyle publications. The formal arrangement of furniture and its symbolic fit in the house have indeed changed meaning as people have begun to show a preference for ease, choice, and comfort. China, an old country, in its present pursuit of economic betterment, a higher standard of living, and growth has embraced new social and cultural values and has become a country eager for change, and in the process appears very young.

NANCY BERLINER　　　*8　Sheltering the Past*

The Preservation of China's Old Dwellings

The preservation of regional vernacular—that is, nonelite—residential architecture protects not only specific monuments or historic moments, but also physical manifestations of living cultures, past and present, and offers them as investigative opportunities for future generations. This chapter will examine the present situation of such preservation efforts in China, reviewing in the process the efforts that are being pursued to slow destruction or deterioration of vernacular structures, as well as various methodologies that are being practiced in order to carry out preservation efforts.

Across the expanse of China, from small villages to Beijing, many individuals and institutions have awakened to the architectural treasures in their midst and the immediate need to preserve them. As economic growth pressures have increased, voices have become louder and preservation efforts have become more plentiful.[1] Among the more substantial developments is the state-sponsored creation of a set of preservation guidelines for valuable heritage sites in China. In 2002 the State Administration of Cultural Heritage, working with the Australian Heritage Commission and the Getty Conservation Institute, after four years of endeavor, completed the *Principles for the Conservation of Heritage Sites in China,* demonstrating a commitment to take on the responsibility of preserving architecture.[2] On the local level, counties, villages, and individuals are daily facing decisions and coping with deteriorating residences and monuments in a variety of manners.

As the topic of vernacular architecture's preservation in China is massive, this chapter will concentrate on the preservation activities in one region in southeastern Anhui province. The region, traditionally known as Huizhou and now officially called Huangshan municipality, today encompasses four counties (Qimen, Yixian, Xiuning, Shexian) and three districts (Huizhou, Tunxi, and Huangshan), covering 9,807 square kilometers with a population of over 1.4 million people. (In the following text, I will refer to the region by its pre-1987 name, Huizhou.) The local population considers its culture to be "Hui culture," its architecture to be "Hui architecture," and its cuisine to be "Hui cuisine."[3] Recently, there has been discussion at official levels in the municipality to revert to the region's traditional designation as

Huizhou. Architectural preservation in Huizhou is unique to its local characteristics but parallels circumstances and efforts being carried out in much of China.

A great percentage of the Huizhou region is covered with mountains, leaving little flat land for rice cultivation. The situation forced many of the inhabitants, through the centuries, to become traveling merchants in order to afford to purchase rice, to feed their families, from regions beyond. The merchants of Huizhou, who comprised a majority of the adult men in the region since the Ming dynasty, carried, in addition to rice, large profits back to their homes, constructing large ancestral shrines, Buddhist pagodas, bridges, and magnificent residences to shelter their families and descendants. The houses, many of which are two or even three stories high, with a timber-frame structure to support the roof and a white, lime-plastered stone and brick exterior curtain wall, articulated a unique and elegant Huizhou style of architecture. Local Huizhou artisans, with their well-honed skills, produced finely wrought details to decorate these homes. Intricately carved stone, tile, brick, and wood house components became a famed regional tradition (Figure 8.1).

The mountains around the villages, while impeding food cultivation, often protected the population and its architectural structures from the intrusive and destructive forces of wars and, for many years, from intensive industrialization and development. As recently as the 1990s, the villages of Huizhou were still primarily filled with the Ming and Qing houses built by these merchants or more recently constructed houses built in the traditional, timber-frame Hui style of architecture (Figures 8.2–8.4). Since the mid-1990s, as in many areas of China, a variety of factors

Fig. 8.1. *Village in Huizhou region.* Source: Photograph by Nancy Berliner 1987.

Fig. 8.2. *Eighteenth-century home, still inhabited, Guanlu village, Yixian county.* Source: Photograph by Richard Gordon 1998.

Fig. 8.3. *Entrance to home in Guanlu village, Yixian county.* Source: Photograph by Nancy Berliner 1998.

Fig. 8.4. *Entrance to seventeenth-century home.* Source: Photograph by Richard Gordon 1998.

have begun to alter the man-made landscape of the Huizhou region, and, in reaction, individuals and administrative units have begun to reach out for options to preserve their cultural heritage.

Changing Factors, Changing Fashions

With the national economic reforms of the 1980s and 1990s, more young people of the Huizhou region began, like their male ancestors, to seek fortunes, or at least earnings, by traveling to larger cities beyond the Huzhou borders. Men began to journey to Shanghai, Huzhou, and Hangzhou to work in construction or factories, and women went off to Shanghai and even Beijing to work as household domestics or hairdressers in beauty salons. Again, following in the footsteps of their past generations, those working away from home send funds back to care for the elders and, when they can afford it, to build new houses. Inspired by the new-style houses they see in the cities, many construct fashionable homes of concrete in what is called *yang,* or "foreign," style.

Fig. 8.5. *Window lattice recycled for use as vegetable garden barrier. Yuetan village, Xiuning county.* Source: Photograph by Nancy Berliner 1996.

Fig. 8.6. *The dismantling of a traditional home and the construction of a new home, Xiuning county.* Source: Photograph by Nancy Berliner 2001.

Tearing down the family's old home is the most efficient manner of constructing a new house, as it provides both a plot of land on which to build and plenty of building materials, particularly bricks. With a scarcity of wood and restrictions on felling trees in Huizhou, building out of bricks and concrete has become more economical (Figures 8.5 shows how parts are recycled.) Fashion, more than finances, is the primary driving force behind the new facades of Huizhou villages. I have heard young people repeatedly anecdotally voice the following grievances against their

Nancy Berliner

parents' traditional-style houses: they are too cold in the winter; it is difficult to place *yang*-style furniture in them (for instance, a sofa cannot easily be placed up against a wall with a round column); they are too expensive to repair; and it is difficult to find a bride who would be willing to move into an old-fashioned house.[4] This last criticism is not trivial in a country where there is a shortage of marriageable women in the population and where continuing the family line with the birth of a male child is an imperative (Figure 8.6).

The Reactions and the Solutions

Countering many of the young people's desire for new-style homes are not only their grandparents desires to retain the ancestral home, but also the interests of the preservationists, local intellectuals, cultural bureaucrats, and tourism officials in maintaining the traditional and historic appearances of Huizhou. Concerned government officials have enacted laws to prevent the demolition of Ming and Qing edifices. After tea, tourism is the most lucrative industry for Huizhou today, and local government is hoping for, and relying on, an expansion of this industry. Several projects—joint ventures between local governments and private companies—have increased architectural preservation in Huizhou by creating sites that both protect the history and draw ticket-purchasing tourists. In addition, a number of private individual and institutional champions of Huizhou architecture—Chinese and non-Chinese—have financially supported specific preservation projects. And, last, a few local individuals, living in houses they inherited from generations of ancestors, have passionately taken to preserving their own homes. Below I review several of these meaningful solutions.

The Law

In 1998, a new Anhui provincial law, "Regulations Regarding the Preservation of 'Old Dwellings' of the Wannan Region of Anhui Province," went into effect in an attempt to protect and preserve as many as possible of the still standing traditional homes of years past.[5] The first article of the law notes that the regulations were written in order to strengthen the protection of "old dwellings," *gu minju,* of the Wannan region.[6] The second article defines *gu minju* specifically as "dwellings south of the Yangzi River in Anhui province, dating from before 1911 and having historical, artistic and scientific value—ancestral halls *[citang],* memorial archways *[paifang]*, academies *[shuyuan]*, towers *[lou]*, stages *[xitai]*, pavilions *[ting]*, and other architectural structures used by people."

The regulations project an urgency of bringing all members of the local bureaucracy into responsibility, asking "all ranks of the people's government . . . to bring the protection of *gu minju* into the scheme of local economic and social development." Moreover, they require "the responsible leaders of the governments of counties and municipalities to organize surveys of the *gu minju* . . . and make categories to rank them in accordance with their historical, artistic, and scientific value." To further publicize the regulations and prevent harm to identified structures, the law also calls for signs to be hung up in selected buildings, designating their status as protected *wenwu* [cultural relics or heritage sites] (Figure 8.7). In addition to architectural structures, the regulations call for the designation of "protected cultural districts" *[wenhua baohu qu]* within villages with numerous *gu minju* and other structures. Within such districts, plans for new construction, renovation, or demolition may be sent for approval only after the agreement of the cultural relics management departments in the region. The law also provides for the relocation of protected *gu minju* whose original locations are not beneficial to them. However, such relocation may happen only with the approval of the appropriate cultural relic authorities.

To further protect the structures, the regulations outlaw the illegal trade in house components. The components are defined as "ancient building materials such as ceilings *[tianhua]*; lattice panels *[ling]*; doors *[men]*, windows *[chuang zi]*, and brackets *[dougong]*; beams and columns *[liangzhu]*; door hoods *[menzhao]*; furniture *[jiaju]* and other pieces of wood carving *[mudiao]*; stone carvings *[shidiao]*; brick carvings *[zhuandiao]*; bricks *[zhuantou]*; painted bricks *[caihuazhuan]*; patterned or inscribed tiles *[you huawen tuan de wa]*; glazed ceramic or metal pieces *[liuli jinshu jian]*; and drainage pipes *[shuiguandao]*." The souvenir and antique stores of "Old Street," a series of older and traditional-style buildings along the original main shopping street in the city of Tunxi, the governmental center of the Huangshan municipality, offer an abundance of beautifully carved brackets, lattice windows, doors, decorative bricks, and other finely carved house parts. Though the works are affirmation of the fine workmanship of days gone by, they are also evidence that hundreds of older houses are being dismantled in the area.

The enactors of the law presumed that outlawing the trade in house parts would shut down their marketing and therefore discourage home owners from dismantling the decorative elements of their dwellings. The law states that when the local

Nancy Berliner

Fig. 8.7. *County-protected Ming residence, still inhabited by a local family, with a county registration plaque, in Shoucun, Xiuning county.* Source: Photograph by Nancy Berliner 1998.

forestry department, which has wood and bamboo inspection stations to seize illegally cut down lumber, discovers old house components, it must immediately inform local cultural relics management departments. Local cultural relics authorities in the counties of Huizhou have indeed apprehended large trucks carrying house parts on their way to antiques dealers and have confiscated the property. However, five years after the law took effect, the dealers in Tunxi were still displaying house parts in their shops.

The law goes beyond the mere protection of the "old dwellings" and provides direction in preservation work. Article 17 notes that any repairs to those buildings "should adhere to the principle of not changing the original appearance of the cultural relic." This principle can be interpreted to mean that the repaired building should appear as it did when it was first built or that it should be stabilized but generally appear in the aged manner as it did before repair.

Finally, the regulations delineate punishments for those who break the law. "Seizing or harming *gu minju*, risking the safety of *gu minju*, or illegally trading in architectural components of *gu minju* are criminal activities, and those who participate in such activities must restore the *gu minju* to its original appearance, pay for losses, and may be fined up to 10,000 yuan. Those who build new construction within the culturally protected districts without approval must cease the work, demolish all illegal construction, and pay a fine not to exceed 20,000 yuan."

When the regulations were first enacted in 1998, they were well publicized and printed in full in local newspapers so that the local population would be well aware not only of the concern for these structures of cultural and historical significance, but also of the criminal offense of violating them. The local county and municipality cultural relics authorities took seriously their appointed responsibilities to create full surveys of the "old dwellings" in the region. According to a January 2003 report, there are now almost two thousand protected architectural structures in the Huangshan municipality and several thousand more still being processed. Among the structures are residences, ancestral halls, memorial archways, pagodas, bridges, stages, pavilions, and gardens.

A year after the law was put into effect, the house seen in Figure 8.7, built in the sixteenth or seventeenth century by a Ming official, was in the midst of being dismantled. The lotus leaf struts on the window lattice are characteristic of Ming architectural decoration in the region and, with other decorative features, date it to that period. Two peasant families owned the building, but neither could afford to repair it. Nor, because of its dilapidated condition, could they safely inhabit it. The preferable course of action was to dismantle the house and use what they could of the building materials (primarily the bricks) to construct a new house, or two new houses, on the same piece of land. While the county was aware of the situation, there were no available funds in the government's budget to repair a privately owned home—never mind public historical structures. Unable to offer a more viable solution, the county could only turn its back to the violation of the well-intentioned law (Figure 8.8).

Nancy Berliner

The primary tourist destination in the Huizhou region is, and has been since the seventeenth century, Huangshan, the 1,800-meter-high mountain range with two cable cars that annually receives over five hundred thousand visitors. The mountain range is so popular that, in a bid to boost tourism in the late 1980s, the name of the entire region was changed from Huizhou to Huangshan municipality.

In its desire to expand the tourist route—and therefore the tourists' time and money spent—in the region, the government and private tourist development companies have turned to welcoming visitors to other sites, including "old dwellings" and villages of "old dwellings." The tourism expansion plans overlap—though occasionally conflict—with the preservationists', historians', and cultural authorities' goals, and they are, at the present, the primary activities concerned with architectural preservation. In many ways, the Huizhou sites resemble U.S. enterprises and institutions such as Colonial Williamsburg (Virginia), Old Sturbridge Village (Massachusetts), and Shelburne Museum (Vermont) in their concern for preservation, education, and tourism.

There are two major types of "old dwelling" destinations in Huizhou: assemblages of Ming and Qing houses from various villages that have been dismantled, relocated, and re-erected on one site (similar to the "open-air museums" in Europe) and long-established functioning villages that retain primarily older homes, ancestral halls, and other traditional building types. Both types of destinations require paid tickets and offer guides and tours.

Open-Air Museums. Among the first group are Qiankou Guminju Bowuguan (translated on websites as "Qiankou Folk House Museum" and "Qiankou Dwelling Museum"), on a hill beside the town of Qiankou in Huizhou district *[qu]* and the more recently established Gu Cheng Yan of Wan'an Village in Xiuning county. A passionate professor of architecture history, Shan Shiyuan, formerly associated with the National Palace Museum in Beijing, initiated the Qiankou Folk House Museum with the primary goal of preserving the houses. In 1982, the National Ministry of Cultural Relics produced a plan to gather together twelve typical Ming-period Huizhou structures and protect them together as a group. Ming dynasty houses, ancestral halls, one bridge, one stone archway, and a pavilion, all from neighboring villages, were thus relocated to a hillside by the town of Qiankou. All had historical and artistic value and were precious examples for architectural historians for

Fig. 8.8. *Dismantling of a Ming dynasty home in Huizhou.* Source: Photograph by Nancy Berliner 1998.

▼

▲

research. (Among the justifications for preservation noted in the Qiankou litera-ture, in addition to preservation of cultural inheritance, is "to further the tourism industry.")

The Qiankou project took six years and succeeded in preserving the twelve Ming structures in a conservative manner. According to the museum's publications, one of the primary policies in the relocation was "not to change the original appearance" of the buildings. This policy is, according to the literature, in strict adherence to the regulations of the national Cultural Relics Law, which calls for "repairing the old to appear old [as opposed to repairing it to look new] and to maintain the original appearance." The policy, as interpreted at Qiankou, is to retain as much of the original fabric as possible and to leave the outer surfaces of the fabrics showing the effects of time. There are no efforts to relacquer or repaint aged surfaces. This policy of con-serving a building without "restoring" it to an appearance of an earlier time period is a very progressive strategy, even in the United States. In major Beijing historic sites, structures are often reconstructed and repainted (Figures 8.9–8.11).

Certain aspects of the Qiankou museum, like many open-air museums in the United States and Europe, can create false impressions. The houses are dispersed across a hillside, an available parcel of land that was not cultivatable. In most Hui-zhou villages, houses are clustered together on flat land between hills. The placement of the houses in Qiankou therefore presents a relationship among the buildings and within the landscape that would rarely, if ever, exist in Huizhou. The houses at

Nancy Berliner

Fig. 8.12. *The Sun Gaosong house, a three-story Ming residence, relocated to the Huangshan Municipal Museum.* Source: Photograph by Nancy Berliner 2001.

Qiankou also lack kitchens. The director, Hu Huaduo, has explained that when the houses were found, none had their original Ming kitchens, so the kitchen aspect of the buildings was omitted. Aided by funding from provincial authorities, the Qiankou museum is now expanding to include a new section, on an abutting parcel of land, of ten relocated Qing buildings. At least one of these will include a kitchen.

The Gu Cheng Yan of Wan'an Village was, unlike Qiankou, a joint venture between Xiuning county and a private Hong Kong tourist development company. Like Qiankou, the Ming and Qing houses now standing on the Wan'an village hillside were all dismantled, relocated, and re-erected. Like Qiankou, the wooden and stone surfaces of the houses retained their "as old" appearances. No original surfaces were newly lacquered or painted. The project was developed both as a way to save older buildings that were endangered by modernization and as a potential income resource from tourists.

Fig. 8.13. *Interior of the Sun Gaosong house, where newspapers and other papers, pasted on the walls over the years, were preserved.* Source: Photograph by Nancy Berliner 2001.

An additional architectural relocation in the region was carried out by the Huangshan Municipal Museum with the goal of saving a rare, three-story Ming merchant's residence that was endangered by an expanding industrial neighborhood in the Tunxi district. The project was jointly funded by the Anhui Provincial Cultural Relics Department, the Huangshan Municipal Cultural Relics Department, and a cultural exchange program with the Peabody Essex Museum (Figures 8.12–8.13). The building, traditionally named Yi Yi Tang, or the Sun Gaosong house, was dismantled and re-erected next to the Huangshan Museum in the city of Tunxi. The preservationists and artisans involved with the project held strictly to the principle of *xiu jiu ru jiu,* "repairing old like old." Only building components that were structurally unsound were repaired or replaced. The new wood was treated so that it blended with the old wood but not so much that it was indistinguishable. The craftsmen working on the building preserved the patina of time not only on the wood, but also on old newspapers, Cultural Revolution posters, and other ephemera pasted onto the walls over many years. This policy, which does not attempt to replicate a four-hundred-year-old appearance that could only be speculative, is a daring and admirable approach in China, where many examples of traditional architecture in tourist sites are glossily repainted.

Nancy Berliner

Villages of Old Dwellings. The buildings of the "Villages of Old Dwellings," unlike the open-air museum, are all located on their original sites, and many retain their original functions. Though the ancestral halls and traditional public buildings have occasionally been transformed into places for informative visual displays for visitors, most people still reside in their traditional houses, many of which date to the mid-Qing period.

Among the villages that have been developed and promoted are three in the county of Yixian: Xidi, Hongcun, and Nanping. In these villages, there are large expanses full of houses built during the Qing period, with some from the Ming, almost all in excellent condition. The preservation of the many buildings, their original sitings in the landscape, the evolved organization of the architecture, and the paths through the villages and the waterways makes visiting these villages a rewarding and educational experience. The villages preserve both the architectural details and the complete environment.

For a fee, tour leaders will guide visitors through the villages, down narrow, stone-paved pedestrian paths and in and out of people's private homes, some of which have been transformed into antiques or souvenir shops. Visitors are also free to wander through the very scenic villages. A parking lot for buses and taxis is conveniently and appropriately located outside the village, and visitors to Hongcun must walk over an arched bridge, spanning a man-made lake, to enter the town. In the village itself there are 125 Ming and Qing dwellings and three ancestral halls.

The villages of Xidi and Hongcun were admitted to UNESCO's World Heritage List in 2000, demonstrating the acknowledgment of the importance of preserving these villages and others like them. UNESCO's description of the two villages underscores their significance and urges that more villages follow along the same path:

> The two traditional villages of Xidi and Hongcun preserve to a remarkable extent the appearance of non-urban settlements of a type that largely disappeared or was transformed during the last century. Their street plan, their architecture and decoration, and the integration of houses with comprehensive water systems are unique surviving examples.

> The Committee [of world heritage sites] decided to inscribe this property on the World Heritage List on the basis of *criteria (iii), (iv), and (v):*

> *Criterion (iii):* The villages of Xidi and Hongcun are graphic illustrations of a type of human settlement created during a feudal period and based on a prosperous trading economy.

Fig. 8.14. *The preservation of Jin Shi Di, a sixteenth-century shrine in Xiuning county, entailed the replacement of a twenty-seven-foot-long beam that had deteriorated due to a leaking roof.* Source: Photograph by Nancy Berliner 1999.

Criterion (iv): In their buildings and their street patterns, the two villages of southern Anhui reflect the socio-economic structure of a long-lived settled period of Chinese history.

Criterion (v): The traditional non-urban settlements of China, which have to a very large extent disappeared during the past century, are exceptionally well preserved in the villages of Xidi and Hongcun.

The committee recommended that the State Party consider nominating other historic villages in southern Anhui to extend the site.[7]

Yixian county is researching the protection of more well-preserved villages within its borders, including Pingshan and Guanlu, and other counties, such as nearby Jixi, are also in search of funds to do the same. The village of Chengkan in the Huizhou district has more Ming structures than any other village in the region—including the grand Baolun Ge ancestral hall, the ancestral shrine of the Luo clan that was first built during the Jiajing period (1522–1566). Local cultural authorities as well as outside private groups have mobilized to protect and preserve many of the historic buildings there, some of which had deteriorated after 1949 as they were used as schools and granaries. Chengkan has benefited greatly by assistance from the China Heritage Arts Foundation of Hong Kong, a nonprofit organization, initiated by Robert H. Ellsworth that helped fund the restoration of Baolun Ge and Changchun She, "The Studio of Everlasting Spring," whose foundations

Nancy Berliner

date to the Song dynasty (960–1279) and the interior to the early sixteenth century. More recently, a fourth structure, Laowu Ge (in Xixinan village), which dates from the 1470s and is known as the earliest Ming-period private residence in China, was restored ("Huizhou Revisited" 2002). The generosity of several international organizations and individuals has spurred the local government to preserve some sites as well and, perhaps more important, has instilled pride among some local residents in their homes and villages (Figure 8.14).

Individuals' Solutions

The majority of fine old dwellings in the Huizhou region are in the hands of private families who have inherited them from their ancestors. Discussions with members of these families reveal conflicts between generations and occasional resolutions. An elderly man and his wife, his son and son's wife, his son's two sons, and their children—a total of ten people from four generations—occupy a seventeenth-century home in a small village in Xiuning county. The house is large and easily contains all of these people. However, the two grandsons, both with their own children, want their own separate, more modern houses. Their only solution is to take down the old house and use the bricks to construct two new houses on the same site. The grandfather is attached to the beauty of the house and its history in their family. He has pleaded with his grandsons not to dismantle the house, but the grandsons have remarked that they will eventually prevail.

Elsewhere in the same village a schoolteacher, his wife, and their son occupy another seventeenth-century house. The village is located far off the main road of the county. When the schoolteacher's son was getting ready to marry, he told his father he would never be able to find a bride who was willing to live in an old house that was so far off the main road. He requested that his father tear down the old family home and construct a new, modern one. His father refused, saying he liked the design of the old house, the view from the second floor, and the piece of culture he had inherited. After much discussion and negotiation, the father and son found a compromise. The father gave the son 2,000 yuan to redecorate his own room in any manner that he pleased as long as it was reversible. The result, as is seen in Figure 8.15, was the transformation of one bedroom into a suite of two rooms. The front room has a new floor, new walls (painted pink), built-in cabinets and mirrors, and a shaped doorway leading into a tiny rear room with a bed. A year after the son completed the renovation, he found a bride. By the following year, she had given birth to a son, and the family line was continuing in the ancestral home.

Fig. 8.15. *Interior of a son's redecorated bedroom in his family's seventeenth-century home.* Source: Photograph by Nancy Berliner 1999.

In a desire to further promote traditional Huizhou architecture and increase an international audience's understanding of its peril, the Huangshan authorities established a cultural exchange program with the Peabody Essex Museum. As part of the program, Yin Yu Tang, a mid-Qing house from a small village in Xiuning, was relocated to the museum in Salem, Massachusetts. The cultural exchange program, with funds and some preservation philosophies contributed by the American participants, has additionally supported the preservation of a number of Ming and Qing structures and residences in the Huizhou region. These projects include the restoration of Jin Shi Di, a grand shrine built in a small Xiuning village in 1531, and the relocation and restoration of Yi Yi Tang and several seventeenth- and eighteenth-century private homes that neither the owners nor the county could afford to repair. For the local cultural authorities, it is an opportunity not only to preserve the specific buildings, but also to instill pride among the local population in its traditional architecture.

While economic practicalities do not allow for protecting and preserving the thousands of distinctive "old dwellings" in Huizhou and while fashions will inevitably fluctuate through the years, the efforts of the present local, provincial, and national authorities to make a statement and take a lead in Huizhou's preservation activities have the potential to affect many future generations.

NOTES ————————————

1. In his book *China's Old Dwellings,* Ronald G. Knapp (2000) discusses the impact of many economic factors on the preservation of vernacular architecture and the many ways the regional governments and others are attempting to remedy the situation.

2. The report is available in Chinese and English on the Internet at http://www.getty.edu/conservation/resources/reports.html.

3. In this context, of course, "Hui culture" represents the culture of historical *Hui*zhou and *not* the "Hui culture" associated with the ethnonym "Hui," the minority nationality also called Chinese Muslims.

4. Since 1996, I have spent many months in the Huizhou region researching architecture for the Yin Yu Tang house project at the Peabody Essex Museum.

5. The law was passed at the thirty-third meeting of the Eighth People's Representatives Assembly on September 21, 1997, and took effect on January 1, 1998.

6. I will use the term "old dwellings" as a translation for the Chinese term *gu minju,* which literally means "ancient people's residences" and refers to nonimperial architectural structures.

7. See http://whc.unesco.org/archive/repcom00.htm#1002.

Nancy Berliner

Part Two

The Home and the Family

9 The Meaning of Jia

An Introduction

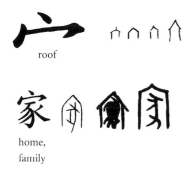

roof

home,
family

Fig. 9.1. *The three strokes ⌒ , drawn at the top, represent a roof, with early calligraphic forms alongside. The Chinese character jia, meaning "house," "home," and "family," is shown in its contemporary form (bottom left), including the abstract representation of both a roof and a pig. Next to it, archaic forms of the jia character, as represented on oracle bones and on bronze vessels, more clearly show a dwelling with a pig within.* Source: Lindqvist 1989, 272.

The Chinese character for "family" is *jia,* the same Chinese word, as discussed above, that is used for "house" and "home." As an ancient written form with a meaning relevant even today, the ideogram for *jia,* 家 , pictographically depicts a pig 豕 underneath three brushstrokes, ⌒, signifying a roof (Figure 9.1). While the precise definition of *jia* is debated, most agree that the symbolism of a pig under a roof, or in the house, is remarkably apt.[1] For many, the essential feature of the Chinese family is that it is a related group of people who "eat out of one pot," either literally, as in a daily family meal—eating pork—or figuratively in terms of sharing income—amassing and storing wealth by raising pigs. Beyond that, the character *jia* implies that the family members live together within the structure of the house represented by the overarching roof. The *jia* pictograph signifies, moreover, that the family is not only an economic unit—a unit of production (pig-*making*) as well as consumption (pig-*eating*). In this reading, the presence of the pig—the "pig under the roof"—represents affluence since eating pork or any other meat was often an ideal that was not often attainable except during periodic festivities. Thus, through this single nine-stroke Chinese character, we can gain some clues to the nature of the Chinese family in terms of its economic features, as well as its relationship to the architectural structure encapsulating it.

Types of Families

Most Chinese families continue to belong to one of three main types: conjugal, stem, or joint. Conjugal, or nuclear, families are composed of a husband and wife and their children. Stem families include, in addition, the father and/or mother of one of the married pair; in the case of Chinese families, this is usually either the husband's father or his mother. Throughout Chinese history, stem families have been the most frequently found living arrangement, and until recent times average family size has remained relatively constant at about 5.2. The People's Republic of China reported average household size as 3.44 persons in 2000, or 0.52 persons fewer than the 3.96 persons reported in the 1990 census. Joint, or extended, families include two or more fraternally related conjugal families in the same generation, plus usually other members such as parents and/or unmarried siblings. Joint families have been said to represent the Chinese ideal and have been celebrated not only in twentieth-century novels like Ba Jin's *Family [Jia]*, but also in those of the past, such as Cao Xueqin's *The Dream of the Red Chamber [Hong lou meng]*, as well as in poetry. Joint families also were understood for decades by social scientists such as the famous anthropologist Fei Xiaotung and others to be organizations of the wealthy classes in that joint families were associated with multiple wives and concubines, for example, and it had been argued that impoverished peasants could not afford to maintain large families and therefore never lived in them.

Myth and Reality

Myron L. Cohen, in his groundbreaking book *House United, House Divided* (1976), called this traditional view into question. He observed that even in Taiwan's poor, dirt-farming communities, as many as 70 percent of the population lived in joint families, contrary to expectation. This led Cohen to see the different family types as different stages in any family's life cycle. According to Cohen, families should not be classified as conjugal, stem, or joint. Instead, each type should be viewed as being a different stage in a process that extends over time. One family form becomes another through the process of marriage and birth, on the one hand, and family division, or *fen jia,* on the other. In studying family division, Cohen called attention to the importance of family contracts and focused on the economic aspect of Chinese families. While he challenged the notion that joint families were organizations of the rich, at least on Taiwan, other studies on the mainland seemed to reinforce the idea that poor families did not live in big houses.

Chinese families are essentially corporate entities and operate as *the* basic unit of production and consumption in society. Members often pool their individual incomes, which are then redistributed by the family head, usually the family patriarch, matriarch, or eldest brother. Optimally, the pooling of income and/or property permits some form of capital accumulation that might not otherwise have been possible, giving rise to the ideal of the big, or undivided, joint family and to the myth that it was exclusively an organization of the rich. In *fen jia*—which traditionally was a formal procedure—rights to all family property were divided among brothers equally, and income was no longer pooled. A contract is written, and everything is recorded in detail. Each conjugal unit then becomes its own *"jia,"*

Nancy Jervis

——兒子剛週歲，就蓋好結婚新房

Our son is just a year old, so we've just built him a new marriage house.

Fig. 9.2. *One-child family poster in the county town near the village in Henan studied by the author. In 1982, the year the photo was taken, posters depicted boys as the only child. Later posters depicted a girl as the only child, as officials recognized the hidden message in such posters and as the pressure to have only one child accelerated.* Source: Photograph by Nancy Jervis 1982.

Fig. 9.3. *Accompanying the economic boom in China during the 1980s was a surge in house building, including, as is pointedly criticized in this cartoon, the construction of a new house for a son who is just a year old. This no doubt should improve his ability to attract a suitable bride.* Source: Drawing by Li Jinqun in *Renmin ribao—haiwai han*, September 20, 1987, 1.

or "family," and the process of forming stem and joint families begins again, to solidify and grow and at some point to weaken and change. Women are normally not involved in the *fen jia* process. They are considered members, or potential members, of their husband's families and generally have no formal rights or, for that matter, obligations to their natal families. Even when the government formally grants rights to family property, it appears that traditional practice will override them, and women remain excluded.

That families go through cycles is clearly demonstrated by the way houses are constructed, a subject explored in both the first and second parts of this book. Clues to prospective plans and resultant conditions are observable in homes throughout China, which to some degree reflect the changing nature of the so-called "one-child policy" (Figure 9.2). Houses are usually built with "extra" rooms for one-day-to-be-married sons and their wives and in anticipation of the later development of a stem or even joint family structure. These rooms, once inhabited only by the couple, increasingly become private space belonging to the conjugal unit. In some cases during the economic boom in China in the 1980s, as seen in the Chinese cartoon in Figure 9.3, it was said that new houses were even being built for male infants. Yan Yunxiang in his chapter on domestic space and conjugal privacy describes the process of private space emerging within a home and influencing in the process new models for acceptable houses. Where once several conjugal units shared one large sleeping space, houses are now generally built with separate rooms for each couple. As a consequence, according to Yan, family members increasingly prefer their new-found "privacy." In Hubei province, presumably in a more affluent area, Cohen observes that a freestanding house is now a prerequisite to marriage. In

The Meaning of Jia

situations where a family is too poor to build a freestanding house for a son, as in Yan's village in the northeast and the village in northwest Henan that I studied, a room is simply refurbished for the newlyweds (Jervis 1992, 245–257). This room, which may earlier have been considered communal territory, now becomes the "private" space of the couple within the larger family home.

David Faure examines how "families" in southern China are constituted not by coresidence within a cluster of houses or co-ownership of all properties, but by operating through common budgets. Utilizing old floor plans and records, he is able to demonstrate that a *whole* compound of separate dwellings can be seen as analogous to a *single* dwelling and thus *one* family. Through ceremonies, especially ancestral ritual, those who do not live under one roof are bound together. The dynamism of family life at several scales is often mirrored in the residential space, reflecting aspirations for the extended family as well as demonstrating wealth and status. Faure concludes that—at least in the Pearl River Delta—coresidence as an aim *and* ritual sacrifice at a common ancestral shrine together feed into the ideal of the large extended family

The Informal or Woman's Family

While we should not underestimate the patriarchal power of this formal and patrilineal family system, it is worth noting that an informal family system that is somewhat more empowering of women seems to have coexisted with the formal one. Margery Wolf, in her seminal book *Women and the Family in Rural Taiwan* (1972), describes what she terms "the uterine family," which is composed of the mother and her children. In this arrangement, the mother maintains close ties with her daughters even after they have been married off and left the village. In my own fieldwork in Henan, I saw this informal family system at work in the 1970s as a matriarch called upon her daughters and their respective husbands' families to aid her son when he needed help and was estranged from his formal or patrilineal family. The existence of unoccupied rooms and unopened doorways serves to anticipate the future visitations of married daughters. In much of the literature on Chinese families, the tendency has been to delineate only the formal family.

Francesca Bray shows in her chapter that even the poorest and most humble families in late imperial China set apart a portion of their homes as a secluded space for women in order to reduce physical or even social contact with males in a family. Bray traces the history of gender separation, revealing that the "inner quarters"

Nancy Jervis

offered constraints and opportunities, advantages and satisfactions, and that, when possible, private quarters were auspiciously located (Figure 9.4). With abundant visuals, she is able to illustrate the expansive nature of family leisure and family ritual across classes, as well as the productive work of women, in which they contributed to family finances by spinning and weaving, raising silkworms, and doing embroidery. Bray introduces some of the revisionist ideas of Dorothy Ko regarding the fact that cloistering sometimes had a positive effect on women's culture. Even as a woman had to contend with the structural difficulties that emerged from women brought together by marriage—for example, being forced to share space in a home in which she was an outsider—women individually and in groups within families were sometimes able to forge strong bonds of affection and companionship. Paradoxically, the patriarchal and patrilineal Chinese family seems to have provided spaces of safety, enjoyment, and even empowerment for women even as women were physically and socially segregated from men.

Fig. 9.4. *Women and children at leisure in the "inner quarters."* Source: Wu 1983, vol. 2.

Houses can be read as templates that met social needs by structuring family relationships based upon hierarchies of generation, age, and gender, expressed in the placement of individual rooms and pathways in addition to the actual relationships between and among rooms and pathways. In her wide-ranging book *Technology and Gender: Fabrics of Power in Late Imperial China,* Francesca Bray has shown how one can view a Chinese home as such an inculcating "text" and as a "template." Indeed, Bray shows that as a place of ritual, each Chinese home traditionally was "a space of decorum, an embodiment of neo-Confucianism" in which patriarchy was encoded (1997, 59–172).

As a domain to express a family's propriety and a repository of its heritage, the home was a metaphor for "order" more broadly. It was within the home that the duties and obligations of three of the Five Relationships basic to Confucian morality operated (affection between father and son, attention to their separate functions between husband and wife, proper order between old and young).[2] Indeed, as Roger Ames has stated, "it is not an exaggeration to say that in the Chinese world, all relationships are familial. The ruler, referred to as *tianzi,* 'the son of Heaven,' is *fumu,* 'father and mother' to the people, who are the *minzi,* 'people children'" (2001, 1). It is clear that the state itself had its model in the ordered family.

Periodic rituals performed according to a prescribed calendrical sequence helped guide behavior and affirm relationships within the family, sometimes extending to the broader lineage, as well as between the living and the dead (Figure 9.5). Some rituals were performed daily while others were semimonthly or seasonal. Most rituals were carried out either at an altar in a main hall or at the stove in the kitchen, but others were performed in nearby buildings that were grand. James Flath, whose chapter emphasizes the nature of the paper prints used in household ritual including Menshen or Door Gods, writes of how the environment of an individual family led to personalized pantheons of tutelary deities in homes in North China (Figure 9.6). As a representative of the Jade Emperor, the Stove God was ubiquitous as the domestic deity *par excellence.* Found in every home—rich and poor—and in response to rather standardized rituals held on the twenty-third day of the twelfth lunar month, the Stove God was sent on his annual New Year's journey to report to the supreme Jade Emperor in heaven on the comings and goings of the family during the year (Figure 9.7). As discussed also in Chapter 4, Flath illustrates the range of calligraphic and pictographic prints used to ensure protection for the family and its home.

Nancy Jervis

a ▶

Fig. 9.5a–b.

a. *In rather simple circumstances, a father is instructing his son in the ritual necessary for honoring ancestors.* Source: Bard 1905, 44.

b. *Among the* Twenty-four Tales of Filial Piety [Ershisi xiao] *is the tale of Ding Lan. Because his parents died when he was very young, he was burdened with the fact that he had been unable to serve and support them. To remedy these unfortunate circumstances, he carved two lifelike statues and placed them on an altar and regularly treated them as if they were alive. However, his wife mocked his behavior and one day pricked the finger of one of the statues. Unexpectedly, blood flowed from the statue, and Ding Lan began to cry and worry about their treatment by his wife. Subsequently, he cast her out and focused all his attention on his parents.* Source: *Ershisi xiao* 1993, 12.

Fig. 9.6. *At the lunar New Year, the double gates of houses throughout China are decorated with posters depicting a pair of Door Gods, who symbolically protect the inhabitants from harm throughout the coming year. Henan.* Source: Photograph by Nancy Jervis 1982.

b ▼   9.6 ▶

Fig. 9.7a–b.

a *The altar niche for the Stove God is above the stove. Although it is ornamented with the expected pair of couplets and two large characters invoking the "Five Good Fortunes," there is no image of Zaojun in the niche. Fenglin village, Luci township, Tonglu county, Zhejiang.* Source: Photograph by Ronald G. Knapp 1988.

b. *A paper image of the Stove God with a drawing placing him within the "palace where good fortune is determined." The image is replete with auspicious symbolism, including a treasure urn, or jubaopen, with glowing ingots and young boys aspiring to be officials. Ningbo, Zhejiang.* Source: Photograph by Ronald G. Knapp 1987.

The visual vocabulary scripted within and about traditional Chinese homes is extraordinary and varied. Much more than mere ornamentation, words and pictures express and embody a family's aspirations for good outcomes, including good fortune generally, as well as longevity, (male) progeny, prosperity, and peace (Figures 9.8 and 9.9). Some serve didactic purpose in that they narrate moral principles and help guide proper behavior. Maggie Bickford utilizes the auspicious imagery associated with "counting the nines" to show how it traversed boundaries of class, education, and taste, from sumptuous imperial palaces to humble peasant homes. She demonstrates well that many of the auspicious printed motifs were "vulgar in the literal sense of that word—they were used by everyone," even if some were magnificent woven or painted tapestries while others were merely crude, woodblock-printed sheets of paper. The layers of meaning represented by auspicious motifs were explicit as well as implicit as they used the repetitive idioms of numbers, images, patterns, and puns, among many other vehicles.

According to the Chinese American anthropologist Francis L. K. Hsu (1948),

Fig. 9.8. *Fu, Lu, and Shou are an auspicious triad, sometimes called Stellar Gods. Here they are carved in low relief on bricks that face a spirit wall. Each is an emblem for something desired:* fu *for good fortune,* lu *for emolument or income, and* shou *for longevity.* Source: Photograph by Ronald G. Knapp 2003.

Fig. 9.9. *Placed as a dominant ornament on the gable end of this side building, this stylized* shou, *or character for "longevity," is an invocation for a long life.* Source: Photograph by Ronald G. Knapp 2003.

Fig. 9.10a–b.

a. Courtyard of a one family house in the winter. Henan. Source: Photograph by Nancy Jervis 1982.

b. For more than two decades now, new village houses have increasingly been two-storied. For the most part, such houses are built on the site of and with the same physical layout as the old house. In this house, as in many other new ones, instead of one room for the married son and his wife, the couple receives a suite with a living room, bedroom, and small kitchen, exemplifying the trend toward greater conjugal intimacy discussed by Yunxiang Yan. Source: Photograph by Nancy Jervis 1999.

each Chinese family "lived under the ancestors' shadow" in that the living and the dead in a family were linked through ritual. James Flath introduces the notion of ancestralism and the use of simple ancestor prints, which provided a direct representation of the ancestral cult in a majority of homes throughout North China. While paper prints sufficed for most in North China, some used wooden tablets arranged on a cascading shrine in their main hall.

As Puay-peng Ho illustrates, expansive and imposing ancestral halls in many parts of southern China were "architectural statements of the strength of lineages, whose existence extends the concept of familism beyond individual families to include all those sharing a common patrilineal descent from a single ancestor." Not only in terms of scale and ornamentation, but also in terms of the elaborateness of the rituals carried out within them, ancestral halls in many of the villages of southern China make manifest the expansive nature of the "family," helping to consolidate and reinforce lineage structure while recognizing the fundamental family unit, whether conjugal, stem, or joint family, as its multiple nuclei. Through ritual and decorative motifs, ancestors were commemorated in branch and focal ancestral halls in ways that enhanced the solidarity of the lineage, affirmed the significance of patrilineal descent, and refashioned the "living" family in both its abstract and actual forms.

Nancy Jervis

Current Trends

Chinese families are dynamic entities, just as are their houses and homes. Over time there has been a transformation of both familial structure and domestic spatiality. First in Taiwan and more recently throughout the modernizing mainland, Chinese families, houses, and homes are continuing to be transformed (Figure 9.10). Some of this is rather simple, such as the increasing trend for married sons to move away earlier and earlier from their parental homes and families to their own nearby houses, to new abodes down the road, or even to the anonymity of apartments in distant towns and cities. As Yan Yunxiang tells us in his chapter, "the horizontal, conjugal tie" is replacing "the vertical, parent-son relationship" as the axis of family relations, marking "the triumph of conjugality over patriarchy, a structural transformation of family relations." Yet it appears that even new houses continue to be constructed with the additional rooms and domestic spaces that acknowledge that such a family, too, will move through a cycle, that it will grow, and then, quite likely, divide.

NOTES

1. Both pigs and dogs have histories as domesticated animals that reach back to neolithic times. Han period stone-relief carvings, mural paintings, and pottery models found in tombs attest to the significance of these animals, as well as chickens, in Chinese homes. Pigs, dogs, and chickens are scavengers and are all efficient converters of household waste into protein and fat, providing in the process some 70–80 percent of animal calories in the rural diet in the twentieth century. Moreover, while eating scraps, crop residue, human excreta, pond scum, and garbage, they destroy parasites as their digestive systems convert "waste" to nutrients. Even at the beginning of the twenty-first century, it is still possible to find any of these animals in some Chinese villages, where they move freely in and out of courtyards and sometimes homes. Raising pigs historically was a prime component of the rural economy, as a source of cash income and a measure of financial security for peasants. Nearly half of all pigs in the world today are found in China, with most of them raised by households with four or fewer pigs. In addition to their traditional significance, pigs play a role in the modernization of the country in that they provide critical biogas needed for the heating and cooking in countless households. For additional information about the significance of domesticated animals in China, see Chang (1977); Simoons (1991, 295–297).

2. The remaining two are righteousness between ruler and minister and faithfulness between friends.

10 House United, House Divided

Myths and Realities, Then and Now

House United, House Divided, the title of this chapter, is also the title of my book on the Chinese family published in 1976. Based on fieldwork between 1964 and 1965 in Yanliao, a small Hakka village in Meinong township in southern Taiwan, the book focused on family organization and family development, in the process exposing myths and offering new interpretations in an attempt "to understand the extent and direction of social change in modern times" (Cohen 1976, xv). Analyzing historical information and data derived from the histories of families that span more than forty years, this chapter further explores and explains many of the dynamics inherent in Chinese families over time: how they are formed and sustain themselves, how they prosper and seemingly inevitably decline, and then how they reform as reinvigorated small units ready to progress in new patterns of development. I focus especially on the changing dynamics of family organization and family development during recent decades. It should be apparent from the process described below that a family's living arrangement—the form and extent of its housing— is inextricably related to its own form and extent (Figure 10.1). Also evident is the complexity of understanding and generalizing about the nature of Chinese families across time, space, and status, a subject dealt with in several of the chapters that follow. While it is not possible for families in any single village to represent completely the variegated forms of families found throughout China, those living in Yanliao and other villages discussed in this chapter indicate the "pronounced adaptability of the Chinese family to many of the changes it has encountered in modern times" (Cohen 1992, 362). Yunxiang Yan, in the last chapter, carries forward some of the ideas presented in this chapter as he explores similar transformations of families in Heilongjiang province, from complex corporate groups to relatively simple private nuclei in which family life revolves around the husband-wife's pursuit of financial independence, privacy, and personal space.

When I arrived in Yanliao in 1964, I was familiar with what the sinological wisdom of the day would lead one to expect in Han Chinese families, and this was confirmed in some respects by what I found. But not at all verified was the belief that in family life there was a vast divide between China's wealthy gentry or elite, on the one hand,

Fig. 10.1a–b. *Views along village lanes of Yanliao in the mid-1960s* **(a)** *and 1990s* **(b)** *that suggest the nature of changes over time.* Source: Photographs by Myron L. Cohen

and the masses, on the other. Supposedly characteristic of the former were large, extended, or "joint," families, so defined by the presence in one family of two or more husband-wife units of the same generation. Typically the joint family consisted of several married brothers living together with their wives and children; usually the parents were also present, but in some cases the married brothers continued to live together after the parents had passed away. As to the rest of the population, it lived

Myron L. Cohen

either in poor, simple, and tiny families defined as "conjugal"—meaning a married couple, the conjugal unit, with or without unmarried children—or in "stem" families—that is, two married couples, one in each generation, with the usual arrangement being parents living together in one family with their son and his wife.

The prevalent understanding at that time was that the contrast between the families of the wealthy "gentry" and merchants and those of the poor "peasants," the farmers and the masses, was an aspect of broader cultural differences, such that the complexity of joint familial life was an expression of elite culture. So I was quite unprepared for what I encountered when I walked into the village for the first time and found that joint families were common in this community of dirt farmers, growing mainly rice and tobacco. Later I determined that 386 people, or 55 percent of the 700 village residents, were members of joint families.

During my second day in the village, it was brought home to me how daily life was conditioned by the prevalence of the joint family form. In the family with which I was now living, I saw a man in his mid-forties, married and with children, ask his father for cigarette money. The older man looked at his son and gave him some change. This was an interaction between people living in one family, for under other circumstances it was hardly the usual pattern for people to make such requests of their elderly parents.

My encounter with the reality of family life in Yanliao revealed as just a myth the earlier notion that the joint family was an elite phenomenon in circumstantial and in cultural terms. The new reality, now well confirmed by my subsequent work on the China mainland, is that living in a large or joint family was a phase in the lives of many if not most people. This then reflects how the joint family was not as much a form of family as it was but one characteristic phase in a cycle of family development (Cohen 1992, 1998). Another phase could be a conjugal family, which, if there were several sons, would assume stem form upon the marriage of the first; when the second son married, it would become joint and might continue to grow in number as each son married and began to have children. At some point or other, the family would "divide," which meant that the family estate, the family's property, was split into smaller units, with each brother participating in the division getting in principle an equal share.

Upon a brother's receipt of a share in the family estate, he has basically become head of a new family corporation, a new *jia*. In other words, he does not obtain his share of land or other family assets as an individual, but rather as head of the new, smaller *jia*, and this share of the old family estate becomes the foundation of the new *jia*'s corporate holdings. Once it is understood that the brother's "share" goes not to him but to his smaller family unit, then certain problems regarding the relationship between women and the families into which they marry are clarified. In this smaller family, created by a larger one's partition, husband and wife are now co-managers of the new family estate. Given that marriage was an arrangement between the families of bride and groom, it is not surprising that a man with many brothers was considered a poor match in light of the smaller portion of family holdings he was likely to obtain upon family division. So it is the *corporate* nature of the traditional Chinese family that first must be appreciated in order to understand other aspects of family life.

Understanding the *jia* as a corporation complicates our appreciation of yet another myth regarding the Chinese family that has held sway for many decades: that with modernization traditional family arrangements give way to newer, smaller families. On the face of it, my experiences in Yanliao in the mid-1960s would appear to explode this myth, given the large number of joint families then living in a world largely formed by the industrial era. But during the decade following my departure from the village, developments I elaborate below resulted in vast change in residential patterns, with conjugal or, in a few cases, stem families now the rule. Nevertheless, in certain respects the modernization myth can still be taken as such, given the complex interactions between the family as residential unit and as corporation, a circumstance illustrated by the following story. In June 2000, while I was visiting Taiwan, a close friend from Meinong told me that his family had "just divided." He was the sixth of seven brothers. In 1965, when I was in the village, they were members of a joint family with twenty people, which was not large by then prevalent standards, for some had forty or forty-five members. Their widowed mother, then 58, was the domestic boss, while the oldest brother was the family head, or *jiazhang,* as far as the outside world and family farm management were concerned. At that time, save for brothers four, five, and six, all family members lived together in one residential compound, including the three oldest brothers, their wives and children, and the youngest unmarried children. The mother had her own room, as did each of the married couples. Among those living together, labor and earnings were pooled, and the entire family shared meals produced in one kitchen, thus manifesting the commensality that classically has been an aspect of Chinese family corporate life. Living apart but not yet married, brother four was a policeman in Taibei, brother five a military officer, and brother six a student. Having careers in the military or the police was premised upon free, state-provided advanced train-

Myron L. Cohen

ing; such careers were common choices those days for families with some land but too poor to pay for their children's educations after middle school.

When I returned in 1991, only the oldest brother and his children were still in the village and still farming family land. Everyone else had moved to Kaohsiung [Gaoxiong], Taibei, or other urban centers. So in 2000 what was my friend talking about when he said that his family had "just divided" when in fact they had not lived together for many years? In order to answer this question, I need first to review some of the major changes in village life and livelihood during the forty plus years since I lived first in Yanliao.

I have been returning to Meinong township for short visits almost annually since 1991, always going to Yanliao village, where I carried out the 1964–1965 fieldwork, and to Meinong town, the township center, where I resided and did research during 1971–1972. I had made only a couple of very brief revisits prior to 1991, but that year I spent two weeks in Yanliao so as to familiarize myself with some of the changes that had occurred since my earlier fieldwork. One focus was on changes in family organization. In the course of several visits beginning in 1991, I managed to interview people from every family with members still in the village. Changes in family organization are connected with broader social, political, and cultural developments. Accordingly, I first consider some features of village life as I saw them during recent visits in the 1990s and compare them with the past before turning to a discussion of changes in family organization. Notwithstanding the continuing formidable energy of ordinary villagers as they go about their lives, my basic impression is of remarkable economic and social change marking movement from the "third world" to the first. By earlier standards the village is now rich; most families own cars, for example, whereas thirty-five years ago there were no automobiles in the village, and the few persons in the larger Meinong township possessing them were a tiny, wealthy elite.

As the twenty-first century began, Yanliao in many ways was still a farming village, with tobacco its major crop, a subject I described at length more than a quarter century ago (Cohen 1976, 46–55). However, with Taiwan's membership in the World Trade Organization in January 2002, the government no longer was able to protect the lucrative crop as a monopoly, and, as a result, many if not most farmers have recently given up the cultivation of tobacco. In the past, the annual crop of tobacco was grown during the winter season, between two crops of rice (Figure 10.2). Sweet potatoes also were commonly grown, mainly for pig feed; they too have been replaced by commercial animal feed products. Moreover, agriculture has become

Fig. 10.2a–b. *Although taken thirty years apart, these two images illustrate the continuing harvesting of tobacco by hand, even as much production has become increasingly mechanized. The curing of tobacco leaves is now done in diesel-powered, computer-regulated metal chambers instead of in large wooden "tobacco houses," or* yanlou, *seen in the background.* Source: Photographs by Myron L. Cohen.

increasingly mechanized and specialized. Even before 2002 there were fewer tobacco farmers, but they grew more than in the 1960s, with the government's Taiwan Tobacco and Wine Monopoly Bureau increasing quotas for farmers still growing the crop. Thus until 2002 the village consisted of tobacco growers renting land in order to meet their quotas and other villagers renting out land to the tobacco growers. Many villagers simply rented out land and did no farming on their own, a circumstance related to changing patterns of family organization discussed below.

In tobacco production, field preparation is now mechanized and tobacco planting done by hired specialists, in contrast with the past—before tractors—when the family took care of all production, using both preindustrial farm tools and animals, as well as a small number of power tillers. Now tobacco leaves are cured in diesel-powered, computer-regulated metal chambers instead of in wooden curing houses, called "tobacco houses" *[yanlou],* fueled by wood and requiring twenty-four-hour supervision so as to maintain a constant temperature. The transition to computerized curing has been the greatest of all labor-saving innovations in tobacco production. Picking tobacco leaves and then sorting them after curing are the only remaining labor-intensive phases of tobacco production. Farmers estimated that labor

Myron L. Cohen

Fig. 10.3a–b. *In the past, the court-yard within the embrace of a family's home served as important work space for drying harvested rice in the sun* **(a)**, *and family members carried out the bulk of the work. It was here also that the bagged rice was put on a cart, drawn by a water buffalo, to storage* **(b)**. *Today, rice is dried in special heated drying chambers, and thus the prospect of damaging rain is no longer a constant threat. Trucks today are used to transport grain. Mechanization and specialization have brought nonfamily members into the sequence of agricultural production.* Source: Photographs by Myron L. Cohen

requirements have been halved for tobacco. For picking tobacco leaves, farmers still resort to labor exchange arrangements of the kind I saw forty years ago, whereby families join into larger work teams so as to mobilize sufficient labor in the successive harvesting of each other's tobacco fields.

If anything, rice cultivation has been even more transformed by the mechanization of all major phases of production: plot preparation is now by tractor; seedlings are no longer grown in seed beds, then uprooted and transplanted by hand, but are rather purchased and then mechanically transplanted by a tractor modified for that purpose; tractors are also used for rice harvest, which in the past was entirely dependent on manual labor, and the harvested grain is no longer dried in the sun but in special heated drying chambers, such that the prospect of damaging rain is no longer a constant threat (Figure 10.3). Some farmers own most of the equipment they must use, especially if they have substantial land and a large tobacco quota (this before 2002); otherwise the equipment and its operators are hired, usually simply by an appointment set up over the telephone. Chemical insecticides and weed killers are still applied using hand sprayers, however, but while this kind of work can stretch over a considerable time, on a daily basis it demands little labor.

House United, House Divided

Fig. 10.4a–b.

a. A traditional U-shaped, single-story family compound with new, multistory housing behind, and **(b)** *a refurbished courtyard with new, flat-roofed buildings. Atop the new buildings are television antennas and a water storage tank. On the facades of both the old and new homes, traditional New Year ornamentation remains relatively unchanged.* Source: Photographs by Myron L. Cohen.

Thus lack of family labor beyond a married couple is no longer an obstacle to growing rice or even tobacco, which had been one of Taiwan's most labor-demanding crops. Mechanization and specialization have redefined agricultural production at the same time that there has been a massive outflow of the younger generation to the cities for work involving salaried positions or their own enterprises, with enterprise operators comprising a substantial minority. A considerable portion of the village's farmers now consists of middle-aged and late-middle-aged couples.

In conjunction with such demographic and economic developments there have been truly revolutionary changes in family organization. During the period of my first fieldwork, as noted above, most villagers were members of joint families, but such entities no longer exist insofar as they are characterized by the pooling of income, common residence, and common kitchen. All of this has been replaced by a pronounced conjugalism, much of it contributing to the out-migration of younger married couples. But even those still living in the village tend to form themselves as independent economic units, apart from their parents (Figure 10.4).

At the same time, the local definition of the family remains linked to the notion of family division *(fen jia)*, in spite of the fact that the vast majority of families so defined consist of several economically autonomous units. The typical pattern is for the middle-aged parents to be farmers in the village while their married sons live outside with their wives and children and are self-supporting. The usual responses to my questions on this matter were that the sons "are independent" but that "we are one family" and "we have not yet divided" and that "they all come home for the New Year." There are still quite a few cases where one married son still lives with his parents, and the common arrangement under such circumstances is for the son and his wife to hold on to their earnings; in some cases the son helps with the purchase of food, but many fathers told me that they paid for all household expenses. The son and his wife bear the cost for tuition, clothing, and other such expenses that he, his wife, and his children may have. Unmarried sons and daughters usually are expected to turn over their earnings to their parents in anticipation, I was told, of the marriage expenses that the parents will later bear. But here, too, there are exceptions: wealthier parents permit their unmarried children to keep their earnings.

It must not be assumed that prior to the changes we have been discussing, conjugal units were totally absorbed within a larger family (Cohen 1976, 99–148). In the past, married couples were well defined, usually both in terms of where they lived and what they owned in common. Key to all this was the idea of the room, or *fang.* The relationship between physical rooms and conjugal units was almost one of identity because the same term, *fang,* also referred to the married couple. Thus the room taken up by a newly married couple is the "new room," or *xinfang.* But *xinfang* sometimes refers to the newly married couple itself, and by extension the patrilineal line of descent deriving from the marriage of that couple is also a *fang,* now with the meaning of "branch." This image of the room as defining a fundamental unit within the family is powerfully reinforced by the fact that the room is considered to be the property of the husband-wife unit. This is known as *fangchan,* or "*fang* property," and covers the room's furnishings, some provided by the husband's natal family but also including what is brought in by the wife as dowry. Such conjugal property coexists with family property, or *jiachan,* as well as with "women's private property," known in standard Mandarin, interestingly enough, as *sifangqian,* or "private room money," the room again signifying separation from the larger *jia* or family corporation, but this time in the form of a woman's individual holdings. Thus within the family context there are three property arrangements. These kinds of coexisting property relationships can only blossom and develop their full complexity when the corporate family has assumed joint form, such that there are two or more conjugal units at the same generational level, usually brothers and their wives. Through these arrangements the conjugal unit was imbedded within the larger *jia* economy at the same time that it was well defined in a variety of ways. Thus greater conjugal independence, even to the extent of residential and economic separation, does not entail any radical redefinition of the hierarchy of social units within the *jia* framework.

I now return to the story with which I began this chapter. The fact that "division" is seen to be a significant event, even though those involved have already lived separately for several decades, is a reflection of how important links are maintained among residentially and economically separate units within what is locally defined as an undivided *jia*. For example, parents often assist married sons in the purchase of expensive items such as cars or housing. Also, on Sundays and holidays, sons living relatively close to parents, as in Kaohsiung and Tainan, often come home and help on the farm. If their parents are under economic pressure, sons frequently give them money on the New Year, as well as at other times. Thus within the common *jia* framework there remains the potential for many forms of financial cooperation. Finally, it is recognized in principle that if a son living outside should have to return due to economic failure or other problems, he and his wife and children have the right to move back to the family house in the village. However, no one ever was able to provide me with an example of such an occurrence, since recent years have hardly been characterized by economic failures here. Many people living and working outside have told me they intend to return to the village when they retire, but the connection between such aspirations and notions of *jia* unity remains to be seen.

In the past, there were also a few cases of married couples living outside but still considered as belonging to a *jia* mainly resident in the village. But then sons not living at home were expected to fully participate in the unified family economy by contributing their labor, if they lived close enough for this to be feasible, or, if salaried, through remittance of their income to their father. A major—indeed revolutionary—change is that it is now the expectation and the practice that a son be economically independent upon marriage, but this does not preclude cooperation in business among *jia* members. Indeed, such cooperation within the undivided family framework is precisely what characterizes the organization of larger enterprises. Internally, the family is a collection of independent conjugal units; externally and under proper circumstances this family can take the form of a massive enterprise. By remaining undivided in terms of corporate identity, but in all other respects establishing totally independent family units, people preserve for themselves options for future cooperation. This requires little sacrifice, is ideologically rewarding, and also makes perfect sense as a strategy in contemporary Taiwan, which, while prosperous, has its share of political and economic uncertainties.

That formal *fen jia* does at some point still occur appears connected to property distribution among those eligible for shares. Family division is still among males only, as they become actual or potential family heads. As before, some legal work is required so that the division agreement is in accordance with Taiwan's law. With

Myron L. Cohen

division after the father's death, daughters normally waive the property rights conferred upon them by Taiwan's law code, which recognizes no inheritance distinction between women and men. In Yanliao there have been no cases of women refusing to do this and only very few in Meinong township as a whole, but these date even from before the period of my first fieldwork in the 1960s.

The process of family division has changed very little over time. Outsiders are still called in to help, and a division contract is drawn up. Formal division is necessary because "fuzzy" property relationships among otherwise economically autonomous married brothers are one reflection of their close ties within the *jia* framework. Frequently enough, a man remaining in Yanliao will till all fields owned by the *jia* if his brothers have moved out, married, and are holding nonfarming jobs of one sort or another. The man still in Yanliao may live with his parents and pay the land taxes, but he certainly cannot give his brothers rent in consideration of their shares, precisely because the distribution of shares can be determined only in the context of formal division. Thus, such division is precipitated only when the brothers determine that it is in their interests to decide exactly who owns what.

The major changes in marriage procedures are linked both to the vast improvements in income and living standards and to the transition from the arranged marriages common more than forty years ago to the love matches of today. Postmarital residence remains virilocal in those cases where the couple remains in Meinong and, more generally, the family is still male-oriented; women who marry out are the responsibility of the husband's family. Marriages with non-Hakka—be they the majority, Minnan-speaking Taiwanese or "mainlanders"—are far more frequent than in the past, and parents no longer object. The "mainlanders," now overwhelmingly Taiwan-born, in most cases are in fact the children or even grandchildren of those who fled to Taiwan during 1949–1950, but at least one man married an overseas Chinese woman from Burma. In Meinong township, there have been several marriages between local men and overseas Chinese of Hakka descent who were born and raised in Indonesia, enough for there have to have been organized on their behalf special Chinese literacy classes. These "mail order" marriages reflect the fact that Meinong men who stay in farming have difficulties finding women in Taiwan who are willing to marry them.

The parental generation still disapproves of same-surname marriages, which now do occur, whereas in the past they were out of the question. The old attitude in Meinong, as demonstrated in the case of the well-known Meinong novelist Zhong Lihe, was of such hostile opposition that any person so marrying would be disowned by his or her family. Nowadays, I was told, while "parents are still unhappy about it, often there is not much they can do." In local cases of such marriages the parents on both sides usually still agree to sponsor wedding banquets; but in one instance the bride's parents refused to hold a wedding celebration, and in another, while the groom's side agreed to hold one, the groom's father wept throughout the banquet.

The sequence of events preliminary to marriage as I observed it in 1965 (Cohen 1976, 149–177) is now largely abandoned. Go-betweens *[meiren* or, in Hakka, *moignin]* are no longer involved in spouse selection, although they still have a ceremonial role to play later; they are recruited by the groom's family, but only after the son informs the family that he wants to get married. Likewise ended is the old practice of "seeing the girl" *[kan ximei* or, in Hakka, *kon semoi]* so as to give the potential bride and groom an opportunity to meet and accept or reject the match. Even the term is rarely used, for now it is almost always the case that the couple have met on their own and already determined to marry. Exceptions would be the overseas Chinese "mail-order brides," but here again the local man and the foreign bride must agree to the match, and the involvement of their families is vastly different from what it was in the past. The bride and groom's *bazi* ["eight characters," signifying year, month, day, and hour of birth] are no longer compared so as to horoscopically determine a couple's compatibility, since this is now for the pair itself to decide. In a minority of cases the groom's parents will have the *bazi* matched by a specialist to determine an auspicious date for the wedding ceremony, but I was told most people do not even bother to do that anymore. Still practiced is the *la gamen,* as it is known in Hakka; it used to refer to the inspection visit of members of the bride's family to the groom's home, where they were served a meal and still might reject the match if they found that the groom's side had economic or other problems. Now *la gamen* has been totally ceremonialized, with the groom's side inviting the bride's for lunch, as in the past, but under circumstances where the couple have on their own accord decided to marry. The subsequent betrothal feast is now at the groom's side, whereas in the past the bride's family hosted it. This change may be one aspect of the shift of the economic burden to the groom's family.

A payment of "betrothal money" *[pinjin]* is still given to the bride's side (in 1991 it was NT$200,000 or US$8,000) but under vastly changed circumstances. As before, the money is presented to the bride's parents in a red envelope. But whereas in the past the money, supplemented by what was usually a smaller amount from the bride's family, was used to purchase dowry, now it is usually returned, while

Myron L. Cohen

only the empty red envelope is retained by the bride's parents. Thus the ritual is now known as "receiving a happiness" *[tao ge xi;* Hakka: *t'ao ke hi]* in contrast to receiving money. The groom's parents then give this bundle of cash to the son who is to be married for use by him and his wife. This major transformation took hold in the late 1970s and early 1980s and is linked to the elimination of dowry in most cases and its replacement by cash payments. Likewise, the common pattern is for the bride's parents to give her NT$80,000–100,000 (US$3,200–4,000), representing their smaller contribution to what will be the new couple's conjugal fund. Such a gift to their daughter, in conjunction with their returning the betrothal money to the groom's family, means that no dowry will be provided.

There are still a few cases where *pinjin* is accepted, but under such circumstances the intent of the bride's side is to provide a dowry in the form of an automobile. It was estimated for me in 1991 that such dowries were given by "fewer than 10 percent" of the families, generally wealthier, with their contributions representing the minority of cases where the bride's side assumed the heavier burden of conjugal endowment as far as dowry was concerned. But wealth is not the only factor involved, for the presentation of a car is precluded for the many men who already have one. Even if the bride's family does give the new couple a car, the total contribution of the groom's family will be greater if, as is commonly the case, it helps the couple either purchase or build a new home or apartment, usually outside of Meinong.

The demise of dowry is linked to the fact that in the minority of cases where bride and groom remain with the groom's parents, the groom's side will already own many items that in recent decades have been included in dowry, such as refrigerators and television sets. More important, the sending of dowry has become impractical because in most cases bride and groom now make their home at some distance from Meinong. I was told that parents now let the bride and groom have the money to buy what they need. The end of dowry represents the triumph of the individualistic consumer economy, where the desires of bride and groom as individuals and as a couple now dominate the exchange of wealth in the wedding process. The traditional role of dowry presentation was to endow a newly married couple in the context of their economic and residential integration into a larger family. As consumers within Taiwan's contemporary culture of consumerism, couples now select each other based on individual desire, and likewise they choose the material possessions paid for with the funds provided by their parents.

This heightened consumerism pervades Taiwanese culture today; in the village,

Fig. 10.5a–b.

a. *View across the courtyard to the old ancestral hall at the center, with piles of dried rice that have been covered with rice straw and a tarpaulin to prevent damage from rain.* Source: Photograph by Myron L. Cohen.

b. *The three-story structure is the new, vastly enlarged ancestral hall, which overlooks the open space, embraced on two sides by a combination of older and newer buildings.* Source: Photograph by Myron L. Cohen.

grand new houses are being built, and now it is the rule to equip them with air conditioners. Consumerism is hardly restricted to the young. Travel abroad is now common, especially in the generations of parents ranging in age from their late fifties to early seventies. Linked to such travel, and to Taiwan's heavily export-dependent economy, is vastly more knowledge about the world on the part of ordinary villagers, who are forging wide-ranging links on the basis of reinterpreted traditional ties, taking the form, for example, of involvement in the World Hakka Association (about ten villagers belong) and attendance at its annual meetings, held each year in a different city (and country!). Villagers also contribute to the recon-struction of ancestral halls in mainland China villages from which their ancestors migrated to Taiwan. Even more generous than such expenditures on the mainland are the many contributions to local temples and festivals or to those at important religious centers on Taiwan. Community religion flourishes in this context, in spite of the fact that religious events are not nearly as well attended as in the past—a reflection of the growth of recreational alternatives—but domestic worship of the ancestors and gods remains very strong, as does participation in temple banquets if not ritual. So the manifestations of consumerism on the part of young people with regard to family and marriage fundamentally are in accordance with the values of their parents: there is cultural consensus.

As with betrothal, wedding rituals have also been simplified since 1965, with

Myron L. Cohen

more cash transactions and fewer involving goods. Ancestor worship remains important (Figure 10.5). Prior to the wedding day the groom still proceeds with the *kin ngoe-tsou,* the Hakka phrase meaning "to honor the matrilateral ancestors," whereby he worships at the natal ancestral compounds of his mother and his father's mother; later he and his bride will worship the ancestors at his own compound. Cash payments have replaced the presentations of the *tchou-p'ien,* the Hakka term for the large cut of pork traditionally sent to the bride's side by the groom's, and the *a-p'o niouc,* also pork but for distribution by the bride's family to the bride's maternal grandmother's natal family. If the bride's maternal grandmother, or *a-p'o,* is still alive, she will be given cash, but if she has passed away, then, as of old, there must be a distribution of pork (first purchased by the groom's family) among her descendants. The transition from meat to cash presentations has been supported by many factors. Most families no longer raise pigs, so cash in any event would be required to obtain the pork. More important are the growing strength of the consumer culture and the not unrelated improvement in subsistence patterns; rich and high-quality food is now consumed on a daily basis rather than only during banquets associated with "good and bad events" *[hao shi huai shi;* Hakka: *ho-se fai-se]*—weddings, funerals, religious celebrations, and the like— as was the case even in the recent past.

Like in other contexts, the presentation of cash allows the recipients to dispose of it as they desire, in a consumer-oriented environment presenting numerous possibilities. Furthermore, the message of heightened, especially desirable, and delicious consumption—previously conveyed by pork or other desired foods—has lost much if not all of its force nowadays, when such foods are routinely consumed or, indeed, avoided because they are held to be dangerous to one's health, thus signifying a total departure from previous standards. The basic change, then, is that there has been a severing of the previous linkage between the ceremonies and rituals of "good and bad events," on the one hand, and a dramatic transition from subsistence-level consumption to the consumption of rich banquet fare, on the other.

The contrast between ordinary consumption and the feasting highlighted by ceremonial occasions has not necessarily been reduced, but the standards on either side of this contrast have gone up considerably. Both the bride's side and the groom's side give elaborate wedding banquets, now usually held in restaurants or halls hired for the occasion rather than in their residential compounds, with professional chefs preparing dishes that are costly even by present-day standards—bird's nest soup, abalone, shark fin soup, not to mention lobster and other expensive dishes not ordinarily taken as daily fare. The groom's banquet is held on the wedding day, while the bride's is now held on what had been the customary "third day" return of the bride to her natal family. When I first did fieldwork, the bride's feast was held early in the morning of the wedding day, in conjunction with the arrival of the groom's party to fetch her. But at that time some brides' families were already changing their main wedding feast into a lunchtime banquet held the next day. The present arrangement represents the fusion of what had originally been two very separate ritual undertakings. Cash gifts for weddings remain a major family expense: the standard minimum in 1995 was NT$1,200 (US$48), up from NT$1,000 two years earlier; the usual ordinary gift in 1995 was NT$1,600 (US$62).

Traditionally incorporated into the various wedding rituals were procedures designed to provide the bride with *sifangqian,* her "private money," known in Hakka as *segoi* (Cohen 1976, 177–191). Many of these are no longer practiced, such as the bride's presentation of shoes to the groom's close relatives. These had been brought with the dowry and have shared in its demise. However, during the wedding banquet the bride, as in the past, seeks out female relatives for the "insertion of flowers" into their hair. Traditionally and when I did my first fieldwork, this was a very public means for the bride to accumulate her "private money," and it still has the same function, with such payments to the bride ranging from about NT$300 (US$12) to NT$500 (US$20). One big change, however, is that the term *segoi* is now

Myron L. Cohen

far more frequently used interchangeably with the standard Mandarin *sifanqian*, albeit with the latter given a Hakka pronunciation. This is one example of a more general mandarinization of the Hakka vocabulary as used in Meinong, perhaps in part encouraged by the appearance of Hakka-language television broadcasts often involving exactly the same scripts as are read in Mandarin in other programs. It is ironic that the programming in Hakka has come about as a result of Hakka agitation for language treatment in Taiwan equal to that provided Mandarin and Hokkien or Taiwanese speakers. This effort to establish the authenticity and autonomy of Hakka ethnicity has resulted instead in an accelerated replacement of Hakka vocabulary, not to mention localisms in the Hakka-speaking areas, by terms shared with standard Mandarin and differing only in how they are pronounced.

During my first fieldwork in Yanliao, women's "private money" was still significant in family economic life, for in stem or joint families such funds defined for the daughters-in-law a sphere of property rights that in fact, and in the final analysis, served to give some economic protection and autonomy to the husband-wife unit within the larger family. Brothers could not look out for the economic interests of their own wives and children without imperiling the unity of the larger family, while their parents in the senior generation could be loyal only to this larger family if they wanted to preserve it and avoid family division, so it was left to each daughter-in-law to look after her and her children's interests. One important instrument for achieving this was her store of private money or private property. At the time of family division this private fund was merged with the husband's share of the old family estate so as to comprise the new smaller family's economic foundation. This, at least, was the husband's expectation, but given the secretive nature of his wife's holdings, it was frequently possible for her to hold on to a portion.

Present-day *sifangqian* seems to have completely lost its gendered quality, another remarkable change. It is no longer "women's private money" but simply "private money." I was told repeatedly that now everybody had *sifangqian*. One important use of such private money by men and women alike is in the numerous *piaohui*, or rotating credit clubs. It would appear that there are few if any able-bodied adults in Meinong who do not belong to one or more such clubs. For example, one village family with whom I have been on very friendly terms since my original fieldwork falls easily into the bottom quartile of village family incomes. Yet in this family the husband belongs to two NT$20,000 (US$800) rotating credit clubs while his wife belongs to one NT$20,000 club and one NT$10,000 club. The procedures are well understood and derive straight from late imperial culture. The amounts refer to the periodic payment each member must make to create a pool of funds given out through a variety of methods to a different member each club session (usually once a month). Their participation in such clubs did not precisely confirm one local resident's remark that an ordinary person would belong to no less that three of them, but given their economic circumstances, the extent of their involvement certainly showed that his remark was rather close to the truth.

The universalization of the notion of private holdings seems related to several broader trends. First, as noted above, is the transformation of family structure and family roles in the context of the emergence of a powerful consumer culture. Consumption in this context is by definition individualistic, so with the breakdown of the tightly integrated pooled economy characteristic of traditional families (stem and joint as well as conjugal), people give expression to their independence as consumers by expanding the traditional notion of "private" to include just about anybody. But this new consumer orientation is also conditioned by a traditional orientation toward wealth and money, which, together with education, were major determinates of social standing in late imperial China, given the famous deemphasis of hereditary class or castelike social alignments among the Han Chinese. That wealth was an important goal was expressed rather fabulously in late imperial culture in the famous and widespread trinity of desired ends: wealth *[fu]*, official position *[lu]*, and longevity *[shou]*. This traditional orientation has been both reinforced and individualized in modern Taiwan, and for many people it represents an aspiration far more realizable than it ever had been before.

In Yanliao in the late 1990s, as in the past, color prints expressing hopes for wealth were commonly pasted on walls inside homes. Some simply were inscribed with sayings such as "Generate wealth daily" *[Riri jiancai],* while others were adorned with images expressive of wealth and the other desired goals. People constantly talked about investments, especially regarding land speculation. In 1995 one person complained that he had lost NT$250,000 in a bad mainland China investment, while several men who had been dirt farmers when I first knew them in the 1960s compared the advantages of investing in bowling alleys in Hanoi as opposed to Shenyang or discussed how they were raising flowers for export to Japan, in some cases using seeds or bulbs imported from Holland. It is hardly the case that the substantial entrepreneurial energy manifested by village residents during the last years of the twentieth century and the first few of the twenty-first marked a significant departure from traditional orientations. Rather, at play was precisely the continued expression of these orientations under vastly enhanced opportunities for investment.

Myron L. Cohen

◄ a   b ►

c ▼

Fig. 10.6a–c. *A principal difference between the "old" village landscape and the newer one is the horizontality of older structures, as well as building materials and furnishings.*

a. *As the view along a village lane shows, single-story, red brick houses abut each other along open ditches. Rice is being dried on the road.* Source: Photograph by Myron L. Cohen.

b–c. *Whether viewed along a lane or across a field, multi-story houses made of prestressed concrete dominate, as do electrical and phone lines. The old drainage ditch has now been covered, and, even along the narrow lane, potted plants help to soften the environment.* Source: Photographs by Myron L. Cohen.

I now want to flesh out the description and analysis given above by providing an example of family arrangements in the late 1990s, including the nature of homes (Figure 10.6). My focus here is on the various arrangements within the *jia* framework. Huang Binghong's *jia* consists of eighteen people: Binghong (b. 1931), his wife (b. 1932), his three sons (b. 1953, 1955, 1960), their wives, and their children. His two daughters (one b. 1963 and one after 1965) are married and so have left this *jia*. Binghong is a tobacco farmer and also raises pigs (five hundred at the time of my visit). This is a wealthy village family whose new home, built in 1992, is one of the more impressive houses in Yanliao. Huang Qingwen, the eldest son, works for the Taiwan Railroad Administration and lives with his wife and children in their own home in Fengshan, a city not far from the much larger city of Kaohsiung. Binghong helped Qingwen build the house, splitting costs evenly with him. Also living in Fengshan with his wife and children is Huang Qinghe, Binghong's second son, who works for the municipal Water Supply Bureau. Like his older brother, he has a house, likewise built with his father covering half the cost. Huang Qingmu,

Fig. 10.7. *Although these are not the homes of the Huangs, they portray the exterior and interior styles of prosperous dwellings in Yanliao as the twenty-first century begins.* Source: Photographs by Myron L. Cohen.

the third son, and his wife and children live with his parents in the Yanliao house; they take their meals together with his parents, and he and his father jointly run their farm. Although Binghong says that his first and second sons are "economically independent," he adds that they "have not divided." When I visited the family, it was a Sunday, and the oldest son was there helping. According to Binghong, "Both sons come back to help on Sundays; they will do what has to be done." Also living with Binghong is his younger brother Yonghong, whose "health is not good" and who has never married. In this *jia* Binghong has his own car, as do each of his sons. Yet another indicator of their prosperity is that Binghong and his wife have gone on tours to mainland China, Japan, and Korea. While Binghong's second son's marriage was a love match, those of his other two sons and two daughters were arranged, a reflection of how new the present-day almost total dominance of love marriages is (Figure 10.7).

In 1965 Binghong had already married and was living with his parents (who are now deceased), his younger brother, and his own young children. This, then, was a stem family, and because Yonghong never married or otherwise separated, there had been no instance of *jia* division as of 1994. The economic independence of Binghong's two eldest sons is typical of such circumstances prior to *jia* division. Their father's help in setting up their homes in Fengshan really represents a continuation of the *jia*'s traditional endowment of a new conjugal unit, but now in the context of the modernizing trend toward conjugal independence. Although the sons living outside keep their salaries, they return to Yanliao on Sundays and holidays to help on the farm. And, of course, they return for the lunar New Year, when the *jia* lives and feasts together in the *tuannianfan*, a display of commensality that in fact defines the *jia* as a kind of moral unity no matter what the economic ties among its constituent individuals or conjugal units may be. In fact this overriding unity allows just for the flexibility and adaptability in cooperative relationships among *jia* members that makes continuing membership in the *jia* so attractive to most people. So *fen jia* remains of importance precisely because it continues to signify a massive change in the social ties among those involved, given the continuing importance of the *jia*.

In spite of the major transition from the economically and socially highly integrated family units that still dominated Yanliao in the mid-1960s to an individualization of finances by the 1990s, expressed as private holdings common to men and women, the corporate dimension of the family is still an important factor in villagers' lives. Linked to the continuity of *jia* as a corporation is the maintenance

Fig. 10.8. *This rural homestead compound in Sichuan sits amid a rice paddy. Here the rice harvest is in progress.* Source: Photograph by Myron L. Cohen.

of its strong patrilineal and patrilocal (virilocal) orientation, such that when women marry they are still considered to have moved from membership in their natal *jia* to their husband's. This membership transfer is with respect to the *jia* as a corporate entity, irrespective of the fact that the newly married couple resides as a conjugal unit in its own home and perhaps in a city where neither the husband's nor the wife's parents are. What has changed markedly in Yanliao are the relationships among people belonging to such a family corporation. On the China mainland there have been parallel changes, as I noted during fieldwork in the Hebei village of Yangmansa in 1986–1987, and in one village near Shanghai and one in Sichuan, both studied during 1990 field research. I have already written on family life in Yangmansa (Cohen 1998), where the term *danguo,* to "go it alone," refers precisely to sons or brothers living apart and with economic autonomy prior to formal family

Myron L. Cohen

division. As in Yanliao, Yangmansa parents commonly help their sons establish residential separation, but in this Hebei village the common procedure during the period of my fieldwork was for the parents to build a new separate house for each son, except that the youngest frequently stayed with his parents and succeeded to their home. *Danguo* would follow, and then, at a later date, formal division with a written division contract. While the term *danguo* is used elsewhere in North China (see Yan 2003), it was not commonly employed in the other mainland villages that were my field sites. Nevertheless, the process to which it refers characterized the village near Shanghai where, in the absence of sufficient space for new housing, it was common to rebuild and expand the parental home, adding additional stories so as to accommodate sons and their wives within the common residence but as economically autonomous units. Such a residential pattern was also observed in mid-1970s Taibei, where conjugal autonomy, combined with the maintenance of *jia* ties, received similar expression (see Tang 1978). In the Sichuan village, located on the Chengdu Plain, new residences were built or compounds expanded; again married couples commenced living independently shortly after marriage but avoided formal family division until many years later (Figure 10.8).

In spite of the vastly different historical experiences on Taiwan and mainland China during modern times, modernization has similarly impacted family life and led to changes in housing forms. The moral and strategic importance of the *jia* continues to receive expression in the face of forces of consumerism and conjugalism, which encourage smaller residential families focusing on the husband and wife. Conjugal units are the important parties to *jia* division, and it of course means that there must be at least two of them for the *jia*-family distinction to have any force. Current demographic trends throughout China are working to blur this distinction due to declining birth rates. Whether these are the results of state-imposed restrictions on family size or free choices under circumstances of rapid modernization, the smaller size of families and the consequent increase in the number of one-son families—or families with daughters only, such that even if a man marries in there will be only one conjugal unit in that generation—have the ironic consequence that *jia* and residential family increasingly are becoming one and the same thing. This indeed was the traditional pattern, but because the new equivalency of *jia* and family is based upon the absence of more than one son, it may in fact finally spell the end of the *jia* as a structure of social and moral relationships.

FRANCESCA BRAY

11   The Inner Quarters

Oppression or Freedom?

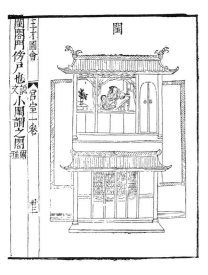

Fig. 11.1. *Women's quarters, as depicted in an encyclopedia of 1609. The image is accompanied by two definitions from classical dictionaries of the Han dynasty.* Source: *Sancai tuhui* 1609, 1009.

In late imperial China even the poorest and most humble families set apart some portion of their domestic quarters as a secluded space for the women. Men and women who were not related were not supposed to have any physical or even social contact, and within the family, male and female in-laws were supposed to keep their distance—eating at separate tables, for example. Men were expected to leave the inner quarters for work early in the morning, and except in rare circumstances respectable women were supposed neither to leave the house nor to allow anyone from outside the household to enter.

To the modern Western mind, the very existence in imperial China of *neifang,* "inner quarters," or *gui,* "women's apartments," suggests an oppressive patriarchal order in which men confined women, the better to control and exploit them (Figure 11.1). Yet feminist historians recently have shown that within the context of late imperial society and its cultural ideals, the existence of "separate spheres" could offer some advantages and satisfactions and that it was not uncommon for life in the inner quarters to be experienced as active and gratifying. In this essay I discuss the constraints and the opportunities that the segregated lifestyle of late imperial China might have offered to different women, depending on their class, their age, and their rank within the family.

Strict doctrines of gender segregation can be traced back well into pre-imperial times. As early as the fifth century B.C., Confucius had difficulty persuading one hard-line disciple that if he saw a woman drowning, it was not improper but humane to grab her by the hand to save her. Even at that early time, women were assigned to the "inside," *nei,* and men to the "outside," *wai.* These terms referred not simply to inside and outside spaces, but also to the activities and concerns appropriate to each, and the boundaries between the two were strictly policed. According to the *Book of Rites,* one of the five Confucian classics, "Male and female should not sit together, nor have the same stand for clothes, nor use the same towel and comb, nor let their hands touch in giving and receiving. A sister-in-law and brother-in-law do not interchange inquiries. . . . Outside affairs should not be talked of inside the threshold [of the women's apartments], nor inside affairs outside it" (translated by Raphals 1998, 224).

It is probable that in the early dynasties such ideals of rigorous separation of male and female were largely confined to the elite. However, beginning in the Song dynasty, about a thousand years ago, neo-Confucian philosophers further elaborated the precepts regulating relations between men and women in terms that gradually became the orthodoxy at all levels of society (Bray 1997, 151–172). In a work on domestic etiquette, the statesman and scholar Sima Guang (1019–1086) set down detailed instructions for the spatial segregation of the sexes, and for communication between the inner and outer domains, as they should be practiced in an elite household. Sima Guang's prescriptions were soon almost universally familiar, for they were incorporated by the famous neo-Confucian master Zhu Xi into his *Family Rituals* of ca. 1169. The *Family Rituals* gave instructions for the correct performance of ancestral worship, weddings, and funerals; it was widely quoted in works for popular circulation, and the ceremonial practices laid out by Zhu Xi were incorporated into the official legal code a century later by the Yuan emperors (Ebrey 1991a, 1991b).

Sima Guang writes:

> In housing, there should be a strict demarcation between the inner and outer parts, with a door separating them. The two parts should share neither a well, a wash room, nor a privy. The men are in charge of all affairs on the outside, the women manage the inside affairs. During the day, without good reason the men do not stay in their private rooms nor the women go beyond the inner door. . . . [Menservants were supposed to enter the inner quarters only to conduct repairs or in emergencies; maids were not supposed to go outside.] The doorman and old servants serve to pass messages and objects between the inner and outer quarters of the house, but they must not be allowed to enter rooms or kitchens at will. (Translated in Ebrey 1991a, 29)

Referring to this passage, the well-known moralist Yuan Cai (fl. 1140–1195) commented: "This is over half of what is needed to manage a household" (Ebrey 1984, 286). Sima Guang writes of a large compound in which the front courtyards were the "outer quarters" used to receive visitors and conduct business. The inner quarters were at the back of the compound, separated from the rest of the house by an interior gate. In many large houses the inner quarters were a separate building in a back courtyard. A Japanese book of 1799 entitled *Shinzoku kibun* [Qing customs], gives detailed and lavishly illustrated first-hand accounts of merchant affairs and everyday life in the prosperous cities of the lower Yangzi, the region known as Jiangnan. It says that in the merchants' houses of the southern cities the

Fig. 11.2. *Ordinary houses and shops. "Ordinary" means that the houses do not belong to officials. The big house in the foreground is probably a merchant house. The front courtyard and hall are where guests would be received; the room in the center, up the steps, is where the ancestral tablets were placed. The inner quarters are at the back. At the top left we are shown a simple peasant's house, with a stall for the ox at the front. The two shops at top right are a physician's consulting room and pharmacy on the left and a cloth shop on the right.*
Source: *Shinzoku kibun* 1799, 72–73.

doors to the women's quarters were covered with a curtain, but at night the double doors were closed and locked. In more ordinary houses, consisting of a single building, male visitors were received in the main room or on the front veranda, and the side rooms served as the inner quarters. In a poor family's cottage, a curtain hung across the kitchen door might demarcate the inner quarters, behind which the women retreated when male visitors occupied the single living room (*Shinzoku kibun*, 112ff.) (Figure 11.2).

Within the house social and generational rank was clearly marked by the allocation of rooms. According to geomantic principles, the cosmically most auspicious room was the one facing south at the center of the main hall, and this is where the family altar and ancestral tablets were placed. The private quarters or bedrooms of the senior couple and their eldest son (the ritual heir) and his wife would also be auspiciously located, south-facing and centrally placed. Younger married sons and their wives and children would usually occupy south-facing rooms in a different courtyard or further to the side of the hall. Chinese law allowed a man to have only one wife who was his legal and ritual partner. Concubines were much lower in status, and their rooms were located less auspiciously, in east- or west-facing wings.

Young children of both sexes lived with their mothers, but Sima Guang described the usual practice when he said that boys must move out of the inner quarters at the age of ten (Ebrey 1991a, 33). Although a married man spent the night

The Inner Quarters

Fig. 11.3. *A man with his wife in front of her bed.* Source: *Lu Ban jing,* edition of ca. 1600, as reproduced in Ruitenbeek 1993, 2/15b.

in the room of his wife or concubine (Figure 11.3), during the day he would leave for the fields or for his office or shop; an educated man who was not a serving official would repair to his study in another part of the house (Bray 1997, 136–139). Men who tarried in the inner quarters were not true gentlemen and were likely to come to a bad end. Baoyu, the hero of the eighteenth-century novel *The Dream of the Red Chamber* (also called *The Story of the Stone*), is the despair of his ambitious father, for he avoids the outer sphere entirely and spends all his time with his female relatives. If it were not possible for men to go out, the inner spaces would be reclassified during the day to accommodate them. In the northern provinces the winters were bitterly cold; no outside work could be done, and everyone had to stay indoors to keep warm. The typical village house in the Beijing region consisted of three rooms: a main room containing the altar in the center, and on either side a bedroom containing a *kang,* a hollow brick platform heated by flues that led from the stove. At night one bedroom would be occupied by the senior couple, the other by their eldest son and his wife and children. But during the winter days all the men and boys would occupy one bedroom, while the women and children would crowd into the other (Körner 1959, 6).

There were occasions when inner and outer worlds met in the same space. Perhaps the most significant of these were domestic rituals, including the ceremonies of the ancestral cult; the rituals of maturity for children, such as capping for sons and

Francesca Bray

Fig. 11.4. *Ancestral sacrifice in the main hall. The patriarch is prostrated in the center, with his four sons beside him. Behind each married man stands his wife. A grandson is also present. Daughters and concubines did not participate in these ceremonies since they were not members of the lineage.* Source: *Shinzoku kibun* 1799, 496–497.

pinning up the hair for daughters; betrothals; weddings; and funerals. The ritual unit was the married couple, and wives played an essential role in all Chinese domestic rituals. The liturgies laid down by Zhu Xi and other authorities describe performances that resemble dances, where senior man and woman match movement for movement and gesture for gesture, repeated by all the married couples in the family in order of birth and generation (Figure 11.4). Where the man presents a cup of wine, the woman presents a bowl of tea; where the men ascend the right hand staircase, the women ascend the left. A man became a full ritual member of his family by virtue of having a wife as a ritual partner. A concubine had no ritual status; even if her husband's legal wife died, she could never move up to fill the wifely role because she had not been presented to the ancestors when she entered the household. Concubines therefore played no role in domestic rituals, and their inferior status was reflected in the relatively inauspicious geomantic location of their rooms.

Other occasions when inner and outer worlds met might include mealtimes. But even in relatively easy-going households, like those described in the *Shinzoku kibun,* no promiscuous mixing was allowed at meals. Until they were twelve or thirteen, boys and girls ate together at the same table, sitting with their immediate family group of the father, his children, his wife, and his unmarried sisters. Once they reached puberty, the boys had to sit separately. A bride might not eat at the same table as her father-in-law, nor could a wife sit with her husband's brothers. Sima

The Inner Quarters

Fig. 11.5. *An old couple eats together as their son and his wife pledge them. From a Wanli (1573–1620) edition of the Yuan dynasty collection by Gao Ming,* Pipa ji *[Tales of the lute].* Source: Zhou 1993, 302–303.

Fig. 11.6. *Celebrating an old lady's birthday. Her sons, who have become officials and are wearing their official robes, have returned home for the occasion and are attending the old lady with their wives. From a Wanli edition of* Chuxiang wulun quanbei zhongxiao *[Tales of surpassing virtue and of perfect filiality].* Source: Zhou 1993, 90.

Fig. 11.7. *An official and his wife celebrating the Lantern Festival (the first full moon after Chinese New Year) with a puppet show. From a Wanli edition of the moral story* Zhaoshi guer ji *[The tale of Orphan Zhao].* Source: Zhou 1993, 70.

Guang's rules of etiquette allow only the senior couple to eat together. They are served first, at a separate table (Figure 11.5), and then the men sit down at one table, the women at another, ranked in order of age. The children too sit at a separate table, with the boys on the left and the girls on the right, in order of age (Ebrey 1991a, 27). A more common practice was for men to eat together in the outer room and for women to eat together in their own quarters (*Shinzoku kibun*, 155).

There were various occasions where married couples spent leisure time together. Illustrations of family scenes depict couples presenting their respects to the widowed matriarch (Figure 11.6), celebrating the festivals of the year (Figure 11.7), or simply enjoying a meal together. All respectable social activities involving people who were not family, however, were single-sex. Dorothy Ko (1994, ch. 5) documents how a busy official, living under the same roof as his wife, might lead a very separate life. Even if her social life was active, it was almost exclusively female. As an ethnographer of Guangdong in the 1920s put it, "There is no social life between men and women in the villages. The custom and ethical teaching of the Chinese are that men and women, unless they are members of the same family, should keep apart as much as possible; so even the male and female members of the same class never join together in a party, a feast, or a celebration. In making calls, extending congratulations or consolations, the men visit the men and the women visit the women" (Hayes 1985, 89). This pattern of behavior was already well established in

Francesca Bray

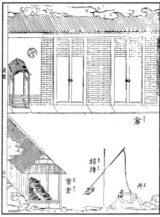

Fig. 11.8. *"Two mothers longing for their sons."* On the right the older lady talks to her younger visitor, while on the left her steward shows in a fortune teller who will divine how their respective sons are doing. From a Wanli edition of the Ming fiction collection by Gao Lian, Yuzan ji [Tales of the jade hairpin]. Source: Fu 1981, 150–151.

Fig. 11.9. *The back courtyard of a late-eighteenth-century Jiangnan merchant house, with the kitchen on the right; a well, storerooms, and the toilet (left); and shower room (right) in the shed next to the kitchen.* Source: Shinzoku kibun 1799, 142–143.

the Ming and Qing dynasties, as we can tell from sources like novels or the etiquette sections of encyclopedias (Figure 11.8).

Observing the proper separation of the sexes was considered essential to the social and cosmic order, and not only space, but also work was strictly divided. The idea was that upper-class men studied and went into government; lower-class men were farmers, craftsmen, or merchants. Women's work was essential and complementary to that of men. Women were responsible for preparing food (Figure 11.9), for looking after the children and elderly, and for producing textiles and making clothes. The inner quarters might include heated rooms for raising silkworms (Figure 11.10) or sheds housing elaborate draw-looms (Figure 11.11) or reeling machines (Figure 11.12); in poorer families the equipment might include no more than a simple cotton loom and a spinning wheel (Figure 11.13) in a corner of the living room. The cloth that women spun and wove was not just for family needs. Until the late sixteenth century families were taxed in equivalent amounts of grain (produced by men) and cloth (produced by women), and many families would sell surplus cloth for cash. So although women conducted their work secluded within the inner quarters, what they produced tied them to the wider world as productive subjects of the Chinese state and as contributors to the family finances (Bray 1997; Gates 1996; Mann 1997).

Although women's work was ideally all performed indoors, it was recognized

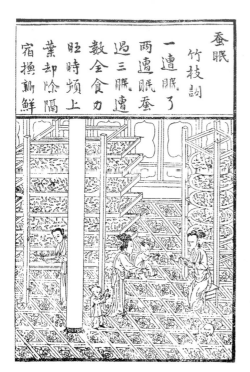

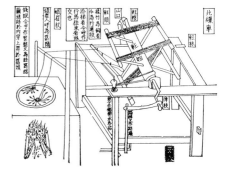

▲ **Fig. 11.10.** *Feeding the silkworms. The worms are set out on wicker trays, round or square, stacked vertically in wooden frames. The woman on the left is adding chopped mulberry leaves to the trays.* Source: *Bianmin tuzuan;* edition by Shi and Kang 1982, section 2:18.

Fig. 11.11. *A draw-loom. A tall, spacious room was required for these looms, which were used for weaving expensive figured silks. Here the loom is shown in a shed in the women's quarters of a well-to-do household.* Source: *Gengzhi tu,* Kangxi imperial edition of 1696.

that certain duties took a wife outside. In many regions peasant women would help out in the fields at busy seasons, even though they were hampered by their bound feet, and certain field tasks, like picking tea or cotton (Figure 11.14), routinely fell to women. If the family rice paddies were too far from the house for the farmer to come home for a quick meal at noon, he would have his wife or daughter bring a meal in a bamboo basket, together with bowl and chopsticks (*Shinzoku kibun,* 182). Women did a lot of farm work near the house or in the courtyard—for instance, husking and grinding millet on the small rim-mills common in North China. The rooms of the house were not big enough for dressing looms, so that had to be done outside (Figure 11.15), and washing clothes, going to market, or fetching water from the well were other necessary tasks that were likely to take women outside their walls.

In principle upper-class women were expected to work productively too, sitting at their looms or supervising tasks in the kitchen. But by late imperial times, the most productive work that many well-off women did was a little embroidery (Figure 11.16). Embroidery was in fact often seen as important cultural work, both by women and by men. Men saw it as a symbol of domestic female harmony, while women were aware that the quilts and shoes they embroidered together would pass beyond the walls of the inner chambers to serve as one of the few material links

Francesca Bray

11.15
◄

◄ **Fig. 11.12.** *Machines for reeling silk thread from cocoons. The cocoons were floated in a pan of water heated by a stove. The hot water loosened the gum around the cocoon so the single long fiber could be wound off. The threads from several cocoons were fed together through an eyelet (the square hole in a copper coin), and as they emerged from the water, they were twisted into a single yarn and wound onto a reel.* Source: *Nong shu*, 1530 edition, 22/26a–27b.

Fig. 11.13. *Spinning wheel for cotton. These wheels were found in almost every rural home in late imperial China.* Source: *Nong shu*, 1530 edition, 25/6b.

Fig. 11.14. *Picking cotton. A group of young women is hard at work on the left, while on the right a granny and a little boy, helpfully carrying a wicker basket around his neck, look on. A woodblock print of 1808 based on an original painting of ca. 1765.* Source: *Shouyi guangxun* 1808, 1/14b–15a.

Fig. 11.15. *Dressing a cotton loom. The forty-foot warp threads must be threaded through the heddles, wound onto the warp-beam (bottom right), and sized with starch to prevent fraying (top left). This task was most conveniently performed in the courtyard or even outside the compound.* Source: *Shouyi guangxun* 1808, 2/18a.

Fig. 11.16. *Young ladies at their embroidery.* Source: *Shinzoku kibun* 1799, 338–339.

between the senior women and the family daughters, who took such objects with them as part of their trousseau when they left home to get married (Bray 1997, 265–269). *Shinzoku kibun* (p. 155) tells us that in wealthy homes the ladies did not make clothes for the family themselves, but some did handicrafts or embroidery as a hobby. For many less-well-off urban families, embroideries produced both for domestic and for Western markets became an important source of income starting in the eighteenth century (Mann 1997).

The Inner Quarters

The inner quarters were a place for leisure and family life as well as working and sleeping. In the inner quarters of a merchant family, as described in *Shinzoku kibun*, the married ladies' rooms were on the ground floor of the building, and the upper floor contained the daughters' bedrooms. It was reached by a staircase and had small windows covered with blinds to protect the young ladies from intruding glances. The floor was of polished boards, and the entrance was a double door. There were mats and rugs on the floor, with tables, chairs, and stools. The panels of the door stood open, but a woven blind hung inside. At the front of the top story was built the *lutai*, or "dew platform," a large balcony supported on pillars, with balustrades of wood or bamboo on three sides and an awning overhead to keep off the sun. With pots of orchids arrayed against the balustrade, the dew platform was a fragrant and breezy refuge from the summer heat (Figure 11.17). It served as a family sitting room, a place where women would work at their embroidery and other tasks and where the men of the family joined them to chat over breakfast and to relax over a pipe in the evenings (*Shinzoku kibun*, 122). Family parties for viewing the moon in the eighth month were held on the dew terrace. So too was the girls' ceremony of the Double Seventh, the night when the constellations figuring the legendary lovers, the Herd Boy and the Weaving Girl, met in the sky and when offerings of fruit and cakes were made as young girls prayed to be given skills

Fig. 11.17. *The dew platform. There is a Buddhist altar flanked by calligraphy scrolls inside on the left and a small table holding books and writing implements against the back wall; in the room beyond on the left is a bed with a rush mat, suitable for warm summer weather.* Source: *Shinzoku kibun* 1799, 132–133.

Francesca Bray

Fig. 11.18. *Lady's chamber.* Source: *Shinzoku kibun* 1799, 114–115.

with the needle. In the homes of poor families without a dew platform the offerings had to be made at ground level, in the courtyard (*Shinzoku kibun*, 40–43).

The *Shinzoku kibun* illustration of the dew platform shows a glimpse of a Buddhist altar. In late imperial China, Buddhist piety was particularly associated with women and with the lower classes. Since Song times at least, women had been particularly attracted by the boddhisattva Guanyin, a merciful goddess to whom women who were pregnant or childless turned for protection and help. Although popular Buddhist doctrines held that women were intrinsically polluted and therefore barred from immediate salvation, the prospect of reincarnation and eventual admission to paradise and the possibility of improving one's spiritual status through good works and piety made Buddhism an attractive escape for women from the shackles of the Confucian order.

In well-off households the inner quarters provided each married woman with a room of her own, where she kept her private belongings. Woodblock illustrations of sixteenth- and seventeenth-century novels and the pictures commissioned for the *Shinzoku kibun* at the end of the eighteenth century show the inner quarters of homes as elegant retreats with every creature comfort. A lady's bedroom would contain an elaborate alcove bed, a dressing table, tables and chairs, and a washstand with bowl and towels, most of which she would have brought with her as part of her dowry. She was well provided with toilet articles, mirrors, and sewing boxes. Musical instruments might be hung on the wall, and in a separate alcove, which could be locked, were piled her clothes chests, jewelry boxes, and household goods (Figure 11.18). The elaborate canopy bed, carved or lacquered and hung with

Fig. 11.19. *Ming dynasty bed. Nelson-Atkins Museum of Art, Kansas City, Missouri.* Source: Used with the permission of The Nelson-Atkins Museum of Art, Kansas City, Missouri (Purchase: Nelson Trust 64-4/4).

Fig. 11.20. *A young lady's chamber with a spotted bamboo bed on which a book lies open; sewing implements and boxes that might contain either makeup or writing implements are lying on the table by the bed. From the 1602 edition of* Jingchai ji *[Tales of the thorn hairpin], collected by the Yuan author Ke Danqiu.* Source: Fu 1981, 132–133.

draperies, symbolized the woman's status as a wife and mother, and in illustrations it is always shown as the most prominent feature of a lady's quarters (Figure 11.19). A table in front of the bed served as a dressing table or as a desk for reading, writing, and painting (Figure 11.20).

Sons inherited equal shares of the patrilineal property, of which land was usually the most valuable component. But patrimony was communal property, held in trust for future members of the lineage. At no stage in their lives could Chinese men be said to own it outright. By late imperial times women did not inherit family property, but their families provided them with a dowry when they wed. The ownership of this incoming property was in constant dispute. The strict Confucians claimed that it became part of the joint family property of the groom's lineage; when she came to her new home, the bride should give it over to her parents-in-law, or at least ask their approval for any use she made of it. If Confucian moralists made so strong a point of this, it is because a contending school of thought saw dowries as women's private property, to use as they would—not least because they had often produced or acquired it by their own hard work, weaving fine cloth for their own use or selling it for cash to buy other necessaries. Cases are recorded where women used their dowry wealth to start a business or buy land on their own account, lend money to their husbands, or make gifts to a temple (Bray 1997, 139, 188).

Francesca Bray

A poor woman's dowry might consist at best of some pots and pans, quilts, and a few clothes. A rich woman in late imperial times would take to her new home a bed carved in precious wood, a chest of clothes for each season, jewelry, fine textiles, and cash, as well as household goods. All these were kept in the woman's own room. In the houses described in *Shinzoku kibun* the wives kept their belongings in a locked alcove, and even the maids had a key for their rooms, but the men had nothing to lock up. Paradoxically the patriarchal order sought to control women by confining them, but in the process it created private spaces that served as sites of resistance to its control.

The relation between female virtue and seclusion was construed in two different ways in late imperial thought, with very different implications for the status of women. Either women were capable of moral choices and the pursuit of virtue, or they were innately immoral and lacking in self-control so that female "virtue" was in fact an absence of vice imposed by male control and strict spatial segregation. The first position was consonant with the view that male and female spheres had equal dignity and worth and was based on the premise that women, just like men, were naturally capable of moral and intellectual cultivation. The wife of a busy official would often be expected to run not only the household, but also the family property. The husband of Miss Li (1104–1177) was able to concentrate entirely on his responsibilities in government, "never having asked about family supplies." Miss Li took on the management of their property as her responsibility, buying fertile fields and building a house by a stream. Once a peasant came into the courtyard carrying a sack of rice on his back, to the amazement of Miss Li's husband, who had no idea who he was or what he carried. She just laughed and said, "That is our rent" (Ebrey 1993, 191). Wives commonly took on these managerial tasks, which brought them into contact with stewards, builders, tenants, and other men not of their family, right through the late imperial period (Ko 1994; McDermott 1990).

By the sixteenth century it was also becoming common for scholars to exalt the role of mothers as educators and to advocate more and better education for women (Ko 1994). A literate woman could teach her sons the basics of reading and morality by taking them through the simpler classics. When boys reached the age of seven or eight, they would go on to a tutor or to school, but many distinguished men continued to consult their mothers as they progressed with their studies and careers (Hsiung 1994). In some circles women were considered no less capable of intellectual or literary achievement than men (Figure 11.21), and the fact that they were debarred from public affairs was thought to confer on them a heightened purity

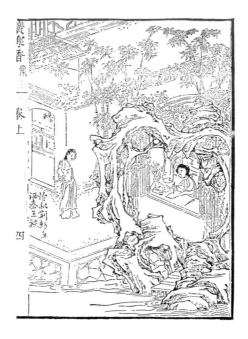

Fig. 11.21. *A young lady's room, here a garden studio such as a man of literary tastes might have, except for the prominence of the bed and its draperies. The young woman is shown sitting at her writing desk in front of the bed. From a collection of magical tales,* Guang han xiang *[The cold fragrance diffused], published in the Kangxi period (1662–1722).* Source: Fu 1981, 920.

of understanding and refinement of judgment in moral matters. Providing a formal education for daughters gradually spread from a few refined families to a more general practice of the urban well-to-do, and the perils of hiring a tutor for one's daughters became a standard element in the plots of plays and novels.

From this perspective, then, women were worthy partners of men, and a woman's virtue was not the product of her seclusion but stemmed from her moral character. But another view, which was probably more widespread in late imperial China, held that moral education and decorous behavior within the confines of the inner quarters offered no safeguard against the perils of the outer world. A woman found in the wrong place was given no credit for purity of intention. This was certainly the perspective embodied in the law. Qing legal records include cases where a woman of a country family was seen in the company of a man in some place such as the garden of the house; the conclusion automatically drawn was that she was involved in an illicit sexual relationship (Sommer 2001). That women were morally inferior and untrustworthy and that they must be kept locked up if the honor of the family was to be preserved was certainly the view most frequently expressed in the patriarchal genre known as "household instructions," or *jiaxun,* a genre extremely popular among the petty gentry of the late imperial period (Furth 1990).

Strict patriarchs were especially nervous of the people to whom they referred contemptuously as *liu po,* "the six kinds of old crone": matchmakers, Buddhist and

Francesca Bray

Daoist nuns, women herbalists, fortune-tellers, and midwives. Such women regularly entered the inner quarters of strange houses for professional purposes. Except for the matchmakers, without whose help no marriage could be arranged (and whose role was sanctioned in orthodox liturgies), orthodox males viewed all of these women as a threat to the morality of their wives and daughters; they also feared that they would swindle money out of them for nefarious purposes. These women peddled wares and knowledge of which such men had no need or of which they actively disapproved: fertility drugs and abortifacients, religious comfort and promises of salvation, charms, and fortune-telling. In fact it seems probable that many of the herbal remedies and other services for which respectable women paid were much less seditious than the men liked to think. Probably one of the greatest attractions of these women's visits for the ladies was that they brought in news from the world beyond the walls of the inner quarters.

Although it was easier for well-off families to follow the stricter rules of gendered segregation, the majority of ordinary women in late imperial China shared the commitment of ladies to demure behavior. Even in the Song dynasty poor women seem to have done their best to dress modestly and keep out of men's view whenever possible (Ebrey 1993). Poor families were just as jealous of their women's respectability as gentry, but apart from the seasonal farm tasks mentioned above, their women routinely left the home to buy fresh food at the market, to get water from the well, or to do washing at the river. These were the places where poor women could chat to other women and exchange the gossip that Chinese men condemned so strongly—perhaps because, as Margery Wolf (1968) argues, it often operated as a powerful form of social control over people abusing their authority, whether it was a man who beat his wife or a woman who mistreated her daughter-in-law.

Some outings were permissible for women of all classes. Many women looked forward to a visit to the operas put on in villages and cities all over China to celebrate festivals or lineage commemorations. Some operas, usually those chosen by elders for lineage celebrations, told morally exalted tales of successful sons and virtuous daughters-in-law; others had plots of romantic love or featured young women who won fame as warriors or who triumphed (albeit disguised as men) in the imperial examinations (Tanaka 1985). Women of all classes also liked to visit temples and to go on pilgrimages, if their husbands would give them permission. Childless women offered incense to the Goddess of Mercy, Guanyin, or to the many other deities of the late imperial period associated with fertility. Old women, as

Fig. 11.22. *Student Zhang falls in love with Oriole at the Monastery for Eternal Salvation. Attributed to Qiu Ying (ca. 1494–ca. 1552). Illustration to* Xixiang ji *[The story of the western wing], a Yuan dynasty collection.* Source: Courtesy East Asian Library, University of California, Berkeley.

death approached, wanted to pray for salvation or reincarnation in a better life. Elite men, even when they studied Buddhism and visited temples, affected to be free of vulgar religiosity and the emotionality that went with it. They regarded women's participation in such outings with deep suspicion: in operas as in novels, Buddhist and Daoist temples were depicted as promiscuous places where love affairs were likely to occur (Figure 11.22) (Leung 1983). And when women grouped together for a pilgrimage, even if no worse mischief occurred, they were sure to lose all sense of decorum and start behaving like spendthrift hoydens, casting dignity to the wind and literally kicking up their heels in unaccustomed physical freedom. A typical male view of these pious expeditions is conveyed in the scene depicted by a seven-

Francesca Bray

teenth-century novelist where "like a pack of wolves and dogs, the whole herd of women stampeded their donkeys, overtaking one another turn by turn" (Dudbridge 1992, 52).

Elite women probably had the fewest opportunities to venture beyond their own walls. Dorothy Ko (1994) discusses various forays outside the walls of the house that some women might make: scenic outings, boating and picnics, drinking and poetry parties with women relatives and friends, or long journeys accompanying a husband to official duties in a new part of the country. But only a privileged few had this degree of freedom, and their more secluded friends often envied their exposure to broad horizons and dramatic nature. The only travels most ladies experienced were proxy journeys, made by reading, looking at paintings, or sending letters to other women equally confined.

What effect did female seclusion have on women's ideas about themselves? In the case of gentry women, Dorothy Ko argues that seclusion provided freedom and dignity:

> In Ming-Qing households, the innermost realm of the private sphere was the prerogative of women. The women's quarters, tucked away in inconspicuous corners of the gentry housing compound, were off limits even to adult men in the family. In facilitating the development of her self-image and identity as woman, this cloistering had a positive effect on women's culture. Mothers and housewives, who took pride in their calling to be the guardian of familial morality, welcomed the identification of women with domesticity. Hence women did not feel the need to challenge the age-old ideology prescribing the functional separations between the sexes. (1992, 14)

Ko argues that gentry women in this period were "oblivious" to the hierarchical dimension of this doctrine of separate spheres. In my opinion, it is more likely that they were conscious of it but accepted it as a natural fact.

The evidence from the merchants who contributed accounts to *Shinzoku kibun* tends to confirm Dorothy Ko's revisionist interpretation, except that they portray an agreeable intimacy between men and women. They describe a train of life in which they pass perhaps the most relaxed and agreeable hours of the day in the inner quarters. After the household head had washed and combed his hair in the mornings, we are told, he would repair to the women's quarters to drink tea and smoke a pipe, and then the whole family would sit down to breakfast together (*Shinzoku kibun,* 155). The merchants describe the lives of their wives as cloistered but do not mention moral inferiority or the perils of cuckoldry. Poor women's lives they portray as necessarily less confined. Though many neo-Confucians railed against the moral perils of embroidery, the merchants speak of it as a charming and companionable occupation. Though they do say that of course girls cannot leave the house to go to school, they do not condemn educating daughters at home. The sequestered quarters of the women emerge in these descriptions as the most pleasant and relaxed part of the house, the place for family parties and cheerful evenings, cool in summer and well warmed with braziers in winter.

The moralists, however, commonly represented women as emotional, willful, and likely to quarrel among themselves. Was this true, and if so, was it a natural outcome of seclusion? Were women the worst enemies of other women, or did they see each other as friends and allies, as Ko's work suggests? Here I think it is essential to distinguish between women who were related by birth and those who were thrown together by marriage—an experience of alienation to which Chinese men were never exposed. The moralistic literature that depicts women as quarrelsome and selfish focuses on the tensions among women related by marriage, and they were undoubtedly considerable.

Incoming brides had no preexisting ties to their new family, and relations between insiders and outsiders were often very difficult. In gentry households a new bride was unlikely to receive physical ill treatment, but she would still find herself outside her own home for the first time, as a very junior member of the hierarchy. Many families struggled to provide their daughters with good dowries so that their new family would treat them with respect and kindness. Sometimes poor families would drown newborn girls because they knew they would not be able to afford a decent dowry. Local magistrates tried to ban this practice, which they regarded with horror; sometimes they even attempted to raise money to provide small dowries for poor families (T'ien 1988, 26). Even with a dowry, in poor households a new bride was likely to be treated as an unpaid servant and set to do all the unpleasant chores. Peasant mothers taught their daughters lengthy songs of despair that were part of the wedding ceremony: torn from her mother, aunts, and sisters, as she set off for her new home, the young woman felt as if she had died and was making the descent into hell (Johnson 1988).

Relationships among women brought together by marriage were fraught with structural difficulties, and this was undoubtedly exacerbated by the fact that seclusion threw these women into each other's company with few opportunities for avoidance or escape. In many poor families the relationship between mother- and

Francesca Bray

Fig. 11.23. *The childbirth chamber. The new mother is sitting on her bed, propped up by piles of quilts to prevent sudden movement and hemorrhaging. A maid or perhaps the wet nurse is holding the baby.* Source: *Shinzoku kibun* 1799, 317.

Fig. 11.24. *A couple present their newborn son to the matriarch while the younger brother and his wife look on. From a Wanli edition of the anonymous Ming fiction collection* Qingpao ji [Tales of the dark robe]. Source: Zhou 1993, 113.

daughter-in-law, at least before the birth of a son, was that between tyrant and slave, and it was common for unmarried sisters to despise and exploit their brothers' new wives. Another source of friction was the rivalry between a wife and her husband's concubines and any of the maids he might choose to favor with his sexual attentions. It was not unknown for a wife to beat a concubine or maid to death; since she was mistress in her own domain of the inner quarters, her husband was often unable to intervene effectively (Ebrey 1993, 167–168). Once a woman bore a son (Figure 11.23), she became a full ritual member of her marital family: she was now the mother of a member of the patriline, a future ancestor entitled to worship by her male descendants when she died. So a new bride's hopes lay in the future—in becoming a respected wife and mother and eventually a matriarch, mistress of her own houschold living in the best quarters, with daughters-in-law of her own under her control and grandsons to dandle on her knee (Figure 11.24).

Yet there was another side to relations among women; the attachments between female relatives—far less prominent in moralist writings, jokes, or proverbs—were

pleasant and loving. Ko (1994) proposes that the inner quarters were a place where women forged strong bonds of affection and companionship and it turns out that the women concerned were usually kinswomen, mother and daughter, sisters, cousins, or other blood relatives. In the case of the women writers from seventeenth-century Jiangnan that Ko has studied, poems between mother and daughter express not just tenderness but a bond of intellectual and aesthetic sensibilities. While she acknowledges that few women of the period were as well educated as her subjects, Ko believes it is likely that the mother-daughter bond shaped social experience, at least in the gentry families of late imperial China, just as much as the father-son bond, to which Confucian male scholars gave pride of place, or even the mother-son bond (the "uterine family") that Margery Wolf (1972) saw as providing the strongest emotions in the lives of Taiwanese peasant women and that Hsiung Ping-chen (1994) has argued formed the emotional and moral focus of many elite men's lives in late imperial times.

Among women of lower social status, too, evidence for a female society of solidarity is emerging. In her ethnographic study of social practices in Shandong, Ellen Judd (1989) documents a long tradition of continuous visits between a mother and her married daughters; in some cases newly married women even returned home to have their first child. The astonishing collection of letters in "women's script" [nü shu] recently brought to light in southwestern Hunan reveals the intensity of affection that could develop among young women of relatively humble families who became close friends, vowing eternal friendship, staying in each other's houses, learning embroidery patterns together, and singing the same songs until they were torn apart by marriage and could communicate only by the occasional but heartfelt letter, written in the form of a long poem (Silber 1994). The studies of girls' houses and marriage avoidance or delayed marriage in nineteenth- and early twentieth-century Guangdong also show that sharing a space created enduring bonds among women (Stockard 1989; Topley 1978).

The bonds between mother and daughter, aunt and niece, sisters, or girl cousins growing up under the same roof were bonds of tenderness and devotion made bittersweet by the threat of marriage. The emotional bond between sister and brother was very strong too, and brothers were often treated as the guardians of their sisters' interests after marriage. Married women clung to such friendships as best they could. Letters were one way to cross the forbidden spaces between their husband's house and their natal home, to invite their dear ones into their own secluded quarters and cultivate the precious friendship. A few women were accomplished literary

Francesca Bray

writers, and the poems and letters they exchanged have been preserved; they were able to maintain friendships with other female writers and acquaintances, as well as with their own relatives. Ordinary women's scope was more limited, and exchanges of gifts, especially of embroidered objects such as slippers, handkerchiefs, or fans, were often important in cementing such bonds. Very few women received formal schooling, and the "women's script" of Hunan was an anomaly. Even so, it is possible that letters played a greater role in women's lives than is usually supposed, permitting them to exchange news with their natal family and friends. Guides to letter writing had been in popular demand since early times, separately published or included in household encyclopedias. Such books "included many letter forms for use between relatives on both the male and female side and across three generations, between friends and between business associates. . . . The female side is more prominent in these books than might be expected" (Hayes 1985, 86). "Basically a woman has no business writing," concludes the 1560 edition of a popular encyclopedia—after a long section describing exactly what forms of address a woman should use when writing to her natal relatives, friends, and other correspondents (*Jujia biyong*, 1: 83–84).

In conclusion, men and women in China had very different ties to domestic space and correspondingly different experiences of identity and personal ties. A man was born, grew up, and died within the same walls and with the same male kin around him. He never had to leave his parents or his home; he knew to which lineage and which landscape he belonged from the time he began to understand the world. His house was his home for life, and yet he could walk outside the family compound whenever he pleased. He lived in a kind of commune of shared patrimonial goods, in which his first loyalty was supposedly to the group. A girl grew up on borrowed time. When she married, she had to leave the house of her birth, her mother, and her sisters, whom she loved and depended on, to move into an unknown house and a new group of women, many of whom might regard her with hostility. She would have to be self-reliant until she built up alliances and, as a mother, became an acknowledged member of her new family. Few wives questioned the system, because as time passed, they gained power and authority. Such resistance to neo-Confucian patriarchy as there was seems to have hinged on privacy and property. A married woman was virtually a prisoner within her husband's compound, and yet within this space she had freedoms that her husband did not. She had a room of her own where she could retreat with her children and where she kept her dowry in locked trunks under her own control.

DAVID FAURE

12   Between House and Home

The Family in South China

Chinese texts are adamant that the ideals of a successful family can be expressed in phrases such as "coresidence and common property" *[tongju gongcai]* and "five generations under one roof" *[wushi tongtang]*. They cite examples of families that indeed survived for five generations undivided, living under the same roof and holding in common, so to speak, the family properties. By all reports, instances of such families were extremely rare. The rarity of successful families living together within an extensive dwelling, however, does not nullify the prevalence of the ideal. Therein is posed the problem for the social historian: in what sense would clusters of houses occupied by people of a common surname claiming a common ancestor constitute a "family"?

A starting point for an answer could be the succinct discussion by Shiga Shuzo (1978, 109–150) on the development of Chinese family law. He downplays living together in the same house as an objective and stresses the importance not of co-ownership of all properties, but of operating through common budgets. He argues that inheritance is predicated upon the continuation of the ancestor's person, represented in ritual terms in sacrifice to the deceased by his offspring. While Shiga's reinterpretation of the family ideal provides the insight needed for any venture into Chinese family history, the insight is helpful only if there is documentation concerning coresidence and budget sharing. It is unfortunate that we know next to nothing regarding the historical context of how space was used in Chinese houses over time or about budget sharing, especially in terms of the relationship of the very few family accounts still extant to the family structures of the account holders.

A focus on residence and budgets is obviously so fundamental to family life that it is certain that changes in house style and budget keeping have implications on families. Such changes can be documented in southern China's Pearl River Delta in Guangdong province. For example, the use of bricks for building houses was introduced into the area from the sixteenth to the eighteenth centuries, along with the spread of Chinese writing, official practices, schools, and the literati ideal. As practices such as these spread, the local population in time generally abandoned living in boats or bamboo sheds on stilts for houses made of bricks, sometimes on

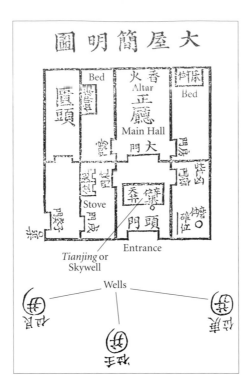

Fig. 12.1. *"Simplified Plan of the Big House"* [Da wu jianming tu]. Source: *Xixi jiacheng* 1913.

a foundation of stone, with a tiled roof. As literacy spread and as county governments became more effective, title deeds came to be written, and land emerged as the principal form of tradable property. Yet the records of individual families are scanty. In all the genealogical records I have read of the Pearl River Delta, only two show floor plans of houses. These drawings will be used below to reveal some aspects of Chinese families over time in the Pearl River Delta.

Although floor plans are uncommon among genealogical records, they were quite often prepared by geomancers, who included samples in their handbooks. Figure 12.1 shows the "Simplified Plan of the Big House" *[Da wu jianming tu]* that was built by a man who lived between 1698 and 1773 (*Xixi jiacheng* 1913). Taken from the pages of the genealogy of the Zhang surname of Xiangxi village in what once was the Shenzhen district and is now the Shenzhen Special Economic Zone, the text accompanying this diagram indeed indicates that it was drawn in the context of geomancy. The front entrance to this almost square dwelling opens into a small sunken courtyard, called a *tianjing* or skywell, which leads then to an entry to the main hall, at the end of which is the domestic shrine. Away from this central axis, the main hall provides access into a pair of flanking bedrooms. Adjacent to the

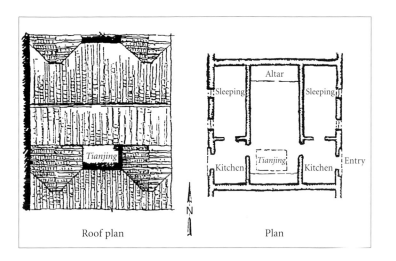

Roof plan   Plan

Fig. 12.2. *Roof plan, floor plan, and view across the roof of a small contemporary dwelling in Guangdong province.* Source: Hammond 1992, 99–100.

court is a kitchen with a built-in stove, as well as a preparation room in which the rotary rice polisher and the foot-operated mortar and pestle are located. In this preparation room, one corner is shown as "inauspicious." There are also two outside rooms, which may be entered also through a side entrance. The function of the outer side room is unspecified, but the inner side room is used as a storeroom. There would have been few windows in any of the walls and probably only a skylight in the roof. The slanted roofs draw rainwater into cisterns located in the sunken skywell, and a drain opening, shown in the diagram as a small circle, provides the drainage for the house. Three wells for fresh water are located at the front of the dwelling. There is no doubt that this is an elaborate variation of a common arrangement still seen in village houses throughout many parts of Guangdong province (Figure 12.2), where the stores are kept in one of the bedrooms indicated here or in a loft that is built into the main hall (Hammond 1992; Lu and Wei 1990).

The Zhang of Xiangxi claim to have been the owners of Shenzhen market, and the man who built the house was known for having defended the family's rights in the village, a reputation implying that he was a fairly wealthy and influential man by local standards. While he had a wife and three sons, there is no record of daughters

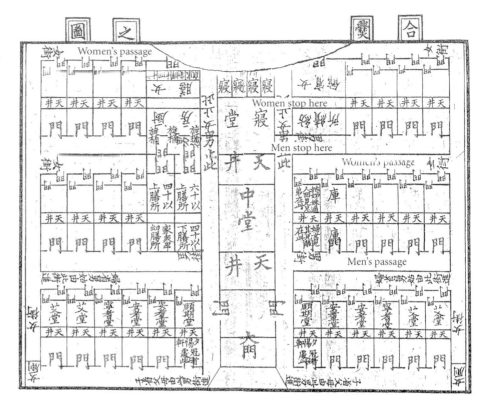

Fig. 12.3. *"Diagram of the Collective Stove"* [He chuan zhi tu] *shows a detailed plan of the walled residential compound that is made up of individual modular residential units, most of which are separate "houses" even as the walled compound or village is a unit for "shared cooking."* Source: Huo ca. 1529.

in the genealogy of his lineage branch. The house mentioned above, with only two bedrooms, was probably not designed for a family of more than four to five people. The dwelling itself was one among a cluster of similar houses, probably in a single or several rows, that were built together. The house cluster or hamlet would appear as a village, or part of one, hence the name "New Village" applied to it. It is likely that Zhang's brothers and cousins, and then the families of his and their sons, occupied the other houses. The collection of his brothers, cousins, grandsons, and nephews also constituted a "family" of sorts. Calling the single-structure entity in Figure 12.1 "a house" implies that the full array of relatives was not coresident in the same house; thus, the architecture embraces the notion of family division.

Figure 12.3, titled "Diagram of the Collective Stove" *[He chuan zhi tu],* actually shows a residential compound, walled on three sides, made up of individual modular units, most of which are separate "houses," even as the compound is a unit for "shared cooking." The diagram is found in the Ming dynasty family manual, *The Family Admonitions of Huo Weiya [Huo Weiya jiaxun],* which is ascribed to the authorship of Huo Tao (1487–1540). Huo Tao was a very senior court official, staunch supporter of the Jiajing emperor (1522–1566), and a very important man in the transformation of rituals in the Pearl River Delta in the sixteenth century. Among his achievements was to popularize the custom of conducting lineage rituals in buildings officially known as "family temples," and which today are referred to in English as "ancestral halls." The architectural style of the family temple was, prior to a change in law in 1529, maintained as the preserve of the aristocracy. In recognition of this restriction, Zhu Xi in the twelfth century had proposed in the widely circulated *Family Rituals of Master Zhu* that ancestral sacrifice be conducted by commoners at a shrine placed within a "bedchamber." The difference between the two is fairly intuitive: the family temple was a detached building in a unique style, while the altar set up in the bedchamber would have been looked upon as a domestic shrine. It was very much owing to the efforts of Huo Tao and people close to him that the imperial government recognized the right of commoners to build ancestral halls in their villages.

We know that in 1525 Huo Tao built an ancestral hall, a representation of which is indeed shown in Figure 12.3 as embedded in the residential compound of three rows of houses. Thus, the entire compound was to function as a "family" unit that ate its meals from a common stove (Huo Tao ca. 1529). As seen in Figure 12.3, the walled compound consists of a three-compartment building that runs from front to back through its middle, with numerous individual living units lined up in three parallel rows on both sides. In the overall plan of Figure 12.3 the layout shows not only the essential elements of individual village houses as depicted in Figure 12.1, but the *whole* compound itself could likewise be seen as analogous to a *single* dwelling. This can be seen clearly if one regards the main doors in both drawings as equivalent, so that the living units shown in Figure 12.3 are equated to the bedrooms of Figure 12.1. Village layouts similar to this type are still commonly found in richer villages of the Pearl River Delta (Figure 12.4).

Figure 12.3 clearly illustrates the segregation of men and women within the compound and serves therefore as a rationalization for its unity. Men enter the compound through the openings of the side lanes just inside the main entrance, but they proceed no further than the beginning of the bedchamber. Women, presumably, enter individual dwelling units from the rear entrances, and they have a monopoly of the circulating lane that runs on the two sides and back of the compound and then terminates at one of the women's latrines located in the front corner of the compound. The segregated lanes are connected to the central chambers through two passages, again separately for men and women. Near the central chambers are segregated

a ▼

 b ▼

c ▶

d ▶

e ▶

Figs. 12.4a–e. *Front row of houses at Shitou village, Nanhai county, the exact location where Huo Tao built his ancestral hall. The hall depicted in Fig. 12.3 would be the right-hand side building of figure* **(c)**, *continued into the left-hand side of building* **d**. *The passageways as indicated in Fig. 12.3 are clearly visible in* **(c)** *and* **(d)**. *Two halls have been added to the side of the main hall, and the residential compounds have been rebuilt.* Source: Photographs by David Faure.

functional areas, such as dining halls, a spinning and weaving room, and a guest-room for women. Special provisions are also made for daughters who had married out: they enter the compound through a separate entrance from the women's lane, and they are able to see their brothers in specially designated rooms.

While it is tempting to read into the plans shown in Figures 12.1 and 12.3 the architectural representations of the nuclear and the extended family, it is doubtful that the difference can be so discretely described. In reality, both fall somewhere between the two ideals.

Family Budgets

Shiga Shuzo's emphasis on common budgets and their relation to the continuation of the ancestor's person beyond death in maintaining the family comes across very clearly in Huo Tao's *Family Admonitions,* in which a ceremony, described in religious terms, is conducted in front of the ancestral altar immediately after the ancestral sacrifice at the New Year. For this ceremony, the spirit tablet of the ancestor is moved to the central chamber, and, as the head of the family stands to its side, the men of the family line up in the corridors and approach the spirit tablet individually to report their achievements for the previous year. The achievements in question are not an abstract description in general terms; the text is very precise in grading the achievements to be reported. A contribution of 5 *mu* of farmland or 30 taels of silver to the ancestral estate counts as an upper-grade achievement; 2 *mu* or 15 taels amounts to a medium-grade achievement; 1 *mu* or 5 taels, a lower-grade achievement; and a report of no contribution renders the individual as "incapable." An upper-grade achievement entitles the achiever to an award, a medium- or lower-grade achievement carries no award, but the "incapable" for three continuous years are to be punished. Lest there is any doubt that the ancestor is personally drawn into the ceremony, it may be noted that the ritual for the report of the "incapable" consists, in the third year, of the lineage head announcing the punishment on the ancestor's behalf. As members of the lineage are given ancestral land and funds for their livelihood, the contribution to the ancestral estate would have represented a profit that was raised on the entrusted capital.

This ceremony in front of the ancestral spirit tablet is not commonly reported, and only two other references are known, both in the Ming dynasty, one in Anhui province and the other in Guangdong.[1] The practice must have died out along with the custom of distributing landed property to male members of the family for use even as the title remained with the ancestral estate. All other reports I have seen indicate that managers were appointed to look after the ancestral estate, and in the Pearl River Delta the common practice was to rotate management among branches of the lineage. The practice of keeping written accounts and posting them at the ancestral hall during the New Year, at which time management changes hands from one lineage branch to another, continues to the present.

People like Huo Tao, who sought to extend the neo-Confucian ideals of the family in the sixteenth century, were practical men of affairs, understanding well that common ownership of property required the maintenance of accurate accounts, which were kept in a cupboard located in the lineage's schoolhouse. The financial reports, which Huo required in his *Family Admonitions,* were therefore clearly spelled out. The income book recorded rents collected in two seasons of the year, while expenditures were kept for specified sacrifices, replacement of sacrificial objects, repair of the ancestral hall, payments for impoverished members of the lineage, payments for descendants of the principal line, disbursements for tax collection, and military dues. Whatever balance of income there was over expenses was to be entered into savings. Pang Shangpeng (1524–1581), Huo Tao's near contemporary and another senior official who came from the Pearl River Delta, specified similar accounting requirements in his equally famous family regulations. Pang made one significant addition: books were to be kept for income and expenses related to funerals and celebrations (Pang 1939). He did not give a reason for the stipulation, but it can be surmised that these records kept track not only of money matters, but also of connections among kin and friends.

It is significant that written accounts took over from the oral reports made directly to the ancestors. Managers of common property owed their responsibility not only to their living kinsmen, but also to their ancestors and descendants to come, the continuation of an income from the property being a condition whereby sacrifice to the ancestors might be maintained. The managerial act of keeping accounts and the use of property income for ancestral sacrifice, however, also indicate the precise manner in which Huo Tao's house plan must have served only as an ideal. It is unlikely that families held properties in the name of only one ancestor and therefore maintained only one set of accounts. As descendants maintained separate accounts in the names of multiple ancestors and participated in the sacrifices offered to them in different groupings, they defined themselves, in ritual terms, as concomitant members of multiple families. The families that occupied different houses in New Village at Xiangxi, therefore, like the Huo family in the common-stove compound, would have been members of the larger families defined by the accounts they kept and the multiple ancestors to whom they sacrificed. The layout of individual houses, as shown by the plan in Figure 12.1, signified quite clearly that each house might store and polish its own grain, but in ritual terms, the residents would have been, in the presence of the ancestors, also part of larger families.

Naturally, families might also divide, and there are quite a few examples of family division contracts extant. Such contracts deal specifically with plots of land and houses that go separately to different sons or their lines of descent, and it was not uncommon to stipulate also that property was to be set aside for the provision of sacrifice for the patriarch whose efforts had created the estate and whose demise had led to a situation where division was necessary. Divided families, therefore, may be thought of as families founded on a new set of accounts, if indeed new accounts were kept. Yet if one continues to define a family only with reference to accounts, this would leave coresidential groups out of the definition. Such coresidential groups usually were the poorer families, whose resources consisted not of land and houses, but of manpower, receipts from the annual harvest, and income from odd jobs and cottage industry. Farmers who kept accounts of their harvests must have been few and far between, as most would not have been sufficiently literate to do so even if they had seen the point. Thus, average farmers usually kept no written record since such records would not have served any particular purpose.[2] Divided families, eating apart, would have drawn on different hoardings of the harvested grain. Family division, therefore, would have matched residence with the use of common resources, only some of which for a portion of the coresidential groups would have been kept in written accounts. That does not in itself violate the "common property" principle as the basis of family life, but it does mean that the combinations of cohabitation and common property holding become quite complex.

Yet perhaps "family" is not quite the word that should be applied to kin groups built around ancestral sacrifice. It may be pointed out that what appear to us as lineages—that is, groups in which the tracing of descent across numerous generations is at the center of recognized relationships—actually begin as discrete families. This, of course, does not rule out fictitious kinship, examples of which were common enough. However, even when kinship is set up fictitiously, it is set up among coresidential and common-property groups. The point has to be made that with migration—if only from one part of the village to another—and family division—when coresidence is realigned with the common holding of property— the group comes closer to the model of a patriarch dominating his immediate descendants than to the ancestor around whom lines of descent are traced primarily through the written genealogies and participation in rituals.

When Huo Tao set up his ancestral hall in 1525, he claimed to be only in the sixth generation in descent from the first ancestor who had settled in his village, and there were in the "lineage" no more than forty male members aged 21 and above, most of whom were descended from his great-grandfather.[3] Their descendants eventually became a lineage, but up to Huo Tao's time, when the rituals were established, they were set up not for lineage but for a large family group using a common set of accounts and devoted to the single patriarch—the great-grandfather. Coresidential and common-property groups did combine to build larger lineages, but lineages were also created when families continued.[4]

House, Home, and Family

The idealism of the undivided family aside, therefore, the two plans shown in Figures 12.1 and 12.3 represent the view of "the family" as seen from both the individual domestic unit and the ancestral hall. One might draw a distinction between daily meals cooked in the house and ceremonial banquets served at the ancestral hall, but the drawings and the accompanying texts argue that the occupants of the house were members of both the domestic group *and* the lineage community as "family."

David Faure

The choice of words, which so far has been left out of this discussion, underscores this position. In the text that accompanies Figure 12.1, the structure represented by the floor plan is called a *wu,* or "house," and the walled compound of houses is termed *cun,* "village." The text accompanying Figure 12.3 refers to the practices within the unit of shared cooking as *jujia,* or "home-living," a term, as one might say in English, that suggests these are activities that take place "at home," as opposed to activities that take place "away from home." Neither concept adequately portrays "family," with all the connotations of coresidence, common ownership of property, and inheritance. In the Pearl River Delta from the sixteenth century onward, the ideal of coresidence and common property holding would have found its institutional support in the maintenance of ancestral sacrifice, with common property being held for that purpose. Where sacrifice was offered to more than one ancestor, as would have been quite common, it would have been common for many domestic groups to be members of more than one "family."

It is true that any meaningful analysis of this topic must come to include a discussion of the development of emotional bonds, companionship, marriage, the sale of women as brides, and the emergence of the cult of gentility. Indeed, some of these subjects had a great deal to do with the ritual changes of the sixteenth century. No doubt, also, in the cruel competition for scarce resources, many people were pushed out of their families and not allowed to propagate within them. Historical records tend to speak only about the successful families, while the losers disappear without a name and without mention.

Coresidence and common property holding draw attention to the dynamism of family life in terms of its changing fortunes, conditions that are often mirrored in their residential space (Cohen 1976). A house is built or claimed, property controlled by a patriarch is shared, the family grows, and space is functionally divided. With family division, some property continues to be held in common, while each coresidential unit might set up its own accounts, with the cycle continuing as a group moves out and builds it own house. In the New Territories of Hong Kong, a very good example of a family that went through such a dynamic and organic cycle is that of the Tsang [Zeng] surname at Shan Ha village; the residence was popularly known as Tsang Tai Uk, or the "Tsangs' Big House" in Sha Tin (Figure 12.5). Tsang Tai Uk was built over twenty years for a single family and completed by 1867 as a rectangular fortified "village" of three rows of houses surrounded by massive walls, with watchtowers at its four corners. Tsang Koon-man (ca. 1808–1880), who built the compound, had made his fortune in Hong Kong city in the early days of the

Fig. 12.5. *Oblique photograph showing Tsang Tai Uk, or "the Tsangs' Big House," in Sha Tin.* Source: Photograph by Ivan Chi Ching Ho 2003.

colony and moved as an outsider into Sha Tin district. The architecture reflects, therefore, both his aspirations for the extended family and an ostentatious demonstration of wealth and status as he moved up in the Sha Tin community. An ancestral hall with a spirit tablet devoted to his ancestors is located at the far end of the compound, directly facing the front entrance. A chamber in the middle row of houses along the line connecting the hall and the entrance was, some time in the later years of the nineteenth century, turned into a "meeting hall," not for "lineage" affairs—for there would have been none such—but for meetings of the principal intervillage alliance at Sha Tin. In this hall, Koon-man and then his descendants displayed the finely carved panel recording his achievement and purchased official title, written by leading Guangdong scholar and official Dai Hongci. Koon-man had six sons and four daughters, so to the end of the nineteenth century, there could not have been many inhabitants in the compound. It was built as much for display as for the housing of posterity (Lee 1995, 162; Zeng 1981).

An example in the Pearl River Delta, where there are fewer case studies with the same level of detail as those in Hong Kong's New Territories, is that of the Ye surname, a lineage that consists of a group of people who, at least for a while, were coresidential in Yejia Zhuang, or "Ye Family Estate," in the town of Foshan. The walled compound was built in 1877 by one of two twin brothers (Ye Yibin [1820–1875] and Ye Yunbao [1820–1888]), with houses for members of the family located on the two sides of the ancestral hall, which was dedicated to their father, who died in 1830. Thus, the houses could not have been occupied by more than two to three

David Faure

generations. As the Ye family prospered, partly through business in Hong Kong, part of the family moved away. In 1917, family members registered their common holdings in Hong Kong and Foshan under Hong Kong company law, with the Kwong Tai Company serving as holder of the ancestral property and bound by legal requirements regarding accounting disclosure and managerial liability (Zhong 1999). The family had obviously outgrown coresidence, but it continued to be bound by common property and periodic ritual observance.

Coresidence as an aim *and* ritual sacrifice at a common ancestral shrine together feed into the ideal of the large extended family. The existence of individual living units, wherein domestic groups cook and eat apart, speaks of the reality of frequent family divisions and small families. Yet when the living units are arraigned in or around an ancestral compound and sacrifice at the shrines is supported by properties held in common by different subgroups within the extended family context, a semblance of the exercise of common budgets is created, reified by the sharing of the annual meal held after ancestral sacrifice. The family is never quite as extensive as the aims of coresidence might suggest or ever as small as the group enclosed by a living unit. As domestic groups are nested one within another, sharing different roofs and budgets, the family takes shapes in between the two boundaries of the house and the village.

NOTES

1. *Bashi zongyou zongzhi tushuo* 1374; in Zhou and Zhao (1993, 15–16.)

2. A very interesting diary-cum-account of a southern Anhui farmer in the 1840s has nevertheless recently been published in Shao Hong and Huang Zhifan (2002).

3. The genealogy *Shitou Huoshi zupu* enumerates 141 biographical entries up to the seventh generation. Of these, dates of birth and death are given for 126 cases—that is, there are 15 cases of missing data. Eliminating the entries of men who were either born after 1525 or died before 1525, 74 cases are left, made up of 47 cases born in 1496 or after. In other words, 27 men living in 1525 were recorded as being older than 20 years of age, and this number might be increased to 42 if all 15 cases of missing data fitted into this category. That is quite unlikely, however. No one among the entries that include the dates of birth in the eighth generation (127 out of 156 reported) was born before 1525.

4. This is inherent in Zheng Zhenman's (2001) study of lineage organization and social change in Fujian during the Ming and Qing dynasties.

PUAY-PENG HO

13   Ancestral Halls

Family, Lineage, and Ritual

The most conspicuous buildings found in village landscapes in southern China are usually ancestral halls, architectural statements of the strength of lineages whose existence extends the concept of familism beyond individual families to include all those sharing a common patrilineal descent from a single ancestor. By their size, height, and ornamentation, as well as the extent of the ritual carried out within them, the halls usually dwarf surrounding houses and stand as imposing structures in what are often rather monotonous compact villages of similar buildings. In villages throughout southern China, ancestral halls often are numerous, ranging from a handful to as many as twenty or thirty. There are also villages with extraordinarily high numbers of ancestral halls, such as Liukeng village in Jiangxi province; it listed ninety-five ancestral halls in the 1826 lineage registry (Li and Chen 2001, 149–158) (Figure 13.1). The ancestral halls in single-lineage villages are normally hierarchically organized, ranging from large, focal ancestral halls to medium-size branch halls to very small family halls; all are dotted throughout the village with no apparent pattern or, in some villages, following discrete branch settlement clusters. While the main purpose of ancestral halls is to make regular sacrifices to the ancestors of the lineage, branch, or family, following the prescriptions of neo-Confucianism, the building of an ancestral hall involves much more than this simplistic functional reason. Ancestral halls also serve a symbolic end, just as the compilation of written genealogies served to proclaim distinct identities and boost prestige. During the early Ming dynasty, when freestanding ancestral halls were first allowed to be built, only the scholar elites were permitted the privilege. Such a status was contested among members of the lineage and among villages. When the permission needed for building ancestral halls was relaxed during the subsequent Qing dynasty, not just the scholars, but also the merchant elites constructed them. As ancestral halls proliferated during the late imperial period, it is natural to ask a number of questions: for whom were ancestral halls built, what were the motivations for their construction, and how were the function and meaning expressed in the building itself?

Although ancestral halls are distinguished both as a building type in architectural studies and a community entity in sociological and anthropological studies,

Fig. 13.1. *Maps of Liukeng village, Le'an county, Jiangxi, showing the location of the focal ancestral hall, branch ancestral halls, and family ancestral halls in 1582 (top) and 1826 (bottom).* Source: Adapted from Liu 2000, 34.

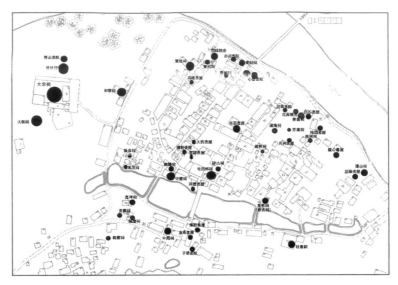

they are rarely the center of major research. Historians of Chinese architecture are traditionally divided into those studying classical and official architecture, such as palaces and temples, and those studying vernacular architecture, houses. Despite their importance in the physical and symbolic landscape of the village, ancestral halls seem to have been relegated to a category of semi-official or semi-religious structures outside the research focus of either group of architectural historians. The situation has been rectified in recent years with the publication of several

Puay-peng Ho

books on individual villages whose ancestral halls are measured, drawn, and described in terms of their architectural characteristics, as well as the historical patterns of lineage development and the elements contributing to the building of ancestral halls. Only recently have ancestral halls been studied in depth both architecturally and as a social institution within their village environment by using textual evidence found in lineage registries (Liu 2000; Liu 1993; Zhang 2002). In addition, there are increasing numbers of socio-anthropological studies of ancestral halls that yield a more complex picture. When the local history of a village or region is studied, for example, the importance of the ancestral hall within the local community is often underscored not only as a symbol for communal identity, but also as a means to express the multivalent motives for which the ancestral halls were constructed (Faure and Siu 1995; Segawa 1996; Szonyi 2002). These readings of the patronage, function, and utility of ancestral halls suggest that although there is a general underlying pattern, each case is unique, and the richness of the phenomenon is the most rewarding aspect of the study of ancestral halls in China (Ho 2001).

Settlement and Lineage Structure

Chinese villages are often compact, even as large and densely populated as a medieval European town. To some degree, ancestral halls in Chinese villages in the south stand prominently like churches in medieval towns in Europe, but they serve very different functions. Two basic types of village settlements are found in China: those that were settled by a number of different surname lineages and those occupied by a single-surname lineage. In a multi-surname settlement, there may be an ancestral hall for each of the lineages residing in the village. These halls tend to be small. In a single-surname village, a focal ancestor, or *kaijizu*, the ancestor who established the base of the lineage—the earliest ancestor of a particular lineage who migrated to a new locality—can usually be traced as the founder of the settlement, with the size of the village dependent on the length of settlement, the number of inhabitants, and the prosperity of the lineage. Some villages in southern China trace their origins back more than a thousand years and as a result are large in scale and densely populated. In cases where the population of a particular village reached a level where the agricultural land could not sustain its population and anticipated growth, some members of the lineage might have branched out to settle in other locations, thus founding a new village. In many cases, the records show that when a focal village branches out into surrounding areas through the out-migration of some of its

Fig. 13.2. *Map showing the nine villages of Ping Shan, Hong Kong.*
Source: Drawn by Henry Lo.

residents, common surname satellite villages emerge in locations around the focal village. This pattern can be seen clearly in many areas along the coastal region of southern China, where a larger main village has a focal ancestral hall, while smaller surrounding villages may contain branch ancestral halls.

Ping Shan village in Hong Kong, for example, was first settled around six hundred years ago. Today, there are two main villages and seven satellite villages in the general area with residents surnamed Tang [Deng], all of whom are related to the focal ancestor who established Ping Shan village (Figure 13.2). The two main villages in the center of the settlement each have around six hundred inhabitants. Walls surround three villages, and some, housing up to five hundred inhabitants, even have a moat. The remaining villages all were set up in the last two hundred

Puay-peng Ho

Fig. 13.3. *Map showing the main settlements of the five segments of the Tang [Deng] lineage.* Source: Drawn by Henry Lo.

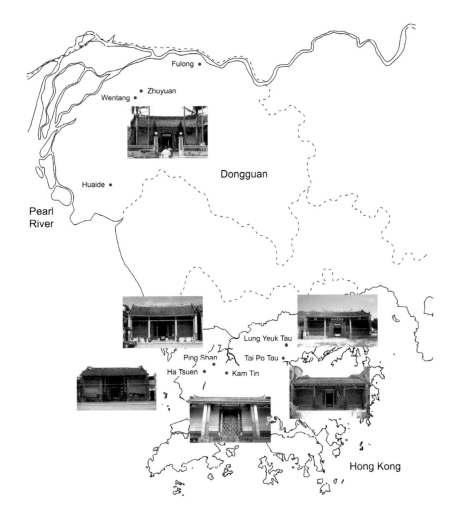

years and thus are smaller, with more compact housing for between two to three hundred residents. Each of these villages shares the same ancestry and would partake in the sacrifices offered at the focal ancestral hall in the central villages. In a few cases, some members may choose to move to far away localities and thus share very little in the common ritual activities of the main village. Indeed, the same Tang clan of Ping Shan was once a member of the main Tang family in Kam Tin, where the focal ancestor's five sons opted for different settlement sites: one continued to live in Kam Tin, and his descendants branched out to Ha Tsuen, Tai Po, and Lung Yeuk Tau; one son settled in Ping Shan, and three sons moved to Dongguan, Guangdong province (Figure 13.3). At the present, members of the five main branches of the Tang lineage still come together once every few years for common activities.

Ancestral Halls

Although a village group or even a branch village does not stand independently within the overall lineage genealogy, some choose to establish their own ancestral hall in order to declare independence from the main lineage. Thus, the building of an ancestral hall can be seen as a tangible means of establishing identity. Moreover, a village may have ancestral halls serving different ancestors, each holding a particular position in the communal structure. The rituals performed in each ancestral hall help to consolidate and reinforce the lineage structure, which has the family as its most fundamental unit.

The kinship web of blood relationships is formed with simple families at its core and with extended families, segments, lineages, and clans as outer rings. According to neo-Confucianist principles, an individual has no particular position in the ordered social web unless he is a descendant of the major descent line of the eldest son of the apical ancestor—in anthropological terminology, "the ancestor at the apex," the founding ancestor. Practically speaking, however, in late imperial China, any son whose achievements in state examinations or business were outstanding also enjoyed certain privileges and status within the lineage hierarchy. What is more important in traditional society, moreover, is the collective identity represented by the lineage. Each individual is placed between the ancestors and descendants in what Hugh Baker calls "the continuum of descent," in which many lines of descent come together to form the lineage, defined as "a group of males all descended from one common ancestor, all living together in one settlement, owning some property in common, and all nominally under the leadership of the man most senior in Generation and Age" (1979, 26–28, 49). In late imperial China, it was increasingly common to have the head of the lineage elected from the scholar elites to take care of lineage affairs, while the eldest son along the focal descent line, *zongzi,* performed ceremonial roles at the sacrifices. As noted, the lineage may live in a village where the kin and physical territories coincide or with lineages of other surname sharing the same locality. Single-surname villages are more common in South China than in North China (Freedman 1966, 5). Ancestral worship also takes a different form in North China, as discussed in the next chapter, where the focus of ritual is not in the ancestral hall but at the grave and the representations of the ancestors are ancestral tablets and ancestral scrolls (Cohen 1990).

The hierarchical and authoritative structure of the ideal society is constructed with each individual placed in appropriate position and is maintained in harmony by Confucian codes of propriety. What is asked of an individual in this structure is filial piety, or *xiao,* shown toward one's parents (Baker 1979, 102–106). Such filial

Puay-peng Ho

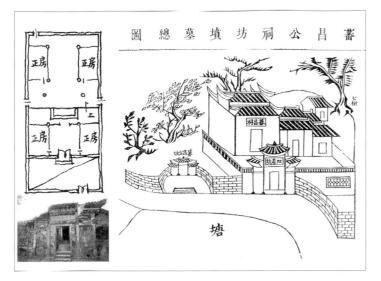

蕃昌公祠坊墳墓總圖

正房 正房

正房 正房

塘

piety is shown not only when the parents are alive, but also after they have passed away since it is believed by many Chinese that the world of the dead often replicates the world of the living. Thus, existing only in spirit, the dead are served as if they are still living since they continue to require similar sustenance (Baker 1979, 72–73). In addition, descendants are required to pay respect not only to their immediate parents, but also to ancestors in earlier generations. Various rituals have evolved to maintain the coherence of such an intergenerational structure in order to sustain communal solidarity. While rituals have traditionally been performed in a variety of different communal buildings, the most important continue to be the ancestral halls.

Rituals that have been carried out in ancestral halls are known collectively in English as "ancestor worship" and include practices with a history stretching back to the Shang dynasty (sixteenth–eleventh centuries B.C.). Many Chinese continue to believe that even though the body of the deceased is buried underground, his soul survives and has to be housed and taken care of. Before the Song dynasty, which began in 926, a spirit tablet, or *shenzhu,* representing the soul of the deceased, one's immediate ancestor, was placed in a family shrine, or *muci,* located near the tomb site (Figure 13.4). In such a shrine, it was required that ancestors of four previous generations be worshiped. After four generations, the *shenzhu* tablet would be buried beside the tomb of the ancestor. Later, the spirit tablets were moved into the home so that the spirit of the deceased could be worshiped and served with daily offerings. This is ancestor worship at the most rudimentary level. On the tablet was written the name of both the immediate ancestor and past ancestors; together they served as the center of family worship. Elaborate feasts were held in honor of the ancestors during various festivals and on the anniversaries of their birth and death. At the Qingming Festival, soon after the spring equinox, ancestors are commemorated with ritual sacrifices at their grave sites.

After the Song dynasty, families came to erect a separate building next to the house that served as the worship hall, called *citing* or *jiaci,* the family ancestral hall. In this hall, spirit tablets of up to four generations of ancestors were housed and offered sacrifices. Instituted chiefly by Zhu Xi and other neo-Confucianists, this new practice of separate ancestral halls is often said to have been meant for restoring social order after the chaotic times of the Five Dynasties. It was not until the edict of 1536, which allowed for the setting up of lineage ancestral halls specifically for making sacrifices to the lineage-founding ancestors, that freestanding ancestral halls began to proliferate throughout China's rural landscape. Known as *zongci,* these lineage halls were dedicated to the worship of the earliest ancestor of the lineage, the focal ancestor. As noted, in the early part of the Ming dynasty, only degree holders and high officials were allowed to build ancestral halls of this type, although in regions far away from the central government, such as in the southeastern coastal areas, there were numerous cases of defiance. By the late Ming period, however, such controls were relaxed, and substantially more ancestral halls were erected than in the early period.

Zongci, usually found at the center of the village, were built with contributions collected from all members of the lineage, who also sometimes donated pieces of land to form a "common field" whose income would provide for the upkeep of the hall and for the common welfare of the lineage. In some cases, when the income from the pooled land was insufficient, it was necessary for the lineage to purchase additional land for this common purpose. Corporate property of this type was used not only to endow funds for the upkeep of the ancestral hall, but also to educate the youth of the lineage and sometimes to build defensive structures in times of need. Corporate estates held in common and, presumably, in perpetuity helped guard against the decline in assets of individual families within the lineage, a condition that might have impacted their ability to perform required rituals. This picture of the building of the focal ancestral hall in a village should be seen as an ideal from which there emerged many variations.

It is common to see a small ancestral hall built after only a few generations of settlement in a village. However, a large focal ancestral hall would be built only if a member of the lineage achieved high official position; or when someone within the

Puay-peng Ho

Fig. 13.5. *Ren Branch Ancestral Hall [Ren Pai Zongci], Ouyang lineage, Diaoyuan village, Ji'an county, Jiangxi.* Source: Photograph by Puay-peng Ho 2000.

Fig. 13.6. *Bilugong, a small family ancestral hall, in Liukeng village, Le'an county, Jiangxi.* Source: Photograph by Puay-peng Ho 2000.

lineage, usually a learned elite, rallied members of the lineage to start fund-raising for building a hall; or when a member had gotten rich and decided to build a hall for the focal ancestor. The building process in reality was usually far from smooth. For example, the person who had achieved high government position might not have the means to build a hall, and it would be left to his descendants to gather together sufficient funds to eventually build the hall. In the case of collective fund-raising initiatives, it indeed might take the lineage several generations to complete the building because of ongoing disagreements, as well as shortages of funds. Richer members of a lineage who want to build a hall might face opposition within the lineage because of their peripheral position in the lineage structure.

Since the early years of the Qing dynasty, the branches of a lineage or even individual families who could afford a building began to erect branch and family ancestral halls. Since no official position was needed as a prerequisite for the building, a village could now contain many ancestral halls. In the village of Diaoyuan, Jiangxi province, there are five segments of one lineage living in the same settlement, and each has an ancestral hall in the area where it lives (Figure 13.5). Many of the small ancestral halls found in Liukeng village in Jiangxi are family and branch ancestral halls (Figure 13.6). On Nantai Island in Fuzhou, Fujian province, three different forms of ancestral halls can be seen today: official halls built with specific imperial permission; gentry halls built by high officials who might not have received official permission but claimed to be able to build a hall by virtue of their high position; and popular halls built to strengthen kinship bonding (Szonyi 2002, 96–97). Even in urban locations, where migrants from a rural area may now live, an ancestral hall

Fig. 13.7. *Main hall of the Chen Ancestral Hall, Guangzhou, Guangdong.* Source: Photograph by Puay-peng Ho 2002.

is often established so that sacrifices can be made to ancestors whose tablets remain housed back in the home village. As commercial activities intensified during the Qing dynasty and traders settled in main cities for business, merchants who seldom returned to their home villages resorted to this remedy to meet their filial obligations. One imposing extant example is the ancestral hall of the Chen clan (sometimes known as Chen's Academy) in Guangzhou, built in 1894 for the Chen surname of seventy-two counties of Guangdong province (Figure 13.7).

The effects of wealth and political power may lead to a departure from what might appear to be a perfect hierarchical order of ancestral halls in villages, thereby creating what Watson (1985) and Cohen (1990) call "asymmetrical segmentation." In some cases, for example, the focal ancestral hall is neither the largest nor the most ornamented building in a village because a wealthy member of a lineage was able to coerce other members to allow the building of an ostentatious hall to remember a particular ancestor; this otherwise would not have been permitted according to strict neo-Confucian stipulations. Another circumstance in which the ancestral hall of a family might outshine that of the main lineage is when a member of a particular family held a very high governmental office and then set out to com-

Puay-peng Ho

Fig. 13.8. *Main gate of Baolun Ge, the Luo Dongshu ancestral hall, Chengkan village, Shexian county, Anhui.* Source: Photograph by Puay-peng Ho 2001.

Fig. 13.9. *Baolun Ge, "The Pavilion of Precious Encomiums," Chengkan village, Shexian county, Anhui.* Source: Photograph by Puay-peng Ho 2001.

memorate his own ancestors. One of the grandest and largest examples can be found in the village of Chengkan, Shexian, Anhui province, where the most elaborate ancestral hall belongs to the family of Luo Dongshu, who lived during the Yuan dynasty in the fourteenth century (Li 1994, 37–40). Built by his descendant of the twenty-second generation, Luo Yinghe (1540–1630), in 1617, the magnificent ancestral hall, which was restored in 1993, is befitting the first rank official position of Luo Yinghe rather than that of either his ancestor Luo Dongshu, who was a renowned scholar but had never attained official position, or the founding ancestors, who settled in Chengkan during the late Tang dynasty, tenth century (Figure 13.8). Neither Luo Dongshu nor Luo Yinghe was from the descent line of the eldest male descendants from the founding ancestor; thus strictly speaking, neither was entitled to build the most elaborate hall in the village. Originally called the "Shrine of the Virtuously Tranquil Luo Dongshu," the immense and soaring Baolun Ge, or "The Pavilion of Precious Encomiums," venerates Luo Dongshu and celebrates the numerous encomiums or formal expressions of praise offered by emperors over the centuries (Figure 13.9)

Ancestral Halls

The location of a focal ancestral hall in a village differs greatly from settlement to settlement. In general, there are four broad patterns: near a grave site, at the center of the village, at the outer edge of the village, or at the best *fengshui* site, such as the *shuikou* (literally the "mouth of water," where a stream exits from a settlement). In the early years of the Ming dynasty, it was common to build an ancestral hall near the grave, as stipulated in dynastic codes. At imperial tombs, a temple staffed by officials would be set up for offering sacrifices to the deceased emperor. Likewise, the son of the deceased would observe a three-year period of mourning by the grave. Thus the setting up of an ancestral hall by the grave, the *muci* or tomb hall, was a long-established tradition.

When permission was granted by imperial edict for the building of ancestral halls in the mid-Ming period, it became legitimate to build the halls within the village settlement itself. In rural settlements in the New Territories of Hong Kong, ancestral halls were usually located at the center of a village, facing the distant hills

Fig. 13.10. *Aerial photo of Ping Shan village, Hong Kong in 1949, showing the imposing focal ancestral hall located in the center of the village.* Source: Used with the permission of the Mapping Office, Government of Hong Kong SAR.

Fig. 13.11. *Focal ancestral hall of Peitian village, Liancheng county, Fujian.* Source: Photograph by Puay-peng Ho 2001.

Fig. 13.12. *The remains of Dazongci, the "Great Focal Ancestral Hall," Liukeng village, Le'an county, Jiangxi.* Source: Photograph by Puay-peng Ho 2000.

and with unobstructed vistas, according to fundamental *fengshui* principles (Figure 13.10). Ancestral halls in villages elsewhere in southern China were built at various sites—in the center of the settlement, near the house of a major donor, or on land donated by a member of the lineage. The hall might be embedded in the village when houses were built later in front of it, as is the case in Peitian village, Longyan county, Fujian province (Figure 13.11). However, in the development of a village, the location of the focal ancestral hall might be moved around the settlement, and if the land in the middle of the village was not sufficient, land outside the village boundary might be secured for its building. Liukeng village in southern Jiangxi is a case in point. Its first focal ancestral hall was constructed near the grave between 1333 and 1335, but in 1369 a small hall was built in the middle of the village, next to a study hall, to replace the first hall, which was far away from the village. The hall was again rebuilt in 1524 at a site half a kilometer outside the village since its large size could not be accommodated within the existing settlement. When the hall was destroyed, an even larger hall, the Dazongci, the "Great Focal Ancestral Hall," was rebuilt on the same site in 1565, and that too burned down in the 1920s (Figure 13.12).

Fig. 13.13. *Focal ancestral hall of Tangyue village, Shexian county, Anhui.* Source: Photograph by Puay-peng Ho 1999.

Fig. 13.14a–b.
a. *Focal ancestral hall, Dongshanci, of Shiqiao village, Nanjing county, Fujian, located at the* shuikou. *In the distance is the silhouette of the round, rammed-earth tower of the village.*
b. *Decoration of double happiness in Dongshanci.* Source: Photographs by Puay-peng Ho 1996.

Fig. 13.15. Fengshui *map of Ping Shan village showing the* fengshui *of the ancestral hall.* Source: Unknown; ca. 1905.

Fig. 13.16. *The focal ancestral hall (left) and the ancestral hall of Yu and Qiao ancestors* [Yu Qiao er gong] *(right) at the center of Ping Shan village, Hong Kong.* Source: Photograph by Puay-peng Ho 1994.

The ancestral halls of Tangyue village, Shexian, Anhui province, are also located just outside the village for the same reason (Figure 13.13). In Shiqiao village, Nanjing county, Fujian province, the ancestral hall is located even further away from the village, right next to the *shuikou*, where the river flows out of the village (Figure 13.14). It is clear that *fengshui* was carefully considered in the siting of many ancestral halls since the fortuitous siting of the building itself was believed synonymous with the *fengshui* of the lineage, with both contributing to the good fortune of the village and its inhabitants (Figure 13.15).

Branch ancestral halls were usually located within the area or neighborhood of the village occupied by the branch. In villages where there was no clear pattern of distribution of houses according to kinship relationship, the branch ancestral halls were located where the donor/donors owned or bought land for them. Yet even here, exceptions seem to be the rule since, on the one hand, not all branches or segments of the lineage could afford to build an ancestral hall, and, on the other hand, as mentioned above, prosperous branches of the lineage might construct an ancestral hall that might be equal to or even surpass the focal ancestral hall. Reflecting the wealth of the eleventh-generation ancestor, the Tang branch ancestral hall in Hong Kong's Ping Shan village was built adjacent to the focal ancestral hall and was approximately the same size (Figure 13.16). Family ancestral halls are usually located next to the family residence or on land owned by the family.

0 5 10 20 m

Fig. 13.17. *A diagram showing plans of a number of ancestral halls in Hong Kong, ranging widely in size and arrangement.* Source: Drawn by Henry Lo.

The architecture of the ancestral hall occupies a unique position in the spectrum of building types in China. Neither an official building nor a common structure, its position is somewhere in between because of the wide variety of sizes and multiplicity of construction traditions. The ancestral hall of a smaller lineage that is not significant is usually similar in form to that of a common house, with very few clues setting it apart from surrounding dwellings. In contrast, with full imperial sanction and assistance or with a great amount of money, an ancestral hall can be as elaborate as an official building, although it probably would not have glazed roof tiles (Figure 13.17).

The form and construction of ancestral halls, like other buildings, are very much influenced by local vernacular traditions and practices. Thus, a northern Shanxi ancestral hall is very different from a southern Fujian hall (Figure 13.18). Even in a relatively small area, there often is a great range of building forms, which derive from a number of factors, including the social status of the builder of the hall; financial capacity; available building lot for the structure; local construction techniques, materials, and building traditions; and decorative preferences. For example, some villages in Longyan district, Fujian province, consist of rammed-earth houses, and others consist of timber-frame houses. The ancestral halls of the former villages, in the south of the county, are usually timber-frame buildings with low-pitched roofs, much like coastal Fujian houses, while the ancestral halls of the latter villages,

Puay-peng Ho

Fig. 13.18a–b. *Ancestral hall of* **(a)** *Zhangjiata village, Xikou, Linxian county, Shanxi, and* **(b)** *Chengqilou, Yongding county, Fujian.* Source: Photographs by Puay-peng Ho.

such as in Peitian in the northwest of the county, are built in the same manner as big houses in the building traditions of southern Zhejiang province.

As described in Ming ritual codes, the ideal ancestral hall, as seen in Figure 13.19, is a building complex consisting of an entrance hall, a main hall, and a tablet hall, but the actual features are quite diverse from place to place, depending upon size, construction form and method, and the specific nature of the hall. For a freestanding family ancestral hall, the form is usually very similar to that of a house, consisting of a narrow entry doorway, a small courtyard, and a hall measuring around five to seven meters across. Such a simple ancestral hall may be built to the side of the original residence of the deceased, and it might just be another building in a row of houses, with only the name plaque of the hall to distinguish it from the houses alongside. This type is commonly seen in villages in the New Territories of Hong Kong, where houses are arranged in parallel rows, with the ancestral hall occupying one of the row houses (Figure 13.20). In some villages, where the dwelling units are relatively small, two adjacent houses along a row or two straddling adjacent rows might be combined to form the ancestral hall. In the rammed-earth fortresses, or *tulou*, of southwestern Fujian province, families installed the ancestral tablets in a hall built in the center of the structure (Figure 13.21). Other large, defensive rammed-earth or brick strongholds located in southern Jiangxi and northern Guangdong provinces also have their ancestral halls built at the core of the compound. In many

Ancestral Halls

Fig. 13.19. *The ideal ancestral hall, as described in the ritual code of the Ming dynasty.* Source: Cheng 1530, juan 6, 15.

▼

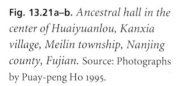

Fig. 13.20a–b. *A small ancestral hall of Cheung Uk village, Sha Lo Tung, Hong Kong.* Source: Photographs by Puay-peng Ho 1999.

Fig. 13.21a–b. *Ancestral hall in the center of Huaiyuanlou, Kanxia village, Meilin township, Nanjing county, Fujian.* Source: Photographs by Puay-peng Ho 1995.

▼

13.23 ▲

South China villages, a study hall, built by an individual family primarily for the education of its offspring, might also be used as a family ancestral hall as a result of installing the ancestral tablets at the center of its main hall. Examples abound in the many study halls in Liukeng village, for which the ritual schedules were also found in the lineage registry. In Ping Shan village in Hong Kong, the well-known mid-eighteenth-century Kan Ting Study Hall (which was built to the edge of the village because a large parcel of land was not available in the village) is a two-building type, with the ancestral tablets placed at the center of the rear hall (Figure 13.22).

The overall size of a branch ancestral hall varies according to the status and wealth of the patron. Most are freestanding complexes of two or three buildings with courtyards in between them, not too different in form from that of small local temples. In a two-building structure, while proportions and construction are determined by local practices, the first building is normally used as the entrance hall, while the inner building is where the ancestral tablets are housed and ritual is conducted. In the Nanxijiang region of southeastern Zhejiang province, ancestral halls are mainly of the two-building type, with a theater or stage built to the back of the entrance hall and facing the main hall. Throughout this region, as seen in Figure 13.23, ancestral halls

Ancestral Halls

Fig. 13.24. *The bracket system of the ancestral hall of the Li lineage, Yanlong village, Nanxijiang area, Yongjia county, Zhejiang.* Source: Photograph by Puay-peng Ho 2001.

generally are three bays in width, with each bay being about 5–6 meters wide. Ornamentation can be seen in many building elements, particularly the wooden members of the building, such as elaborate timber bracketing systems, which are widely employed in ancestral halls throughout the Jiangnan region, where they add a sense of elegance to the buildings (Figure 13.24). If a member of a lineage had gained success in the imperial examinations, a pair of flagpoles would be erected in front of the hall, with the exact number of flagpoles being an indication of the status of the lineage. One of the most flamboyant examples is seen in front of the ancestral hall of the Zhang lineage in the village of Taxia, Fujian province (Figure 13.25), where there are thirteen pairs of flagpoles erected in an arc around the half-moon *fengshui* pond in front of the hall.

The largest ancestral hall, typically the focal ancestral hall for the lineage, consists of three or more buildings lined up along a central axis. The first structure serves as the entrance hall *[xiating]* and includes a central entrance gate with two side chambers *[xiangfang]*, with a courtyard separating it from the second or "middle" building *[zhongting]*, which is used as both a meeting hall and a place to offer sacrifices. The intervening courtyard between these two structures is usually rather large in order to accommodate a gathering of villagers for communal activities (Figure 13.26). Beyond and behind the second structure is a small courtyard and then a third building, or *shangting*, in which the ancestral tablets would be maintained (Figure 13.27). A line of movable screen panels is usually located at the rear of the central hall to preserve the privacy of the tablet hall. In addition, the narrow courtyard between the middle hall and rear hall also helps to preserve a sense of mystery to the tablet hall, known also as the "sleeping chamber," or *qin*, where the ancestral spirit is said to rest. During communal sacrifices offered to the ancestral spirit, the screen panels may be removed to allow an unobstructed view of the ancestral tablets in the third building and in order for the spirit to enjoy the sacrifices. While this represents a basic arrangement for a large ancestral hall, it is not uncommon to encounter further embellishments related to the official rank of the ancestor or indeed the wealth of the person who built the hall.

The most significant expression of high official rank and great wealth is the frontal width of the hall. A three-bay width can be seen as the standard, while a five-bay width is a clear indication of position and wealth, as it is the maximum width allowed by the imperial codes for nonimperial buildings (Figure 13.28). In some cases, indeed, the ancestral hall has a seven-bay frontage, a clear violation of the imperial sumptuary code, as only the emperor was to have a hall that size.

Puay-peng Ho

Fig. 13.25. *Flagpoles of the Deyuan Tang, ancestral hall of the Zhang lineage of Taxia village, Shuyang township, Nanjing county, Fujian.* Source: Photograph by Puay-peng Ho 1996.

Fig. 13.26a–b. *The courtyard between* **(a)** *the entrance ceremonial arch and the entrance hall, and* **(b)** *the entrance hall and the main meeting hall of Baolun Ge, the Luo Dongshu ancestral hall, Chengkan village, Shexian county, Anhui.* Source: Photograph by Puay-peng Ho 1999.

◀ 13.26a   13.26b ▼

Fig. 13.27. *The courtyard between the main meeting hall and the rear tablet hall of Baolun Ge, the Luo Dongshu ancestral hall, Chengkan village, Shexian county, Anhui.* Source: Photograph by Puay-peng Ho 1999.

Fig. 13.28. *A five-bay ancestral hall of the Hu lineage, Yingzhou village, Jixi county, Anhui.* Source: Photograph by Puay-peng Ho 2001.

Fig. 13.29. *The nine bays of Baolun Ge are arranged in three sections, with the central section and a bay on each side shown here. Chengkan village, Shexian county, Anhui.* Source: Photograph by Puay-peng Ho 1999.

▼

Cleverly, the patrons of these megastructures often were able to conceal the actual size by manipulating the bay width or eaves line in order to make the huge hall appear as if it were composed of only three bays. A good example of this subterfuge can be seen in Baolun Ge, whose nine-bay frontal width was clearly broken into three sections, each with three bays, by the device of adjusting the width of each bay and the separation of the hall interior into three sections (Figure 13.29). By comparison, the hall for a county magistrate would have a three-bay and three-building arrangement, much like that of a large ancestral hall. Further additions include side chambers or corridors on either side of both courtyards; a progressive increase in level and height of building from the entrance to the tablet hall; and the use of a major structural system, post-and-beam construction, with decorative brackets called *dougong*. One example of an exceptionally elaborate ancestral hall and an impressive symbol of solidarity is that of the He lineage at Shawan, Panyu, Guangdong province, where a ceremonial arch is located in the courtyard between the entrance hall and the sacrificial hall and the buildings are all five bays wide (Figure 13.30) (see Faure and Siu 1995, 28–34). In the case of the ancestral hall of

Puay-peng Ho

Fig. 13.30. *Liukeng Tang, the ancestral hall of the He lineage, Shawan township, Panyu city, Guangdong province.* Source: Photographs by Puay-peng Ho 1992.

the Luo lineage at Chengkan, Shexian, Anhui province, a gate structure with vertical wooden poles was placed in front of the entrance hall, and the tablet hall has two stories. Given the relatively small size of ordinary houses in these villages, the ancestral halls are indeed impressive structures that are distinguished symbolically and physically as the center of the lineage community.

Decorative motifs are found throughout ancestral halls and usually relate to good wishes for descendants, including prosperity and wealth, as well as abundant offspring. While ornamentation is particularly notable in the wooden members, such as those associated with the roof structure, the facia board, and the door, other ornamentation includes brick carving on the walls, stone carvings of the column bases and door drums, and stucco ornamentation on the walls and the ridges, as well as painting on various surfaces. Apart from iconography associated with good wishes, didactic calligraphy and edifying couplets were placed throughout each ancestral hall. Among the most common motifs are those expressing virtuous acts and conveying wishes for many offspring, subjects in line with the very purpose of the structure. The virtuous acts—promoting filial piety, loyalty, friendship, and

Fig. 13.31. *A wood carving showing the story of filial piety in the focal ancestral hall of the Zhou lineage, Huayang village, Jixi county, Anhui.* Source: Photograph by Puay-peng Ho 2001.

13.32 ▲

Fig. 13.32. *Pomegranates on the roof of the focal ancestral hall of Hang Tau village, Ping Shan, Hong Kong, expressing the wish for many offspring.* Source: Photograph by Puay-peng Ho 1993.

Fig. 13.33. *Stone carving of plum blossoms in the ancestral hall of the Zhou lineage of Huayang village, Jixi county, Anhui.* Source: Photograph by Puay-peng Ho 2001.

13.33 ▶

Fig. 13.34. *The form of an ancestral tablet, as described in the ritual code of the Ming dynasty.* Source: Cheng 1530, *juan* 6, 17.

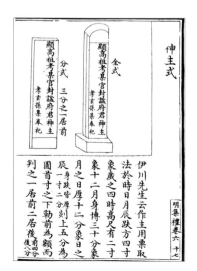

benevolence—are depicted in scenes from well-known stories and historical episodes (Figure 13.31), while wishes for posterity are expressed metaphorically via representations of melons and pomegranates with their many seeds (Figure 13.32). Other common messages are conveyed using auspicious signs and animals, such as the bat for good fortune or the unicorn for luck (see Knapp 1999, 81–157). The subjects of literati painting, such as plum blossoms and bamboo, are also found in the ornamentation of ancestral halls, perhaps to add a sense of the scholarly milieu (Figure 13.33). The names given to each ancestral hall also usually served a didactic purpose related to the corporate body. One good example is that of Dunben Tang, or the "Hall for Respecting the Root [of the lineage]" in Tangyue village, Shexian, Anhui. In many ancestral halls, as noted, there is a progressive increase in height as one moves farther inside. It is said that the number of steps carries with it a good omen in that *bubugao*, or "rising at every step," expresses wishes for a rise in the hierarchy of officialdom.

Wooden ancestral tablets are arranged in rows on an altar in the interior tablet

Puay-peng Ho

▲ **Fig. 13.35.** *The ancestral tablets of the focal ancestral hall of the Tang lineage (Chung Ling Tang Ancestral Hall), Lung Yeuk Tau; Fan Ling village, San Tin, New Territories, Hong Kong.* Source: Photograph by Puay-peng Ho 2003.

Fig. 13.36a–b.
a. *The three sections of ancestral tablets in the Cao lineage hall, Caofang village, Liancheng county, Fujian.*
b. *The ancestral altar of a small branch ancestral hall of the Wu lineage, Donglong village, Ningdu county, Jiangxi.* Source: Photographs by Puay-peng Ho 2001.

hall (Figures 13.34–13.35). In Fujian and Guangdong provinces, such altars are composed of decorative niches, similar to those found in temples to house images of deities. In the Jiangnan and Huizhou regions of central China, the niches are not decorative but are elegantly sculpted and enclosed by lattice panels, which may be opened during ritual but serve generally to protect the tablets. Usually there are three or more sets of niches dividing the ancestral tablets into distinct groups, with the central niche housing the tablets of the main ancestors in successive generations (Figure 13.35). From the top row, the central position is given to the tablet of the focal ancestor, with his first-generation descendant on the left and his second-generation descendant on the right, the third on the next left and the fourth on the next right, and so on. The niches on either side of the central niche are for people who sponsored the building of the ancestral hall and descendants who did significant deeds, performed righteous acts, or showed extraordinary filial piety (Figure 13.36a). In a small branch ancestral hall, the altar with decorative surrounds can be very small, with only enough room for a few spirit tablets (Figure 13.36b).

Ancestral Halls

The most important events at the ancestral halls were always the spring and autumn sacrifices. These were times when the halls would be swept clean, large red lanterns hung, doors and columns decorated with paper and cloth, and the altar draped with red cloth. These periodic sacrifices involved the participation of all male members of the lineage and were usually conducted in a solemn and orderly manner in order to induce awe and inspiration. Lineage elders led the ceremonies by "kneeling three times and bowing the head nine times"—known in English as kowtow *[ketou]*—an act that provided a model for the younger members of the lineage. Sacrifices made to the ancestors included whole animals, such as a lamb, pig, or fowl, in addition to vegetables, fruits, and wine. The ancestral tablets would be moved from the niche or altar closet into the open altar, an action that was seen as tantamount to inviting the ancestors to take a seat at the banquet prepared for them. A lengthy sacrificial text, composed by the most learned member of the lineage, would be read, and after the ancestors had indicated that they had taken the meal, the sacrifice would be deemed over. Thereupon, the villagers would distribute the sacrificial offerings to each person on the lineage registry, by order of their position in the village, starting with the lineage head. Each registered member would have an equal share of the sacrifice except for those above sixty years of age and those who had passed state examinations, who would receive double or triple portions. Members of the lineage who had been guilty of misdeeds and had been punished by the elders of the lineage were denied any share of the sacrifice; this denial would be expressed in a humiliating way in order to uphold discipline within the lineage and enhance the solidarity of lineage members. The dates for sacrifice at branch and family ancestral halls would be different from those at the focal ancestral hall so that members of the lineage could participate at all rituals. The list of ancestral halls of the lineage and dates for spring and fall sacrifices were usually found in the lineage registry.

Another prominent celebration at the ancestral hall occurred on New Year's Day, when offerings were again made to the ancestors (Figure 13.37). During these festivities, the elder of the lineage would read the regulations of the lineage and exhort all members to good conduct, brotherly love, and filial duty. Operas were performed on stages built in the ancestral hall, or temporary stages inside or outside the ancestral hall complex, not only to entertain the ancestral spirits and their living descendants, but also to present didactic tales of moral persuasion. Another significant occasion in the past was associated with entering a newborn son into the

Puay-peng Ho

Fig. 13.37. *A lineage meal cele-brating the New Year in the focal ancestral hall of Ping Shan village, San Tin, New Territories, Hong Kong.* Source: Photograph by Puay-peng Ho 1996.

lineage registry in order for him to be rightfully recognized as a member of the lineage and to enjoy its privileges. In southern China, this was done in a ceremony involving the lighting of a lantern during the New Year festivities. In Huizhou, the newborn was entered into the registry only after he had reached the age of three, when his chances of surviving were considered much stronger.

The ancestral hall was also where marriages took place and where the bride was brought to inform the ancestors of the happy occasion, as well as to acknowledge that she had married into the family and the lineage (Figure 13.38). The ancestral hall was also where major decisions of the lineage were made. These included accounting for lineage property, upholding lineage regulations, judging disciplinary cases, and providing schooling for children. As positions in officialdom could be gained only if one passed the imperial examinations, providing a good education for the children was of paramount importance. Thus, there was no better place for the village school than the ancestral hall, with its spacious and light interior, as well as its didactic ornamentation. Ancestral halls were also used for the funeral services of important members of the lineage. Since some believed that it was desirable to die in an ancestral hall, those approaching death sometimes came to live in one of

Fig. 13.38. *A bride entering into, crossing the narrow entry courtyard, and then standing in the inner courtyard of the focal ancestral hall. On the right, she is standing on bamboo chopsticks, the pronunciation of which is homophonous with "sons coming quickly." Xinwei village, Longnan county, Jiangxi.* Source: Photographs by Puay-peng Ho 2000.

its side rooms or were moved there to await the final moment. After death, the body would be moved to the main hall, and, after the right time was determined by a *fengshui* master, proper funeral rituals would be held. It is still common to see coffins stored in various places in the ancestral hall (Figure 13.39). While the hall was considered sacred space during periodic sacrifices, in normal times the open areas provided room for children to play and for older folks merely to gather, chat, and pass time.

Ancestral halls represent a collective tangible symbol of common patrilineal descent from a designated ancestor. By their scale, scope, and ornamentation, they express the historical solidarity of the lineage, as well as its significant economic achievement. Moral admonitions, honorific statements, and didactic ornamentation provided substantial reminders of correct conduct and mutual obligations to guide individual and community behavior. By participation in periodic rituals within such grand edifices, individuals and their immediate families saw that the lineage was not merely an abstract concept but one that was bound by blood in a collective identity that went beyond the present, embracing not only the past, but anticipating the future as well.

Fig. 13.39a–c.

a. *The body of the deceased interred in the main hall of the Weishang ancestral hall of the Wu lineage, Donglong village, Ningdu county, Jiangxi.* Source: Photograph by Puay-peng Ho 2003.

b. *The setting of a funerary ritual hall with the coffin placed in the rear and seating for visitors in the main hall of Tanfu ancestral hall in the same village.* Source: Photograph by Puay-peng Ho 2003.

c. *Coffins stored for future use in the ancestral hall, Diaoyuan village, Ji'an county, Jiangxi.* Source: Photograph by Puay-peng Ho 2000.

JAMES A. FLATH

14   Reading the Text of the Home

Domestic Ritual Configuration through Print

Fig. 14.1. *Doorway with Door Gods attached to both leaves in Yangjiabu, Shandong.* Source: Photograph by James A. Flath 1999.

In the early decades of the twentieth century, a visitor to any Chinese town or village would have encountered colorful Door Gods [Menshen] affixed to the double-leafed doors that led to the courtyards of the traditional Chinese home. As seen in Figure 14.1, this is a representation epitomizing the traditional Chinese home as quaint and earthy, yet also a closed entity of walls within walls that never revealed more than a glimpse of what lay within. The image, however, also suggests a way to decode some of the meanings ascribed to the structure by its inhabitants, since the Door Gods indicate that the traditional Chinese home was, among other things, spiritually configured through transcendent qualities assigned to various aspects of its architecture. From the stalwart Door Gods to the sanctity of the Jade Emperor, or Yu Huang, and even the humble Spirit of the Pigpen [Da Zhu Gui], the mortal inhabitants of the traditional home were intensely aware of household deities and spirits and the respect that they demanded. This is demonstrated nowhere more directly than through the votive woodblock print images called *nianhua*, or "New Year pictures," that were designed for use in the home as icons and ritual aids.

Nianhua were, and in some cases still are, available in both secular and ritual forms, but it is the latter in particular that help to explain two divergent but complementary perspectives on the home. First, it can be demonstrated that ritual *nianhua* gave concrete identity to the domestic spaces for which they were designed and that social values were embedded in the physical structure of the house through the practice of domestic cults. Second, the study of domestic social values through print serves to place home and family within the wider social and cultural landscape and especially helps to illuminate the relationship between local society and higher authority.[1] These perspectives are linked by a third: all of the images under consideration here originated as woodblock prints. As such, these icons must be evaluated not as the parochial text of the individual home, but as part of the wider print culture that produced, disseminated, obtained, displayed, and read printed representations. Print penetrated and transformed domestic social relations, and it tied the individual household into the universal understanding of what it meant to live in the home and to be a member of a family. Nonetheless, while printed ritual images

Fig. 14.2. *Woodblock printing shop in Yangjiabu, Shandong.* Source: Photograph by James A. Flath 1999.

Fig. 14.3. *Although separate blocks with different colors of ink are used to produce most woodblock prints, in some cases prints are colored and detailed by hand, as the spaces left by the inked outline block are filled in. Yangliuqing, Tianjin.* Source: Photograph by James A. Flath 1999.

played a role in configuring the household, the conditions of display and reading also informed the final interpretation of the text, ultimately providing the means for adapting abstract domestic cults to the realities of domesticity.

Print Production in Rural China

When considering the social impact of printed items, one must consider how they were produced and generally made available to the public. This factor is especially important in appreciating how widely certain images circulated and to understanding that even though locally produced, print was capable of integrating regional cultures and promoting a universal structure of domestic iconography.

The actual practice of traditional woodblock printing was simple but remarkably efficient and capable of delivering large quantities of identical images to the market. The standard method of woodblock print production first involved pasting an outline of the desired picture onto a block of hardwood and then carving it out in relief. Separate blocks containing the color forms were then produced for each of the four to six colors used in the picture. The printing process then involved pressing paper onto the inked outline block and repeating the procedure for each of the colors until the picture was complete (Figure 14.2). In some instances, in Yangliuqing in particular, finer prints are colored and detailed by hand, as seen in Figure 14.3.

In the late nineteenth and early twentieth centuries, the *nianhua* industry was dominated by a handful of large printing centers. While these centers could be found in all corners of China—including Mianzhu in Sichuan, Suzhou in Jiangsu,

James A. Flath

and Foshan in Guangdong—the discussion in this chapter will focus on several whose products were particular to North China. Yangliuqing, in the Tianjin suburbs, controlled the largest share of the popular print market in North China and consistently produced the finest representations, which entrepreneurs were then able to distribute to rural and urban consumers as far away as Xinjiang (Chinese Government Bureau of Economic Information 1927, 51). The county of Wuqiang in central Hebei was oriented more toward the rural markets of the North China plain, but printers were still known to market their goods as far off as Shaanxi (*Wuqiang xianzhi* 1996, 277–280). The former commercial center of Zhuxianzhen in Henan was in decline by the close of the nineteenth century owing to infrastructural changes that had choked off its trade with the south, but in the early twentieth century the remnants of its once booming *nianhua* industry could still be found there and in nearby Kaifeng. Finally, the eastern Shandong village of Yangjiabu and its subsidiaries controlled much of the Shandong *nianhua* market and shipped prints as far off as Manchuria (*Yangjiabu cunzhi* 1993, 25).

While precise statistics do not exist, each of these industries is believed to have produced and distributed print runs numbering in the tens of millions during the last months of the lunar year. The *nianhua* printing industry was thus highly centralized and capable of extending large quantities of print over considerable distances. This says much about the nature of cultural integration in rural China generally, but the most important implication for this discussion is that even if the popular print industry did not exactly promote a universal domestic religion, it at least promoted a relatively standard household iconography that was vital to the successful propagation and collective understanding of domestic cults.

The Ritual Configuration of the North China Home

The consecration of the home had been a part of domestic life since at least ca. 500 B.C., when the *Analects [Lunyu]* mentioned the stove and "recess" as sites of veneration. Robert Chard's (1999, 259) discussion of imperial household cults demonstrates that subsequent dynasties continued to promote domestic sacrifices through various configurations of household spaces and accessories down to the end of the Ming dynasty, when they were described as the "Five Sacrifices." The Qing dynasty briefly reinstated those sacrifices, and although they ceased to be officially observed in 1661, they were never formally abolished and continued to be popular throughout the dynasty.

Fig. 14.4. *"Enjoying New Year Together."* Yangjiabu, Shandong. *Contemporary reprint of an early-twentieth-century print. This image shows in serial form the major sacrifices and activities performed by the family at New Year. These include, from top to bottom and left to right, sacrifices to Heaven and Earth, Stove God [Zaojun], and God of Wealth; preparing food, paying respect to the ancestors, setting fireworks, greeting friends and family, and sending wife to visit family. Note that male family members perform all of the sacrifices, including that to the Stove God. Women remain in the background.* Source: Collection of James A. Flath 1996.

The official description of these practices, however, says little about the highly animated cults that took over and transformed the former state sacrifices. As the home was the most personal environment, it was the place that was most deeply inscribed with the personified cults associated with key sacrifices (Figure 14.4). Henri Doré (1966, 4:417) wrote in the early twentieth century that there were six household deities *[jinjishen]*, or "tutelary gods of the house," belonging to the "Ministry of Exorcism." These included the generic household gods *[jiatang]*; ancestral tablets *[muzhu]*; the Stove God [Zaojun]; Gate or Door Gods [Menshen]; the exorcist Zhong Kui; and the male and female Genii of the Bed [Chuang Gong and Chuang Mu]. In addition to these household deities, it was possible to use the historical hero Jiang Ziya as an exorcist and to give the seat of honor to the Bodhisattva Guanyin, among others.

Other configurations of household deities can be found in woodblock prints representing the "six household gods" (Figure 14.5). An unpublished print in the Alekseev collection held at St. Petersburg's Hermitage Museum, for example,

James A. Flath

Fig. 14.5. *Household gods. Yangliu-qing, Tianjin. Contemporary reprint of an early-twentieth-century print.* Source: Wang 1992.

Fig. 14.6. *The Jade Emperor. North China, early twentieth century. This image shows the Jade Emperor before an altar set with offerings and flanked by his immortal attendants in official dress. Images of this type were known as "paper-horse" prints and were intended to be ceremonially incinerated rather than permanently posted.* Source: Wang 1992.

includes Door Gods [Menshen], the Lad of the Well [Jingquan Tongzi], the Earth God [Tudi Gong], the three Niang Niang goddesses [Sangu Furen], the God of the Family [Hushen], and one other unnamed deity, presumably the Jade Emperor.[2] Another from Baoding includes the Stove God [Zaojun], the God of Wealth [Caishen], Door God [Menshen], the Earth God [Tudi Gong], the Well God [Jingquan], and another known as Gouliu, possibly the God of the Latrine (Wang 1999, 62). This evidence shows that the selection of household gods varied from place to place and from situation to situation, with each household having a favored subgroup determined by local custom and family precedent. Whatever the personal identity of the gods may have been, they all shared in being closely attached to a specific part of the household. Some were synonymous with their station in the house, others were more abstract, but all had a distinct physical space in which their cult was centered and their printed likenesses posted. The four principal cults of Heaven and Earth—Jade Emperor, the Stove God, the Door Gods, and the ancestral spirits—are discussed in detail below.

Reading the Text of the Home

The Courtyard: Heaven and Earth. In 1752 Zheng Banqiao (also Zheng Xie), the magistrate of Wei county in the province of Shandong, commemorated the renovation of the local City God temple with a discourse on the nature of Heaven and Earth:

> So what we gaze upward and behold of an azure appearance *is* Heaven; what we look down and come in contact with, massive . . . *is* Earth. Between *Heaven and Earth, endowed with* ears, eyes, mouth, nostrils, arms and legs, having the ability to speak and to clothe himself, ceremonious and capable of observing the proprieties [rites], *is* Man. But does this imply that the Azure Heaven is also a personal being with ears, eyes, and nostrils? Since the time of the Duke of Chou, it has been styled the Supreme Ruler, and the vulgar have also called it the Gemmeous Emperor [Jade Emperor], and have thereupon given it ears, eyes, mouth, nostrils, arms and legs, a crown with pendant ornaments, a jadestone scepter, and a personal existence. . . . They have given it a retinue of youthful officers, and fierce generals as companions; and the people of the Empire following *en masse* the footsteps *of their predecessors* have also personified it . . . but Heaven, Earth . . . the Corners of the House, the Well, and the Kitchen Furnace, although deified have no personal existence, and should not be sacrificed to as though they had. Yet from ancient times even the sages have all sacrificed to them as though they had a personal existence. (Cited in McCartee 1869–1870, 173–177; emphasis in original)

Zheng recognized that the concept of Heaven and Earth could be understood as formally abstract, but he also understood the irresistible urge to imbue the abstract with personal qualities. This had changed little by the early twentieth century, when Juliet Bredon and Igor Mitrophanow (1927, 145–146) reported on the ceremony of the "One Hundred Gods" [Bai Shen] in Beijing, noting that it was observed on the nineteenth day of the first moon, when "all the gods of heaven and earth" would gather to report to the Jade Emperor (Figure 14.6).

The pantheistic prints that were used in this ceremony represent various configurations of tutelary spirits, hierarchically arranged for the convenience of sacrifice. These demonstrate concretely which sets of deities were considered important enough to be included and how they stood in relation to one another. "One Hundred Gods" prints have been thoroughly analyzed by Bent Pedersen (1988), and so it will suffice to say that these large prints included thirty to fifty gods of various affiliations, with key deities like the Jade Emperor, Buddha, Guanyin, and Guandi placed most prominently (Figure 14.7). These prints were intended strictly

James A. Flath

for the New Year sacrifice, and, according to regional practice, the print was wrapped around a wooden or sorghum stalk tablet or simply folded into the shape of a spirit tablet. This would then be placed before an incense burner on the "contacting gods table" *[jieshen zhuo]* in the courtyard, as seen in Figure 14.8. For indoor use, a less populous depiction of "Nine Buddhas of Heaven and Earth" could be decorated with various offerings. Other versions of the pantheon were sacrificed to and/or installed in the niche or under the eaves of the house (Figure 14.9). These were simplified prints exhibiting a central spirit tablet inscribed with words to the effect of

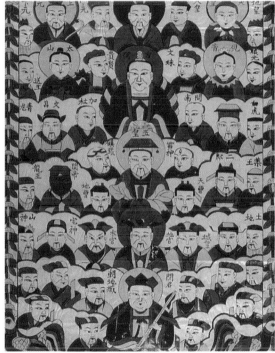

"Ruler of Heaven and Earth, Three Realms, Ten Directions, and Unlimited Wonders" [Tiandi sanjie shifang wanling zhen zai] (Figures 14.10, 14.11). According to Nagao (1971, 73–81), the prints represented the gods of the house and were worshiped on the first and fifteenth of the month, at the same time as the generic household gods and the Stove God. These representations would garner continuing attention throughout the year and on important occasions, such as weddings, when bride and groom bowed before them.

Pantheons were frequently accompanied by a set of "paper-horse" [zhima] prints (Figure 14.12). Rough and simple compared to other nianhua, these prints were kept year round in shops devoted to the sale of paper gods to members of various social groups, occupations, and trades, each of which had its own patron. Paper-horse prints were also available for every malady and social occasion, thereby multiplying their numbers manyfold. In addition to retail shops, individual paper-horse prints were to be found in markets, temples, and other venues. The sum total of these images is impossible to calculate, and even educated observers like Doré could say only that the varieties of paper-horse prints were "almost countless" (1966, 4:427). In the mid-1920s Clarence Day too could write only that one particular shop stocked "a thousand or more" types of such prints (1927, 280).[3] Yet it should not be assumed that most people were more than vaguely aware of most of them because many deities belonged to specific guilds or were managed by ritual specialists who apportioned the gods much as a physician managed a pharmacopoeia. Otherwise, they could be bought in bulk and incinerated as a package.

The printed representations of Heaven and Earth have several important implications for the spatial configuration of the home. While on some occasions the "Nine Buddhas of Heaven and Earth" or similar groupings of gods were invited into the front hall during New Year, most of the one hundred gods were respectfully left out in the courtyard. The main sacrifices to Heaven and Earth (and its personification as the Jade Emperor) were conducted out of doors, and the permanent throne of Heaven and Earth was also posted in an external niche or on an outside support overlooking the courtyard. This meant that the awesome power of these deities was conscripted for the overall protection and cultivation of house and family, and they were accordingly positioned so that nothing spectral could enter or leave the house without their scrutiny, thus making them a key link in the spiritual defense of the home. At the same time, when the Jade Emperor was positioned outside, he could be kept at arm's length from the family, thereby permitting the household residents to avoid his overwhelming gaze. The Jade Emperor certainly

James A. Flath

Fig. 14.10. *Printed shrine to the Jade Emperor. Beijing, 1927.* Source: Nachbaur and Wang 1926.

Fig. 14.12. *Spirit of the Insect King. North China, early twentieth century. This image is classed as a "paper-horse" print to be ceremonially burned, probably as a response to infestations.* Source: Collection of the Muban Foundation.

Fig. 14.11. *Heaven and Earth. Yangjiabu, Shandong. Contemporary reprint of early-twentieth-century original. This image suggests a shrine or temple with dragon-entwined pillars, lanterns, and steps leading up to a plaque inscribed with the words, "The True Ruler of Heaven and Earth, Three Realms, Ten Directions, and Unlimited Wonders."* Source: Collection of James A. Flath 1996.

represented ultimate authority, and the family legitimated that authority through
domestic ritual. Insofar as that cult was represented by a print, however, the ultimate interpretation depended upon the treatment and reading of the text. In that
sense the family could manipulate the cult to its own advantage and moderate any
supervisory privileges the Jade Emperor may have carried as an agent of external
authority.

The Kitchen and the Stove God. While the Jade Emperor was isolated from the
family, he was not without a representative in the home. The Stove God [Zaojun],
also known as the "Lord of the Family," the "Overseer of Fate," and the "Heavenly
Spy," was the lowest-ranking member of the heavenly bureaucracy and technically
subordinate to the Jade Emperor. There is little question, however, that qualita-
tively the Stove God was the central domestic deity. Of the five household obser-
vances documented in 1833 in Shanghe, Shandong, for example, the worship of
the Stove God was most important (Ding 1992, 134). Conventional wisdom also
instructed families that if they could buy only one *nianhua* a year, that print must
be of the Stove God (Figure 14.13).

Establishing the identity of the Stove God is much more complicated and in many
respects counterproductive, since as Robert Chard (1990, 1995) has demonstrated in
his studies of the legends and scriptures of the Stove God, there is no simple way to
account for the deity's folkloric significance. In respect to North China, however, it
is worthwhile citing Arthur Smith (1899, 27), who noted at the close of the nineteenth
century that the Stove God was widely believed to be Zhang Gong, who maintained
peace and harmony in his household despite its being inhabited by nine generations
of the family. The secret to Zhang's success was his shared civility, which extended
even to his hundred dogs, who were known to wait patiently if any of their number
was late for a meal. When the emperor sent for the patriarch to learn his secret, Zhang
called for a brush and repeatedly wrote the character *ren,* or "forbearance," on a sheet
of paper. It was due to his example that Zhang Gong was given the household throne.
Another popular account relates the story of Zhang Layue, a lecherous husband who
abandoned his wife in favor of a prostitute. When he finally returned to his virtuous
wife, Zhang was so taken with remorse that he killed himself by leaping into the stove,
where he became the Stove God (Yu 1994, 7). An elite view of the Stove God's origin
is found in the 1935 annals of Qingcheng, Shandong, which cite a popular verse concerning the Stove God: "The Stove God is originally named Zhang, a bowl of rice and
bowl of soup." The compiler, however, noted that he understood the Stove God to be

James A. Flath

Fig.14.13. *Stove God [Zaojun]. North China, 1911. This print represents the Stove God and his wife, along with a host of servants, the Heavenly Official, God of Wealth, and the Eight Immortals. Beside the Stove God and his wife is the instruction, "Go up to Heaven and speak positively, return to palace and bring auspiciousness." At the top is a lunar calendar for the year of Xinhai—1911.* Source: Collection of the Muban Foundation.

the spirit of Emperor Yandi, the patron of fire, and that he did not know the origin of the name Zhang (Ding 1992, 180).[4]

In being only a few among many interpretations, these legends cannot be taken as literally representative, but they establish some of the representative characteristics of the Stove God. First, as verified by the popular saying, "Men don't worship the moon, women don't offer sacrifices to the Stove God," the Stove God is a patriarch, and his cult is essentially patriarchal. Second, as the wide variety of scripture on the subject indicates, the Stove God supports familism either as a responsible patriarch such as Zhang Gong or as a wayward patriarch like Zhang Layue, redeemed by the grace of heaven.

While details varied from region to region, the basic structure of the common ritual was, in contrast to the folklore, remarkably standard across China (Chard 1995, 18). The ritual involving the Stove God print began with removing the poster from the wall on the twenty-third day of the twelfth lunar month and ritually burning

Fig. 14.14. *Stove God [Zaojun] in context. Yangjiabu, Shandong. This museum reconstruction represents a traditional North China stove set with sacrificial offerings to the Stove God, whose image is pasted to the wall above.* Source: Photograph by James A. Flath 1999.

it. This observance was supposed to send the god on his annual New Year's journey to make his report on the comings and goings of the family to the supreme Jade Emperor in Heaven. The Stove God, however, appears slightly corrupt or, as Lu Xun (1964, 243) wrote, slightly stupid since on the evening before his dispatch to Heaven the family would take a bit of honey or a confection known as "teeth-sticking sweet" and smear it on his mouth. This might have been considered a bribe, but generally it was believed that with his mouth either stuck shut or full of candy, the Stove God could only mumble forth his unintelligible report to the Jade Emperor and return home, where the family had prepared a new "throne" for him in the form of the new *nianhua* bearing his image. For the remainder of the year the Stove God would receive sacrifices on the first and fifteenth day of each month.

The "palace" or "throne" of the Stove God was invariably found above the family stove, sometimes in the form of an actual niche but usually consisting only of a two-dimensional structure conveniently included in the body of the print that was posted on the wall, as seen in Figure 14.14. There are regional variations in the details of the Stove God print, but the basic form remains virtually the same throughout China. In most cases the Stove God, often accompanied by his wife, is suspended below a calendar that occupies the upper register of the print. The lower register of the print is essentially the Palace of the Stove God (Zaojun Fu), and he resides in the space with his own family, retinue, and symbols of abundance.

As a printed representation, therefore, the Stove God configured the kitchen as a patriarchal ritual space, but the more serious implications of having the "heavenly spy" watching over the women's working environment were undermined by the casual treatment that the deity was likely to receive. It is possible, even likely, that the Stove God cult took on more complex characteristics drawn from scriptures and folklore, but the basic form of the deity and cult was extended through the mass production of the simple and essentially benign Stove God print, and the basic reading of that print was, as Robert Chard (1995, 54) argues, informed by the casual exercise of annual ritual.

Door Gods. In the late nineteenth and early twentieth centuries, an outsider might have observed that the ritualistic inscription of the home began at its outer extreme, with the double-leaf front gate affixed with a pair of Door Gods, or Menshen (Figure 14.15). Dun Lichen wrote that legends surrounding Door Gods were strictly popular interpretation, and, according to his learning, false: "In reality these explanations are . . . false, and it is only correct to say of them that they are gate gods. In

James A. Flath

Fig. 14.15. *Martial Door Gods. Left, contemporary reprint of early-twentieth-century original, Yangjiabu, Shandong. Right, Shandong 1907–1908. These figures represent the Tang dynasty generals Qin Qiong and Yuchi Gong.* Source: Collection of James A. Flath 1996 and V. M. Alekseev Collection, Museum of Religion, St. Petersburg.

fact the gate is the chief of the five household things sacrificed to, and hence is not a heterodox deity. Thus when people of the Capital regard them as gods, but do not sacrifice to them, they have failed to grasp their significance" (1906, 100).

In the common household, Door God rituals were indeed far less developed than were the mythological trappings of the deities. As Dun complained, most people failed to sacrifice to them, and it was necessary to place the Door Gods in the right order. "The Door Gods, wrongly pasted, trouble to the right and to the left," as a proverb advises; this simple requirement hardly compensates for the extensive corpus of lore and legend that surrounded them (Plopper 1926, 185). Unlike the Stove God, the Door Gods had variable but clearly defined identities drawn from well-known sources. One of the most commonly held beliefs is taken from the ever-popular first-century B.C. *Shanhaijing* [Classic of the mountains and seas], which notes that the Door Gods Shen Tu and Yu Lei originated as guardians of the celestial peaches of Dushuoshan (De Groot 1892–1907, 6:954). As related in Wu Chengen's Ming dynasty novel, *Journey to the West,* Qin Shubao and Hu Jingde have equally classic origins and were said to have been so effective in ridding the Tang emperor's palace of ghosts that they were honored by having their images posted on the palace doors. In similar spirit, the seventeenth-century *Enfeoffment*

Reading the Text of the Home

Fig. 14.16. *Civil Door Gods. Zhuxianzhen, Henan, 1920s–1930s. These civil Door Gods, suggesting the figure of Dou Yujun, are surrounded by children holding traditional symbols of fortune and wealth, including the* ruyi *scepter (receive all that you wish for), a lantern (rise to officialdom), and lotus (continuity of honorable sons).* Source: Collection of the Muban Foundation.

of the Gods supplies the "Ran Deng (Lamp Lighting) Daoist" riding a deer and Zhao Gongming on his tiger-mount. Finally, the classic *Romance of the Three Kingdoms* contributes Guan Yu (Guandi), while *Outlaws of the Marsh* adds his lineal descendant Guan Sheng.[5] The common denominator and central component of all front gate Door Gods is trustworthiness, strength, and loyalty, supported by a fierce martial countenance and impressive weaponry.

The jurisdiction of these gods was limited to the outer gates, while interior doors were delegated to other agents more appropriate to those spaces. After passing through the outer gate, one would approach the house, where s/he would encounter the door to the house and its associated deities. The prints used on this second entrance were normally smaller than those used for the front gate and incorporated certain cultural and civic heroes. In the interests of maintaining balance, not only do the secondary Door Gods appear in perfect internal balance, but also their civility balances the martial nature of the Door Gods at the front gate. One common figure is Dou Yujun (Dou Yanshan), a philanthropic poet who sired and educated the "five dragons" of the Dou family (Figure 14.16). As told in the classical poem *The Five Cassia's of the Dou House,* all attained honor by passing the imperial civil service exams and receiving coveted *jinshi* (metropolitan) degrees (Gan 1962, 32).

James A. Flath

Fig. 14.17. *Zhong Kui. Zhuxianzhen, Henan, 1930s.* Source: Collection of the Muban Foundation.

Other interior Door Gods include the "Three Stars" of fortune, longevity, and emolument (rank and salary) or the wealth- and happiness-summoning icons, "Tianguan (the heavenly official) Grants Fortune" *[Tianguan cifu].* In each case, the civil gods supplement the security of the home with the requirements of learned cultivation. An even smaller set of deities could be used for bedroom doors or secondary buildings. Where a household was home to a married woman who had not yet given birth, the bridal chamber could be decorated with fertility symbols such as "Qilin Sends Children" *[Qilin song zi]* or other depictions of honorable male children to promote the birth and proper cultivation of any male heirs.

A final use of deities and charms to protect doorways of home and business alike was during the Duanwu Festival and the "evil fifth month," when all manner of negative forces were set loose in the world (Knapp 1999b, 76–78). According to Dun Lichen, Beijing residents followed these practices in order to protect themselves from disaster: "Every year at the time of the *Duan Ying,* shops have yellow streamers a foot long, covered with vermilion seal impressions, or perhaps painted with figures of the 'Heavenly Master' or of Zhong Kui, or with the forms of the five poisonous creatures, which serve as charms. These are hung up and sold, and the people of the Capital compete with one another in buying them. They are pasted up on the second gate of one's house to ward off evil influences" (1906, 44).

Zhong Kui, the most formidable exorcist, began his rise to fame in the Song dynasty, when his story was related in Shen Gua's *Mengxi bitan* [Jottings from Mengxi]. The story relates how Zhong Kui, having failed to serve the emperor during his life, swore to serve him in the afterlife by exterminating all spectral evil. In appreciation, the emperor ordered the painter Wu Daozi (fl. 710–760) to render a portrait of Zhong Kui to be posted as a deterrent against demons, thus the common appellation "demon queller" (De Groot 1892–1907, 6: 1174–1175).[6] Most people in the early twentieth century, however, would likely have known Zhong Kui better for his role in popular dramas, such as "Zhong Kui Marries off His Sister," which tells how the scholarly Zhong Kui was denied his rightful examination honors because of his hideous appearance. The humiliation caused him to commit suicide, but because he had earlier promised his sister's hand in marriage to his friend and benefactor, Zhong Kui returned in spirit to fulfill the pledge (Figure 14.17).

Another powerful exorcist came in the form of the "Heavenly Master," Zhang Tianshi (A.D. 34–156), a historical Daoist priest who founded a Daoist satrapy during the Han Dynasty period. Despite his personal demise, Zhang's works carried on through his putative lineage as late as the twentieth century, when his descendants

Fig. 14.18. *Zhang Tianshi. Beijing, 1927. Zhang Tianshi wields his heaven-sent sword, which emits powerful* yang *energy to dispel the poison represented by the toad.* Source: Nachbaur and Wang 1926.

Fig. 14.19. *Five poisons* [wudu]. *Beijing, 1927. The "five poisons" of snake, centipede, scorpion, salamander, and toad are surrounded and dissipated by positive energy.* Source: Nachbaur and Wang 1926.

continued to exercise their spiritual domain from their base in Longhushan, Jiangxi, before being disentitled under the Republic. The image of Zhang Tianshi, therefore, had an immediate connection with the historical exorcist through popular history and the practice of his sect or the Daoist religion, and with his lineal descendants who performed services in the present, including the manufacture of exorcistic prints.[7] Zhang's exorcist prints were especially in demand during the fifth month, when they were needed to dispel the five poisons, or *wudu*. Several of these yellow-colored prints are found in Nachbaur and Wang's 1926 collection, including a depiction of the cosmic neutralization of the "five poisons," represented by serpent, toad, centipede, salamander, and scorpion (De Groot 1892–1907 6: 1182–1185) (Figures 14.18–14.19).

In comparison to Dun Lichen's account that the Door Gods were simply "the chief of the five household things sacrificed to," in other accounts Door Gods came

James A. Flath

with specific heroic identities that guaranteed their qualification as capable defenders and also allowed them to double as a source of entertainment for the householder. From the perspective of Confucian orthodoxy, in which scholars like Dun were still being trained at the end of the Qing dynasty, such attributes distorted the original intention of household ritual as a means of exerting orthodox behavior at home. Therefore, what may have most bothered Dun Lichen was the fact that the Door Gods were not worshiped as derivatives of orthodox deities but as independent and widely celebrated heroes from history and mythology. As in the case of the Stove God, what was perceived in some circles as a means to effect domestic ritual standards had little bearing on domestic experience, simply because elite circles did not have the capacity to produce and distribute their messages on the same scale as the *nianhua* industry. And while there was a very general success in convincing people of a need for household ritual, the final interpretation of the specific form was left up to the imaginations of the print specialists, who responded not to the occasional critique of an obscure literatus, but to the demands of their discerning clientele.

Ancestralism and the Family Hall

Patricia Ebrey (1995) has argued convincingly that the propagation of the elite model of ancestral sacrifice is the greatest achievement of those literati who sought to encourage domestic ritualism, a subject treated in greater extent in the previous chapter. While Ebrey is primarily concerned with the Song dynasty, Chow Kai-wing (1994) supports the case for an equally energetic propagation of ancestor ritual in late imperial China and especially in the Qing dynasty. But if ancestralism was widely promoted by the social elite, even considering the increased publication of ritual texts in late imperial China, it is still improbable that the vast majority of people had more than a vague awareness of these orthodox interpretations of *zong* (patriline) and *jia* (home/family). It may be shown that this vague awareness did not seriously inhibit the adoption of such concepts in common households, but to understand how these concepts were appreciated it will be necessary to turn *not* to Zhu Xi's eleventh century *Family Rituals* or any of the other classic ritual texts, but to the simple "ancestor prints" that gave the most direct representation to the ancestral cult in the great majority of North China homes (Figure 14.20).

In *Family Rituals,* Zhu Xi was direct in his instructions concerning how the ancestral shrine should be constructed as an elaborate, freestanding structure and

Fig. 14.20. *Paper family hall. Jiangzhuangzhen, Shandong. This elaborate image represents a wealthy family of officials and their attendants preparing to enter a family ancestral hall. The upper half of the print portrays the founding ancestors behind a sacrificial altar and ancestral tablet. The blank spaces on either side are intended for the names of later ancestors.* Source: Photograph by James A. Flath 1999.

equipped with ritual books, clothes, and sacrificial vessels (Ebrey 1991, 7). While ancestral halls were not unknown in North China, the expense of building and maintaining such structures was beyond consideration for the average farm family, who was far more likely to replace the ancestral hall with a simple graphic representation. The 1936 County Annals from the perpetually impoverished Dongping county in western Shandong refer to such prints and pictures literally as the "paper family hall" *[zhi jiatang]* and note that they were put up for New Year and stored away after the fifteenth day of the first month (Ding 1992, 284). Martin Yang (1968, 93) gives due respect to the importance of ancestral pictures as literal representations of the ancestors, who were integral members of the family and critical to the outcome of family fortunes. Myron Cohen's informants in a village south of Beijing also recalled that "poorer people had ancestral scrolls, richer ones had ancestral tablets." The scrolls were described as either revered objects passed down from generation to generation and updated whenever necessary or as simple printed "forms"

James A. Flath

Fig. 14.21. *Ancestor picture. Yangjiabu, Shandong. Contemporary reprint of early twentieth-century original.* Source: Photograph by James A. Flath 1999.

Fig. 14.22. *Ancestor print. North China, 1907–1908. This simple image nonetheless contains all the essential elements of the family hall, including a gate guarded by Door Gods, tablets for three generations inscribed with the words "Throne of the Ancient Spirits," and the portraits of the founding ancestors at the top, with a final tablet reading "Three Generations of Paternal Lineage."* Source: V. M. Alekseev Collection, 1907 1909. Museum of Religion, St. Petersburg.

that could be filled in with the names of recently deceased relatives (Figure 14.21).[8] The latter were described as "cheap, but more expensive than ordinary lunar New Year's Prints" (Cohen 1990, 516).

Although these pictures were far less expensive than the prescribed ancestral apparatus, their size and detail might still have made them too expensive for purchase by the poorest families. In this case the *nianhua* industry could provide a printed version that would cost no more than a few cents. An image from the Alekseev collection, probably found in Shandong in 1907, portrays Door Gods standing before the front gate as noble family members approach bearing festive goods (Figure 14.22). Inside, more family members gather before the ancestral tablets, inscribed with the words "throne of the ancient spirits." Behind a table filled with sacrifices is a central tablet reading "ancestors of three generations," which corresponds to the *zong* orientation of the Chinese family. In the poorest circumstances, such prints might simply have been pasted on a bare wall, although,

Fig. 14.23. *The family shrines in this house along the Shandong coast are shown here prepared for the New Year. Although barely visible behind the decorations, the main shrine contains an ancestor print of the type seen in Fig. 14.22. The smaller shrine to the left represents the Palace of the Stove God, complete with a Stove God print, which has been moved to the front hall from its usual place in the kitchen. Above the Stove God shrine one can make out a* nianhua *of the type produced in Yangjiabu, showing a festive theme of spring renewal. Weihaiwei, Shandong, ca. 1940.*
Source: Courtesy of Hedda Morrison Collection, Harvard-Yenching Library, Harvard University. © 2003 President and Fellows of Harvard College.

as seen in Figure 14.23, every effort was usually made to install the print in a wooden niche, where it could receive actual offerings on appropriate occasions. The inclusion in the print of family members and other honorable personages indicates that these prints were designed not simply for the family to reify the presence in the home of the ancestors, but also to help the ancestors reify the presence of the living family. By depicting the family as part of high society, the family could symbolically escape a more humble appointment in life and present itself in a position that brought sufficient honor to its predecessors.

Ancestral images, therefore, demonstrate a wide disparity in the practice of the ancestral cult among those few who owned proper ancestral halls, those who used more elaborate ancestral portraits and prints, and those who would simply buy a print intended to be incinerated when its purpose had been served. While the basic recognition of the *zong* and respect for departed spirits is retained at all levels of representation, in their most basic form the ancestors are not only nameless, but also mass-produced. Ancestral prints and pictures demonstrate that there had been considerable success in propagating the ancestral rites, but they also demonstrate that the wishes of the Confucian elite were seldom met in the home of the commoner.

James A. Flath

The traditional Chinese house, in addition to being a structure and a shelter, must be understood as an interpretive space through which the social world was understood. I have argued that the interpretation of the home was largely defined by domestic cults and that cults were in turn defined and propagated by print. Print extended throughout late-traditional Chinese society, entered the house, and connected home and family to the universal moral and ritual structures descended from elite values and sacrifices. Print thereby penetrated and transformed the social relations of the family, and in that sense the late-imperial state had infiltrated—and in some respects invented—the inner sanctum of the family, where the values represented by domestic cults continued to be relevant even after the state and elite that invented them had effectively died. However, the simple fact is that state and social elites could not produce sanctioned texts in sufficient numbers to put a copy of them in every home, so while elites patronized print culture, the bulk of print was still managed by entrepreneurs having little obligation to reproduce orthodox messages, except insofar as they proved to be popular and marketable commodities. This had the effect of carrying some quasi-orthodox forms into the domestic environment, but given the independent circumstances of production, distribution, and reading, those forms would seldom have been viewed in the explicit knowledge

Fig. 14.24. *Clothing store advertisement featuring a Mianzhu Door God. Taibei, Taiwan.* Source: Photograph by James A. Flath 1999.

Fig. 14.25. *Liquor advertisement featuring the wealth-summoning figure of Liu Hai. Jinan, Shandong.* Source: Photograph by James A. Flath 1999.

of their relative propriety to orthodoxy. The print world spread domestic cults and thereby exposed the family to the raw materials of ideological indoctrination, but in the end domestic politics were determined less through respect to higher institutions than by how the family extended, organized, and read those materials in the home.

At the beginning of the twenty-first century, ritual *nianhua* and the figures they represent have typically lost their place of privilege in the home. Mechanically printed Door Gods do still appear intermittently on rural gateways, the God of Wealth has made a fitting comeback in the era of economic reform, and, against all odds, a handful of village printers are still actively producing woodblock *nianhua*—some as tourist novelties and others for their original manifestation as New Year's harbingers of happiness. Most families, however, appreciate that *nianhua* and their iconography are something that belongs to the past and at present survives only out of respect to tradition. But as such, *nianhua* at least serve to remind us that however much times may change, tradition and history will always be embedded in Chinese domestic spaces (Figures 14.24–14.25).

James A. Flath

A longer version of this chapter, as well as a comprehensive account of the printing industry, is available in my book, *The Cult of Happiness:* Nianhua, *Art and History in Rural North China* (2004).

1. This subject, as well as the extent of state penetration into local society, has been widely debated. See in particular studies by Duara (1988), Faure (1999), Szonyi (1997), and Watson (1986).

2. Unpublished print catalogued by the author at the Hermitage Museum, St. Petersburg, February 2002. Other images from this collection may be seen in Alekseev (1928, 1966) and Rudova (1988).

3. Because these authors have made extensive surveys of the material, it will not be necessary to give comprehensive treatment to this particular print form. In addition to Doré and Day, accounts can be found in Goodrich (1991), Po and Johnson (1992), and Wang (1992).

4. This applies also to the compiler of *Chiping xianzhi* (Ding 1992, 312).

5. Kardos (1998) mentions a number of other Door God figures, although most are little known in northern *nianhua*.

6. While embedded in mythology, this story has a grain of historical fact to it as well; in 1072, a Song dynasty edict called for the reproduction of five thousand copies of the Zhong Kui painting by Wu Daozi for distribution in the courts of the Western and Eastern capitals (Lust 1996, 27).

7. Images collected in Shanghai by H. G. C. Hallock and retained in the Cleveland Public Library include this information in the body of the print.

8. Nagao Ryuzo (1971, 76) mentions that where a family could not write, the forms would be left blank.

15 The Symbolic Seasonal Round in House and Palace

Counting the Auspicious Nines in Traditional China

The shapes of good fortune pervaded visual daily life in traditional China, and these lucky motifs continue to be a mainstay of modern design. In the homes of East Asia and around the world Chinese graphs for "blessings" or "good fortune" *[fu],* "long life" *[shou],* and "happiness in marriage" *[shuangxi]* take ten thousand decorative forms as they ornament doors and windows, chairs and tables, curtains and carpets, soup bowls and spoons. This is because for millennia people in China have expressed and embodied their aspirations for good outcomes—longevity, (male) progeny, prosperity, and peace—in words and in pictures. Auspicious imagery forms the longest and broadest traditions of visual culture in China. As impressive as their ubiquity and endurance are the ways in which these visual traditions traverse boundaries of class, education, and taste. Pasted on the window panes of poor and modest households, the double-happiness papercuts that wish newlywed peasants and factory hands good luck find their counterparts in the bedsteads, cupboards, and candlestands of imperial Qing bridal chambers and in the decorations of Chinatown wedding palaces (see Knapp 1999: Figures 7.36–7.44; Wan et al. 1988: Plates 403–404). Thus, visualized desires for a good life for family and friends continue to join people together across time, space, and circumstance.

During the early part of the last century, impressed by the auspicious images that surrounded him on the streets and in the homes of Tianjin, Nozaki Nobuchika (1928) compiled a manual in which he categorized, illustrated, and explained the lucky motifs that he saw everywhere on metalwork, stone and wood carvings, architectural elements, paintings, prints, and pottery. His systematic survey of Chinese auspicious motifs became the basis for many handbooks that are available today. In the West, meanwhile, sinologists sometimes turned their attention to the ornamental repertory of auspicious graphic devices (Chavannes 1922). Since that time, especially since the mid-twentieth century, folklorists, ethnographers, art historians, and graphic designers have compiled an ever-growing literature on auspicious imagery, especially with regard to popular prints or *nianhua* (Bickford 1999; Bo 1995; Rudova 1988; Wang Shucun 1997). Most relevant to this volume on house, home, and family is Ronald G. Knapp's *China's Living Houses,* with its examples of auspicious motifs as architectural ornament and domestic ornamentation. While Knapp focused on auspicious motifs in vernacular architecture, in this chapter I take a different approach, focusing instead on a pivotal point in the seasonal round—the shortest day of the year, the winter solstice—and I explore how different groups of people at different times and in different circumstances expressed their shared hope for returning light and, with it, new beginnings through visual means.

The festivals that marked the seasonal round in imperial China were moments of social, as well as celestial, synchronization. Whatever distinctions of birth and status, wealth and poverty, or education and illiteracy divided people from one another in the social hierarchy and in their daily lives, there regularly arrived during the course of each year particular moments when these barriers were overwhelmed by the sheer force of shared aspirations for attracting good fortune and averting harm. This becomes especially clear if we consider daily visual life in traditional China.

Everywhere we look, we see emblems of distinction, reminders of division, of perquisite and deference: the palaces of princes and mansions of ministers; the modest courtyards and hovels; the blue robes of the scholars; the rank badges and hat buttons of officials; the five-clawed imperial dragon. Some of these marks were a matter of custom and means, some of statute and stipulation. And beyond these gross visual indicators were more nuanced strategies of distinction, deployed through what we call "taste"—the self-conscious selection or avoidance of various kinds of art and articles of daily use through which members of the elite (and those aspiring to join their ranks) marked themselves as persons of culture.

In contrast, the images produced for festival display were relentlessly inclusive. They were vulgar in the literal sense of that word: they were used by everyone. And they freely combined elements that came from the visual traditions of all times and of all segments of society. They drew from ancient and modern art, from literati and peasant culture, from the court, from the scholar's studio, from the village market, and from the city streets. This was not merely a matter of emperors, officials, and scholars playing at being commoners by appropriating folk art, nor of commoners slavishly imitating their betters in vermilion and gilt. The visual displays that marked the festivals were the outcomes of centuries of productive interactions among imperial, scholarly, and popular practices, each influencing the evolving forms of the others, as everyone made his passage through the year and hoped for the best.

More than the great sacrifices of state, it was the family celebrations of the seasons in which this very strong cultural coherence was made manifest in a myriad of

Maggie Bickford

images. For some, the site of celebration lay deep within the walls of the Forbidden City. For others, it was a humble dwelling, down winding alleys or dusty country lanes. A case in point are images made to mark the winter solstice *[dongzhi]*, the shortest day of the year in house and palace alike.

The magnificent, six-foot-tall tapestry shown in Figure 15.1 was made for the Qianlong emperor (r. 1736–1795) in the late eighteenth century.[1] The cheap paper print, about ten by twenty inches (illustrated in Figure 15.2), was made a hundred years later.[2] One is a unique object, created by imperial commission and woven by the best Suzhou craftsmen to hang in a palace hall. The other was mass-produced by an unknown print shop, to be purchased for a copper at mat sheds at the market and pasted up on the walls of common households. Both are *Jiujiu xiaohan tu,* as the print title proclaims and the emperor's colophon explains—that is, "Nine-Nines Disperse the Cold Pictures (or Charts)."

What is the "Nines"? It is a sequence of nine nine-day periods between the winter solstice and the spring season. The first "Nine" begins at the solstice (during the eleventh lunar month, approximately December 22 of the Western calendar; some counts begin the next day). The nine-nines, or *jiujiu,* are completed eighty days later, entering the bitterest cold, traversing the Beginning of Spring [*lichun,* end of the twelfth or early in the first lunar month], the official New Year [*yuandan,* first day of the first lunar month], and exiting into warmer weather.[3] *Jiujiu xiaohan tu* are visual aids for counting the nines, marking the days from winter to spring. In counting off the days, the counter helps to bring on warmth for everyone and, in doing so, brings good fortune to himself and to his family.

The images in Figures 15.1 and 15.2 show two basic approaches to envisioning the Nines. The pictorial textile *embodies* them in the figures of nine sheep and goats. The print *charts* them: The Nines take the form of eighty-one white polka dots, arranged in nine nine-dot clusters that decorate the nine colorful belly-bands of baby boys. Flanking the infants are twin lotus columns, where inscriptions direct the user to count the Nines *actively* by filling in the dots day by day. Typical of such charts, these directions explain the code for marking each day's weather on the circle:

> Fill the top half for clouds; the bottom for a sunny day;
> Left for rain; right for wind;
> A dot at the center if it happens to snow;
> A hollow dot within a dot for mixed clear and cloudy weather.

Fig. 15.1. Jiuyang xiaohan tu *[Nine yang disperse the cold picture]. Anonymous artist(s), eighteenth century. Colophon by the Qianlong emperor (r. 1736–1795) dated 1781/1782. Kesi silk tapestry with added embroidery, 213 cm x 119 cm.* Source: Courtesy of Palace Museum, Beijing.

Fig. 15.2. Jiujiu xiaohan tu *[Nine-Nines disperse the cold chart]. Anonymous artist(s), nineteenth or early twentieth century. Woodblock colored print, 35 x 59 cm. Hermitage Museum, St. Petersburg.* Source: Rudova 1988, no. 52.

After all of the dots have been marked, the cold times are over and warm weather has come back.[4]

In the emperor's tapestry and in the commoner's print, the image makers have *visually* ensured that the counting and marking will take place under the most auspicious circumstances. Each uses the same strategy to pack his image with as many good wishes as it can hold. That device is the lucky rebus, or visual pun, explicated by Qianlong's inscription (on the pink paper mounted along the top edge of the tapestry) and invoked in text along the top of the print—both in rhyme. I shall turn to the emperor's colophon in due course. Let us continue to examine the auspicious amplification of the print.

Into the chubby hands of the boys, the designer put auspicious fruits and flowers. And around their plump little bodies, he has strewn lucky motifs. This is not a random display. It is a systematic invocation of blessings, as the cartouche inscription makes clear. The words say, "May noble sons be born to you continuously and may all be as you wish!" *[Lian sheng gui zi yi ruyi]*. Vividly, the wish for the continuous production of sons is visualized as five baby faces are joined to continuous bodies so configured that, as the eye travels along the circumference of each roundel, the images read as a total of ten, plump baby boys—a visual perpetual motion device for the generation of male offspring (Wang 1997, no. 169, *"Lian*

The Symbolic Seasonal Round in House and Palace

sheng gui zi"). Linked images reiterate this message by means of rebus and symbol: Lotus, *lian* (in the hands of the babes) is homophonous with the word for "continuous," *lian;* and the musical instrument (at the lower-right corner of the left panel) is called *sheng,* which sounds like "give birth," also *sheng.* The branch of cassia, *gui,* sounds like "noble," *gui,* and also symbolizes success in the civil service examinations. The idea of "many sons," *duo zi,* is embodied also as symbol and rebus by the many-seeded pomegranate—commonly called *duozi*—held in the hand of one of them (at the upper-left corner). As for "everything as you wish," *ruyi,* a *ruyi* scepter crowns the left-hand panel (Nozaki 1928, no. 101). In a manner typical of auspicious amplification, the image also is equipped with lucky motifs that do not directly relate to this text (or to the next one that I shall discuss): wishes for wealth are cast as ingot and coin displayed on the left-hand panel.

Still more wishes are called for. "May you garner the Three Abundances and the Nine Analogs!" *[Ding yao Sanduo Jiuru pian].* The "Three Abundances," Sanduo— long life, blessings, and progeny—here are symbolized by the Peach of Longevity *[shou tao]* (left panel, upper-right corner); the bat *[(bian) fu],* homophonous with "blessings" *[fu]* (right panel, lower right); and (on the left panel, upper-left corner), the pomegranate *[duozi]* (see Rudova 1988, no. 52; Nozaki 1928, nos. 18 and 23).

This visual invocation is completed at the top of the left-hand panel, where the *ruyi* scepter, which first was read as "as you wish," now doubles as an indicator of the "Nine Analogs," or Jiuru. The Nine Analogs is a sequence of nine comparisons that use the word *"ru,"* 如, which in English means "like," and occur in a litany of blessings invoked on behalf of the king in a poem collected in the *Shijing—The Book of Songs*—China's earliest collection of poetry. The relevant passages of this poem, which is called "Heaven Protects," from the invocation of its first line, read, in Arthur Waley's (1937) translation (modified) as follows:

> May Heaven guard and keep you,
> Cause there to be nothing in which you do not rise higher,
> *Like* the mountains, *like* the uplands
> *Like* the ridges, *like* the ranges
> *Like* a stream coming down in flood
> In nothing not increased.
> . . .
> *Like* the moon advancing to its full
> *Like* the sun climbing the sky
> *Like* the everlastingness of the Southern Hills

Maggie Bickford

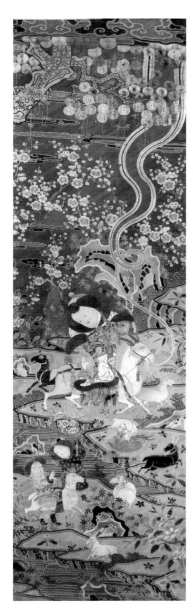

Fig. 15.3. Kai Tai tu *[Kai Tai picture]. Anonymous artist(s), Yuan (1279–1368) or Ming (1368–1644) dynasty. Hanging scroll, silk tapestry with silk embroidery, 217.1 cm x 64.1 cm. National Palace Museum, Taiwan.* Source: Palace Museum Photographic Distribution (PMPD), University of Michigan, Ann Arbor.

Without failing or falling
Like the pine-tree and the cypress in their verdure
All these blessings may you receive.[5]

Having expanded the Nine-Nines jingle and explicated the picture's minor motifs, we find this cosmic invocation is lodged in a cheap little print.

The questions then arise: Did the people who bought this print know how to read? Did the readers among them know the Jiuru's *locus classicus* in the *Shijing* or, for that matter, the Sanduo's origins in the *Zhuangzi* (*Hanyu da cidian* 1995, 1:197)? Could they chant all of "Heaven Protects" from memory? Did they know its classical commentaries by heart? It did not matter. One need not have been an exegete to get the message or to get the benefit of the talismanic display. In the raggedy rhymes and vulgar pictures of auspicious imagery, the entire Great Tradition was made available for action—to be pressed into the service of bringing good fortune to anyone and everyone.

"Everyone" included the emperor. In his service, with the even-handed protocols typical of auspicious visuality, the lucky motifs of the common people provided the pictorial program for the Qianlong tapestry depicted in Figure 15.1. During the winter of 1781–1782, between the winter solstice and the New Year, the emperor wrote an inscription for this tapestry and had it mounted along the top. The emperor proudly pointed out that his tapestry was a contemporary Suzhou copy, after a Song period original. Perhaps his weavers copied it from an earlier pictorial textile (Figure 15.3) that also was in Qianlong's collection and that now is in the collections of the National Palace Museum, Taibei.[6]

The emperor's colophon reads as follows:

The meaning of the nine *yang* 羊 resides in the nine *yang* 陽 ,
And so we have [before us this] "Dispersing the Cold by
    Counting the Nines Image."
Halfway through the eleventh month, in our mind we could
    see the returning spring:
The meaning of "Males [numbering] three initiate the Tai"
    is even more fitting.
[This] imitation by Su[zhou] craftsmen is without deviation.
It is wrong to say that the moderns are not as good as the
    ancients.
And therefore I say [this] return to simplicity humbles me
    (translated in Bickford 1999, 132).[7]

The emperor began interpreting the image with explication that hinges on a visual pun. The "nine 'yang' 羊," he tells us, stand for "nine 'yang' 陽 ." That is, nine sheep and goats (*yang* 羊, which we can see) stand for nine male [*yang* 陽] units of something that we cannot see. He then explains that this *yang/yang* correspondence directed the configuration of the tapestry, which he identifies as a "'Dispersing the cold [by] counting the Nines' image" *[Xiaohan shu jiu tu]*.

But this is not the end of the tapestry's story, nor the end of its auspicious visual punning. The eighty-one days of the Nine-Nines and the nine goats that represent them comprise and embody another, shorter significant temporal interval—that is, the Sanyang, or "Three Males." Like the Nine-Nines, the Sanyang cumulatively completes the transit from winter to spring, from the old year to the new, specifically the interval between the winter solstice and the first lunar month, or the official New Year. Thus, Qianlong continued his exegesis by turning our attention away from the nine sheep and goats and toward the three little boys who attend them. In doing so, he extracted this second, interlocked rebus: "Males [numbering] three initiate the Tai" is even more fitting" *[Nan san kai Tai yi you fu]*. The boys embody the term Sanyang, as it occurs in the phrase, *"Sanyang kai Tai."*

Why is this time span called the Sanyang, and what is the Tai? The Sanyang indicates the three *yang* 陽, or unbroken, lines that form the bottom of the Tai hexagram (Figure 15.4), which is associated with the first month of the new lunar year. The winter solstice (in the eleventh lunar month) is the pivot of the solar cycle, when light and the male *yang,* having reached their nadir, begin to wax again. The month before the solstice (the tenth lunar month) manifests the apogee of female, *yin,* darkness, as the Kun, or "The Receptive," hexagram, which is composed solely of broken, *yin* lines. During the solstice month, the shift in *yin-yang* balance is embodied as the Fu, or "Return (the Turning Point)," hexagram, in which a single unbroken *(yang)* line appears at the bottom of this configuration. In the last month of the old year (the twelfth month), two unbroken lines rise from the bottom half of the Lin, or "Approach," hexagram. At last, the old year ends and the new year begins in the first month, when the three solid, or Sanyang, lines rise, open up *[kai]* the Tai, or "Peace," hexagram, and manifest the sure ascension of light, warmth, and the male principle.

This happy course of events is embodied by the *Sanyang kai Tai* rebus, doubled and displayed as interlocked images. Reading along with the emperor, we count the three boys *[nan san]* as the three males of the Tai hexagram. Or we may focus on the outsized central motif, the detail seen in Figure 15.5, where three sheep and

Maggie Bickford

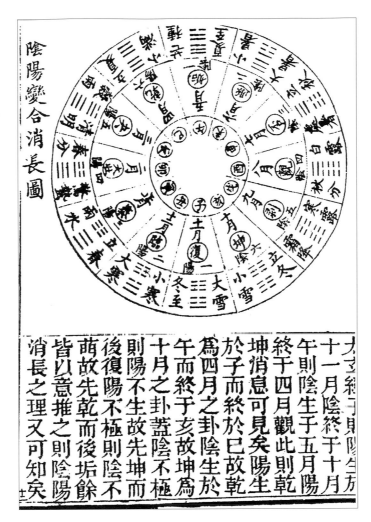

Fig. 15.4. Yin-yang bianhe xiaochang tu *[Diagram of the waxing and waning transformations of* yin *and* yang*].* Source: Chen n.d., n.p.

goats stand for the Sanyang—the three solid lines—and the richly robed royal child, or *taizi,* stands for the lucky Tai hexagram that comprises them.

Like the printmaker, the weavers proceeded to load up their image with luck. They framed the main image with symbols of the New Year, long life, rebirth, and virtue. There are camellias, together with pine, bamboo, and plum, the Three Friends of the Cold Season. Each of these plants has a long history of its own in poetry and painting, and here, in their role as subsidiary motifs, each brings its own symbolic stores of luck and virtue and makes its contribution to the auspicious payload of the *Sanyang kai Tai* image. Some of their associations—like the longevity pine and New Year's plum—come from popular culture; some—like the Three

The Symbolic Seasonal Round in House and Palace

Fig. 15.5. *Detail of Fig. 15.3.*

Friends—also were mainstays of the scholars' Iconography of Virtue, where they stood for the noble scholar under pressure but uncompromised during troubled times. No matter where their origins lay, all were made to converge here to embody aspirations for a good new year (Bickford 1999).

At the outset, we noted that the print in Figure 15.2 and the tapestry show two different ways of envisioning the Nines: the former *charts* them; the latter *embodies* them. We have seen how the printmaker appropriately embellished his chart by sprinkling it with auspicious motifs: cash and ingot, cassia branch and bat, *sheng* pipes and *ruyi* scepter; each was displayed clearly as an isolated image. The designer of the tapestry took a different approach: he or she took pains to *integrate* each auspicious element into a plausible picture of figures in a landscape. Goats, sheep, little boys, pine, bamboo, plum, and rock purposefully were organized and were woven together visually into an image, as seen also in Figure 15.6, that at once appears to be an innocent wintry vignette of children playing at goatherds in a garden and at the same time delivers a multitude of auspicious wishes in pictorial form (Bickford 1999, 2002).

Maggie Bickford

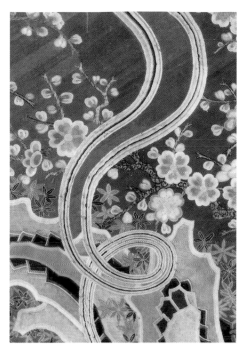

Fig. 15.6. Yuanren Xiying tu
[(Yuan artist) infant at play].
Anonymous artist, Yuan dynasty.
Hanging scroll, ink and color on
silk, 90.4 cm x 56.1 cm. National
Palace Museum, Taiwan. Source:
Courtesy of the National Palace
Museum, Taiwan.

Fig. 15.7. *Detail of Fig. 15.3.*

This process of incorporating lucky motifs extended to every element of the picture: the ribbon issuing from the mouth of the goat, seen in Figure 15.7, is not just goat's breath; it is *yangqi,* or male vapor, associated with the winter solstice and the official New Year. It points to the powerful generative force marshaled in these massed *yang* motifs. *Yangqi* produces boys; and boys replete with young *yang* produce more *yang* and more boys . . . and so forth, forever. Thus the tapestry visualizes the same wish for the perpetual production of male descendants that we saw dynamically configured in the wheeling baby boys displayed on the Nine-Nines print. In this way the emperor, like his subjects, counted the days until spring and hoped that good outcomes of many kinds would attend this cyclical turning toward light.

Counting the Nines in verse, song, pictures, and charts had a long history before Qianlong's time and after it, well into the twentieth century. From Song times on, there was a steady interaction between vulgar and elite practices. Amateur folklorists, from the Song literatus Fan Chengda (1120 1193) to those of the late Qing and early Republic, collected the Nine-Nines counting songs, which seem to have begun with southern farmers and then spread to other regions and to cityfolk and scholars, each group adapting the songs to their climatic and social environment (Bickford 1999).

Fig. 15.8. Welcoming Spring. *Anonymous artist, Yuan [1279–1368] or Ming [1368–1644] dynasty. Silk, horsehair, and embroidered gauze, 213.3 cm x 63.5 cm. The Metropolitan Museum of Art, New York. Purchase, the Dillon Fund Gift, 1981 (1981.410). Source: Courtesy* of The Metropolitan Museum of Art.

Fig. 15.9. Kai Tai tu *(Fig. 15.3) and* Welcoming Spring *(Fig. 15.8) conjoined.*

Visualizations of the winter solstice Nines seem to have begun during the Yuan period. Qianlong's goats and boys find their predecessors in pictorial textiles, such as the *Kai Tai* tapestry (Figure 15.3), and in paintings, such as *Infant at Play (Yuan-ren Xiying tu)* (Figure 15.6), and their many contemporaries and successors. Often the Nine-Nines were expanded fully to show all eighty-one goats.[8] It seems to me to be likely that the *Kai Tai* tapestry (Figure 15.3) and the *Welcoming Spring* tapestry that matches it (Figure 15.8) once were the center and right panels of such a fully configured display (Figure 15.9).

In contrast to naturalizing auspicious images by means of pictorial elaboration, the weavers of solstice festival brocades (Figures 15.10–15.12) achieved their auspicious

　Maggie Bickford

Fig. 15.10. *Festival brocade with repeat pattern of boy riding a ram. Anonymous artist(s), Ming dynasty (1368–1644). Textile-art, London.* Source: Photograph courtesy of The Textile Gallery, London.

◄ **Fig. 15.11.** *Panel with rams and* yin-yang *symbols on a ground of* prunus *branches. Anonymous artist(s), Ming dynasty, Wanli reign period (1573–1619). Silk and gilded paper wrapped around a silk core, 165 cm x 67.5 cm. John Eskenazi, London.* Source: Photograph courtesy of John Eskenazi, London.

Fig. 15.12. *Sixteenth- or seventeenth-century Ming festival textile for the winter solstice; robe fragment patterned with rams, taiji disc, and plum blossoms. Anonymous artist(s). Silk brocaded with silk and gold-metallic thread, 37 cm x 27.5 cm. Museum of Fine Arts, Boston. 07.850. Gift of Denman W. Ross, 1907.* Source: Photograph © 2004 Museum of Fine Arts, Boston. All rights reserved.

Fig. 15.13. *Drawing of a knee wrapper,* duan, *embroidered with* Sanyang kai Tai. *Ming dynasty, Wanli reign period (1573–1620). Excavated from the tomb of the Wanli emperor and his empress Xiaoduan, née Wang (buried 1620).* Source: Zhongguo shehui kexue yuan kaogu yanjiu suo 1990, 2: Fig. 241. Used with the permission of the Cultural Relics Publishing House.

ends through a combination of condensation and repetition. Employing a strategy that went back as far as the auspicious textiles of the Han and Tang periods, they epitomized key elements, combined them into a composite motif, and maximized luck by repeating that auspicious emblem again and again along the length of silk. The design demands for repeat motifs that could be replicated any number of times in a bolt of silk and that would remain intact on pieces cut from the bolt for use fostered this approach to weaving good fortune into cloth and clothing that was worn at special times of the year. These festival textiles became popular during the Ming and Qing periods (Cammann 1953, 66–70; Zhao Feng 1999, nos. 02.00a–d, 02.03, 03a–b, 02.04, 02.06, 06a–b).

In Figure 15.10, a pattern that is closely related to the paintings and pictorial textiles that we have seen, the boy rides his goat into spring, back and forth, again and again, surrounded by lucky filler motifs, as he bears his glad tidings along the length of this colorful festival textile.[9] The ultimate in concentrated effect was achieved in solstice festival brocades upon which goats prance back and forth, *yang* vapors emanating from each mouth, rising aloft toward *taiji* discs, and interspersed with New Year's plum blossoms (Figures 15.11 and 15.12).[10]

Ming texts record festival textiles that were displayed and worn at court; today, the fragments that we illustrate and others like them connect these literary descriptions to the material record. The principal textual record of these courtly festival practices is the memoirs of Liu Ruoyu (1584–ca. 1642), the deposed grand eunuch who, from his prison cell, recollected the details of palace accoutrements and cuisine through the rounds of the festival year. Liu wrote of "*yang*-producing textiles" [*yangsheng mian*] and "*yang*-producing badges" [*yangsheng buzi*] that were worn at the Ming court during its winter solstice festivities (Liu 1641, 19.9a, 20.9a).

While the fragments that we illustrate are unprovenanced, the excavations of the Ming imperial tombs have yielded many festival textiles, costumes, badges, and accessories that are securely dated and connected to Ming imperial use. Among them is a pair of "*Sanyang kai Tai*" knee wrappers (Figure 15.13) from the tomb of the Wanli emperor (r. 1573–1620) and his empress Xiaoduan, née Wang, who were buried in 1620. Here the "big sheep" at the center stands for *taiyang* (Zhongguo 1990, 2, Figure 241).

These pictures and patterns all auspiciously *embody* the solstice and the transit from winter to spring. Turning now toward visually actively counting off the Nines, we find the earliest *textual* evidence in the late fourteenth century, when Yang Yunfu nostalgically recalled the customs of the Mongol capital and court. Tracking the

Maggie Bickford

Fig. 15.14. Jiujiu xiaohan zhi tu [*Nine-Nines disperse the cold chart*]. *Anonymous artist(s), dated 1488. Ink rubbing.* Source: Wang 1985, 17.

seasonal round through a sequence of poems, Yang evoked a Nine-Nines counting chart in this quatrain:

> Try counting off the window's nine-nines [counting] chart
> Then lingering cold has all run out and warmth's returning starts.
> [When] the plum-blossom dots show no trace of white spots
> What you see this morning is flowering apricots.

Yang then supplied a note in which he explained what a "Nine-Nines Chart" was and how to use it: After the winter solstice, people paste a bare, painted plum branch on their windows. Thereafter, every morning, when the ladies put on their makeup, they take a dab of rouge and draw a circle. At the point when they complete eighty-one of them, just then warm weather returns, transforming those rouge-painted wintry plums into springtime apricot blossoms (Yang 1368+).

Suggestive of Yang's account is the center panel of a Nine-Nines Disperse the Cold Chart, dated in correspondence to 1488 (Figure 15.14).[11] It is the earliest visual evidence of such charts known to me. Here, a flowering-plum spray, bearing nine clusters, each comprising nine buds or petals, makes up the eighty-one white spots to be filled in day by day. Notice that the Nine-Nines bouquet is inserted in a vase [*ping*], itself an auspicious rebus for "peace," *ping'an.* Surrounding this central chart are nine panels that replicate the sequence by means of landscape pictures that are inscribed with poems. From the lower left in clockwise fashion, the snowy landscapes grow more and more forbidding as the cold deepens, then indicate moderation and the return of warmth, with farmers ploughing in the eighth frame and, in the ninth, a garden filled with blossoming trees as the Nines exhaust their course. Sealing the sequence in the (tenth) bottom-center frame is an especially auspicious image (Figure 15.15) that epitomizes the transit from winter to spring in the form of three boys and a goat, now familiar to us as the embodiment of *"Sanyang kai Tai."* Thus, the action of bringing on spring by dotting plum blossoms at the center is framed by poetry and pictures that evoke and display the successful completion of the cycle.

During the three hundred years between the engraving of this image on stone and the weaving of Qianlong's tapestry in colored silks, references to "Nine-Nines Disperse the Cold" charts increased in frequency and detail in the guidebooks and memoirs of the late Ming and early Qing. For instance, in their guide to the capital city, Liu Tong (d. 1637) and Yu Yizheng (d. ca. 1635), writing on the eve of the Manchu conquest, recorded the winter solstice customs of the common people.

Fig. 15.15. *Detail of Fig. 15.14.*

They described the eighty-one plum blossoms charts and a plain printed chart that displayed nine clusters of nine circles together with a "Nine-Nines song" *[Jiujiu zhi ge]*. The contemporary song that they quoted clearly descended from the songs that were transcribed by Song dynasty amateur ethnographers. The simple circle charts still find use in modern times (Liu and Yu 1957, 2.29; Bickford 1999, 138–139).

Meanwhile, through the memories of Liu Ruoyu, we can see that preparations for the solstice were under way also within the walls of late Ming palaces. Out came the festival brocades (Figure 15.11) and robes (Figure 15.12), and out came the emperor's Sanyang knee wrappers (Figure 15.13). People would hang up paintings of goats and royal boys, and they would paste up Nine-Nines Disperse the Cold poetry charts that were printed by the Directorate of Ceremonial, or Sili jian. Liu recalled only that these imperially printed charts displayed a vulgar quatrain for each of the nines. He did not know how they were transmitted, just that they had been followed for a long time. He proceeded then to modern improvements on custom: two or three kinds of (what he called) "new-style poetry-line charts (or configurations)" *[xinshi shiju zhi tu]*.[12] We do not know just what they looked like. The old-style charts may have resembled the 1488 rubbing (Figure 15.14), which combined a seven-character quatrain with a landscape image in each of its nine Nine-Nines panels. Later imperial charts and configurations, based on the emperor's poetry and calligraphy, may have reflected the new, improved approach.

Several Qing imperial charts survive from the nineteenth and twentieth centuries (Fu 1982; He 1990; Li 1987). A chart attributed to the Daoguang emperor (r. 1820–1850), shown in Figure 15.16, still hangs in the Forbidden City (Wan et al. 1988, Figure 376). The chart, entitled *Guan cheng chun man* [Brush strokes complete the spring], displays an appropriate line of imperial poetry that comprises nine characters, each of which is constructed in nine strokes. Commentators record that in charts like this one the emperor's hand was copied in double-outline characters by Hanlin scholars and printed for distribution.[13] These, in turn, were the models for mass-produced charts for the market. Thus, as others counted the Nines by dotting on plum petals or filling in circles, the Nine-Nines counter who used this chart filled in day by day one outlined brushstroke in one of the nine nine-stroke characters of the imperial brush.

Outside the palace, the populace counted the Nines on cheap, colorful charts sold at market. Many of these survive today—for instance, Figure 15.2, with which we began. These charts display impressive ingenuity in the ways in which they display the Nines. On a print made in 1899 (Figure 15.17), nine flower fairies, gracefully posed among auspicious clouds at the top of the image, invite us to fill in the nine

Maggie Bickford

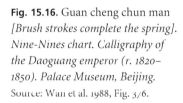

Fig. 15.16. Guan cheng chun man
[Brush strokes complete the spring].
Nine-Nines chart. Calligraphy of
the Daoguang emperor (r. 1820–
1850). Palace Museum, Beijing.
Source: Wan et al. 1988, Fig. 3/6.

Fig. 15.17. Jiujiu tu. *Flower fairies*
Nine-Nines chart. Anonymous
artist(s), dated by inscription to
1899. Woodblock print with added
color, 60 cm x 107 cm. Location
unknown. Source: Bo 1995, no. 27.
Used with the permission of the
Cultural Relics Publishing House.

petals of each of the nine flowers that twine about them. Inscribed to their left is a Nine-Nines song. Below them, the image fixes a most auspicious moment in the sequence. About to enter the sixth Nine, the emperor conducts the celebration of Lichun, the Beginning of Spring, surrounded by the Spring Ox, *chun niu,* the boys of Union and Harmony, He He, and the God of Wealth, Caishen, rushing in with his barrow full of riches (Bo 1995, no. 27). Thus the lucky Nines come to preside over an image of an empire blessed with peace and plenty.

The annual market for Nine-Nines charts urged printers on to imaginative variations. Like the image of the wheeling babies with which we began, a print that was made at the end of the Qing dynasty, shown in Figure 15.18, ingeniously combined the Nine-Nines count-off with the wish for many sons by depicting infant actors (Wang 1997, no. 216).[14] Against a backdrop of trellised vines, framing a panoramic view of hills beyond a river, the little boys play at ancient generals and heroes. They strike their dramatic poses beneath the cartouched titles of three operas: *Nanyang guan, Hongyang dong,* and *Pohong zhou.* Each of these three opera titles comprises three characters, making nine in all, and each double-outlined character is constructed of nine strokes, making eighty-one strokes to be filled in, one each day, until spring comes. (The chart we illustrate was never used—its hollow strokes remain unfilled.)

We come to the end of this dialogue between imperial and commoner culture

The Symbolic Seasonal Round in House and Palace

Fig. 15.18. Jiujiu xiaohan tu. *Infant operas Nine-Nines chart Anonymous nineteenth- or twentieth-century artist(s). Tianjin, Yangliuqing. Colored print with additional color, 33 cm x 59 cm.* Source: Wang 1997, no. 216.

with the last emperor, Pu'yi (r. 1908–1911). In the files at the Number One Historical Archives Administration of China [Zhongguo Diyi Lishi Dang'an], there survive a number of Nine-Nines charts that were made for the emperor while he still lived in the Forbidden City. One of them, entitled "Nine-Nines Disperse the Cold Chart," took the piscine form of the *taiji* pattern as its basic counting unit (Figure 15.19). These *yin-yang* fish [*yin-yang yu*] were organized in nine nine-unit blocks, each block labeled with its sequential number and notated with dates of entering and completing its Nine. In a variation on the farmers' traditional practice of recording the weather by marking a portion of each Nine-Nines circle, the executant of this chart ingeniously rotated the black and white "fish" to indicate the weather of the day. Another chart, entitled "Song of Dispersing the Cold and Increasing *Qi*" [*Xiaohan yi qi ge*], shown in Figure 15.20, is said to have been based on lyrics composed by Pu'yi's staff to relieve their listless master. Each of its nine blocks is surmounted with the title of one song and notation of the dates of beginning and ending the Nine; the text of named verse—each starting by invoking the Amithaba Buddha—was transcribed along the left and right sides. In the center of each box, nine circles were configured in a schematic visualization of the imagistic title. The title "Three Stars at the Door" (lower-right corner) was matched with a diagonal string of three circles enclosed by a "doorway" formed from the remaining six; simi-

Fig. 15.19. Jiujiu xiaohan tu. Yin-yang *Nine-Nines chart. Pu'yi or assistants. Dated 1922–1923. Collections of Number One Historical Archives Administration of China.* Source: Li 1987, 19.

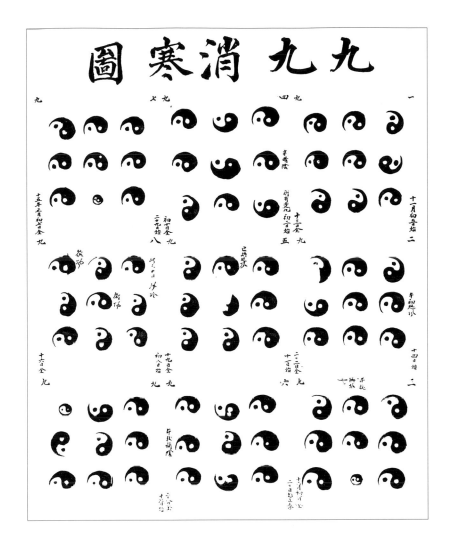

larly, at the center of this chart, the fifth Nine, "Five Blessings [within] One Gate" [Wu Fu Yimen], displays a five-circle cluster within a four-circle "gate" (Li 1987).

These charts are datable calendrically or by inscription. They were made for Pu'yi during the winter of 1922/1923. Like any of his former subjects, he or his servant patiently took things a dot at a time, as he marked the day's weather on diagrams inscribed with notations dated to the fifteenth year of a reign that had only three.

A Nine-Nines poetry chart made during the following winter (1923/1924), as seen in Figure 15.21, continued the *Guan cheng chun man* tradition (Figure 15.16) of Pu'yi's imperial Qing predecessors and introduced an innovation in marking the weather. Here the nine nine-stroke characters form the phrase *Chun qian ting bo*

The Symbolic Seasonal Round in House and Palace

Fig. 15.20. Xiaohan yi qi ge *[Song of dispersing the cold and increasing qi]. Pu'yi or assistants. Dated 1922–1923. Collections of Number One Historical Archives Administration of China. Source: Li 1987, 70*

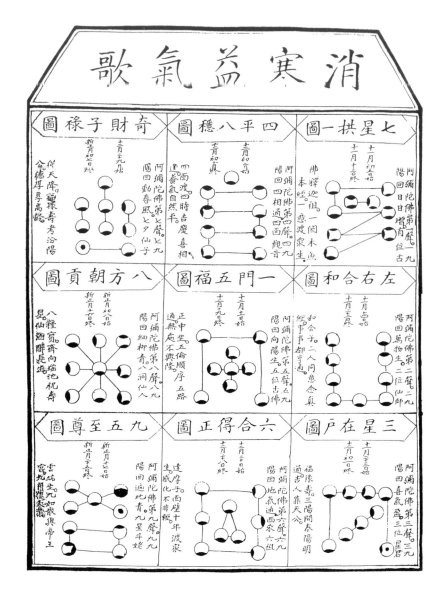

feng song xiang ying shi. As in similar charts, the date of beginning and completing each Nine was noted to the right and left of each corresponding character. Pu'yi's variation was to inscribe each stroke of each character with a textual description of that day's weather—the sequence of dates conveniently embedded in the stroke order of execution. Each inscription conformed to the size of the stroke and followed the direction of the brush that had formed that stroke. The dots hold only

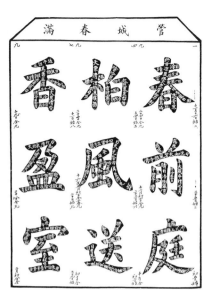

Fig. 15.21. Guan cheng chun man. *Nine-Nines chart. Pu'yi or his assistants. Dated 1923–1924. Qing Palace Collection.* Source: Fu 1982, 32.

Fig. 15.22. *Two Nine-Nines poetry charts configured as double gourds. Pu'yi or his assistants. After 1911. Left: Guan cheng chun man. Right: Hanmei tu yu [The wintry plum spits jade (white blossoms)].* Source: He 1990, 47.

a word or two; the long strokes take entire phrases. Thus, the inscription on the fifth Nine character, *feng*, meaning "wind," at the center of the chart, shows the brief note, "New Year's Day: chilly" *[Yuandan liang]* on the ninth-stroke dot, while a sixteen-character phrase follows the long second stroke—first horizontally from left to right; then, bending with the brush, from top to bottom; and finally, following the upward flick of the brushtip, forming the character *xin* (new) upside down (Fu 1982, 31–32).

The tradition of imperial "Nine-Nines Disperse the Cold poetry Charts" pasted on the walls of the late-Ming palace, as recalled by Liu Ruoyu from his prison cell, took a political (and poignant) turn toward modern times in three double-gourd charts made by the deposed Pu'yi or his assistants during the period of sequestration in the old Qing palace (Figure 15.22) (He 1990, 42; Bickford 1999, 139–141). Like the imperial Ming charts, Pu'yi's traced the Nines through suites of nine seven-character quatrains. And two of Pu'yi's sequences (one of which is illustrated in Figure 15.22, right) began with the very same words (save one character), *Tou jiu chu han cai shi dong*, which Liu had quoted as the first line of the Ming palace poetry chart. But while each of Pu'yi's quatrains began with conventional *jiujiu* counting doggerel, the remaining three lines turned to historical events. As they traced the Nines in poetic lines, configured as auspicious double gourds enclosing lucky endless knots, the texts of two of these charts (Figure 15.22, left and right) also traced the unauspicious aftermath of the 1911 revolution. In contrast to these laments, the third chart, Xiaohan Tu (not illustrated) "Dispersed the Cold" by celebrating the history of emperorship from the legendary times of peace and order, when the "Three Emperors ruled and the ten thousand things flourished"

[Sanhuang zhi shi wanwu sheng], to the time when the Great Qing sat enthroned in the imperial palace.

Still in the Old Palace, the deposed emperor traced these double-knot/double-gourd patterns, composing and configuring his Nine-Nine quatrains. In doing so, he counted the Nines and recounted the history of empire and of recent events. Under these peculiar circumstances, the custom that for centuries had joined emperor to commoner might have brought some comfort to Pu'yi as he made his own transition from one state to the other.

NOTES _____

This chapter was developed from the author's article "Three Rams and Three Friends: The Working Life of Chinese Auspicious Motifs" (Bickford 1999). Some of the material in the present chapter appeared in that article in different form.

1. The tapestry is recorded in Hu Jing (1816, 7:3485B). For a large color reproduction, see Zhu (1986, no. 98).

2. It is reproduced in Rudova (1988, no. 52); other editions and variations are widely reproduced elsewhere.

3. Regulated by the solar calendar, the Winter Solstice and Beginning of Spring Festivals do not fall on fixed days of the lunar calendar. The Beginning of Spring may fall before or after the official New Year's Day. See Bodde (1936); Bodde and Bogan (1994, 4, Appendixes A and B).

4. My discussion is based on Rudova (1988, no. 52), with modifications. For other charts of this type and variations of the weather-marking code, see Bodde (1936, 88–89) and Bodde and Bogan (1994, 54–55).

5. "Heaven Protects" [Tianbao], *Shijing*, Mao no. 166, stanzas 3 and 6, in Hung (1934); translated in Waley (1937, no. 167).

6. Recorded in Wang Jie et al. (1971, 3:1707A); the entry records the object as a *kesi* tapestry with added embroidery. See Watt and Wardwell (1997, Figure 81, 194). Although Hu et al. (1816) enter this textile as a Song dynasty work, Watt and Wardwell consider that Mongol costume and saddled goat are indicative of a Yuan composition. The Metropolitan Museum of Art's *Welcoming Spring* (Figure 15.8), a pictorial textile depicting boys, sheep, and goats dated to the Yuan or Ming dynasties, once may have been contiguous to the National Palace Museum panel, according to a Metropolitan Museum of Art exhibition label, Spring 2000. The composition of the National Palace Museum textile is the same, in central particulars, as that of Qianlong's tapestry, but it is narrower—about half the width of the latter work—suggesting that either the National Palace Museum gauze was trimmed or that its composition was expanded by Qing weavers to produce a wall hanging corresponding in size to Qianlong's desired dimensions. Of course, another earlier pictorial textile might have served as the model for the Qing work.

Maggie Bickford

7. Transcribed under *Fang Song kesi Jiuyang xiaohan tu* [After a Song tapestry, *Nine Yang Disperse the Cold Picture*] in Hu et al. (1816, 7:3485B).

8. Figure 15.6 is reproduced in color in National Palace Museum (1989–, 5:205). The Taibei National Palace Museum collections hold many such paintings (depicting three, nine, or eighty-one sheep and goats); for a sample, see National Palace Museum (1989, 2:75, 79; 3:111, 235, 251, 253, 255; 5:113, 205, 267, 269, 343, 369, 377). Some of these works are assigned to named and anonymous Song artists; the paintings seem later, some much later. Many of these works bear titles that are disconnected from their original function as Nine-Nines or Sanyang images; this, in my view, is a tribute to the painter's success in configuring the requisite rebus elements and auxiliary auspicious motifs into plausible vignettes that stand on their own as figures-in-a-landscape or figure paintings. For an example of a fully expanded eighty-one-goat composition, see *Yuanren Baixiang yan qing* [(Yuan artist) One hundred blessings and abundant joys], reproduced in National Palace Museum (1989–, 5:263).

9. This must have been a very popular pattern because many examples survive in public and private collections in East Asia and the West. For another example, see Zhao Feng (1999, no. 08.09).

10. Cammann (1953, 69) parsed the fragment in Figure 15.12, unpacking its dense store of luck. Focusing on the *taiji* disc (the configuration of which suggested to him the stylized character *shou* [long life]) flanked by swastikas, he decoded these elements as a visual pun for the phrase *Wanwan shou* [Ten thousand, ten thousand years] and concluded that this textile was made to serve a dual function: it celebrated the solstice, and it celebrated the birthday of the emperor. See also Bickford (1999, 151–152).

11. Another rubbing of this chart is in the collections of the Walters Art Gallery, Baltimore, Maryland. I wish to thank Hiram Woodward for supplying a photograph and sharing research notes with me.

12. Liu Ruoyu (1641, 20.9a–b), read together with Lü Bi, compiler, *Ming gong shi* [Ming Palace history]. Lü's text is an abridgement of Liu's work. My discussion here is based on Bickford (1999, 139–140), which has an extensive discussion of the charts and their texts.

13. These charts and their popular modern printed copies are often attributed to the Ming emperor Xuanzong (r. 1426–1436). However, extant charts from the Old Palace (Figure 15.16) are associated with Xuanzong of the Qing dynasty, known as the Daoguang emperor. Some Qing sources attribute to the Qianlong the invention of the *Jiujiu xiaohan tu* bearing the text seen in Figure 15.16, inscribed in the emperor's hand; see Zhao Xinggen (1996, 313). For a palace chart made for the period Guangxiu 31/32 (1905/1906), see Fu (1982).

14. I am grateful to Ellen Laing for sharing her research notes on this print with me.

YUNXIANG YAN

16   *Making Room for Intimacy*

Domestic Space and Conjugal Privacy in Rural North China

The social significance of a house derives from the simple fact that a dwelling provides not only physical shelter for a household, but also an institutionalized and humanized space within which its residents interact with one another, as well as with visitors from the world beyond. Much as in other societies, traditional Chinese dwellings express and model family organization and give shape to the web of social and ethical norms, beliefs, and values, a subject discussed in several chapters. Indeed, the values of whatever family occupies a house, as well as its behavior patterns and interpersonal relations, transform any dwelling into a home. It follows logically that new trends in house design, which are manifested in the physical form of contemporary homes, will be suggestive of important social changes that are occurring within the family.

Anthropologists, including those who specialize in China, have long noticed the close link between house form and the structure of the family. As Francis L. K. Hsu noted a half century ago in his classic work *Under the Ancestors' Shadow,* the differences in size and quality of traditional houses served as important symbols of the social standing of a family and clear markers of economic class (1967 [1948], 28–41). A common patrilineal ideology in the past guided the layout or design of houses, as well as how dwelling space was used in the homes of both well-to-do and poor families. In the homes of prosperous extended families, parents occupied the central stage in the domestic space, yet even when a poor family could not afford a separate functional room, the parents' bedroom became the center of family life and served as the symbol of family continuity (Yang 1945, 40).

U-shaped dwellings are among the housing types that best reflect the continuity of the extended family group in traditional China. This form caught the attention of scholars in many disciplines, particularly those who conducted fieldwork in Taiwan and South China, where they saw the organization of living space in such dwellings as forming templates for human relations. A U-shaped dwelling normally started with a rectilinear base that consists of a central room with one or two rooms on each side (Figure 16.1). Over time, as a family group grew and divided into multiple units, new rooms might be added to extend the rectangle or additions constructed

Fig. 16.1. *U-shaped dwellings of this type (these are in Taiwan) represent a schematic diagram of family relationships within the house.* Source: Lin 1990, 24.

Fig. 16.2. *The progressive development from an I- to an L- to a U-shaped dwelling mirrors the expansion of a Chinese family from its nuclear origins.*

to create a U-shaped compound composed of flanking wings (Figure 16.2). The expansion from the rectilinear core normally was incremental and tied to the fortunes and needs of the household (Knapp 1986, 91–96). Margery Wolf's description of the rectilinear house in Taiwan mirrors those elsewhere in southern China: "At each end of the rectangle . . . there are indications of the ultimate design—an unnecessary door, a carefully made archway clumsily boarded over until the day it will open into a new wing housing the family of a grandson. The rectangle becomes first an L and finally a U whose arms may be extended again and again" (1968, 24) (Figure 16.3). Yet what might appear to be a smooth and natural progression often was frustrated by the natural decline of a family or tensions within a family that forced changes in the use of the residential space:

> At some point the family would divide into smaller units, but there would be no change in the compound's residential arrangement other than the construction of additional kitchens. Except for the central room, all rooms in the compound are distributed among the new families during division, together with other such family property as land, farming equipment, or shops. Because the central room is not involved, the first family partition creates two or more families owning in common this room if nothing else. Thus in most compounds there eventually is a multifamily agnatic group, which continues to increase in its individual membership and in the number of constituent

Yunxiang Yan

Fig. 16.3. *In anticipation of the expansion of this dwelling via the addition of a wing, this bricked-in passageway is designed so that it can be opened in the future as the needs of the family expand. Taiwan.* Source: Photograph by Ronald G. Knapp 1966.

families. At any given time . . . there are compounds (and agnatic groups) at different stages of development; only the base of the U compound is completed in some compounds, others may already have the full U shape and even two or more wings. (Cohen 1976, 21–23; see also Gallin 1966; Wolf 1968)

Doorways might again be boarded up as a family divides its property so that the "physical act of cyclical opening and closing of the doorway becomes one of the concrete symbols of the changing social relations within a family. Since the building itself is much more rigid and predetermined, while the social relations are flexible and fluid, the extent to which family life interacts with the home is necessarily mediated by the more immediate and tangible tasks such as boarding up a doorway" (Liu 1980, 55–56).

As discussed above in Chapter 11, another common feature of the traditional Chinese house was to separate the activities of men and women, both spatially and socially, and to downplay the importance of conjugal intimacy. Among wealthy families, women typically lived in an exclusive part of the household, which created a strictly enforced boundary between the inner quarter and outer portions of the house (see Bray 1997). "But this separation is also psychological, and even extends to rural villages, where it is common to see an obvious indifference between husbands and wives" (Fei 1992 [1947], 86). According to Fei, this is because the axes of relations in a traditional Chinese family are that of father/son and mother/daughter-

Making Room for Intimacy

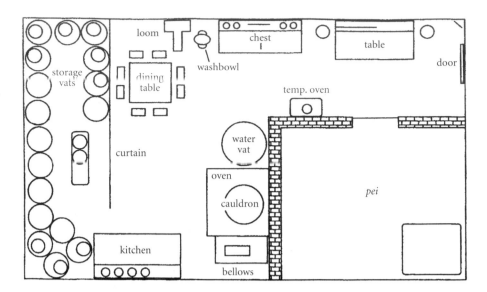

Fig. 16.4. *Within a cave dwelling in Shaanxi province, the interior arrangement of living space continues to be clearly differentiated according to gender: one space centers around the heated bed, or kang (here called a* pei, *according to the local dialect), which women occupy and which is a space of family intimacy, while the other is the (dining) table, which men use as a space of public interaction.* Source: Liu 2000, 44.

in-law, while the conjugal relationship involving husband and wife plays only a relatively minor role. As a result, discipline and hierarchy took precedence over intimacy and emotionality in interpersonal interactions in the domestic sphere (Fei 1992 [1947], 84–86; see also Baker 1979, 11–25). Even in a single-room cave dwelling in northwest rural China, there is still today a sexual division of the domestic space. According to Xin Liu (2000, 42–51), cave dwellings in villages in Shaanxi province are divided into two halves; one centers around the heated brick bed *[kang* or *huo-kang],* which women occupy, while the other is the table, which men occupy (Figure 16.4). Conjugal intimacy and privacy are difficult to develop under such circumstances. This functional divide also symbolizes the opposition between family relationships and public interaction within domestic space.

Given the rapid and often dramatic changes in both the Chinese family and larger social settings in recent decades, several questions may be asked. What has happened to traditional dwellings and to the management of domestic space? Are the continuity of the extended family and the centrality of the parents-son relationship still dominating principles in the design of houses in contemporary China? Is sexual separation and indifference still part of family life inside the house? While it is not possible to give global answers to these questions for China as a whole, ethnographic evidence gathered in villages in Heilongjiang province reveals some interesting clues.

In Heilongjiang, the northeasternmost of China's provinces, the winter season normally lasts for more than five months, and for a substantial part of the season, the temperature often falls 20–30 degrees below zero centigrade. Due to the severe

Yunxiang Yan

winters and widespread economic shortages, villagers in this region have generally lived in quite crowded housing conditions ever since the beginning of settlement in the early nineteenth century. Indeed, until the early 1980s it remained common that a large family—both men and women of two or more generations—slept in the same room and often on the same *kang*. Traditional dwellings and spatial arrangements, however, were largely swept away during a wave of house construction and remodeling that started in the mid-1980s, and by the late 1990s villagers were competing with one another in adopting "modern" house designs. New notions of intimacy and privacy began to emerge as important concerns in family life as individuals began to have their own private lives inside the house. As a result, the home has changed from being a corporate structure to a private haven.

In the following, I will first review patterns of spatial arrangements in old dwellings, as well as in the wave of house remodeling since the mid-1980s, focusing on how villagers defined and were defined by the spatial relations in various types of house plans. In the next two sections I will examine the changes brought about by "modern" housing designs. The quest for privacy has affected all members in a family and thus has altered a number of intrafamily relations, so I will focus on the development of conjugal intimacy and privacy. (For other aspects of the same process, see Yan 2003, chs. 3 and 5.)

Data presented in this chapter were collected over a decade of fieldwork from 1989 to 1999 in Xiajia village, Heilongjiang province; they built on the fact that I lived in Xiajia as an ordinary farmer from 1971 to 1978. With a population of 1,492 in 1998, the village remained a farming community even after the rural reforms brought decollectivization in 1983, but the villagers' livelihood has been closely tied to the market by a new mode of commodity production. To increase profits from farming, the villagers all switched to growing high-yield maize, which is used as commercial animal feed; they sold their maize to state and private buyers and then purchased wheat and rice from the market for their own consumption. Since the late 1980s, temporary jobs in the cities have become an additional important source of cash income. Average per capita income in Xiajia has remained slightly below the national average: it was 528 yuan in 1988 and 616 yuan in 1990, while the national average in these two years was 545 and 623 yuan respectively. The situation was worse during the 1990s, and the living conditions of most villagers showed little sign of improvement in comparison to the 1980s. Official figures during the 1990s, however, were not reliable because while the village economy stagnated, cadres were under pressure to inflate their achievements. For instance, the reported per capita income in 1997 was 2,700 yuan, a figure that even the village cadres openly admitted to being false. Nevertheless, all villagers I interviewed agree that living conditions had improved to a great extent in comparison to those of the earlier collective period. Some households have been able to take advantage of the new opportunities of the reform era and have become quite affluent in recent years, contrasting sharply with others who have been left behind (see Yan 1992).

Spatial Arrangements in Old Houses

Prior to 1949, differences in housing and domestic spatiality in Xiajia could be distinguished only between the limited number of local elite and the general village population. The few rich and powerful landlord families lived in large compounds that were encircled by high walls, with a main dwelling consisting of multiple rooms and smaller, detached ancillary structures, such as simple sheds for the use of hired laborers, draft animals, and storage (Figure 16.5). On the other hand, the majority of villagers lived either in very simple clay and grass houses or, even worse, in small huts that were built by leaning several logs toward the center of a frame, with walls comprised merely of grass mats and twigs that were covered on the outside with thick mud (Figure 16.6).

Fig. 16.5. *A representative walled compound of a richer family in pre-liberation northeastern China is the home of the novelist Xiao Hong, who was born to a landlord family in Hunan county, Heilongjiang.* Source: Wang Zhili and Zhang Zugang 1994, 49.

▼

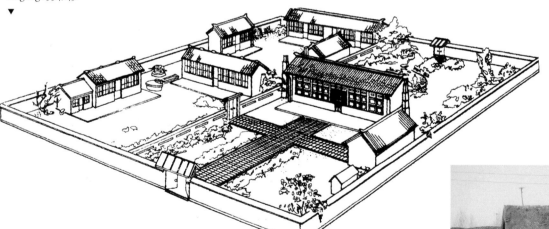

Fig. 16.6. *Simple rural dwellings of this type were ubiquitous in Northeast and North China well into the twentieth century. Surrounded by a stockade of grain stalks to form a modest yard, this nearly collapsed dwelling was built of mud plastered over walls made of grain stalks.* Source: Photograph by Yunxiang Yan.

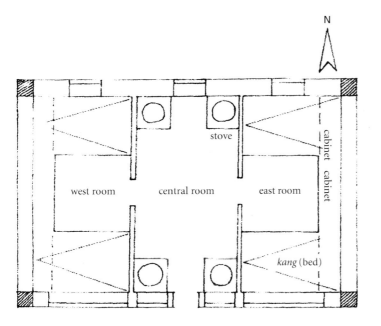

stove

cabinet

cabinet

west room

central room

east room

kang (bed)

Fig. 16.7. *In this schematic representation of a pre-1980 traditional three-bay dwelling, four round stoves in the corners of the "central" or "outer" room are connected to U-shaped* kang *in the adjacent "east room" and "west room."* Source: Drawing by Hu Yanbo.

Fig. 16.8. *As seen from the "outer" or "central" room into the "west room," the relationship between one of the cooking stoves and the nankang, "south kang," is clear. The kitchen space also serves as a hallway into the living/bedroom spaces, as well as for temporary storage.* Source: Wang and Zhang 1994, 45.

According to older villagers, the best thing that the Chinese revolution did for poor people was to make it possible for everyone to marry and build a reasonable dwelling. Indeed, from the 1950s to the early 1980s, Xiajia villagers were able to construct houses that resembled one another both inside and outside, with only minor variations in size. Throughout this period, a relatively common type of three-room house was built with a south-facing wall of windows and an entryway in the middle of the wall. Each dwelling was sited so that its facade faced south in order to absorb maximum sunshine for heat and light, especially during the winter. In overall form and structure, this type of simple dwelling was similar to single-story rectangular houses typical of North China (Knapp 2000, 167–175). The three rooms were called the east room *[dongwu]*, the west room *[xiwu]*, and the outer room *[waiwu]* (Figure 16.7). It is interesting to note that the "outer room" was actually in the center and was where the entrance was located. Some families, like the majority of villagers prior to the revolution, however, were able to build only a two-room house, in which case one room was termed the east room and the other the outer room. Unless the space was absolutely necessary, many families used the west room only for storage or as a bedroom during the summer season. Such a three-room house could accommodate the needs of a family throughout its development.

The central or outer room was used as a kitchen, hallway, and temporary storage space, and some families also kept their pigs in this room during the winter season. Two (in some cases three or four) stoves occupied the corners of the outer room,

Making Room for Intimacy

leaving only limited space in the center for people to walk about and work. Each stove was attached to a nearby *kang* built along the walls in the east room. When the stove was on, the smoke and heat traveled through a set of zigzagged flues or passageways within the heated bed, eventually exiting through a chimney that was located in a back corner along the northern wall of the house. The "south bed" *[nankang]* and "north bed" *[beikang],* named according to their respective locations in the room, as shown in Figure 16.8, were sometimes joined by a narrower and smaller bed called a *yaokang,* literally the "waist bed." To keep warm during the winter, entire families packed themselves onto the *kang* in the east room, which was considered the best of all the rooms, where they sat cross-legged on the heat-dissipating surface. When the children were still young, they usually used only the south bed for most of their activities. Sleeping arrangements were hierarchical. The privileged place, reserved for the most senior male in the household and his spouse (in the next position), was the end of the bed closest to the stove, called the "bed head," or *kangtou.* Other members slept in a row according to their generational rank, sex, and age. Usually, a daughter (or granddaughter in some cases) slept either at the far end of the south bed or in the north bed because she was ranked low and may also have had a special need for privacy.

Until the 1970s, newly married young couples lived in the same rooms with the rest of the members of the groom's family—sometimes eight to ten people—sleeping on the north bed, with only a hanging curtain in front of their bed to separate them from the sleeping space of other family members. When family division occurred, each of the newly established nuclear families got a stove and a *kang* attached to the stove. A house therefore might include four separate families living in two bedrooms, as shown in Figure 16.7. Since the mid-1970s, some young couples have preferred to move into another family's house, where either they alone occupied the west room or they shared the east room with the host family and slept on the north bed of that room. It was not unusual for two unrelated families to live not only in the same house, but also in the same room.

The outer room was not supposed to be used as a family function space other than for cooking and storage. Rather, it was the east room as "bedroom" that in fact served as the household's all-purpose space even though it was not spacious. *Kang* took up most of the physical space of the east room, leaving only a small square in the center, normally 40–60 square feet. It was here on the beds that most family activities took place: corn was husked, other agricultural products were processed, and food was prepared for meals. A family consumed its meals while sitting cross-

Yunxiang Yan

legged on the surface of the bed by utilizing a short-legged raised table. On the *kang* women did their sewing, small children played during cold days, and visiting friends gathered and chatted. When a guest visited a home, the welcome gesture was to call him or her "up to the bed."

From a contemporary urban perspective, there was obviously not much privacy or personal space under such conditions. Everyone was constantly under the watchful eyes and within the hearing distance of everyone else, twenty-four hours a day and seven days a week. The absence of privacy made it especially difficult for couples to develop bonds and mutual attraction and contributed to reinforcing the centrality of the vertical and hierarchical parents-son relationship in family life. Many old and middle-aged villagers indeed recall that when they were young and newly married, they were discouraged by their parents from spending time with their wives at home. "A man should go out and hang out with the men," one villager told me. Thus, it was certainly not accidental that during the collective period, the headquarters of the production teams all had expansive *kang* that could accommodate several dozen people at the same time. Such places became favorite spots for village men during that period, locations where they could chat with fellow team members or play poker. As a result, a young wife would either stay with her in-laws in their limited and confined space or sometimes go out with peers to other homes. The only time for a young couple to be together was at bedtime; however, because of the sleeping arrangements, this was hardly quality time in terms of intimacy.

New House Designs since the 1980s

Significant change occurred in the early 1980s, shortly after the rural economic reforms and decollectivization. The initial success of household farming and the diversified economy increased peasant incomes rapidly and led to a high tide in house construction in Xiajia during the second half of the 1980s. My 1991 survey shows that 102 new houses were built after 1983 (mostly between 1985 and 1988), and 121 houses were rebuilt or enlarged. Traditionally, as noted, villagers had built their houses with clay walls and grass roofs, but most, if not all, of the new houses were built with brick walls and tile roofs. The availability of cement and other modern construction materials enabled villagers to build larger houses or to enlarge their old ones. New aspirations also developed as more and more villagers had opportunities to observe and even to experience urban lifestyles when they had temporary jobs in the cities.

Floor Plan of a 1985 House

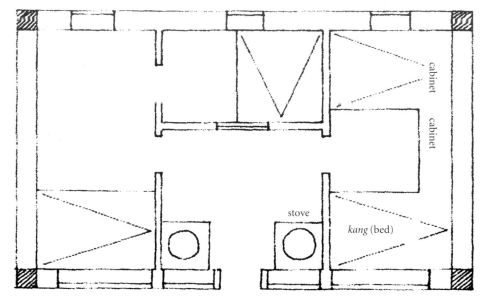

Fig. 16.9. *Among the experimental housing models of the early 1980s is this three-bay dwelling with a traditional large, interconnected* kang *in the "east room" and a* kang *in the "west room" (both of which are connected to large stoves just inside the front door) and also a separate back bedroom. Each of the rooms has a large window along the rear wall.*
Source: Drawing by Hu Yanbo.

The first wave of change was rather moderate and experimental. As represented in Figure 16.9, a new house would typically be a three-bay dwelling with a traditional, large interconnected *kang* in the east room, a *kang* in the west room, both connected to large stoves just inside the front door, and also a separate back bedroom with a window. Then, fairly quickly, came more radical changes, as shown in the floor plan in Figure 16.10. This is a house built in late 1987 by the then village head; it was regarded as the most advanced design at the time. Many villagers copied this model in the following years, thus triggering a new wave of house remodeling. The internal space of this house measures approximately 740–780 square feet, quite large by 1980 standards. The owner made a revolutionary change in house design by dividing the house into three functional areas (even though it is a four-room structure), separating the areas with walls and doors. The entire southern half of the house is made up of two large rooms without *kang,* plus an entrance door in the center. This was the first time in Xiajia village that the notion of a separate room without *kang* was put into practice. Following urban usage this type of room was referred to as *keting,* or simply *ting,* literally meaning the "guest lounge" or "the lounge," but I will hereafter translate it as "living room." In this particular case, there were two living rooms, one for the village head and his wife and the

Fig. 16.10. *Built in late 1987 by the then village head, this dwelling was copied by many villagers. Divided into three functional areas—two large living areas in the front, three bedrooms in the rear, each with a* kang, *and a designated kitchen.* Source: Drawing by Hu Yanbo.

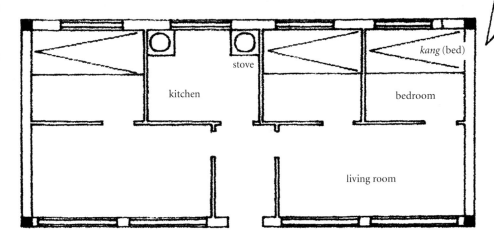

kitchen

stove

kang (bed)

bedroom

living room

other for their grown children. At the time the house was built, the family had an unmarried daughter and an unmarried son, and the mother of the village head also lived with them. To accommodate each individual's needs, the northern half of the house was divided into four equal-sized rooms. The village head and his wife slept in the east room, while his mother and daughter used the adjacent room. The son was given the far west room because he was older than the daughter and of marriage age. The kitchen was moved to the back and used to separate the son's room from his parents' room, hence creating more privacy for both. Through interviews I learned that when the father was not at home, which was normally the case, the daughter and her friends usually occupied the east living room, while the son and his friends used the west living room. The mother spent a lot of time in her own bedroom, either alone or with her friends, sometimes sharing the room with her daughter and other young girls. Both living rooms were furnished with sofas and coffee/tea tables—another new development in Xiajia village in the late 1980s. The east room, however, was better decorated because the father sometimes used it to entertain cadres from the town government or other villages.

Another interesting development is that the size of the beds in this 1987 house was reduced so that there was more ground space in the bedrooms, which were also

Floor Plan of a 1997 House

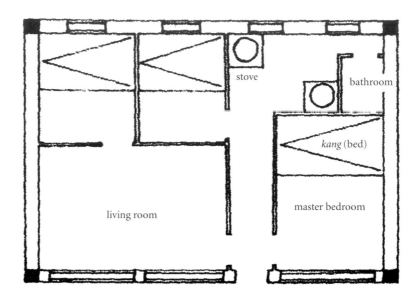

Fig. 16.11. *By 1997, a dramatic reconfiguration of the house had taken place, not only with the shifting of the stoves and kitchen to a rear location, where they continued to be linked to adjacent* kang *in bedrooms, but also with the placement of a "master bedroom" at some distance from other bedrooms. A hallway facilitates movement among the various separate functional spaces. A large family living room now dominates the space in the house, and a significant addition to the design is a separate bathroom, including a full-sized bathtub and a shower.* Source: Drawing by Hu Yanbo.

much smaller. This meant that when the door was closed, the bedroom could function as an independent room, instead of merely as a huge bed. For instance, grooming, a daily task that the men had previously performed in the kitchen/outer room and the women in the old-style east room, was now performed instead in one's own bedroom; thus personal grooming indeed became a more personal and private matter. When the door was closed, each person could also wash his/her bodies in private, a new development that was most appreciated by young women.

The availability of heating resources made it possible to reduce the size of the bed and remove it from the living room. Thanks to the high-yield maize and the heavy use of chemical fertilizer, villagers could harvest not only more grain, but also more corn stems and corncobs—the major source of cooking and heating fuel. Many villagers built a separate heating system in their houses, using the corn stems and corncobs to heat the water-tube boiler. More affluent families increasingly preferred to use coal purchased from the market for winter heating, leaving their extra corn stems and corncobs unused in the field.

The latest and perhaps potentially most important change was the addition of a bath and shower room in a house that was built in 1997, as shown in Figure 16.11. Although it is a three-room structure, it is 150 square feet larger than the 1987 model. Because of the improvements in construction materials in the 1990s, villagers were able to further increase the size of the new houses. Comparing the 1997 house with the 1987 house, we can see that the couple's bedroom—now a "master bedroom"—is larger than the other rooms, imitating urban designs in China's modernizing cities, which boast stylish bedrooms in each apartment unit. Furthermore, in this particular case, a central hallway separates the main bedroom from the other two rooms, used by the couple's three children. The hallway serves as a transit area that links the bedrooms to the kitchen, and when the bedroom doors are closed, the hallway also separates the inner space from visitors. According to my informants, most new houses in the late 1990s bore similar features and these patterns emerged as well in villages all over China.

The major new feature of the 1997 house, however, is the bathroom at the upper right corner, next to the kitchen. The bathroom boasts a full-size bathtub with a shower above, and both the walls and ground are covered with white tiles. There is no running water in Xiajia and the surrounding area, so having a bathroom is quite a luxury. In order to make the bathroom work, the owner of the house dug a well in the backyard and then used pipes to drain water to and from the bathtub. As this operation consumes both time and energy, the family used the bathroom only during the summer. This house was not the first to have an indoor bathroom and certainly was not the last—virtually all new houses built in the late 1990s added this feature. Although several families found the new fashion useless and ended up using the bathroom for storage instead, more and more villagers had begun to use it during the summer season. The happiest beneficiaries were the women, who, unlike the men, who could bathe naked in the nearby small river and ponds, now finally had a sanctuary in which to wash their bodies.

Even with the addition of a bathroom, the family toilet was still placed outside the house (although the form of the family toilet had also changed since the 1980s). In the past, families used a latrine, which was typically located at either end of the house—outside, of course. The entryway was not blocked or covered, and excretions were left for the pigs. When I went to Xiajia village for my first fieldwork in 1989, I was surprised to find that my landlord had built a pit toilet at the front left corner of the courtyard; it was fully walled and roofed, with a door that could be locked from the inside. My landlord proudly told me that his toilet was a model for others, as I was to find out later on. Some older villagers, however, complained that the new-style toilet smelled terrible.

Economic prosperity certainly is a crucial factor motivating villagers to improve their dwellings; the wave of house construction in the early 1980s resulted directly from the rapid increase in peasant incomes in Xiajia and the rest of rural China. However, it would have been easier to merely copy the old styles in order to build better and larger houses than to experiment with new interior designs. Yet it is clear that domestic space is both a physical and a social construct. Behind or underneath the specific house forms, there are indeed underlying principles by which people categorize their relationships and organize their everyday lives. Spatial change in Xiajia thus should not be regarded as merely a one-on-one response to the improvement in economic conditions. Instead it should be understood as part of the overall transformation in the private lives of individuals and families; the transformation is characterized by a rise of autonomy among the youth, a decline of patriarchal power, and, at a deeper level, a rising awareness of the individual. In other words, house remodeling should also be viewed as an effort on the part of villagers to accommodate the demands for conjugal independence and privacy, which can be examined at two levels—that of the family and that of the individual.

Family Privacy and the Notion of Interiority

The aforementioned changes in house form are by no means arbitrary. They are influenced by and in turn reshape the changing ways in which families interact with one another as well as with the official/public. At the same time that a family reduced the size of the *kang* and put them in separate, enclosed bedrooms, it also created a transitional space in the living room where its members could receive and entertain guests. The living room also came to serve as the center of family activities, since the television set, the clock, and sofa or chairs would be placed there. The most obvious result of having such a space is to protect the privacy of the family because people can literally put on a "public face" in the living room when dealing with visitors, while they conduct their private lives behind the closed doors of the bedrooms.

I first noticed the difference during my 1989 fieldwork, when some villagers had separate living rooms while others did not. In the new houses I was invited to sit on a bench, a chair, or a sofa in the living room and chat with my informants as one would normally do either in urban China or in the United States. But when I visited families in traditional-style houses, I reverted to earlier customs—going straight to the heated bed, taking off my shoes, and jumping onto the bed and sitting at the inner corner, the position reserved for family guests. This was all done, of course, with a warm invitation from the host; if not, then I knew I was not welcome. As time passed, at the end of the 1990s, I found myself increasingly directed to the living rooms, some of which were quite fancy, as only the poorest families continued to live in traditional-style houses.

As a visiting anthropologist, I could literally feel the inner-outer boundaries. In the new houses, I could no longer take a quick look around the house and get a basic sense of the economic standing of the family because now a part of the house was hidden from the public gaze. I could no longer keep the entire family together during my interviews. Previously, when I visited and talked with one member of a family, the other members were also present—if they were home—because there was no other place for them to escape. In the new houses, they could stay in their own bedrooms if they wished, no longer having to deal with me. On the other hand, because of the new house design, I was able to have a small room of my own in my host family's house, thus making both my life and my work more convenient and pleasant. My own experience in this connection allowed me to understand and appreciate the meanings of the changing spatial arrangements in a family house.

However, it must be acknowledged that the separation of the bedrooms from the living room is not as rigid as in contemporary American homes. Indeed, what occurs depends on the social distance between a visitor and the host. For example, more often than not, close friends or relatives are invited into the host's bedroom, where some can even take off their shoes and climb onto the *kang*. It is an interesting fact that where the host has a married son living in the same house, the young couple's bedroom is regarded as more private than even that of the parents. During my household survey, I was sometimes invited to the parents' bedroom but never to the bedroom of the married son unless I specifically requested to take a look at the newlyweds' room. Here the significant development is that in the remodeled house, the host or hostess can determine which part of the house is to be open to the visitor. In other words, because of the new house designs, a physical-social threshold emerged in individual dwellings that separated the inside and insiders from the outside and outsiders. In the process, the accessibility of the family to the public was reduced and a sense of interiority at home was created.

When I discussed my findings about the spatial inside/outside divide with two village cadres and one government official from the township, they told me that they had had similar experiences when they visited peasant families to implement state policies (such as collecting levies or enforcing birth control regulations). It was quite common for a housewife simply to tell the cadres that the household head, her husband, was not at home, with the result that there was no way for the cadres to carry out their jobs. This new situation contrasts sharply with the previous circumstances, whereby cadres seemingly had the right to enter any home at will and without notifying the host in advance. Another cadre, who worked as the head of a production team during the collective period, said that during busy seasons he often had to change a scheduled laborer's assignment, going to a team member's home sometimes late at night or in the early morning to reassign the individual. "I sometimes saw a couple still holding one another in sleep, and I simply woke them up from their beautiful dreams," he recalled with an obvious tone of satisfaction. It is important to note that villagers did not lock their houses at night during the collective period.

Conjugal Privacy and Intimacy

In addition to fencing off outsiders, the recent changes in domestic spatiality also enable individuals to have their own personal space in the house, thus protecting the privacy of individuals within the family, especially that of the husband and wife. The direct result of house remodeling such as shown in Figures 16.9–16.11 above is to allow a couple to have its own bedroom and, in many cases, to offer the same to aged parents and grown children. In many families, this spatial reorganization has increased conjugal privacy to a significant extent and contributed to the bonding and affection between husband and wife. This can be illustrated by the experiences of an old friend, a forty-one-year-old man who had worked in the same production team as I during the 1970s. During an informal interview with him in 1997, I started to talk about the implications of a separate bedroom for the intimate life of married couples. With no hesitation, he jumped up and said, "No need to hem and haw. It's straightforward. Let me tell you a simple thing. I never slept naked with my wife until we had our own house, and that was ten years after we married! For two years we lived in the north bed of my uncle's home, and we always had to be quiet—you know what I mean? It was awful!"

This man's experience was by no means unique in the past, as couples normally kept their clothes on in bed. Occasionally, there might be rumors in the village about a naked couple who had accidentally been seen by other people, with the couple then becoming a target of public teasing as well as criticism for its carelessness. Although my data do not provide a systematic account, based on what I heard from villagers, by the 1990s it was rather common for young couples to make love fully undressed. A separate bedroom obviously increased their sense of safety.

When asked about the reasons for choosing to live in a nuclear family, most

Xiajia residents answered with two words: *shunxin,* or "satisfaction/happiness," and *fangbian,* "convenience." The former is not difficult to understand, as many villagers asserted, "Life is always happier when you can manage family life yourself" *[Rizi zongshi ziji guozhe shunxin].* In other words, the power to make decisions and the joy of conjugal independence can make one feel happy. The second term, *fangbian,* however, is more complicated and can be understood only in relation to *shunxin.* When villagers explained that one may feel more *fangbian* in a nuclear family, they did not merely mean "convenience" or "making things easier," as the term usually implies. In most newly established nuclear households, couples frequently encountered "inconveniences" when they needed an extra hand for household chores, or when they lacked the necessary capital for the household economy, or when they needed someone to take care of the newborns. In this context *fangbian* refers to the notion of family privacy, and a couple's demand for *fangbian* represents an effort to reduce the accessibility of the conjugal space to others (see, e.g., Laslett 1973).

In a nuclear family a couple may have more *fangbian* to develop conjugal intimacy, to be left alone, and to make decisions without parental intervention. Because of these special kinds of "conveniences," life in a nuclear family is considered to be more *shunxin*—that is, happier. Thus, it is easy to understand why young villagers—especially young wives—welcome such radical changes in house design. An age-old complaint of women had been that they could not spend much time alone with their spouses when they lived with their parents-in-law and unmarried siblings-in-law in an old-style house. As one young woman put it, "You always felt as though you were being watched, that there were eyes around the house all the time."

The pursuit of conjugal privacy, as reflected in the local notions of *shunxin* and *fangbian,* goes beyond the daily appropriation of domestic space. Young couples now also defend their personal freedom and independence in terms of *sishi,* or "personal matters/business." One of the most common complaints from the young villagers, for instance, had been that their parents were too nosy and always liked to interfere in their personal business. Admittedly, sometimes the younger generation could be quite defensive about "personal business," to the degree that its uncompromising position often triggered serious intergenerational conflicts in stem families (for details, see Yan 2003, ch. 4).

It should be noted that Xiajia villagers do not use the term "privacy" per se, nor are they familiar with the trendy term *yinsi*, which is the Chinese translation of the Western notion of privacy. I doubt Chinese villagers in other regions are familiar with the term either, even though it has been popularized recently in urban areas.[1] As indicated above, a common reason to embrace the new house designs is *fangbian*, and some villagers also use the term *ziyou*, or "freedom," to describe their experience of having more personal space. When pressed further about what they meant by *fangbian* and *ziyou*, several informants simply gave a metaphor: "You can sleep on the bed during the daytime without worrying about being seen or being gossiped about by anyone." To make themselves understood, some villagers also told me that the feeling of freedom was that "you can do whatever you want" [*xiang gansha jiu gansha*]. Less frequently yet regarding a probably equally important notion, villagers maintained that they liked the new house designs because new spatial patterns of organization made one's home *guiju*, or "well organized," as well as *youli youwai*, literally meaning "having an inside and an outside." One of the first reformers of house design in Xiajia, for instance, told me that he had long dreamed of building a new house similar to an urban apartment, because urban dwellings distinguished between inside and outside—he specifically used the phrase *youli youwai*—and therefore they were *fangbian*, or convenient, to live in. Putting these pieces together, I am convinced that without resorting to the urban notion of *yinsi*, Xiajia villagers have begun to pursue and protect their privacy at both the family and individual levels.

According to the legal-liberal approach in the West, privacy as a legal right plays an important role in fostering intimacy, equality, political freedom, and individual autonomy. As a social practice, privacy is crucial to individual development and the formation of diverse social relations. Autonomy and intimacy are at stake in one's life, and they are protected by the notion of privacy when personal matters are stripped of public significance and private space is shielded from public intrusion (see Boling 1996, 19–31; Moore 1984; Warren and Laslett 1977).[2] With regard to private space, Patricia Boling suggests, "We might expand on the spatial sense of private places, and think more metaphorically about the 'territories of the self' we all carry around with us" (1996, 27). Here we can see clearly the close links between Xiajia villagers' notions of *fangbian, ziyou, guiju,* and *youli youwai,* on the one hand, and the scholarly discourse of privacy in the West, on the other hand.

How can Xiajia villagers pursue the ideal of privacy in family life without comprehending the Western notion of privacy? The answer lies in the above-mentioned

Yunxiang Yan

Fig. 16.12. *These drawings represent* siheyuan *in various configurations, from the simplest, with a single courtyard, to those with two, three, and four courtyards. Within each hall-courtyard complex, there is a hierarchical layering, with both "outer" and "inner" space.* Source: Chiu 2000, 142–143.

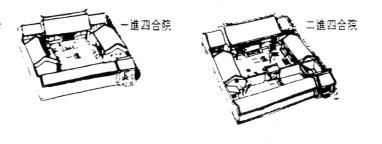

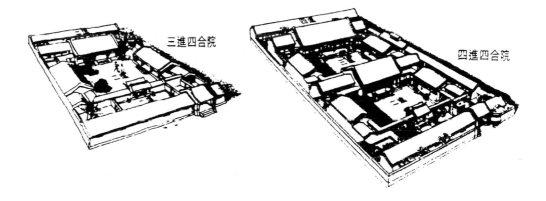

indigenous notions—that is, privacy as a social practice is itself not alien to Chinese culture. On the contrary, a certain degree of privacy has always been carefully protected for some people throughout Chinese history. Suffice it to note that the elite and the rich in Chinese society have always enjoyed some degree of privacy in family life. As far as spatial privacy is concerned, the houses of elite and well-to-do families all drew a clear line between the exteriority of the community and the interiority of the home and between the outer and inner parts within the home, regardless of specific architectural styles or regional differences. Both the courtyard house, or *siheyuan,* in Beijing and the famous garden house in Suzhou, for instance, feature different kinds of physical barriers, such as a sequence of gates, screens, courtyards, and distance, to control the accessibility of the family to the outside world. Whether the *siheyuan* were relatively small or extensive, as seen in Figure 16.12, each embodied a kind of graduated privacy, in which an outer space was employed to accommodate public interactions while an interior *keting* was used to receive visitors and entertain friends (Knapp 2000, 30ff.). Female members in an elite family were generally confined within the inner half of the domestic space, and they played a key role in constructing the private end of the continuum of the family, community, and state, turning a multifunctional house into a private home (Bray 1997, 52–58, 91–150). Similarly, in pre-1949 Xiajia, landlords protected family privacy inside courtyard walls and closed gates and even had armed guards, thus providing examples of houses that were *fangbian, guiju,* and *youli youwai.*

House remodeling in the 1980s and 1990s in Xiajia cannot be viewed as a simple replication of the traditional ideal. For one thing, in the past, privacy was the privilege of the elite and wealthy, far from the reach of the ordinary people, as exemplified by the contrast between the big compounds and small shacks in pre-1949 Xiajia village.[3] Moreover, individual privacy in traditional Chinese culture existed in a hierarchical context—a person could enjoy privacy in relation to those who were ranked lower socially and economically, but not vice versa. This is because privacy was not a legal right but a flexible privilege, the boundary of which varied depending on one's social status in a situation-specific context. For instance, a landlord in a rural community could enter a poor tenant's home without any concern for the latter's privacy, but the opposite was unthinkable. However, when the landlord was facing more powerful local gentry or a magistrate in another context, his privilege of privacy would be reduced or would completely disappear, depending on the degree of the status differences between the two parties. This is like the operation of "social face" in everyday life: an actor normally knows how "big" the other party's face is.[4] In an example mentioned above, the head of a production team in Xiajia village went directly to the bed of a sleeping couple and woke up the husband, and no one complained about the cadre's rude behavior.

Through their efforts to create new house forms, Xiajia villagers actually revolutionized a cultural tradition, turning previously elitist spatial notions into an everyday necessity for ordinary people. Nowadays most families want to build or remodel their houses according to the latest floor plan and control access to their family privacy. Inside new houses, individual family members can have their personal space (or the "territories of the self") due to the new house designs with multiple bedrooms. The previous class/status-based social differentiations in spatial privacy in particular and in private life in general have disappeared. In addition, the previous hierarchy of spatial relations based on generational rank and gender has been undermined to the degree that villagers' efforts to remodel their houses represent a democratization of domestic space in a double sense.

It should be noted that what occurred in Xiajia village is by no means unique. There are reports of similar house remodeling practices in other areas of Heilongjiang province, where the traditional *kang* culture used to prevail, and an increase of conjugal intimacy and privacy in other parts of the country.[5] Throughout China, house remodeling and interior decorating have been hot consumer "ticket items" for years, and urban residents have taken the lead to redefine spatial relations at home (see Davis et al. 1995; Fraser 2000).

Indeed, Xiajia villagers have been inspired by urbanites, and they imitate urban lifestyles in many respects, including overall house design, the use of domestic space, and changes in types and styles of furniture. More important, the mass media, television in particular, have brought villagers in touch with a wide range of contemporary values and ideals that have contributed to changing their mentality and behavior. One of the most important new values is the notion of *ziyou,* mentioned above, which is closely related to autonomy and intimacy—the core values that sustain the notion of privacy. It is not possible to understand the villagers' concern for individual space and autonomy without fully considering the influences of these new cultural values.

From a historical perspective, most urban workers and farmers in France, the United States, and elsewhere in the world often lived in extremely crowded housing conditions. Until the turn of the twentieth century—and, it must be admitted, to some degree today in poorer, remote areas of even economically developed countries—rural homes consisted of a single room, used for both cooking and sleeping, to the degree that privacy and intimacy were nonexistent. In the United States, it was not until the late eighteenth century that people began to divide their homes into three functional areas: the kitchen, the dining and drawing room, and the bedroom. A separate living room that screened public interactions from the inner and private half of the family was a much later invention (see Braudel 1967; Rybczynski 1986). It was only during the first half of the twentieth century that American families began to enjoy a family room and a master bedroom with its own bathroom in their homes (see Pader 1993, 118–120). Prost (1991, 51–67) calls improvements in French housing since the 1950s a true "revolution" in the history of private life. In her study of domestic space in Mexico, Ellen Pader (1993) examines both the family-oriented principles of domestic spatiality in Mexican houses and the recent changes that have resulted from remodeling, separating public interactions from the bedrooms and creating more personal space for individual use.

The Xiajia case, therefore, is a reflection of the historical trend in the transformation of the private life sphere in general and domestic spatiality in particular. As I discuss in greater detail elsewhere (Yan 1997), by the early 1990s conjugal independence had become an accepted feature of family ideology for the majority of Xiajia residents, as it had increasingly become for villagers and city dwellers throughout China. In everyday life the horizontal conjugal tie has replaced the vertical parents-son relationship as the central axis of family relations in both nuclear and stem households. This marks the triumph of conjugality over patriarchy, a structural transformation of family relations. Along with other important changes in private life, such as spouse selection, sex and love, the support of the elderly, and the fertility culture (see Yan 2003), the triumph of conjugality also indicates the transformation of the family from a disciplined corporate group to a private haven, whereby family life revolves around the husband-wife union, and family members have become more aware of their individual rights. As a result, the quest for conjugal space and privacy has become a necessity in the everyday life of ordinary villagers.

NOTES

The ethnographic material used in this chapter was first published in my book, *Private Life under Socialism: Love, Intimacy, and Family Change in a Chinese Village, 1949–1999* (2003), and all rights to that ethnographic material are reserved by the publisher, Stanford University Press.

1. The issue of privacy has drawn the attention of both scholars and the mass media in China. In scholarly discourse, the protection of privacy is regarded as one of the core elements of private rights (see Liu 1996). The mass media mostly focus on legal cases of privacy violation, which reflects the rising awareness of privacy among urban residents. In the first lawsuits, which occurred in 1990, two urban residents sued a novelist for writing a story about their private lives; they won the cases and were awarded 180 yuan and 120 yuan respectively (Li 1999, 8). It is interesting that by the end of the 1990s, while more sensitive about their own privacy, urban residents seemed to gain a new interest in other people's private lives, which resulted in a hot market for privacy-exploration books. The following are a few of the best-sellers published in 1997–1998: *Juedui yinsi* [Absolute privacy], by An Dun; *Feichang yinsi* [Unusually private], by Zi Jun and Xue Mei; *Danshen yinsi* [The privacy of singles], by An Qi; *Zhencao Yinsi* [The privacy of chastity], by An Jing; and *Zuier de yidianyuan* [The sinful Eden], by Yang Bo. For a special report on the importance of privacy in urban life and its commercialization, see *Xinzhoukan* [New weekly] 21 (1998): 13–25.

2. Feminist scholars criticize the efforts to take public significance out of the private sphere because then the unprivileged members—women and children—are put in a helpless situation. For a detailed review of this position, see Boling (1996, 4–19).

3. This is by no means a uniquely Chinese phenomenon. In France, for instance, "For the first half of the twentieth century private life was in most respects subject to communal controls. The wall that was supposed to protect individual privacy was a privilege of the bour-

geoisie" (Prost 1991, 67). As Warren and Laslett note, "The use of privacy is most likely for those whose behavior is not suspect and who have financial and other resources sufficient to draw boundaries around their activities" (1977, 48).

4. The significance of "face" in Chinese society is widely known by now, so much so that the term has entered the English-speaking world. In general, scholars distinguish two kinds of face: social face, based on one's achievements and dignity, and moral face, based on a person's feelings of shame. The former works as a type of prestige and is subject to the evaluation of others, while the latter functions as a moral self-constraint. Social face is achieved and possessed by people in the upper classes, while ordinary people do not care much about their social face (see Hu 1944; King 1988). However, my case study of gift exchange in Xiajia village demonstrates that by the 1980s, ordinary villagers not only cared about social face, but also fought to gain it, an important development similar to their quest for privacy. For a detailed ethnographic account of the "face contest" in Xiajia and a review of scholarly discourse on the concept of face, see Yan (1996, 133–138).

5. Wang and Zhang (1995) report a similar pattern of house remodeling in Changwu township, Zhaodong county, which is about two hundred kilometers from Xiajia village. They interpret the change as another positive result of the economic reforms and one more step toward the modernization of the family in rural China. See also Xu (1997) and Shen, Yang, and Li (1999) for quantitative findings of the increase of conjugal intimacy and privacy in different regions in the country.

Glossary

ai 艾, *Artemisia vulgaris,* mugwort

Ailian shuo 愛蓮說, *The Love of Lotus,* by the Song-dynasty philosopher Zhou Dunyi 周敦頤

Analects 论语, by Confucius

Anchang township 安昌镇, Zhejiang

Anhui 安徽

a-p'o 阿婆, bride's maternal grandmother

a-p'o niouc (Hakka) 阿婆肉, pork distributed by the bride's family to the bride's maternal grandmother's natal family

ba 八, number eight; considered auspicious for its phonetic closeness to the word *fa* 發, for "acquiring wealth"

Ba Jin 巴金, author of *Jia*

Bagua 八卦, Eight Trigrams

bagua qian 八卦钱, old copper octagonal coins

Bai Shen 白神, "One Hundred Gods"

baihu 白虎, white tiger; associated with the element metal

baimu 柏木, cypress

Ban Gu 班固 (32–92), historian of the Han dynasty

Bao jia wei guo 保家衛國, "To protect your home is to protect your country"

Baolun Ge 宝纶阁, the Pavilion of Precious Encomiums

Baoyu 寶玉, hero of *The Dream of the Red Chamber*

baxian zhuo 八仙桌, Eight Immortals table

bazi 八字, the "eight characters" signifying year, month, day, and hour of birth

beikang 北炕, "north bed"—that is, a *kang* along the north wall

bi 璧, round, disclike sacrificial object fashioned from jade

[bian] fu 蝙蝠, homophonous with *fu* 福, "blessings" or "good fortune"

Bilugong 必禄公, family ancestral hall

bing 冰, "lumps of ice"; homophonous with *bing* 兵, or sentry duty by troops

Bishu Shanzhuang 避暑山莊, Imperial Summer Villa at Rehe, modern Chengde

bixie 辟邪, "exorcising" object

bonsai 盆栽, literally "tree in a pot"

bubugao 步步高, "rising at every step"

buxiu 不朽, imperishability

buzhai 卜宅, divination of a house site

caihuazhuan 彩化砖, painted bricks

Caishen 财神, God of Wealth

cang lang 滄浪, blue waves

Canglang Tingyuan 滄浪庭園, Surging-Wave Pavilion Garden, the oldest surviving garden in Suzhou, Jiangsu

Cangpo village 苍坡村, Gangtou township 港头乡, Yongjia county 永嘉县, Zhejiang

Cao 曹氏, lineage and surname

Cao Xueqin 曹雪芹, author of *The Dream of the Red Chamber* [*Hong lou meng* 红楼梦]

Caofang village 曹坊, Fujian

chan 禪, meditation chair

chang 昌, prosperous, flourishing

Changchun She 长春社, the Studio of Everlasting Spring

Changjiang River 長江

Changling 長陵, the mausoleum of Yongle 永樂, the third emperor of the Ming dynasty

changpucao 菖蒲草, *Acorus calamus*, sweet flag

Changwu 昌五鎮 township, Zhaodong county 肇东县, Heilongjiang

Changwuzhi 長物志, *Treatise of Superfluous Things*, by Wen Zhenheng 文震亨 (1585–1645)

chanyi 禪椅, meditation chair

chaoshan 朝山, "Worshiping Mountain," found to the south of an optimal *feng-shui* site

chaoting 朝廷, large open area with a courtyard for audiences with the ruler

Chen 陈氏, surname and lineage

Chen Ancestral Hall 陈家祠, Guangzhou

Chen Fuyao 陳扶搖, a Qing scholar, author of *Huajing* 花鏡 [Flower mirror]

Chen Yuanjing 陳元靚

Chengkan 呈坎, Shexian county 歙县, Anhui

Chengqilou 承启楼, Yongding county 永定县, Fujian

Cheung Uk 张屋 village, Sha Lo Tung 沙罗洞, Hong Kong

Chifeng Municipal Museum 赤峰博物館

chiling 勅令, imperial edict

China Institute 華美協進社

Chu 楚, a regional state in central China during the Zhou dynasty (1045–221 B.C.)

Chuandixia village 川底下村, Zhaitang township 斋堂镇, Mentougou district 门头沟区, Beijing

chuandou 穿斗, post-and-tie-beam wooden structural framework

Chuang Gong 床公 and **Chuang Mu** 床母, male and female Genii of the Bed

chuanyi 圈椅, crestrail roundback chair

Chuci 楚辭, *Songs of Chu*

Chun Niu 春牛, Spring Ox

Chunqiu Zuo zhuan zhengyi 春秋左傳正義, commentary on the "Spring and Autumn Annals"

chuomu 綽幕, older term for *queti* 雀替

Chuxiang wulun quanbei zhongxiao 出像五倫全備忠孝, *Tales of Surpassing Virtue and of Perfect Filiality*

Chuyue Xuan 鋤月軒, Hoe-Moon Lounge, in the Yi Yuan Garden 怡園 in Suzhou, Jiangsu

cijiao 側腳, splayed furniture legs

citang 祠堂, ancestral shrine

citing 祠厅, family ancestral hall

cong 琮, cylindrical sacrificial object fashioned from jade

Cuilinglong 翠玲瓏, Delicate Emerald Hall, in Canglangting Garden 滄浪庭, Suzhou, Jiangsu

cun 村, village

cun fa 皴法, texture strokes used in painting

Da sha 打煞, "Vanquish the demons"

Da wu jianming tu 大屋简明图, Simplified Plan of the Big House

da xi ge 大喜歌, rhymed, "luck-bringing" verses

Da Zhu Gui 大猪鬼, Spirit of the Pigpen

Daguan Yuan 大觀園, Grand View Garden, depicted in *Hong lou meng*

daji 大鸡, rooster; homophonous with "greatly auspicious" 大吉

damuzuo 大木作, major carpentry, such as the framework of buildings

danguo 单过, to "go it alone"; sons or brothers living apart prior to formal family division

Dangxiang or Tanguts 党項, Xixia dynasty 西夏

Dao de jing 道德經 *The Way and Its Power*, by Laozi 老子

daojing 倒镜, "inverting mirror"; also called tiger or white tiger mirror [*hujing* 虎镜 and *baihujing* 白虎镜]

Dazongci 大总祠, Great Focal Ancestral Hall

de 德, virtue

Deyuantang 德远堂, ancestral hall of the Zhang 张氏 lineage, Taxia 塔下 village, Fujian

di wen 地文, literally "earthly patterns"

Diaoyuan 钓源, Jiangxi

dili 地理, "earth truth," "earthly patterns," "land pattern"; used today for the discipline of geography

ding (Cantonese) 灯, paper lantern; homophonous in Cantonese with the word for sons, *ding* 丁

Ding yao Sanduo Jiuru pian 定要三多子九如篇, "May you garner the 'Three Abundances' and the 'Nine Analogs'"

Dingcun village 丁村, Shanxi

Dongguan 东莞, Guangdong

Dongping 东平, Shandong

Dongshan 東山, Lake Tai, Jiangsu

Dongshanci 东山祠, focal ancestral hall, Shiqiao village, Fujian

dongtu 动土, groundbreaking

dongwu 尔屋, east room

Dongyue Dadi 东岳大帝, Emperor of the Eastern Peak

dongzhi 冬至, winter solstice

dougong 斗拱, modular bracket systems

Du Mu 杜牧, Tang poet

duan 缎, knee wrapper

Duanwu 端午 or **Duanyang** 端阳, the fifth day of the fifth month

Dui wo sheng cai 对我生财, "Bring riches to me"

Dunben Tang 敦本堂, Hall for Respecting the Root [of the lineage], in Tangyue 棠樾 village, Shexian 歙县, Anhui

Dunhuang 敦煌, Gansu

duo/shao 多/少, quantity, denoted as more/less

duo zi 多子, many sons; embodied as a rebus by the many-seeded pomegranate, which is commonly called *duozi* 多子

duozi 多子, many-seeded pomegranate; homophonous with *duo zi* 多子, "many sons"

Emei Mountain 峨眉山, Sichuan

Emperor Han Lingdi 漢靈帝 (r. 168–189)

Emperor Ming Xuanzong 明宣宗 (r. 1426–1436)

Emperor Qing Xuanzong 清宣宗 [Daoguang emperor] (r. 1820–1850)

Emperor Song Huizong 徽宗 (r. 1101–1125)

Emperor Xiawen 考文帝, Northern Wei dynasty (471–499)

Emperor Yandi 炎帝 [legendary "Fiery emperor"]

Empress Xiaoduan, née Wang 孝端王氏

Ennin 慈覺大師 or 圓仁, Tang dynasty monk

Epang Palace 阿房宫賦, grand palace of Qinshihuang, the first emperor of the Qin dynasty

Facai huan jia 發財還家, Wealth Returns Home

Family 家 *[Jia]*, novel by Ba Jin 巴金

fang 房, room; also the conjugal unit, referring to a married couple

fang 舫, landboat

fang mu (jie)gou 仿木结构, architectural details that imitate a timber (structural) skeleton

Fang Wentai House 方文泰宅

fangbian 方便, convenience

fangchan 房產, *fang* property, including the husband-wife's room and its furnishings

Fangwei Zong 方位宗 or **Liqi Zong** 理气宗, Compass School or Analytical School of *fengshui*

Fei Xiaotung 费孝通, anthropologist and sociologist

fen jia 分家, family division

Fengshan 鳳山, Taiwan

fengshui 風水, geomancy

fengshui ta 风水塔, *fengshui* pagoda

fengshui xiansheng 风水先生, "interpreter of wind and water," or geomancer

Fogong Si Temple 佛宫寺, Yingxian, Shanxi

Foshan 佛山, Guangdong

fu 福, good fortune, blessings

Fu 復, "Return (the Turning Point)" hexagram, in which a single unbroken (*yang*) line appears at the bottom

fu/gui 富/貴, wealth, denoted as riches

fu lu shou 福录寿, wealth, official position, and longevity

Fubai Xuan 浮白軒, Studio of Frothy White

Fujian 福建

fumu 父母, "father and mother"; the emperor's relationship to the people, who are the *minzi* 民子, "people children"

Furong village 芙蓉, Nanxijiang 楠溪江, Zhejiang

Fuwah Hotel 富华大酒店, Weifang 潍坊, Shandong

Gansu, 甘肃

gao/di 高/低, height; denoted as high/low

Gao Lian 高濂, author of *Yuzan ji* 玉簪記 [Tales of the jade hairpin]

Gao Lian 高濂 and Li Yu 李漁, authors of *Xianqing ouji* 闲情偶記 [Occasional records of leisurely sentiments] (1617)

Gao Ming 高明, author of *Pipa ji* 琵琶記 [Tales of the lute]

ge 閣, two-story pavilion

Ge Yuan 个園, Yangzhou 揚州, Jiangsu

gong 功, merit

gong cheng 宫城, palace-city

Gongbu gongcheng zuofa celi 工部工程作法則例, *Engineering Manual of the Board of Works*

gongji 公鸡, crimson rooster, a propitious *yang* creature

gongting 宫廷, home of the emperor, or "palace with a courtyard"

Gouliu 沟流, possibly God of the Latrine

Gu Cheng Yan 古城岩, Wan'an village 万安村, Xiuning county 休宁县, Anhui

gu minju 古民居, old dwellings

Gu Mu Jiao Ke 古木交柯, Intertwined Ancient Tree, in Liu Yuan Garden 留園, Suzhou, Jiangsu

guan 館, guest house

Guan cheng chun man 管城满春, Nine-Nines chart

Guan Gong 关公, Lord Guan, respected man of the Three Kingdoms period (220–265)

Guan Yu 關羽, also Guan Gong

Guandi 關帝, God of War

Guang han xiang 廣寒香, *The Cold Fragrance Diffused*; published in the Kangxi 康熙 period (1662–1722)

Guangdong 广东

Guangxu emperor 光绪 (r. 1875–1908)

Guanlu village 关麓村, Yixian county 黟县, Anhui

guanmaoyi 官帽椅, yokeback chair

Guanyin 觀音, bodhisattva

gui 桂, cassia leaf; homophonous with 贵 "honorable" and "of high rank," as well as symbolizing success in the civil service examinations

gui 閨, women's apartments

guiju 规矩, well organized; a term to describe new spatial patterns of organization in a home

Guizhou 贵州

Guo Xi 郭熙, famous artist of the Song dynasty

guojia 國家, country; defined by a compound of two words: country and family

Ha Tsuen 厦村, Tai Po 大埔, Hong Kong

Hainan 海南

Hakka 客家; also called Kejia

Han Xizai ye yan tu 韓熙載夜宴图, *The Night Revels of Han Xizai,* attributed to Gu Hongzhong 顧閎中

Hangzhou 杭州

Hanmei tu yu 寒梅吐玉, *The Wintry Plum Spits Jade (White Blossoms)*

hao shi huai shi (Hakka: *ho-se fai-se*) 好事坏事, good and bad events—weddings, funerals, religious celebrations, etc.

He 何, surname and lineage

He chuan zhi tu 合爨之圖, Diagram of the collective stove

He He 和合, boys of Union and Harmony

Hebei 河北

heihu 黑虎, "black tiger" amulet

Heilongjiang 黑龙江

Henan 河南

Hengzhi Qingfen 蘅芷清芬, hall in the Daguan Yuan 大觀園, residential garden in Beijing

hetaomu 核桃木, walnut wood

Hetu 河圖, Yellow River Chart

hezhe di bu da zuo chuang ji yi zhuo 合著地步打做床儿椅案, "couches, stands, chairs, and tables, all fittingly installed"

Ho, Ivan Chi Ching 何志清

Hokkien 闽南

Hong lou meng 紅樓夢, known in English as *The Dream of the Red Chamber* and *The Story of the Stone*

hong shi 红筛, red bamboo sieve

Hongcun village 宏村, Yixian county 黟县, Anhui

Hongkeng village 红坑村, Hukeng township 湖坑乡, Yongding county 永定县, Fujian

Houhai area 后海, Beijing

Houwang village, Pinglu county 平陆县, Shanxi

Hsu, Francis L.K. 许烺光

Hu 胡氏, surname and lineage

Hu Jingde 胡敬德, alternate name for Yuchi Gong 尉尺恭 (also known as Yuchi Jingde 尉尺敬德), brave general of the Tang period; together with Qin Shubao 秦叔宝, he serves as a Door God

hua lun 畫論, theories of painting

Huafeng Zhai 畫舫齋, Painted Pleasure Boathouse

Huairou county 怀柔县, Beijing 北京

Huaiyuanlou 怀远楼, Nanjing county 南靖县, Fujian

Huajing 花鏡, *Flower Mirror,* by Chen Fuyao 陳扶搖, a Qing scholar

Huan Cui Tang Yuan Jing Tu 環翠堂園景圖, Garden Scenes of the Encircled Emerald Hall

Huang Yingtai 黃應泰, the first owner of Ge Yuan 个園, garden in Yangzhou

Huangcun 黃村, Shexian county 歙縣, Huizhou 徽州, Anhui

Huanghe Lou 黃鶴樓, Yellow Crane Tower, Wuchang (modern Wuhan, Hubei)

huanghuali 黃花梨, yellow flower pear wood

Huangshan municipality 黄山市, Anhui

Huayang 华阳 village, Jixi county 绩溪县, Anhui

huayuan 花園, flower garden

Hubei 湖北

huchuang 胡床, folding stool with matting; the prototype of later chairs

Hui [Hui nationality] culture 回族文化

Hui [Huizhou] culture 徽州文化

hui liu cheng jian 滙流澄鑑, "converging streams like a pure mirror"

Huizhou 徽州, southern Anhui

Huizhou Mingdai zhuzhai 徽州明代住宅, *Ming Dynasty Houses of Huizhou*

Hunan 湖南

huokang 火炕, heated brick bed; also called simply *kang*

Hushen 户神, God of the Family

hutong 胡同, old residential lanes in Beijing and other northern cities

Imperial City 紫禁城 [Zijin Cheng]

Ji chen dao 吉辰到儿, "The auspicious time has come!"

Ji Cheng 計成 (1582–?), author of *Yuan ye* 園冶 [Manual of garden design]

jia 家, house, home, family

jiachan 家產, family property

jiaci 家祠, family ancestral hall

Jiajing 嘉靖 period (1522–1566)

jiaju 家具, "implements of the house"

jian 间, building module; distance between columns

Jiang Taigong zai ci 姜太公在此, "Jiang Taigong is here"

Jiang Ziya 姜子牙, Zhou-period minister, also known as Jiang Taigong

Jiang Ziya zai ci 姜子牙在此, "Jiang Ziya is here"; variant form for *Jiang Taigong zai ci* 姜太公在此, "Jiang Taigong is here"

Jiangnan 江南, lower Yangzi River area

Jiangsu 江苏

Jiangxi 江西

Jiangzhuangzhen 姜庄镇, Shandong

jiaoyi 交椅, horseshoe and yokeback armchair

jiasheng 家生, "active objects in the house"

jiatang 家堂, generic household gods

jiating 家庭, the domicile of a family; literally "domestic household with a courtyard"

jiaxun 家訓, "household instructions"

jiayuan 家園, home-garden

jiazhang 家長, family head

jichimu 鸡翅木, chicken-wing wood

Jiefangyingzi 解放影子, Inner Mongolia

jieshen zhuo 接神桌, "contacting gods table"

Jiezi Yuan 芥子園, Mustard Seed Garden

Jilin 吉林

Jin 晋 dynasty (265–420)

Jin Mao Tower 金茂大厦, Shanghai

Jin ping mei 金瓶梅, *The Golden Lotus*

Jin Shi Di 进士第, shrine or residence of a man with a jinshi degree

Jinan 济南, Shandong

jing 景, "forms embodied in scenery 'projecting' out of visual images"

Jingchai ji 荆釵記, *Tales of the Thorn Hairpin*, collected by the Yuan author Ke Danqiu 柯丹丘

Jingquan Tongzi 井泉童子, Lad of the Well

Jinjiang county 锦江县, Fujian

jinjishen 禁忌神, tutelary gods of the house

jinshi 進士, metropolitan degree, highest degree, "Presented Scholar"

Jiu Ru 九如, Nine Analogs

jiujiu 九九, Nine-Nines

Jiujiu tu 九九圖, Nine-Nines chart

Jiujiu xiaohan shitu 九九消寒诗圖, "Nine Nines Disperse the Cold" poetry charts

Jiujiu xiaohan tu 九九消寒圖, "Nine-Nines Disperse the Cold" pictures (or charts)

Jiujiu zhi ge 九九之歌, "Nine-Nines song"

Jiuyang xiaohan tu 九羊消寒圖, "Nine *Yang* Disperse the Cold" picture

Jiuzhou 九州, Nine Provinces, a poetic name for China

Jixi county 绩溪县, Anhui

jujia 居家, "home living"; activities that take place at home

Julu county 巨鹿县, Hebei

jumu 樱木, southern elm wood

jun/chen 君/臣, ideal relationships; denoted as ruler/ruled and father/son 父/子

Jurchen 女真 of the Jin 金 dynasty

Kai Tai tu 開泰圖, *Kai Tai* picture

Kaifeng 开封, Henan

kaijizu 开基祖, focal ancestor, the ancestor who established the base of a lineage

Kam Tin 锦田, Hong Kong

Kan Ting Study Hall 觐廷书室, Hong Kong

kan ximei (Hakka: *kon semoi*) 看细妹, "seeing the girl"

kang 炕, heated brick bed

kang ji 炕儿, small, low tables used on a *kang*

Kang Youwei 康有為, philosopher and reform leader (1858–1927)

kangtou 炕头, "bed head"; the portion of a *kang* closest to the stove

Kangxi 康熙, the third emperor of the Qing dynasty (1654–1722)

kanyu 堪輿, alternative name for *fengshui*: "cover and support" and "canopy of heaven and the chariot of earth"

Kaogong ji 考工記, *The Artificer's Record*

Kaohsiung [Gaoxiong] 高雄, Taiwan

Kejia 客家, also called Hakka

kesi 緙絲, silk tapestry

keting 客厅 (or simply *ting* 厅), literally "guest lounge," "lounge," "hall," but today translated as "living room" and "guest hall"

Khitans 契丹 of the Liao 遼 dynasty

kin ngoe-tsou (**Hakka**) 敬外祖, "to honor the matrilateral ancestors"

kuaizi 筷子, chopsticks; the sound has a punning relationship with "sons coming quickly," *kuai zi* 快子

Kun 坤, "The Receptive" hexagram; composed solely of broken, *yin* 隐, lines

Kunlun Mountain 昆仑山

kunmen 壼門, carved or open cusps

kuzi 裤子, men's trousers; in some southern dialects, the sound is close to that of the auspicious Chinese character *fu* 富, "riches"

Kwong Tai Company 光大有限公司

la gamen (**Hakka**) 迂家门, the inspection visit of the bride's family to the groom's home

lanban 欄板, apron, balustrade

lang 廊, covered pathway

Langzhong city 阆中市, Sichuan

Lantian county 蓝田县, Shaanxi

Lanxi city 兰溪市, Zhejiang

Laowu Ge 老屋閣, Huizhou 徽州, Anhui; earliest Ming period private residence still standing

layue 臘月, twelfth month

Li 李氏, surname and lineage

Li Gongnian 李公年 (fl. ca. 1120), Northern Song painter

Li ji 禮記, *Book of Rites*

Li Liweng 李笠翁 (1611–1680), author of *Xianqing ouji* 閑情偶寄 [A temporary lodge for my leisure thoughts]

lian 連, continuous; homophonous with *lian* 蓮, "lotus"

lian 蓮, lotus; homophonous with *lian* 連, "continuous"

Lian sheng gui zi yi ruyi 連生貴子亦如意, "May noble sons be born to you continuously, and may all be as you wish!"

liangzhu 梁柱, beams and columns

Liangzhu cultures 良渚文化 (4000–2500 B.C.E.)

Liaoning 辽宁

lichun 立春, beginning of spring, end of the twelfth or early in the first lunar month

Lin 臨, "Approach" hexagram, consisting of two unbroken lines rising from the bottom

Lin Yutang 林語堂, Chinese American author and translator (1895–1976)

ling 棂, lattice panels

Ling'en dian 祾恩殿, Hall of Awesome Grace, Beijing

lingge chuang 欞格窗, lattice windows

Lingshan village 灵山村, Zhouping township 周平镇, Xihu district 西湖区, Hangzhou, Zhejiang

Liqi Zong 理气宗 or **Fangwei Zong** 方位宗, Compass School or Analytical School of *fengshui*

Liu Dunzhen 劉敦楨, architectural historian (1879–1968)

Liu Guosong 劉國松, painter (born 1932)

Liu Hai 刘海, a benevolent diety usually depicted standing on a toad and swinging a string of coins

liu po 六婆, "the six kinds of old crone": matchmakers, Buddhist and Daoist nuns, women herbalists, fortune-tellers, and midwives

Liu Yuan garden 留園, Suzhou, Jiangsu

Liukeng 流坑 village, Le'an county, 乐安县 Jiangxi

Liukeng Tang 留耕堂, ancestral hall of the He lineage 何氏, Shawan 沙湾, Panyu 番禺, Guangdong

liuli jinshu jian 琉璃金属件, glazed ceramic or metal pieces

liumu 柳木, willow wood

loessial region 黄土高原地区

longmai 龙脉, "dragon veins"

Longmen 龙门石窟, Buddhist grotto, Henan

Longnan village 龙南村, southern Jiangxi

Longyan county 龙岩县, Fujian

longyanmu 龙眼木, longyan wood

lou 樓, tower, multiple-story building

Lu Ban 鲁班, patron of carpenters

Lu Ban chi 鲁班尺, special carpenter's ruler

Lu Ban jing 鲁班经, *Lu Ban Manual*

Lü Bi 呂毖, compiler of *Ming gong shi* 明宫史

luchong 路冲, "road is against a house"

Luo 罗, clan ancestral hall; see Baolun Ge

Luo Dongshu 罗东舒, Yuan-period worthy for whom Baolun Ge was built

luohan 羅漢, arhat

luojing 罗经, also called a *luopan* 罗盘; a saucerlike block of wood with a magnetized south-pointing needle at its center

luopan 罗盘, compass; also called a *luojing* 罗经; a saucerlike block of wood with a magnetized south-pointing needle at its center

Lushi chunqiu 呂氏春秋, *Lu's Annals of Spring and Autumn*

lutai 露臺, "dew platform"; a large balcony supported on pillars, with balustrades of wood or bamboo on three sides and an awning overhead to keep off the sun

mantou 馒头, steamed bread

Maoping village 茆苹村, Luci township 芦茨乡, Tonglu county 桐庐县, Zhejiang

mei 美, lovely

meili 美麗, lovely

Meixian 梅县, Guangdong

menguang chi 门光尺, special carpenter's ruler; also called a *Lu Ban chi* 鲁班尺

Menshen 门神, Door Gods or Guardians of the Gate

menzhao 门罩, door hoods

meiguiyi 玫瑰椅, rose chair

Mianzhu 绵竹, Sichuan

Mianzhu Door God 绵竹门神

mingqi 明器, funerary model

mingtang 明堂, bright or cosmic court; used to describe a semicircular pond

minju 民居, vernacular house

Moganshan 莫干山, Zhejiang

muci 墓祠, family shrine

mudiao 木雕, wood carving

Museum of Chinese History 中國歷史博物館

muzhu 木主, ancestral tablets

nan san 男三, three boys

Nan san kai Tai yi you fu 男三開泰義猶符, "Males [numbering] three initiate the 'Tai' is even a better match"

Nanchan Monastery 南禪寺, Wutaishan 五台山, Shanxi

Nanchizi 南池子 neighborhood, Beijing

nanguanmaoyi 南官帽椅, "southern official's hat" armchair

Nanjing county 南境县, Fujian

nankang 南炕, "south bed"—that is, a *kang* along the south wall

Nankou township 南口镇, Meixian 梅县, Guangdong

nanmu 楠木, a type of cedar

Nanping village 南屏村, Anhui

Nantai 南台 Island in Fuzhou 福州, Fujian

Nanxijiang 楠溪江, Zhejiang

Nanyue wang 南越王, king of Nanyue, Western Han dynasty (second century B.C.E.)

National Palace Museum 國立故宮博物院, Taibei

nei 内, inner

neifang 內房, "inner quarters" for women

Ni Zan 倪贊 (1301–1374), Yuan 元 dynasty painter

Ni Zan xiang 倪瓚像, *Portrait of Ni Zan*, inscribed by Chang Yu 張雨題

Niang Niang 娘娘 goddesses, Sangu Furen 三姑夫人

nianhua 年画, New Year pictures

Ningyuantang 宁远堂, Zhanqi village 瞻淇村, Shexian 歙县, Anhui

Northern Wei 北魏

nu shu 女书, "women's script"

Ou Yuan 耦園, Garden of Couple's Retreat, Suzhou 蘇州, Jiangsu

Ouyang Xiu 歐陽修, Song dynasty poet, historian, and statesman (1007–1072)

paifang 牌坊, memorial archways

Palace Museum 故宮博物館, Beijing

pao liang 跑梁, "runs along the beam"

Patriotic Sanitation Movement 爱国卫生运动

Pearl River Delta 珠江三角洲, Guangdong

Peitian village 培田村, Longyan county 龙岩县, Fujian

penjing 盆景, Chinese precursor form for the better known Japanese *bonsai* 盆栽

Petronas Towers [**Beituonasi dalou** 贝托纳斯大楼], Kuala Lumpur, Malaysia

piaohui 票会, rotating credit clubs

piaoliang 漂亮, pretty

ping 瓶, vase; an auspicious rebus for "peace," *ping'an* 平安

Ping Shan 屏山, Hong Kong

pingan 平安, peace

pingji 平基, leveling the foundation

Pingshan county 平山县, Hebei

Pingyao 平遥, Shanxi

pinjin 聘金, betrothal money

Pipa ji 琵琶記, *Tales of the Lute*, by Gao Ming 高明

Pucheng county 浦城县, Shaanxi

Putuo Zongcheng Temple 普陀宗乘廟 (1771), at the Imperial Summer Villa, Chengde, Hebei

qi 氣, life breath or cosmic energy

qi 棋/碁, chests made of either wood or stone

qi gong shi ye, ti xiang hu tian di, jing wei hu yin yang 其宮室也體象乎天地經緯乎陰陽

Qiankou 潜口, Huizhou, Anhui

Qiankou Dwelling Museum 潜口民宅博物馆

Qiankou Folk House Museum 潜口古居博物馆

Qiankou Guminju Bowuguan 潜口古居博物馆, Qiankou Folk House Museum

Qianliang village 前良村, Huangze township 黄泽镇, Shengxian 嵊县, Zhejiang

Qianxian 乾县, Shaanxi

Qiaojia Manor 乔家大院, Qixian 祁县, Shanxi

Qilin song zi 麒麟送子, "Qilin sends children"

qin 寝, bedrooms in the rear hall of a dwelling, as well as the rear tablet hall, known as the "sleeping chamber," of an ancestral hall

Qin Shubao 秦叔宝 and **Yuchi Gong** 尉尺恭 (also known as Yuchi Jingde

尉尺敬德 or Hu Jingde 胡敬德), pair of brave generals of the Tang period who serve as Door Gods

qing 情, sentiment or feeling, best expressed in a poem

Qingcheng 青城, Shandong

Qinghai 青海

qinglong 青龙, green dragon

Qingming shanghe tu 清明上河圖 *Qingming Festival on the River*, painted by Zhang Zeduan 張擇端

Qingpao ji 青袍記, *Tales of the Dark Robe*

Qiu Wenbo 丘文播, painter of *Literary Gathering* 文會圖 (tenth century)

Qiuxia Garden 秋霞圃, Jiading 嘉定, Shanghai suburbs

qu 区, district

Qu ji bi xiong 取吉辟凶, "Summon good fortune and keep misfortune at bay"

Qu Yuan 屈原 (ca. 340–ca. 278 B.C.), poet and statesman

Quanzhou city 泉州市, Fujian

queti 雀替 (also the older term *chuomu* 綽幕), carved corner pieces positioned between the beam and column in buildings; they resemble spandrels in many forms of furniture

Ran Deng **Daoist** 燃燈道人, Lamp-Lighting Daoist

"Regulations Regarding the Preservation of 'Old Dwellings' of the Wannan Region of Anhui Province" 安徽省皖南古民居保护条例

ren 忍, forbearance

Ren Branch Ancestral Hall [Ren Pai Zongci] 仁派总祠, Ouyang 欧阳 lineage

Riri jiancai 日日建财, "Generate wealth daily"

Rizi zongshi ziji guozhe shunxin 日子总是自己过着顺心, "Life is always happier when you can manage family life yourself"

ru 如, like

Rui'an county 瑞安县, Zhejiang

Ruyi 如意, "Everything as you wish," amulet

san cai 三才, "three powers" (heaven, earth, and man)

Sanduo 三多, "Three Abundances"—long life, blessings, and progeny; symbolized by the Peach of Longevity *shou tao* 壽桃; the bat *[bian] fu* 蝙蝠 (homophonous with *fu* 福, "blessings"); and the pomegranate *duozi* 多子

Sangu Furen 三姑夫人, Niang Niang 娘娘 goddesses

Sanhuang zhi shi wanwu sheng 三皇治世萬物生, "Three Emperors ruled and the ten thousand things flourished"

Sanyang 三陽, Three Males

Sanyang kai Tai 三陽開泰

segoi **(Hakka)** 私颏私房錢, "private room money," or a wife's private property

sha 沙, local eminences

Shaanxi 陕西

shan 善, good

Shan Ha village 山厦圍, popularly known as Tsang Tai Uk 曾大屋, or the "Tsangs' Big House" in Sha Tin 沙田, Hong Kong

Shan Shiyuan 单士元

Shandong 山东

Shangchuan village 上川村, Wuyuan county 婺源县, Jiangxi

Shanghe 商河, Shandong

shangliang 上梁, raising the ridgepole

Shangliang da ji 上梁大吉, "Good luck with the raising of the ridgepole"

shangting 上厅, third building of an ancestral hall, where the ancestral tablets are kept

Shanhaijing 山海经, *Classic of the Mountains and Seas*

Shanxi 山西

Shawan 沙湾, Panyu 番禺, Guangdong

Shen Fu 沈復 (1763–?), author of *Fusheng liuji* 浮生六記 [Six chapters of a floating life]

Shen Tu 神荼, with his brother Yu Lei 鬱壘, and in full martial regalia, he is a Door God

sheng 生, give birth; homophonous with *sheng* 笙, a musical instrument

sheng 笙, a musical instrument; homophonous with *sheng* 生, "give birth"

Shengmudian 圣母殿, Hall of the Holy Mother, Jinci Temple 晋祠, Taiyuan 太原

shengqi 生气, life force or cosmic energy

Shengxian 嵊县, Zhejiang

shenlong anzhuo 神龙安桌, altar table

shenzhu 神主, spirit tablet

Sheung Wo Hang 上禾坑, New Territories 新界, Hong Kong

Shexian 歙县, Anhui

shi 实, substantive or real, in contrast with *xu*

Shi gandang 石敢當, "This stone dares to resist"

shi qing hua yi 詩情畫意, literally "poetic sentiments and artistic conceptions"

Shi Tao 石濤 (Dao Ji or Tao-chi) (1641–ca. 1717), Qing dynasty painter

shidiao 石雕, stone carvings

Shijing 诗经, *Book of Songs*

Shilin guangji 事林廣記, *Compendium of a Forest of Affairs*

Shinzoku kibun 清俗紀聞, *Qing Customs*

Shiqiao village 石桥村, Nanjing county 南靖县, Fujian

Shitou township 石頭鄉, Nanhai county 南海县, Guangdong

shou 壽, longevity, long life

shou 獸, head of a wild animal

shou tao 壽桃, Peach of Longevity

Shoucun 首村, Xiuning county 休宁县, Anhui

Shrine of the Virtuously Tranquil Luo Dongshu 贞靖罗东舒先生祠; see Baolun Ge

shuangxi 喜喜, happiness in marriage

shufu 舒服, comfortable

shuiguandao 水管道, drainage pipes

shuikou 水口, water inlet; literally the "mouth of water," where a stream exits from a settlement

Shuitou township 水头乡, Cangnan county 苍南县, Zhejiang

Shujing 书经, *Book of Documents*

shunxin 顺心, satisfaction, happiness

Shuowen jiezi 說文解字, Han dynasty dictionary

shuyuan 书院, academies

si shen 四神, four deities or four spiritual animals

si shou 四兽, four deities or four spiritual animals

Sichuan 四川

sichutouguanmaoyi 四出頭官帽椅, "lamp-hanger"-style yokeback armchair

Si'ersi Ta 西尔斯塔, Sears Tower, Chicago

sifangqian (**Hakka:** *segoi*) 私房錢, "private room money," or a wife's private property

sihelou 四合楼, two-story courtyard-style dwelling

siheyuan 四合院, courtyard dwellings, especially those found in northern China

Siku quanshu 四庫全書, *Comprehensive Library of the Four Treasuries*

Sili Jian 司體監, Directorate of Ceremonial Rites

Sima Guang 司馬光 (1019–1086), historian and statesman during the Song dynasty

Sin Tian 新田 village, Hong Kong

Songyue Si Temple 嵩岳寺, Henan

State Administration of Cultural Heritage 中华人民共和国国家文物局

Student Zhang 張

su 俗, vulgarity

Suzhou 蘇州

ta 榻, low platform for sitting or reclining

Tai 泰, hexagram with three *yang* 陽, unbroken lines; called the "Peace" hexagram

Taibei 台北, also Taipei

Taigong zai ci 姜太公在此, "Taigong is here"

Taihemen 太和门, Forbidden City, Beijing

taiji 太极, symbol representing the duality of *yin* and *yang*

tailiang 太梁, post-and-beam wooden structural framework

Taipei [Taibei] 台北

Taipei 101 臺北 101, world's fifth tallest building

Taishan shi gandang 泰山石敢当, "This stone dares to resist"

Taishan zai ci 泰山在此, "Taishan is here"

taishi 太師, timber "teacher" or northern wall

Taiwan 台灣

Taiwan Railroad Administration 台灣鐵路管理局

Taiwan Tobacco and Wine Monopoly Bureau 台灣省菸酒公賣局

taizi 太子, richly robed royal child, standing for the "Lucky Tai" hexagram

tang 堂, hall

Tang [Deng] 邓, surname and lineage

Tangyue village 棠樾村, Shexian 歙县, Anhui

Tao-chi 道濟; see Shi Tao

tao ge xi (Hakka: *t'ao ke hi*) 讨个喜, "receiving a happiness"

Tao Qian 陶潛 of the Jin dynasty, author of *Taohua yuan ji* 桃花源記 [The peach blossom spring]

Taohua yuan ji 桃花源記, The Peach Blossom Spring, by Tao Qian 陶潛

Taxia village 塔下村, Fujian

tchou-p'ien (Hakka) 猪片, large cut of pork traditionally sent to the bride's side by the groom's family

Tengzhou Han Dynasty Pictorial Stones Museum 滕州漢畫像石博物館, Tengzhou 滕州, Shandong

ti 體, embodiment

ti xiang 體象, embodied image

tian di 天地, the realm of Heaven and Earth

tian wen 天文, literally "heavenly patterns"

Tian yi cheng shui, di liu cheng zhi 天一成水地六成之, "Heaven and the number one give rise to water, and Earth and the number six complete them"

Tian you shi, di you qi, cai you mei, gong you qiao 天有時，地有氣，材有美，工有巧, "The seasons have their timing, the earth has its crops, materials possess special usefulness, and the crafts display ingenuity"

Tian yuan di fang 天圓地方, "The universe is round and the earth square"

Tianbao 天保, "Heaven protects"

Tiandi sanjie shifang wanling zhen zai 天地三界十方万灵真宰, "Ruler of Heaven and Earth, Three Realms, Ten Directions, and Unlimited Wonders"

Tianguan cifu 天官賜福, "Tianguan (the heavenly official) grants fortune"

tianhua 天花, ceilings

tianjing 天井, skywell, abbreviated courtyard; generally found in southern China

Tianluokeng village 天罗坑村, Shuyang township 书样乡, Nanjing county 南靖县, Fujian

Tianyi Ge 天一閣, private library hall in Wenzhou, Zhejiang

tianzi 天子, the emperor, "the son of Heaven"

tielimu 鐵力木, grayish black hardwood

ting 庭, open court in front of a hall or lounge

ting 廳, hall

ting 亭, pavilion

tingtang 廳堂, main hall of a house

tong 桐, tall, soft-wooded, smooth-barked deciduous trees with leaves that are heart shaped

tongju gongcai 同居共財, coresidence and common property

Tongyin Guan 桐音館, "Music from the Tong Tree Guesthouse" in Nanjing's Xu Yuan 煦園, or "Warm Garden"

Tou jiu chu han cai shi dong 頭九初寒纔是冬

Tsang [Zeng] 曾, surname and lineage

Tsang Tai Uk 曾大屋, the "Tsangs' Big House" in Sha Tin 沙田, Hong Kong

tuannianfan 团年饭, lunar New Year feast

Tudi Gong 土地公, Earth God, tutelary deity

Tuisi Garden 退思園, Suzhou 蘇州, Jiangsu

tulou 土楼, rammed-earth fortresses

tun 吞, to devour or gulp down

Tunxi 屯溪, Anhui

Tuoba people 拓跋珪 of the Northern Wei 北魏 dynasty (386–534)

wa 挖, excavating space

Wa Jiangjun 瓦将军, Roof-Tile General

wai 外, outer

waiwu 外屋, outer room

Wang Meng 王蒙 (ca. 1308–1385), painter

Wang Shixiang 王世襄, furniture connoisseur and scholar

Wang Wei 王維, Tang 唐 dynasty painter

Wang Xizhi 王羲之, the most celebrated of China's calligraphers (303–361)

Wangchuan 輞川, a villa or hermitage by Wang Wei 王維

Wangjia manor 王家大院, Lingshi county 灵石县, Shanxi

Wangshi Yuan 网师園, Master of the Nets Garden, Suzhou, Jiangsu

Wanjuan Tang 萬卷堂, "Hall of 10,000 Volumes" in Master of Nets Garden 网师園, Suzhou, Jiangsu

Wannan 皖南 region, southern Anhui

Wanwan shou 萬萬壽, "Ten thousand, ten thousand years"

Warring States period 戰國 (475–221 B.C.)

wei 围, enclosing space

Wei 魏 dynasty (220–265)

wen 文, writing or words [*wenzi* 文字]

Wen 文氏, lineage and surname

Wen Zhengming 文征明 (1470–1559), Ming dynasty painter

Wen Zhenheng 文震亨 (1585–1645), author of *Zhangwuji* 長物記 [Treatise on superfluous things]

wenhua baohu qu 文化保护区, protected cultural districts

Wenyuan Ge 文淵閣, imperial library hall, Beijing

World Hakka Association 世界客家總會

wu 屋, house or house complex

Wu Daozi 吳道子, painter (fl. 710–760)

Wu Fu Yimen 五福一門, "Five Blessings [within] One Gate"

Wu jun wu fu 無君無父, "Going against your father and your ruler"

Wu, Nelson 吳納孫

Wu Yue 五岳, Five Sacred Peaks, powerful places in Daoist geography

Wu Zhen 吳鎮, reclusive Yuan dynasty painter (1285–1354)

wudu 五毒, five noxious or poisonous creatures

Wufeng village 吾峰村, Shishan township 诗山乡, Nan'an 南安市, Fujian

Wuqiang 武强, Hebei

wushi tongtang 五世同堂, five generations under one roof

Wutaishan 五台山, Shanxi

Wuxing 五行, the Five Agents or Five Phases—wood, fire, earth, metal, and water

Wuyuan county 婺源县, Jiangxi

Wuzhuyouju 梧竹幽居, the Secluded Pavilion amid Wutong and Bamboo, in Zhuozheng Garden 拙政園, Suzhou, Jiangsu

Xiajia village 下岬村, Heilongjiang

Xiamen city 厦门市, Fujian

xiang 象, image

Xiang gansha jiu gansha 想干啥就干啥, "You can do whatever you want"

xiangchong 相冲, mutually antagonistic situations

xiangfang 厢房, side chambers

Xiangxi village 向西村, Shenzhen 深圳, Guangdong

Xianqing ouji 閑情偶寄, A Temporary Lodge for My Leisure Thoughts, by Li Liweng 李笠翁

xiao 孝, filial piety

Xiao han tu 消寒圖, "Dispersing the Cold" chart

Xiao Hong 萧红, novelist (1911–1942)

xiao kang zhi jia 小康之家, contemporary well-off family

Xiaocanglang Ting 小滄浪庭, Little Canglang Pavilion, in Zhuozheng Garden 拙政園, Suzhou, Jiangsu

Xiaohan shu jiu tu 消寒數九圖, "Dispersing the Cold [by] Counting the Nines" image

Xiaohan yi qi ge 消寒益氣歌, "Song of Dispersing the Cold and Increasing Qi"

xiaomuzuo 小木作, minor carpentry, including lattice work of windows, doors, and partitions

xiaopinwen 小品文, essays by scholar-gardeners

Xiaoqi village 晓起村, Wuyuan county 婺源县, Jiangxi

xiating 下厅, entrance hall

Xiaxiaoqi village 下晓起村, Wuyuan county 婺源县, Jiangxi

Xidi village 西递村, Yixian 黟县, Anhui

xie 榭, waterside pavilion

xin 新, new; found upside down on a chart

xinfang 新房, new room, as well as a newly married couple

Xingfeng peitian 星峰配天, "The terrestrial configurations are in agreement with the celestial order"

Xingshi Zong 形势宗, Configurations School, also called Forms School, of fengshui

Xinjiang 新疆

xinshi shiju zhi tu 新式詩句之圖, new-style poetry-line charts (or configurations)

Xinxing village 新兴村, Zhanghua county 彰化县, Taiwan

Xinyang county 信陽县, Henan

Xinyou village, Longnan county 龙南县, Jiangxi

Xinzhoukan 新周刊, New Weekly

xitai 戏台, opera stage

xiu jiu ru jiu 修旧如旧, "repairing old like old"

Xiuning county 休宁县, Anhui

xiwu 西屋, west room

Xixiang ji 西廂記, The Story of the Western Wing, a Yuan dynasty collection

Xixinan village 西溪南村, Huizhou 徽州, Anhui

xu 虛, unsubstantial and empty, in contrast with shi

Xu Yuan 煦園, Warm Garden, Nanjing

xuan 軒, lounge

xuanwu 玄武, black snake and tortoise, representing the element water

xumizuo 須彌座, religious stone pedestal

ya 雅, elegance

yamen 衙门, the traditional office/residence of an official

yan 言, words or discourses, according to the Zuo zhuan 左傳

Yanchun 延春, Shaanxi

Yandangshan 雁荡山, mountain, Zhejiang

yang 阳, male principle

Yangjiabu 杨家埠, Shandong

Yangliuqing 杨柳青, Tianjin

Yangmansa 杨漫撒, Hebei

yangqi 陽氣, male vapor; associated with the winter solstice and the official New Year

yangsheng buzi 陽生補子, *yang*-producing badges

yangsheng mian 陽生綿, *yang*-producing textiles

yangzhai 阳宅, dwelling for the living

Yangzhou 揚州, Jiangsu

Yanliao village 菸寮村, Meinong township 美濃鎮, Taiwan

Yanlong village 岩龙村, Nanxijiang 楠溪江 area, Zhejiang

yanlou 菸樓, tobacco houses

yantao de difang, yige fating ji gongfeng zuxian de jinian tang 廳堂相當於一篇告示及一個內部檢討的地方，一個法庭及供奉祖先的紀念堂, a conference room, a court of judgment, and a miniature ancestral hall

yaokang 腰炕, literally the "waist bed"; a narrow and small *kang* that connects another *kang* along the north wall with one along the south wall

yasheng 压胜, "dominating" object

yaxie 压邪, "suppressing" object

Ye 葉, surname and lineage

Yejia Zhuang 葉家庄, Ye Family Estate, Foshan 佛山, Guangdong

yi 意, conception or idea, best intimated in a landscape painting

Yi Yi Tang 怡怡堂, the Sun Gaosong 孙高松 dwelling, Anhui

Yi Ying bei 乙瑛碑, *Stele for Yi Ying*, Temple of Confucius, Qufu, Shandong

Yi Yuan 怡園, Suzhou garden, Jiangsu

yidou sansheng 一斗三升, "one bracket, three lifts" cantilever system

Yijing 易经, *Book of Changes*

yin 阴, female principle

yin-yang 阴阳, complementary opposites

Yin-yang bianhe xiaochang tu 陰陽變合消長圖, diagram of the waxing and waning transformations of *yin* and *yang*

Yin-yang yu 隐陽魚, *Yin-Yang Fish*

Yin Yu Tang 蔭餘堂, restored Huizhou dwelling at Peabody Essex Museum

yingbi 影壁, also *zhaobi* 照壁, protective screens

Yingzao fashi 營造法式, 12th century Song dynasty imperial building manual

Yingzhou village 瀛洲村, Jixi county 绩溪县, Anhui

yinsi 隐私, trendy term for privacy

yinzhai 阴宅, an abode for the dead

yituo sanya 一脚二牙, "one leg, three spandrels"

Yixian county 黟县, Anhui

Yongding county 永定县, Fujian

Yonghe Palace 雍和宫, Beijing

Yongjia county 永嘉县, Zhejiang

Yongle 永樂, the third emperor of the Ming dynasty (r. 1403–1424)

you huawen tuan de wa 有花纹图案的瓦, patterned or inscribed tiles

youli youwai 有里有外, literally "having an inside and an outside"; term to describe new spatial patterns in a Chinese home

Yu Boya 俞伯牙, a high-ranking official during the Spring and Autumn 春秋 period (770–476 B.C.)

Yu Huang 玉皇, Jade Emperor

Yu Lei 鬱壘, with his brother Shen Tu 神荼 and in full martial regalia, he is a Door God

yu mi zhi xiang 魚米之鄉, land of fish and rice

yuan 院, inner courts or courtyards formed by adjacent buildings and walls

Yuan Cai 袁采 (fl. 1140–1195), Song dynasty author and literatus

Yuan ye 園冶, *Manual of Garden Design*, by Ji Cheng 計成

Yuandan 元旦, New Year, first day of the first lunar month

Yuandan liang 元旦凉, "New Year's Day: chilly"

Yuanming Yuan 圓明園, Qing dynasty imperial garden complex, Beijing

Yuanren Bai xiang yan qing 猿人百祥衍慶, (Yuan artist) *One Hundred Blessings and Abundant Joys*

Yuanren Xiying tu 元人戲嬰圖, (Yuan artist) *Infant at Play*

Yuanxiang Tang 遠香堂, Hall of Distant Fragrance in Zhuozheng Garden 拙政園, known as the Humble Administrator's Garden, in Suzhou, Jiangsu

yuanzhai 院宅, garden-house

yuanzi 院子, inner courts or courtyards formed by adjacent buildings and walls

Yuchi Gong 尉尺恭 (also known as Yuchi Jingde 尉尺敬德 or Hu Jingde 胡敬德), a brave general of the Tang period; together with Qin Shubao 秦叔宝, he serves as a Door God

Yue Fei 岳飞, hero general of the Southern Song dynasty

Yuetan village 月潭村, Xiuning county 休宁县, Anhui

yumu 榆木, northern elm

Yungang 云冈石窟, Buddhist grottos, Shanxi

Yungmingtang Collection 雍明堂藏品

Yunnan 云南

Yuying Yuan 漁隱園, Fisherman Hermit Garden; the name later was changed to Wangshi Yuan 网师園, or "Master of the Nets Garden," Suzhou, Jiangsu

Yuzan ji 玉簪記, *Tales of the Jade Hairpin*, by Gao Lian 高濂

zan 攢/礩, column base that can be made of wood or stone

Zaojun 灶君, Stove God

zhaichong 宅冲, "house is against a house"

Zhan Yuan 瞻園, an early Ming dynasty garden located in Nanjing, Jiangsu

Zhang 張, surname and lineage

Zhang Tianshi 张天师 (34–156), Heavenly Master

Zhanghua county 彰化县, Taiwan

Zhangjiata 张家塔 village, Shanxi

zhangmu 樟木, camphor wood

Zhangwuji 長物記, *Treatise on Superfluous Things*, by Wen Zhenheng 文震亨

zhaobi 照壁, also *yingbi* 影壁, protective screens

Zhaoshi guer ji 趙氏孤兒記, *The Tale of Orphan Zhao*

Zhejiang 浙江

zhen 镇, calligraphic charm used "to stabilize" a bed, stove, well, chicken coop, etc.

Zhen shi Caishen lai dao zan jia 真是財神來到咱家, "Truly a living Caishen [God of Wealth] comes to our house"

zheng ming 正名, Confucian notion of "rectifying names"

Zheng xin, xiu shen, ji jia, zhi guo ping tianxia 正心，修身，齊家，治國平天下, "Think the right thoughts, look after your body, regulate your family, then you serve your country and will bring peace and harmony to the world"

zhenzhai 镇宅, stabilizing the dwelling or guarding the home

zhi jiatang 紙家堂, paper-family hall

Zhi sha! 止煞！, "Resist all demons!"

zhima 纸马, "paper-horse" prints

Zhiyan village 芝堰村, Zhiyan township 芝堰乡, Lanxi city 兰溪市, Zhejiang

zhong gong 中宫, geomantic center of a traditional house

Zhong Kui 钟馗, formidable demon queller

zhong tang 中堂, geomantic center of a traditional house

Zhongguo Diyi Lishi Dang'an 中国第一歷史檔案, Number One Historical Archives Administration of China

Zhongguo zhuzhai gaishuo 中國住宅概說, *Introduction to Chinese Dwellings*

zhongting 中厅, second or middle building of a large dwelling or ancestral hall

zhongyang 中央, power base or center

Zhou 周氏, lineage and surname

Zhou Dunyi 周敦頤, Song dynasty philosopher and author of *Ailian shuo* 愛蓮說 [The love of lotus]

zhu 柱/砫, column; written interchangeably with "wood" and "stone" radicals

zhu shan 主山, master mountain

Zhu Xi 朱羲, Neo-Confucian philosopher (1130–1200)

zhuandiao 砖雕, brick carvings

Zhuangzi 荘子, Daoist philosopher

zhuantou 砖头, bricks

zhuchong 柱冲, "pole is against a house"

Zhuoying Shuige 濯纓水閣, Washing-Tassel Water Pavilion, in Wangshi Yuan 网师園, Suzhou, Jiangsu

Zhuozheng Yuan 拙政園, the Humble Administrator's Garden, Suzhou, Jiangsu

zhuque 朱雀, vermilion phoenix, representing the element fire

Zhushen tuiwei 诸神退位, "All the spirits abdicate in his favor"

Zhuxian township 朱仙镇, Henan

zitan 紫檀, sandalwood

ziyou 自由, individual privacy; freedom and ease

zong 宗, patriline

zongci 宗祠, lineage hall

zongzi 宗子, eldest son

Zuiweng Ting 醉翁亭, Old Drunkard's Pavilion, in the garden of Song poet Ouyang Xiu

zuo/you 左/右, direction, denoted as left/right

Zuo zhuan 左傳, commentary on *Chunqiu* [Spring and autumn annals]

References

Abramson, Daniel. 2001. "Beijing's Preservation and the Fate of the Siheyuan." *Traditional Dwellings and Settlements Review* 13 (1): 7–22.

Ahern, Emily. 1973. *The Cult of the Dead in a Chinese Village*. Stanford: Stanford University Press.

Alekseev, V.M. 1928. *The Chinese Gods of Wealth: A Lecture Delivered at the School of Oriental Studies, University of London, on 26th March, 1926*. London: School of Oriental Studies.

———. 1966. *Kitaiskaia narodnaia kartina: Dukhovnaia zhizn starogo Kitaia v narodnykh izobrazheniiakh* [Chinese popular pictures: The spiritual life of old China in popular paintings]. Moscow: Nauka.

Ames, Roger T. 2001. "Introduction." In Howard Giskin and Bettye S. Walsh, eds. *An Introduction to Chinese Culture through the Family*, pp. 1–8. Albany: State University of New York Press.

An Chunyang 安春阳. 1984. *Yuan lin zhi cheng Suzhou* 園林之城苏州 [Suzhou: City of gardens]. Beijing: Waiwen chubanshe 外文出版社.

An Dun 安顿. 1998. *Juedui yinsi* 绝对隐私 [Absolute privacy]. Beijing: Xin Shijie chubanshe 新世界出版社.

An Jing 安静. 1998. *Zhencao yinsi* 贞操隐私 [The privacy of chastity]. Beijing: Jilin daxue chubanshe 吉林大学出版社.

An Qi 安琪. 1998. *Danshen yinsi* 单身隐私 [The privacy of singles]. Beijing: Tuanjie chubanshe 团结出版社.

Andrews, Julia F., and Kuiyi Shen. 1998. *A Century in Crisis: Modernity and Tradition in the Art of Twentieth-Century China*. New York: Guggenheim Museum.

Arendt, Hannah. 1958. *The Human Condition*. Chicago: University of Chicago Press.

———. 1961. *Between Past and Present*. Revised edition. New York: Viking Press.

Azevedo, J. 1991. "House Building in Shaanxi, China: A Chronicle of the Technique and Ceremony of Raising the Roof Frame." *Traditional Dwellings and Settlements Review* 11:75–82.

Baker, Hugh D.R. 1979a. *Ancestral Images: A Hong Kong Album*. Hong Kong: South China Morning Post.

———. 1979b. *Chinese Family and Kinship*. London: Macmillan Press.

Ban Gu 班固. 1974. "Xidu fu" 西都賦 [Western capital rhapsody]. In *Wen xuan* 文選 [Selections of refined literature]. Tainan: Beiyi chubanshe 北一出版社.

Bard, Émile. 1906. *The Chinese at Home*. London: George Newnes. Translated by Hannah Twitchell from *Les Chinois chez eux, avec 12 planches hors texte*. Paris: A.Colin, 1899.

Bard, Émile, and Hannah Twitchell. 1905. *Chinese Life in Town and Country.* New York: G.P. Putnam's Sons.

Bashi zongyou zongzhi tushuo 八世宗佑宗支圖說 [Comments on the lineage chart by Zongyou of the eighth generation]. 1374. *Weishi zupu* 魏氏族譜 [The genealogy of the Wei surname]. Manuscript courtesy of Yang Baolin 楊寶霖 and Siu Kwok-kin 蕭國健, and Zhou Shaoquan 周紹泉 and Zhao Yaguang 趙亞光, eds. 1993. *Doushan gong jiayi jiaozhu* 竇山公家議校注 [The family comments of the venerable Doushan], pp. 15–16. Hefei 合肥市: Huangshan shushe 黃山書社.

Batteux, Charles. 1746. *Les beaux arts réduits à un même principe.* Paris: Chez Durand.

Bennett, Steven J. 1978. "Patterns of Sky and Earth: A Chinese System of Applied Cosmology." *Chinese Science* 3:1–26.

Berglund, Lars. 1990. *The Secrets of the Luo Shu: Numerology in Chinese Art and Architecture.* Lund: Institutionen för Konstvetenskap, Lunds Universitet.

Berliner, Nancy. 1986. *Chinese Folk Art: The Small Skills of Carving Insects.* Boston: Little, Brown.

———. 2003. *Yin Yu Tang: The Architecture and Daily Life of a Chinese House.* Boston: Tuttle Publishing.

Berliner, Nancy, Jan Lewandoski, and Clay Palazzo. 2000. "Yin Yu Tang: A Moment in the Preservation Process of an Eighteenth Century Huizhou Residence." *Orientations* 31 (1): 58–65.

Berliner, Nancy, and Handler, Sarah. 1995. *Friends of the House: Furniture from China's Towns and Villages.* Salem: Peabody Essex Museum.

Bianmin tuzuan 便民圖纂 [Illustrated compendium of helpful hints for ordinary people]. 1st ed. 1502. Possibly by Kuang Fan 鄺璠. Modern annotated edition, using text of 1544 and illustrations of 1593, by Shi Shenghan 石聲漢 and Kang Chengyi 康成懿. 1959. Reprinted 1982. Beijing: Nongye chubanshe 農業出版社.

Bickford, Maggie. 1999. "Three Rams and Three Friends: The Working Life of Chinese Auspicious Motifs." *Asia Major* 12/Pt 1: 127–158.

———. 2002. "Emperor Huizong and the Aesthetic of Agency." *Archives of Asian Art* 53 (2002–2003): 71–104.

Bird, Isabella L. (Bishop, Mrs. J. F.). 1900. *The Yangtze River and Beyond: An Account of Journeys in China, Chiefly in the Province of Sze Chuan and among the Man-Tze of the Somo Territory.* 2 vols. London: John Murray.

Bo Songnian 薄松年. 1995. *Chinese New Year Pictures.* Beijing: Cultural Relics Publishing House.

Bodde, Derk, translator and annotator. 1936. *Annual Customs and Festivals in Peking: As recorded in Yen-ching Sui-shih-chi* 燕京歲時記 *by Dun Lichen [Tun Li-Ch'en]* 敦礼臣. Beiping: Henri Vetch.

Bodde, Derk. 1981. *Essays on Chinese Civilization.* Princeton: Princeton University Press.

Bodde, Derk, and M.L.C. Bogan. 1994. *Annual Customs and Festivals in Peking with Manchu Customs and Superstitions.* Taibei: SMC.

Boling, Patricia. 1996. *Privacy and the Politics of Intimate Life.* Ithaca: Cornell University Press.

Bourdieu, Pierre. 1990. *The Logic of Practice.* Stanford: Stanford University Press.

Boyd, Andrew. 1962. *Chinese Architecture and Town Planning 1500 B.C.–A.D. 1911.* Chicago: University of Chicago Press.

Braudel, Fernand. 1967. *Capitalism and Material Life, 1400–1800.* New York: Harper and Row.

Bray, Francesca. 1997. *Technology and Gender: Fabrics of Power in Late Imperial China.* Berkeley: University of California Press.

Bredon, Juliet, and Igor Mitrophanow. 1927. *The Moon Year: A Record of Chinese Customs.* Shanghai: Kelly and Walsh.

Bruun, Ole. 1995. "Fengshui and Chinese Perceptions of Nature." In Ole Bruun and Arne Kalland, eds. *Asian Perceptions of Nature: A Critical Approach*, pp. 173–188. London: Curzon Press.

———. 1996. "The *Fengshui* Resurgence in China: Conflicting Cosmologies between State and Peasantry." *China Journal* (Canberra) 36:47–65.

———. 2003. Fengshui *in China: Geomantic Divination between State Orthodoxy and Popular Religion.* Honolulu: University of Hawai'i Press.

Bunjinga suihen 文人畫粹編 [Selections of the finest Chinese and Japanese literati paintings]. 1977. Vol. 2. Tokyo: Chūōkōronsha 中央公論社.

Bush, Susan, and Shih Hsiao-yen. 1985. *Early Chinese Texts on Painting.* Cambridge, Mass.: Harvard University Press.

Cammann, Schuyler. 1953. "Ming Festival Symbols." *Archives of the Chinese Art Society of America* 7:66–70.

Campanella, Thomas J. 2000. "Jin Mao, Shanghai." *Architectural Record* (January): 82–89.

Cao Xueqin 曹雪芹. 1973. *The Story of the Stone.* Vol. 1: *The Golden Days.* Translated by David Hawkes. Harmondsworth: Penguin Books.

Cao Zifang 曹子芳 and Wu Naifu 吳奈夫. 1986. *Suzhou* 苏州. Beijing: Jianzhu gongye chubanshe 中國建築工業出版社.

Chang, Kwang-chih 張光直. 1977. *Food in Chinese Culture: Anthropological and Historical Perspectives.* New Haven: Yale University Press.

Chard, Robert. 1990. "Folktales of the God of the Stove." *Chinese Studies* 8:149–182.

———. 1995. "Rituals and Scriptures of the Stove Cult." In David Johnson, ed. *Ritual and Scripture in Chinese Popular Religion*, pp. 3–54. Berkeley: University of California Press.

———. 1999. "The Imperial Household Cults." In Joseph McDermott, ed. *State and Court Ritual in China*, pp. 237–266. Cambridge: Cambridge University Press.

Chavannes, Éduard. 1922. *De l'expression des voeux dans l'art populaire chinois.* Paris: Éditions Bossard, 1922. Originally published in *Journal asiatique*, 1901. This monograph is available most widely in an English-language adaptation: Elaine Spaulding Atwood, trans., annot., illus., *The Five Happinesses* (New York: Weatherhill, 1973).

Chen Chi-lu 陳奇祿 [Chen Qilu], et al., eds. 1992. *Zhongguo chuantong nianhua yishu tezhan zhuanji* 中國傳統年畫藝術特展專輯 [The art of the traditional Chinese New Year print]. Taibei: Guoli zhongyang tushuguan 國立中央圖書館.

Chen Congzhou 陳從周. 1984. *Shuo yuan* 說園 [On gardens]. Shanghai: Tongji daxue chubanshe 同濟大學出版社.

Chen Mingda 陈明达. 1980. *Yingxian mu ta* 应县木塔 [The wooden pagoda at Yingxian]. Beijing: Wenwu chubanshe 文物出版社.

Chen Qipeng 陳其澎. 1993. "The Spiritual Defence System: Spatial *Yasheng* in Vernacular Taiwanese Houses and Settlements." *Wenhua yu jianzhu yanjiu jikan* 文化与建筑研究季刊 [C + A Culture and Architecture Research] 3:5–25.

Chen Yuanjing 陳元靚 (ca. 1200–1266), comp. N.d. *Suishi kuangji* 歲時廣記 [Expanded annals of the seasonal festivals]. *Shiwan juan lou congshu* 十萬卷樓叢書 (1876–1892). *Baibu congshu jicheng* 百部叢書集成 ed., *shoujuan* 首卷. Taibei: Yiwen 藝文, 1965–1970.

Chen Yuanjing 陳元靚. 1330s. *Shilin guangji* 事林廣記 [Compendium of a forest of affairs]. Issued at the Yuan court in the 1330s. Reprint edition. Beijing: Zhonghua shuju 中華書局, 1999.

Chen Zhihua 陈志华. 1996. *Zhugecun xiangtu jianzhu* 諸葛村鄉土建築 [Vernacular architecture of Zhuge Village]. Taibei: Hansheng zazhishe 漢聲雜誌社.

Chen Zhihua 陈志华, Lou Qingxi 楼庆西, and Li Qiuxiang 李秋香. 1992. *Nanxijiang zhongyou xiangtu jianzhu* 楠溪江中游古村落 [Vernacular architecture of the middle reaches of Nanxijiang]. Taibei: Hansheng zazhishe 漢聲雜誌社.

Cheng Jiamo 程嘉谟, ed. 1530. *Ming Jili* 明集礼 [Ming rituals]. N.p.

Cheng Liyao 程里尧. 1992. *Wenren yuanlin* 文人園林 [Scholar's garden]. Taibei: Guangfu shuju 光復書局

———. 1999. *Zhongguo gudian yualin* 中国古典园林 [Chinese classical gardens]. Kunming: Yunnan renmin chubanshe 云南人民出版社.

Cheng Pei-kai 鄭培凱, ed. 2002. *Lishi dili* 歷史地理 [Historical geography]. Hong Kong: City University Press 城市大學出版社.

Chinese Academy of Architecture. 1982. *Ancient Chinese Architecture*. Beijing and Hong Kong: China Architecture and Building Press and Joint Publishing Company.

———. 1986. *Classical Chinese Architecture*. 2d ed. Hong Kong: Joint Publishing Company.

Chinese Government Bureau of Economic Information. 1927. "*Yangliuqing huaye zhi xianzhuang*" 杨柳青画业之现状 [The present situation in the Yangliuqing printing industry]. *Semi-Monthly Economic Journal* 1 (2).

Chinese Grottoes: Dunhuang Mogao Caves 中國石窟—敦煌莫高窟. 1987. Beijing: Wenwu chubanshe 文物出版社.

Chiou, Shang-chia 邱上嘉, and R. Krishnamurti. 1995. "The Fortunate Dimensions of Taiwanese Traditional Architecture." *Environment and Planning B: Planning and Design* 22:547–562.

Chiu Kwong-chiu [Zhao Guangchao] 趙廣超. 2000. *Buzhi Zhongguo mu jianzhu* 不只中國木建築 [Not merely China's wooden architecture]. Hong Kong: Sanlian shudian youxian gongsi 三聯書店(香港)有限公司.

Choi, Jae-Soon, et al. 1999. *Hanoak: Traditional Korean Houses*. Elizabeth, N.J.: Hollym.

Chow, Kai-wing 周佳榮. 1994. *The Rise of Confucian Ritualism in Late Imperial China: Ethics, Classics and Lineage Discourse.* Stanford: Stanford University Press.

Chūgoku sekkutsu Tonkō Bakukōkutsu 中国石窟敦煌莫高窟 [China's grottoes: Dunhuang Grotto]. 1981. Tokyo: Heibonsha 平凡社.

Clunas, Craig. 1988. *Chinese Furniture.* London: Bamboo Publishing.

————. 1991. *Superfluous Things: Material Culture and Social Status in Early Modern China.* Cambridge: Polity Press.

————. 1996. *Fruitful Sites: Garden Culture in Ming Dynasty China.* Durham, N.C.: Duke University Press.

————. 1997. *Art in China.* Oxford: Oxford University Press.

Cohen, Myron L. 1976. *House United, House Divided: The Chinese Family in Taiwan.* New York: Columbia University Press.

————. 1990. "Lineage Organization in North China." *Journal of Asian Studies.* 49 (3): 509–534.

————. 1992. "Family Management and Family Division in Contemporary Rural China." *China Quarterly* 130:357–377.

————. 1998. "North China Rural Families: Changes during the Communist Era." *Études chinoises* 17 (1–2): 60–154.

Cui Yanhe. 1999. *Pingyang Jinmu zhuandiao* 平阳金墓砖雕 [Carved brick tombs of the Jin dynasty in Pingyang]. Taiyuan 太原: Shanxi renmin chubanshe 山西人民出版社.

Davis, Deborah, Richard Kraus, Barry Naughton, and Elizabeth Perry, eds. 1995. *Urban Spaces in Contemporary China: The Potential for Autonomy and Community in Post-Mao China.* Cambridge: Cambridge University Press.

Davis, John Francis. 1836. *The Chinese: A General Description of the Empire of China and Its Inhabitants.* London: Charles Knight.

Day, Clarence Burton. 1927. "Paper Gods for Sale." *China Journal* 7:277–284.

————. 1940. *Chinese Peasant Cult: Being a Study of Chinese Paper Gods.* Shanghai: Kelly and Walsh.

De Groot, J.J.M. 1892–1910. *The Religious System of China.* 6 vols. Leiden: E.J.Brill.

Ding Shiliang 丁世良, ed. 1992. *Zhongguo difang zhi: Minsu ziliao huibian; Huadong juan*, 1 中国地方志民俗资料汇编 华东卷 [Chinese local annals: Collected materials on customs; East China volume]. Beijing: Shumu wenxian chubanshe 书目文献出版社.

Dirlik, Arif, and Xudong Zhang 張旭東, eds. 2000. *Postmodernism and China.* Durham: Duke University Press.

Dixue tanyuan 地學探原. 1966. [An investigation into the origins of *fengshui*]. Taibei 台北: Chuangyi chubanshe 創譯出版社.

Dong Fangyuan 董芳苑. 1988. *Taiwan minzhai menmei baguapai shouhu gongnong de yanjiu* 台灣民宅門楣八卦牌守護功用的研究 [Research on the defensive function of bagua plaques above the lintels of dwellings in Taiwan]. Taibei: Daoxiang chubanshe 稻鄉出版社.

Doré, Henri, 1914–1938. *Researches into Chinese Superstitions.* Translated from the French with notes, historical and explanatory, by M.Kennelly. Shanghai: T'usewei Press. Reprint edition, Taibei: Ch'eng Wen Publishing, 1966 (11 volumes).

Duara, Prasenjit. 1988. *Culture, Power and the State.* Stanford: Stanford University Press.

Dudbridge, Glen. 1992. "Women Pilgrims to T'ai-shan: Some Passages from a Seventeenth-Century Novel." In Susan Naquin and Chün fang Yü 丁君方, eds. *Pilgrims and Sacred Sites in China*, pp. 39–64. Berkeley: University of California Press.

Du Halde, J.-P. 1741. *The General History of China: Containing a Geographical, Historical, Chronological, Political and Physical Description of the Empire of China, Chinese-Tartary, Corea, and Thibet.* 3d ed., corrected. London: J. Watts.

Dukes, Edwin Joshua. 1885. *Everyday Life in China or Scenes along River and Road in Fuhkien.* London: Religious Tract Society.

Dun Lichen 敦礼臣. 1906. *Yanjing suishi ji* 燕京歲時記. Translated and annotated by Derk Bodde as *Annual Customs and Festivals in Peking: As Recorded in the Yen-ching Sui-shih-chi by Tun Li-Ch'en* 敦礼臣. Beiping 北平: Henri Vetch, 1936.

Eberhard, Wolfram. 1965. *Folktales of China.* Chicago: University of Chicago Press.

———. 1970. "Chinese Building Magic." Revised and translated version in his *Studies in Chinese Folklore and Related Essays*, pp. 49–65. Bloomington: Indiana University Research Center for the Language Sciences.

Ebrey, Patricia Buckley. 1984. *Family and Property in Sung China: Yüan Ts'ai's Precepts for Social Life.* Princeton: Princeton University Press.

———. 1991a. *Chu Hsi's Family Rituals: A Twelfth-Century Chinese Manual for the Performance of Cappings, Weddings, Funerals, and Ancestral Rites.* Princeton: Princeton University Press.

———. 1991b. *Confucianism and Family Rituals in Imperial China.* Princeton: Princeton University Press.

———. 1993. *The Inner Quarters: Marriage and the Lives of Chinese Women in the Sung Period.* Berkeley: University of California Press.

———. 1995. "Liturgies for Sacrifices to Ancestors in Successive Versions of the *Family Rituals*." In David Johnson, ed. *Ritual and Scripture in Chinese Popular Religion*, pp. 104–136. Berkeley: University of California Press.

———. 2003. *Women and the Family in Chinese History.* London: Routledge.

Ecke, Gustav. 1944. *Domestic Chinese Furniture.* Peking: H. Vetch.

Egan, Ronald C. 1984. *The Literary Works of Ou-yang Hsiu* 歐陽修 (1007–1072). Cambridge: Cambridge University Press.

Ellsworth, Robert Hatfield. 1970. *Chinese Furniture: Hardwood Examples of the Ming and Early Ch'ing Dynasties.* New York: Random House.

———. 1996. *Chinese Furniture: One Hundred Examples from the Mimi and Raymond Hung Collection.* New York. Privately published.

Ershisi xiao guobao tu—Fu: Wuni buxiao baoying tu 二十四孝果报图一附：忤逆不孝报应图 [Illustrations of the twenty-four paragons of filiality—Appendix: Illustrations of retribution for unfilial acts]. 1993. Chengdu: Chengdu wenshu yuan 成都文殊院.

Evarts, Curtis. 1999. *C.L.Ma* 馬可樂 *Collections: Traditional Chinese Furniture from Greater Shanxi Region.* Hong Kong: C.L.Ma Furniture.

Fairbank, Wilma. 1994. *Liang and Lin: Partners in Exploring China's Architectural Past.* Philadelphia: University of Pennsylvania Press.

Fan Jinnian 范勁年. 1980. "Huanghe Lou yange yu lidai xingzhi kao" 黃鶴樓严格与历代形制考 [Research into the changes and historical form of Huanghe Lou]. *Jianzhu lishi yu lilun* 建筑历史与理论 [Architectural history and theory] 1:147–163.

Fan Wei 范纬. 1992. "Village *Fengshui* Principles." In Ronald G. Knapp, ed. *Chinese Landscapes: The Village as Place*, pp. 35–46. Honolulu: University of Hawai'i Press.

Faure, David. 1986. *The Structure of Chinese Rural Society: Lineage and Village in the Eastern New Territories, Hong Kong.* Hong Kong and New York: Oxford University Press.

———. 1999. "The Emperor in the Village: Representing the State in South China." In Joseph McDermott, ed. *State and Court Ritual in China*, pp. 267–298. Cambridge: Cambridge University Press.

Faure, David, and Helen F. Siu. 1995. *Down to Earth: The Territorial Bond in South China.* Stanford: Stanford University Press.

Fei Xiaotong 费孝通. 1992 [1947]. *From the Soil: The Foundations of Chinese Society.* Trans. Gary Hamilton and Wang Zheng. Berkeley: University of California Press.

Feuchtwang, Stephan. 1974. *An Anthropological Analysis of Chinese Geomancy.* Vientiane and Paris: Vithagna.

Flath, James. 2004. *The Cult of Happiness: Nianhua, Art and Culture in Rural North China.* Vancouver: University of British Columbia Press.

Fong, Mary H. 1989. "Wu Daozi's Legacy in Popular Door Gods *(Menshen)* Qin Shubao and Yu Chigong." *Archives of Asian Art* 42:6–24.

Fong, Wen 方闻. 1984. *Images of the Mind: Selections from the Edward L. Elliot Family and John B. Elliot Collections of Chinese Calligraphy and Painting.* Princeton: Princeton University Press.

———. 2001. *Between Two Cultures: Late Nineteenth- and Early Twentieth-Century Chinese Paintings from the Robert H. Ellsworth Collection in the Metropolitan Museum of Art.* New York: Metropolitan Museum of Art.

Fraser, David. 2000. "Inventing Oasis: Luxury Housing Advertisements and Reconfiguring Domestic Space in Shanghai." In Deborah Davis, ed. *The Consumer Revolution in Urban China*, pp. 25–53. Berkeley: University of California Press.

Freedman, Maurice. 1966. *Chinese Lineage and Society: Fukien and Kwangtung.* London: Athlone Press.

———. 1969. "Geomancy." In *Proceedings, Royal Anthropological Institute of Great Britain and Ireland, 1968*, pp. 5–15. London: Royal Anthropological Institute.

Fu Lianzhong 傅連仲. 1982. "Jiujiu xiaohan tu" 九九消寒圖 [Nine-nines disperse the cold chart]. *Zijin cheng* 紫禁城 [Forbidden City] 5 (15): 31–32.

Fu Xihua 傅惜華, comp. 1981. *Zhongguo gudian wenxue banhua xuanji* 中國古典文學版畫選集 [Selected woodblock illustrations of premodern literature], 2 vols. Shanghai: Renmin chubanshe 人民出版社.

Fu Xinian 傅熹年. 1998. *Fu Xinian jianjushi lunwen ji* 傅熹年建築史論文集 [Collected works of Fu Xinian on architectural history]. Beijing: Wenwu Press 文物出版社

Fujiwara Sosui 藤原楚水, ed. 1961. *Shu dao liu ti da zi dian* 書道六體大字典 [Dictionary of six styles of calligraphy]. Tainan: Wangjia chubanshe 王家出版社.

Furth, Charlotte. 1990. "The Patriarch's Legacy: Household Instructions and the Transmission of Orthodox Values." In K.C.Liu, ed. *Orthodoxy in Late Imperial China,* pp. 187–211. Berkeley: University of California Press.

Gallin, Bernard. 1966. *Hsin Hsing, Taiwan: A Chinese Village in Change.* Berkeley: University of California Press.

Gan, Tjiang-tek. 1962. "Some Chinese Popular Block-Prints." In Rijksmuseum voor Vollkendunde, ed. *The Wonders of Man's Ingenuity.* Leiden: E.J.Brill.

Gao Yuzhen 高玉珍 and Curtis Evarts. 1999. *Fenghua zaixian: Ming Qing jiaju shoucang zhan* 風華再現：明清家具收藏展 [Splendor of style: Classical furniture from the Ming and Qing dynasties]. 1999. Bilingual Edition. Taipei: National Museum of History 國立歷史博物館.

Gates, Hill. 1996. *China's Motor: A Thousand Years of Petty Capitalism.* Ithaca: Cornell University Press.

Ge Jianxiong 葛劍雄. 2002. *Lishi shang de Zhongguo yu Zhongguo jiangyu* 歷史上的中國與中國疆域 [The Chinese realm in history]. In Cheng Peikai 鄭培凱, ed. *Lishi dili* 歷史地理 [Historical geography]. Hong

Kong: City University Press 城市大學出版社.

Ge Zhaoguang 葛兆光. 2002. *Gudai Zhongguo ditu zhong de tianxia guannian* 古代中國地圖中的天下觀念 [Chinese cosmic concepts as viewed in ancient maps]. In Cheng Peikai 鄭培凱, ed. *Lishi dili* 歷史地理 [Historical geography]. Hong Kong: City University Press 城市大學出版社.

———. 2003. *Zhongguo gudai shehui yu wenhua shi jiang* 中國古代社會與文化十講 [Ten lectures on society and culture in ancient China]. Hong Kong: Shangwu yinshuguan 商務印書館.

Gengzhi tu 耕織圖 [Agriculture and sericulture illustrated]. 1145. Lou Chou 樓璹. The version used here is the Kangxi 康熙 imperial edition of 1696.

Giskin, Howard, and Bettye S. Walsh. 2001. *An Introduction to Chinese Culture through the Family.* Albany: State University of New York Press.

Glahn, Elsa. 1984. "Unfolding the Chinese Building Standards: Research on the *Yingzao fashi.*" In Nancy Shatzman Steinhardt, ed. *Chinese Traditional Architecture,* pp. 47–57. New York: China Institute in America.

Gong Kai 龔愷, ed. 1993. *Tangyue* 棠樾 [Tangyue Village]. Nanjing: Dongnan daxue chubanshe 东南大学出版社.

———. 1996. *Zhanqi* 瞻淇 [Zhanqi village]. Nanjing: Dongnan daxue chubanshe 东南大学出版社.

———. 1998. *Yuliang* 渔梁 [Yuliang village]. Nanjing: Dongnan daxue chubanshe 东南大学出版社.

———. 1999. *Zhifeng* 爹峰 [Zhifeng village]. Nanjing: Dongnan daxue chubanshe 东南大学出版社.

———. 2001. *Xiaoqi* 曉起 [Xiaoqi village]. Nanjing: Dongnan daxue chubanshe 东南大学出版社.

———. 2003. *Zhifeng* 多峰村 [Zhifeng village]. Shijiazhuang 石家庄: Hebei jiaoyu chubanshe 河北教育出版社.

Goodrich, Anne. 1991. *Peking Paper Gods: A Look at Home Worship*. Nettetal, Germany: Steyler-Verlag. Monumenta Serica Monograph Series 23.

Graf zu Castell, Wulf Diether. 1938. *China-flug*. Berlin: Atlantis-Verlag.

Guangzhou bowuguan 廣州博物館 and Xianggang zhongwen daxue wenwuguan 香港中文大學文物館合辦. 1983. *Sui-Gang Han mu chutu wenwu* 穗港漢墓出土文物 [Archaeological finds from Han tombs at Guangzhou and Hong Kong]. Hong Kong: Xianggang zhongwen daxue wenwuguan 香港中文大學文物館.

Guanzi 管子. Chuan xiubian 權修編. 1985. Translated by W. Allyn Rickett. Princeton: Princeton University Press.

Hammond, Jonathan. 1992. "Xiqi Village: Compact with Ecological Planning." In Ronald G. Knapp, ed. *Chinese Landscapes: The Village as Place*, pp. 95–105. Honolulu: University of Hawai'i Press.

Han Baode 漢寶德. 1998. *Fengshui yu huanjing* 風水與環境 [*Fengshui* and the environment]. Taibei: Lianjing chuban shiye gongsi 聯經出版事業公司.

Handler, Sarah. 2001. *Austere Luminosity of Chinese Classical Furniture*. Berkeley: University of California Press.

Hanyu da cidian Editorial Committee 漢語大詞典編輯委員會. 1995. *Hanyu da cidian* 漢語大詞典 [Great Chinese word dictionary], 13 vols. Shanghai: Hanyu da cidian chubanshe. Reprint. Originally published 1986–1990.

Harrist, Robert E. Jr., et al. 1999. *The Embodied Image: Chinese Calligraphy from the John B. Elliott Collection*. Catalog of the exhibition organized by the Art Museum, Princeton University, March 27–June 27, 1999. Curated by Cary Y. Liu and Robert E. Harrist Jr. Princeton: Art Museum, Princeton University.

Hase, P.H., and Elizabeth Sinn, eds. *Beyond the Metropolis: Villages in Hong Kong*. Hong Kong: Joint Publishing Company.

Hayes, James. 1985. "Specialists and Written Materials in the Village World." In David Johnson, Andrew J. Nathan, and Evelyn S. Rawski, eds. *Popular Culture in Late Imperial China*, pp. 75–111. Berkeley: University of California Press.

He Ling 鶴齡. 1990. "Xun Qing huangshi de Xiaohan shitu" 遜清皇室的消寒詩圖 [Dispersing-the-cold poetry charts of the deposed Qing imperial household]. *Zijin cheng* 紫禁城 [Forbidden City] 3 (58): 46–47.

He Xiaoxin 何曉昕. 1990. *Fengshui tanyuan* 风水探源 [Exploring the sources of *fengshui*]. Nanjing: Dongnan daxue chubanshe 东南大学出版社.

Hebei gudai mucang bihua 河北古代墓葬壁画 [Ancient tomb murals in Hebei]. 2000. Beijing: Wenwu chubanshe 文物出版社.

Ho, Puay-peng 何培斌. 1995. *The Living Building: Vernacular Environments of South China*. Hong Kong: Chinese University of Hong Kong, Department of Architecture.

———. 2001. "Rethinking Chinese Villages." *Orientations* 32 (3): 115–125.

———. 2003. "China's Vernacular Architecture." In Ronald G. Knapp, ed. *Asia's Old Dwellings: Tradition, Resilience, and Change*, pp. 319–346. Hong Kong and New York: Oxford University Press.

———. 2004. "Brocaded Beams and Shuttle Columns. Early Vernacular Architecture in Southern Anhui Province." *Orientations* 35 (2): 104–110.

Holm, David. 1991. *Art and Ideology in Revolutionary China*. Oxford: Clarendon Press.

Hou Jiyao 侯继尧, Ren Zhiyuan 任至远, Zhou Peinan 周培南, and Li Zhunze 李传泽. 1989. *Yaodong minju* 窑洞民居 [Vernacular cave dwellings]. Beijing: Zhongguo jianzhu gongye chubanshe 中國建筑工业出版社.

Hou Jiyao 侯继尧 and Wang Jun 王军. 1999. *Zhongguo yaodong* 中國窑洞 [Yaodong in China *(sic)*]. Zhengzhou 郑州市: Henan kexue jishu chubanshe 河南科学技术出版社.

Hou Youbin 侯幼彬. 1995. *Zhongguo jianzhu meixue* 中國建築美學 [Aesthetics of Chinese architecture]. Haerbin: Heilongjiang kexue jishu chubanshe 黑龍江科學技術出版社.

Hsiung Ping-chen 熊秉真. 1994. "Constructed Emotions: the Bond between Mothers and Sons in Late Imperial China." *Late Imperial China* 15 (1): 87–119.

Hsu, Francis L.K. 许烺光 1948. *Under the Ancestors' Shadow: Chinese Culture and Personality*. New York: Columbia University Press.

Hu, Hsien-chin. 1944. "The Chinese Concept of Face." *American Anthropologist* 46:45–64.

Hu Jing 胡敬, et al., comps. 1816. *Shiqu bao ji san bian* 石渠寶笈三編 [Catalog of the Qing imperial painting and calligraphy collection, 3d series]. Facsimile reprint, Taibei: National Palace Museum, 1971.

Hu Wenyan 胡文彦 and Yu Shuyan 于淑岩. 2002. *Zhongguo jiaju wenhua* 中國家具文化 [Chinese furniture culture]. Shijiazhuang: Hebei meishu chubanshe 河北美術出版社.

Huang Changmei 黃長美. 1986. *Zhongguo tingyuan yu wenren sixiang* 中國庭院與文人思想 [Chinese gardens and thoughts of the literati]. Taibei: Mingwen shuju 明文書局.

Huang Hanmin 黃汉民. 1994. *Fujian chuantong minju* 福建传统民居 [Vernacular architecture of Fujian]. Xiamen: Lujiang chubanshe 鷺江出版社.

Huang Minglan 黃明兰 and Guo Yinqiang 郭引強, eds. 1996. *Luoyang Hanmu bihua* 洛阳汉墓壁画 [Han tombs with wall paintings in Luoyang]. Beijing: Wenwu chubanshe 文物出版社.

Huang Nengfu 黃能馥, ed. 1985–1987. *Yinran zhi* 印染織綉 [Printing, dyeing, weaving, and embroidery]. Vols. 6 and 7 of *Zhongguo meishu quanji: Gongyi meishu bian* 中國美術全集，工艺美术编 [Complete series on Chinese art: Arts and crafts section]. Beijing: Wenwu chubanshe 文物出版社.

Huang Weijun 黃為雋 and Shang Guo 尚廓. 1992. *Min Yue Minzhai* 閩粵民宅 [China vernacular dwelling *(sic)*: Fujian and Guangdong provinces]. Tianjin: Tianjin kexue jishu chubanshe 天津科学技术出版社.

"Huizhou Revisited." 2002. *Orientations*. 33 (3): 105–106.

Hung, William 洪業, gen. ed. 1934. *Maoshi yinde* 毛詩引得 [A concordance to the Shih Ching]. Harvard-Yenching Institute Sinological Index Series, Supplement No. 9. Peiping 北平: Yanjing daxue tushuguan yinde bianzuanchu 燕京大學圖書館引得編纂處.

Huitu Lu Ban jing 繪圖魯班經 [Illustrated *Lu Ban jing*]. 1983. Full original title is *Xinjuan gongshi diaozhou zhengshi Lu Ban mujing jiangjia jing* 新鐫工師雕斲正式魯班木經匠家鏡 [Newly engraved official classic of Lu Ban and artisans' mirror for carpenters and carvers]. Taibei: Zhulin yinshuju 竹林書局.

Huo Tao 霍韜. ca. 1529. *Huo Weiya jiaxun* 霍渭厓家訓 [The family admonitions of Huo Weiya]. Reprinted in *Hanfenlou miji* 涵芬樓秘笈 [Secret records of the Hanfenlou]. Shanghai: Shangwu yinshuguan 商務印書館, 1924.

Hwangbo, Alfred B. 2002. "An Alternative Tradition in Architecture: Conceptions in Feng Shui and Its Continuous Tradition." *Journal of Architectural and Planning Research* 19 (2): 110–130.

Jervis, Nancy. 1992. "Dacaiyuan Village, Henan: Migration and Village Renewal." In Ronald G. Knapp, ed. *Chinese Landscapes: The Village as Place*, pp. 245–257. Honolulu: University of Hawai'i Press.

Jessop, T. E. 1964. "The Definition of Beauty." Reprinted in W. E. Kennick, ed. *Art and Philosophy: Readings in Aesthetics.* New York: St. Martin's Press. Originally published in *Proceedings of the Aristotelian Society* 33 (1932–1933).

Ji Cheng 計成. 1932. *Yuan ye* 園冶 [A garden design manual]. 3 vols. Beiping: Zhongguo yingzao xueshe 中國營造學社.

———. 1988. *The Craft of Gardens.* Translated by Alison Hardie. New Haven: Yale University Press.

Jia Sixie 賈思勰. 1996. *Qimin yaoshu* 齊民要術 [Essentials to household enrichment]. Beijing: Tuanjie chubanshe 北京團結出版社.

Jiang Fan 江帆. 1994. "Liaoning nongcun de jianfang xige" 辽宁农村的建房喜歌 [Luckbringing house construction songs in the Liaoning countryside]. Unpublished conference paper. Partial English translation by Jacob Eyferth.

Jin, Qiming 金其銘, and Li Wei 李唯. 1992. "China's Rural Settlement Patterns." In Ronald G. Knapp, ed. *Chinese Landscapes: The Village as Place*, pp. 13–34. Honolulu: University of Hawai'i Press.

Jin Zhong 金忠 and Che Yingkui 車應魁. 1994. *Ruishi liangying* 瑞世良英. Shanghai: Shanghai guji chubanshe 上海古籍出版社.

Johnson, Elizabeth L. 1988. "Grieving for the Dead, Grieving for the Living: Funeral Laments of Hakka Women." In James L. Watson and Evelyn S. Rawski, eds. *Death Ritual in Late Imperial and Modern China*, pp. 135–163. Berkeley: University of California Press.

Johnston, R. Stewart. 1991. *Scholar Gardens of China.* Cambridge: Cambridge University Press.

Judd, Ellen R. 1989. "*Niangjia*: Chinese Women and Their Natal Families." *Journal of Asian Studies* 3 (August): 525–544.

Jujia biyong shilei quanji 居家必用事類全集 [The householder's vademecum]. 1301. Probably by Xiong Zongli 熊宗立. The version referred to here is the revised ed. of 1560 by Tian Rucheng 田汝成.

Kang Youwei 康有為. 1936. "Guang yizhou shuangji" 廣藝舟雙楫 [Expanding on Bao Shichen's 包世臣 (1775–1855) "Twin Oars of the Ship of Art" (1848)]. In *Yilin mingzhu congkan* 藝林名著叢刊 [Collection of famous works in art]. Shanghai: Shijie shuju 世界書局.

Kao Yu-kung. 1991. "Chinese Lyric Aesthetics." In Freda Murck and Wen Fong 方聞, eds. *Words and Images: Chinese Poetry, Calligraphy and Painting*, pp. 47–90. Princeton: Princeton University Press.

Kaogong ji 考工記 [The artificer's record]. 1996. Edited by Wen Renjun 聞人軍. Sichuan: Bashu shushe 巴蜀書社.

Kardos, Michael. 1998. "Gods of the Gate, Protector of the Door." M.A. thesis, University of British Columbia.

Kates, George N. 1948. *Chinese Household Furniture*. New York: Harper.

Keswick, Maggie, and Alison Hardie. 2003. *The Chinese Garden: History, Art, and Architecture*. Cambridge, Mass.: Harvard University Press.

Kieschnick, John. 2003. *The Impact of Buddhism on Chinese Material Culture*. Princeton: Princeton University Press.

King, Ambrose Yeo-chi 金耀基. 1988. "'Mian,' 'chi' yu zhongguoren xingwei zhi fenxi" 面·耻与中国人行为之分析 ("Face," "shame," and the analysis of behavior patterns of the Chinese). In Yang Guoshu 楊國樞, ed. *Zhongguoren de xinli* 中國人的心理 [The psychology of the Chinese], pp. 75–104. Taipei: Guiguan tushu gongsi 桂冠圖書公司.

King, Anthony D., and Abidin Kusno. 2000. "On Bei(j)ing in the World: 'Postmodernism,' 'Globalization,' and the Making of Transnational Space in China." In Arif Dirlik and Xudong Zhang, eds. *Postmodernism*

and China, pp. 41–67. Durham: Duke University Press.

Knapp, Ronald G. 1986. *China's Traditional Rural Architecture: A Cultural Geography of the Common House*. Honolulu: University of Hawai'i Press.

———. 1989. *China's Vernacular Architecture: House Form and Culture*. Honolulu: University of Hawai'i Press.

———, ed. 1992. *Chinese Landscapes: The Village as Place*. Honolulu: University of Hawai'i Press.

———. 1999a. "At Home in China: Domain of Propriety, Repository of Heritage." In Kai-Yin Lo 羅啟妍 and Puay-peng Ho 何培斌, eds. *Living Heritage: Vernacular Environment in China* [*Gucheng jinxi: Zhongguo minjian shenghuo fangshi* 古承今襲：中國民間生活方式], pp. 16–37. Bilingual edition. Hong Kong: Yungmingtang 雍明堂.

———. 1999b. *China's Living Houses: Folk Beliefs, Symbols, and Household Ornamentation*. Honolulu: University of Hawai'i Press.

———. 2000. *China's Old Dwellings*. Honolulu: University of Hawai'i Press.

Knapp, Ronald G., and Shen Dongqi. 1992. "Changing Village Landscapes." In Ronald G. Knapp, ed. *Chinese Landscapes: The Village as Place*, pp. 47–72. Honolulu: University of Hawai'i Press.

Knechtges, David R., trans. and annot. 1982. *Wen xuan: Or Selections of Refined Literature*. Princeton: Princeton University Press.

Ko, Dorothy. 1992. "Pursuing Talent and Virtue: Education and Women's Culture in Seventeenth and Eighteenth Century China." *Late Imperial China* 13 (1): 9–39.

———. 1994. *Teachers of the Inner Chambers: Women and Culture in Seventeenth-Century China.* Stanford: Stanford University Press.

Körner, Brunhild. 1959. *Die religiöse Welt der Baüerin in Nordchina. Reports from the Scientific Expedition to the North-Western Provinces of China under the Leadership of Sven Hedin,* 8: *Ethnography.* Stockholm: State Ethnographic Museum.

Kwong, Charles Yim-tze. 1994. *Tao Qian and the Chinese Poetic Tradition.* Ann Arbor: Center for Chinese Studies, University of Michigan.

Lai Zhide 來知德 (1525–1604). 1971. *Yijing lai zhu tu jie* 易經來註圖解 [*The Book of Changes,* with explanatory notes and illustrations, by Lai Zhide]. Revised by Zheng Can 鄭燦. Taibei: Minle chubanshe 民樂出版社.

Laslett, Barbara. 1973. "The Family as Public and Private Institution: An Historical Perspective." *Journal of Marriage and the Family* 35 (3): 480–494.

Lee, Rosemary. 1995. "Tsang Tai Uk 曾大屋." In Patrick H. Hase and Elizabeth Sinn, eds. *Beyond the Metropolis: Villages in Hong Kong,* pp. 158–172. Hong Kong: Joint Publishing Company.

Lee, Sang Hae. 1986. *Feng-shui: Its Context and Meaning.* Unpublished Ph.D. dissertation, Department of Architecture, Cornell University.

———. 2003. "Traditional Korean Settlements and Dwellings." In Ronald G. Knapp, ed. *Asia's Old Dwellings: Tradition, Resilience, and Change,* pp. 373–390. Hong Kong and New York: Oxford University Press.

Leece, Sharon. 2002. *China Style.* Hong Kong: Periplus Editions (HK).

Legge, James, trans. 1985. *The Chinese Classics.* 5 vols. Reprint ed. Taibei: Southern Materials Center.

Leung, Angela K.C. 1983. "L'Amour en Chine: Relations et pratiques sociales aux XIIIè et XIVè siècles." *Archives des sciences sociales des religions* 56 (1): 59–76.

Lewis, Bernard. 1996. *The Middle East: A Brief History of the Last 2000 Years.* New York: Scribner.

Li chi 禮記 [Book of rites; an encyclopedia of ancient ceremonial usages, religious creeds, and social customs]. 1967. Translated by James Legge. New Hyde Park, N.Y.: University Books.

Li Hong. 1994. "The Quintessence of Huizhou Temple Architecture: Baolunge Ancestral Shrine." *Orientations* 25 (1): 37–40.

Li Jun 李俊. 1999. "Yinsi duoshaoqian yi jin" 隐私多少钱一斤 [How much for a pound of privacy?] *Beijing qingnianbao* 北京青年报 [Beijing youth daily], January 24, p. 8.

Li Lulu 李露露. 1992. *Zhongguo minjian chuantong jieri* 中国民间传统节日 [Traditional Chinese popular festivals]. Nanchang: Jiangxi meishu chubanshe 江西美术出版社.

Li Qiuxiang 李秋香 and Chen Zhihua 陈志华. 2001. *Liukengcun* 流坑村 [Liukeng village]. Chongqing: Chongqing chubanshe 重庆出版社.

Li Songling 李松龄. 1987. "Puyi yu 'jiujiu xiaohan tu'" 溥儀與九九消寒圖 [Puyi and (His) 'Nine-Nines Disperse the Cold Charts'"]. *Zijin cheng* 紫禁城 [Forbidden City] 3 (40): 18–20.

Li Yu 李漁 (Liweng). 1995. *Xian qing ou ji* 閒情偶寄 [A temporary lodge for my leisure thoughts]. Beijing: Zuojia chubanshe 作家出版社.

Li Yuming 李玉明. 1986. *Shanxi jianzhu tonglan* 山西古建築通覽 [A panorama of ancient Chinese architecture in Shanxi]. Taiyuan 太原: Shanxi renmin chubanshe 山西人民出版社.

Li Zehou 李澤厚. 1994. *The Path of Beauty: A Study of Chinese Aesthetics*. Hong Kong: Oxford University Press.

Liang, Ssu-ch'eng [Liang Sicheng] 梁思成. 1984. *A Pictorial History of Chinese Architecture: A Study of the Development of Its Structural System and the Evolution of Its Types*. Edited by Wilma Fairbank. Cambridge, Mass.: MIT Press.

———. 1998. *Zhongguo jianzhu shi* 中國建築史 [History of Chinese architecture]. Tianjin: Baihua wenyi chubanshe 百花文艺出版社.

Lin Huicheng 林會承. 1990. *Taiwan chuantong jianzhu shouci* 台灣傳統建築手冊 [Handbook of Taiwan's traditional architecture]. Taibei: Yishujia chubanshe 藝術家出版社.

Lin Lina 林莉娜. 1996. *Huazhong jiaju tezhan* 畫中家具特展 [Catalog to the special exhibition of furniture in paintings]. Taipei: National Palace Museum 國立故宮博物院.

Lin, Yutang 林语堂. 1935. *My Country and My People* 吾国与吾民. New York: John Day.

———. 1937. *The Importance of Living* 生活的艺术. New York: John Day.

Lindqvist, Cecilia. 1989. *China: Empire of Living Symbols*. Reading, Mass.: Addison-Wesley.

Liu, Cary Y. 1994. "Heavenly Wells in Ming Dynasty Huizhou Architecture." *Orientations* 25 (1): 28–36.

———. 1997. "The Ch'ing Dynasty Imperial Library, Wen-yüan-ko: Architecture and the Ordering of Knowledge." Ph.D. dissertation, Princeton University.

———. 1999. "Song Dynasty Painting of the T'ai-ch'ing-lou Library Hall: From Historical Commemoration to Architectural Renewal." In Cary Y. Liu and Dora C.Y. Ching, eds. *Arts of the Sung and Yüan: Ritual, Ethnicity, and Style in Painting*, pp. 104–109. Princeton: Art Museum, Princeton University.

———. 2000. "Embodying Cosmic Patterns: Foundations of an Art of Calligraphy in China." *Oriental Art* 56 (5): 2–9.

Liu, Cary Y., Dora C.Y. Ching, and Judith G. Smith, eds. 1999. *Character and Context in Chinese Calligraphy*. Princeton: Art Museum, Princeton University.

Liu, Dan. 2000. "Ancestral Hall, Villager and Village: A Case Study of the Ancestral Hall in Liukeng Village." Unpublished M.Phil. thesis. Hong Kong: Chinese University of Hong Kong 香港中文大学.

Liu Dunzhen 刘敦桢. 1957. *Zhongguo zhuzhai gaishuo* 中國住宅概說 [Introduction to Chinese dwellings]. Beijing: Jianzhu gongcheng chubanshe 建築工程出版社.

———. 1993. *Chinese Classical Gardens of Suzhou* 苏州古典园林. Translated and edited by Joseph C. Wang. New York: McGraw-Hill; Beijing: China Architecture and Building Press 中國建筑工业出版社.

Liu Dunzhen, chief ed. 1993. *Zhongguo gudai jianzhu shi* 中国古代建筑史 [History of ancient Chinese architecture]. Beijing: Zhongguo jianzhu gongye chubanshe 中國建筑工业出版社.

Liu, John K.C. 1980. "Housing Transformations: A Study of Family Life and Built Form in Taiwan." Ph.D. dissertation, University of California, Berkeley.

Liu Liming 刘黎明. 1993. *Citang, lingpai, jiapu: Zhongguo chuantong xueyuan qinzu xisu* 祠堂，灵牌，家谱：中国传统血缘亲族习俗 [Ancestral hall, ancestral tablets, lineage registries: The customs and practices of traditional Chinese kinship]. Chengdu: Sichuan renmin chubanshe 四川人民出版社.

Liu Ruoyu 劉若愚. Latest date mentioned 1641. *Zhuozhong zhilüeh* 酌中志略 [Brief anecdotes on making the grade]; *Haishan xian guan congshu* 海山仙舘叢書 (1845–1885).

Liu Tong 劉侗 and Yu Yizheng 于奕正. 1957. *Dijing jingwu lüe* 帝京景物略 [Guide to the capital city] (1635 preface), sect. "Chunchang" 春場; *Zhongguo wenxue cankao ziliao xiao congshu* 中國文學參考資料小叢書 [Condensed compendium of reference materials on Chinese literature], collection 2, vol. 4. Shanghai: Gudian wenxue 古典文學.

Liu Wei 劉煒. 2002. *Tushuo Zhongguo de wenming* 圖說中國的文明 [Pictorial history of Chinese culture]. Hong Kong: Hong Kong Commercial Press 商務印書館.

Liu, Xin 刘新. 2000. *In One's Own Shadow: An Ethnographic Account of the Condition of Post-Reform Rural China*. Berkeley: University of California Press.

Liu Zuoxiang 刘作翔. 1996. "Si quanli: Yige zhide zhongshi de fazhi lingyu" 私权利：一个值得重视的法事领域 [Private rights: A noteworthy area of rule by law]. *Dongfang* 东方 [The Orient] 4:19–23.

Lo, Kai-Yin 羅啟妍, ed. 1998. *Classical and Vernacular Chinese Furniture in the Living Environment: Examples from the Kai-Yin Lo Collection* 中國古典家具與生活環境：羅啟妍收藏精選. Bilingual edition. Hong Kong: Yungmingtang 雍明堂.

Lo, Kai-Yin 羅啟妍, and Ho Puay-peng 何培斌, eds. 1999. *Living Heritage: Vernacular Environment in China* 古承今襲：中國民間生活方式. Hong Kong: Yungmingtang 雍明堂.

Loke, Margaret. 1999. "Chengkan: A Ming Village." *Orientations* 30 (2): 59–64.

Lü Bi 呂毖, comp. *Ming gong shi* 明宮史 [Ming Palace history]. Various editions.

Lu Xun. 1964. *Selected Works of Lu Hsun*. Beijing: Foreign Languages Press.

Lu Yuanding 陆元鼎 and Wei Yanjun 魏彦钧. 1990. *Guangdong minju* 廣東民居 [Vernacular architecture of Guangdong]. Beijing: Zhongguo jianzhu gongye chubanshe 中國建筑工业出版社.

Luo Zhewen 羅哲文 and Wang Zhenfu 王振復, chief eds. 1990. *Zhongguo jianzhu wenwu daguan* 中國建築文化大觀 [Panorama of Chinese architecture culture]. Beijing: Peking University Press 北京大學出版社.

Lust, John. 1996. *Chinese Popular Prints*. Leiden: E.J.Brill.

Ma Bingjian 马炳坚. 1999. *Beijing siheyuan jianzhu* 北京四合院建筑 [The architecture of the quadrangles of Beijing]. Tianjin 天津: Tianjin daxue chubanshe 天津大学出版社.

Mann, Susan. 1997. Precious Records: Women in China's Long Eighteenth Century. Stanford: Stanford University Press.

March, Andrew. 1968. "An Appreciation of Chinese Geomancy." *Journal of Asian Studies* 27:253–267.

Matsuda Naonori 松田直則. 2003. "Japan's Traditional Houses: The Significance of Spatial Conceptions." In Ronald G. Knapp, ed. *Asia's Old Dwellings: Tradition, Resilience, and Change*, pp. 285–318. Hong Kong and New York: Oxford University Press.

McCartee, D. B. 1869–1870. "Translation of the Inscription upon a Stone Tablet." *North China Branch of the Royal Asiatic Society* 6:173–177.

McDermott, Joseph P. 1990. "The Chinese Domestic Bursar." *Ajia bunka kenkyu* アジア文化研究 2:15–32.

Meng Yuanlao 孟元老 and Li Shibiao 李士彪 2001. *Dongjing menghua lu* 东京梦华录. [Reminiscences from the Eastern Capital]. Jinan 济南: Shandong youyi chubanshe 山東友誼出版社.

Moore, Barrington. 1984. *Privacy: Studies in Social and Cultural History*. Armonk, N.Y.: M. E. Sharpe.

Morse, Edward Sylvester. 1885. *Japanese Homes and Their Surroundings*. New York: Harper's.

———. 1902. *Glimpses of China and Chinese Homes*. Boston: Little, Brown.

Mote, Frederick W. 1973. "A Millennium of Chinese Urban History: Form, Time, and Space Concepts in Soochow." In R. A. Kapp, ed. *Four Views of China*. Special edition of *Rice University Studies* 59 (4): 35–65.

———. 1976. "The Arts and the 'Theorizing Mode' of the Civilization." In Christian F. Murck, ed. *Artists and Traditions: Uses of the Past in Chinese Culture*, pp. 3–8. Princeton: Princeton University Press.

———. 1989. *Intellectual Foundations of China*. 2nd ed. New York: McGraw Hill. Originally published 1971.

Moule, Arthur Evans. 1911. *Half a Century in China*. London: Hodder and Stoughton.

Nachbaur, Albert, and Wang Ngen Young. 1926. *Les images populaires chinoises* [Chinese popular pictures]. Beijing: Na che bao.

Nagao Ryuzo 永尾龍造. 1971. *Shina minzokushi* 支那民族誌 [Chinese popular customs]. Reprint edition, Taibei: Dongfang wenhua shuju 東方文化書局. Originally published 1940–1942.

National Palace Museum 國立故官博物院. 1989–. *Gugong shuhua tulu* 故官書畫圖錄 [Illustrated catalog of the National Palace Museum]. Taibei: National Palace Museum 國立故官博物院.

Needham, Joseph. 1954–. *Science and Civilization in China*. Cambridge: Cambridge University Press.

Nong shu 農書 [Agricultural treatise]. 1313. Wang Zhen 王禎. The version used here is the 1530 Jiajing 嘉靖 edition.

"Noted Towers." 1943. *Monumenta Serica* 8:319–327.

Nozaki Nobuchika 野崎誠近. 1928. *Kisshō zuan kaidai, Shina fūzoku no ichi kenkyū* 吉祥圖案解題：支那風俗の一研究 [Explications of auspicious motifs: A study of Chinese customs]. Tianjin: Zhongguo tuchan gongsi 中國土產公司. This book is available most widely in a 1980 Chinese-language adaptation: *Zhongguo jixiang tu'an: Zongguo fengsu yanjiu zhi yi* 中國吉祥圖案：中國風俗研究之一 [Chinese auspicious motifs: A study of Chinese customs]. Taiwan: Zhonghua shuju gufen youxian gongsi 中華書局股份有限公司. Based on the second edition, with additions and deletions, and published in Tokyo by Heibonsha 平凡社 in 1940.

Nylan, Michael. 1999. "Calligraphy, the Sacred Text and Test of Culture." In Cary Y. Liu, Dora C.Y. Ching, and Judith G. Smith, eds. *Character and Context in Chinese Calligraphy*, pp. 16–77. Princeton: Art Museum, Princeton University.

———. 2001. *The Five "Confucian" Classics.* New Haven: Yale University Press.

Oliver, Paul, ed. 1997. *The Encyclopedia of Vernacular Architecture of the World.* Cambridge: Cambridge University Press.

———. 2003. *Dwellings: The Vernacular House World Wide.* London: Phaidon Press.

Pader, Ellen. 1993. "Spatiality and Social Change: Domestic Space Use in Mexico and the United States." *American Ethnologist* 20 (1): 114–137.

Pang Shangpeng 龐尚鵬. 1939. *Pangshi jiaxun* 龐氏家訓 [The family admonitions of the Pang surname]. Reprint of 1571 edition of *Congshu jicheng chubian* 叢書集成初編 [Collection of collected works, first series]. Changsha: Shangwu yinshuguan 商務印書館.

Panofsky, Erwin. 1962. *Studies in Iconology: Humanistic Themes in the Art of the Renaissance.* New York: Harper and Row.

Peasant Paintings from Huhsien County. 1974. Beijing: People's Fine Arts Publishing.

Pedersen, Bent. 1988. "Popular Pantheons in Old China." *Journal of Oriental Studies* 26:28–59.

Peng Yigan 彭一剛. 1986. *Zhongguo gudian yuanlin fenxi* 中國古典園林分析 [An analysis of Chinese classical gardens]. Beijing: Zhongguo jianzhu gongye chubanshe 中國建築工業出版社.

Peterson, Willard J. 1982. "Making Connections: 'Commentary on the Attached Verbalizations' of the *Book of Change.*" *Harvard Journal of Asiatic Studies* 42 (1): 67–116.

Plopper, C. H. 1926. *Chinese Religion Seen Through the Proverb.* Shanghai: China Press. Reprint edition, New York: Paragon Book Reprint Corporation, 1969.

Plotinus. 1962. "On the Intellectual Beauty" (Eighth Tractate of the Fifth Ennead). In *The Enneads.* 3d ed. Translated by Stephen MacKenna. London: Faber and Faber.

Po, Sung-nien [Bo Songnian] 薄松年, and David Johnson. 1992. *Domesticated Deities and Auspicious Emblems: The Iconography of Everyday Life in Village China.* Berkeley: Chinese Popular Culture Project.

Prost, Antoine. 1991. "Public and Private Spheres in France." In Antoine Prost and Gerard Vincent, eds. *A History of Private Life,* vol. 5. Trans. Arthur Goldhammer. Cambridge, Mass.: Harvard University Press.

Raphals, Lisa. 1998. *Sharing the Light: Representations of Women and Virtue in Early China.* Albany: State University of New York Press.

Rapoport, Amos. 1989. "On the Attributes of 'Tradition.'" In Jean-Paul Bourdier and Nezar Alsayyad, eds. *Dwellings, Settlements, and Tradition: Cross-Cultural Perspectives,* pp. 77–105. Lanham, Md.: University Press of America.

Reischauer, Edwin. 1955. *Ennin's Diary: The Record of a Pilgrimage to China in Search of the Law.* New York: Ronald Press. Quotation taken from Japanese translation, *Nitto guho junrei gyoki* 入唐求法巡禮行記

Rossides, Nicos. 1982. "The Influence of Ecomancy on Japanese Living Space." *Ekistics* 49 (295): 278–284.

Rowley, George. 1947. *Principles of Chinese Painting.* Princeton: Princeton University Press.

Rozhon, Tracie. 2001. "Century-Old Chinese House Immigrates to America; An Enthusiastic Welcome from Scholars of Regional Architecture: Yin Yu Tang House to Be Restored and Stand on Grounds of Peabody Essex Museum, Melrose, MA." *New York Times*, February 22, B1.

Ruan, Xing 阮昕. 2003. "Pile-Built Dwellings in Ethnic Southern China: Type, Myth, and Heterogeneity." In Ronald G. Knapp, ed. *Asia's Old Dwellings: Tradition, Resilience, and Change*, pp. 347–372. Hong Kong and New York: Oxford University Press.

Rudova, Maria. 1988. *Chinese Popular Prints.* Translated from the Russian by Viacheslav Sobolev and edited by Lev Menshikov. Leningrad: Aurora Art Publishers.

Ruitenbeek, Klaas. 1986. "Craft and Ritual in Traditional Chinese Carpentry—With a Bibliographical Note on the *Lu Ban jing.*" *Chinese Science* 7:1–23.

———. 1993. *Carpentry and Building in Late Imperial China: A Study of the Fifteenth-Century Carpenter's Manual Lu Ban jing.* Leiden: E. J. Brill.

Rybczynski, Witold. 1986. *Home: A Short History of an Idea.* New York: Viking.

Ryor, Kathleen. 2002. "Nature Contained: *Penjing* and Flower Arrangements as Surrogate Gardens in Ming China." *Orientations* 33 (3): 68–75.

Sancai tuhui 三才圖會 [Illustrated encyclopedia of heaven, earth, and man]. 1609. Wang Qi 王圻. Facsimile edition. Taibei: Chengwen chubanshe 成文出版社, 1970.

Schorske, Carl E. 1998. *Thinking with History: Explorations in the Passage to Modernism.* Princeton: Princeton University Press.

Scruton, Roger. 1979. *The Aesthetics of Architecture.* Princeton: Princeton University Press.

Segalen, Victor. 1988. *René Leys.* Translated by J. A. Underwood. Woodstock, N.Y.: Overlook Press.

———. 1990. *Steles.* Translated by A. Harvey and I. Watson. London: Cape.

———. 1991. *Paintings.* Translated by Andrew Harvey and Iain Watson. London: Quartet Books.

Segawa Masahisa 瀬川昌久. 1996. *Zoku fu: Kanan Kanzoku no sozoku fusui iju* 族譜：華南漢族の宗族，風水，移住 [Lineage registry: The lineage, *fengshui*, and migration of Han people in South China]. Translated into Chinese as *Zupu: Huanan Han zu di zongzu, fengshui, yiju* 族谱：华南汉族的宗族，风水，移居. Shanghai: Shanghai shudian chubanshe 上海书店出版社.

Shang Guo 尚廓. 1992. "Zhongguo fengshui geju de goucheng, shengtai huanjing yu jingguan" [China's pattern of *fengshui*: Its formation, relationship to environment and landscape]. In Wang Qiheng 王其亨, ed. *Fengshui lilun yanjiu* 风水理论研究 [Research of *fengshui* theory (sic)], pp. 26–32. Tianjin: Tianjin daxue chubanshe 天津大学出版社.

Shang Guo 尚廓 and Yang Lingyu 杨玲玉. 1982. "Chuantong tingyuan shi zhuzhai yu diceng gaomidu" 传统庭院式住宅与低层高

密度 [Traditional courtyard style houses and the high densities of ground floors]. *Jianzhu xuebao* 建筑学报 [Architectural journal] 5:51–60, 72.

Shanxi sheng gujianzhu baohu yanjiusuo 山西省古建築保護研究所 (ed). 1984. *Foguangsi* [Foguang temple]. Shanxi: Wenwu chubanshe 文物出版社.

Shanxi sheng wenwuju and Zhongguo lishi bowuguan 山西省文物局，中國歷史博物館 主编, eds. 1991. Yingxian mu ta Liao dai mi cang 應縣木塔遼代秘藏 [Secrets of the Liao dynasty wooden pagoda at Yingxian]. Beijing: Wenwu chubanshe 文物 出版社.

Shao Hong 邵鴻 and Huang Zhifan 黃志繁. 2002. "19 shiji 40 niandai Huizhou xiaonong jiating de shengchan he shenghuo: Jieshao yi fen xiaonong jiating shengchan huodong riji bu" 十九世紀四十年代小农家庭的生产和生活：介绍一份小农家庭生产活动日记簿 [Production and livelihood in a small peasant family in Huizhou in the 1840s: An introduction to a small peasant family's diary on production activities]. *Huanan yanjiu ziliao zhongxin tongxun* 华南研究资料中心通讯 [South China Research Resource Station Newsletter] 27:1–15.

Shen Chonglin 沈崇麟, Yang Shanhua 杨善华, and Li Dongshan 李东山, eds. 1999. *Shiji zhi jiao de chengxiang jiating* 世纪之交的城乡家庭 [Urban and rural families at the turn of the century]. Beijing: Zhongguo shehui kexue chubanshe 中国社会科学出版社.

Shiga Shuzo 滋贺秀三. 1978. "Family Property and the Law of Inheritance in Traditional China." In David C. Buxbaum, ed. *Chinese Family Law and Social Change in Historical and Comparative Perspective*, pp.

109–150. Seattle: University of Washington Press.

Shinzoku kibun 清俗紀聞 [Recorded accounts of Qing customs]. 1799. Nakagawa Chusei 中川子信, comp. Facsimile. Taibei: Dali chubanshe 大立出版社, 1983.

Shisan jing zhushu 十三經注 [Thirteen classics with notes and commentaries]. 1980. Collated by Ruan Yuan 阮元. Beijing: Zhonghua shuju 中华书局.

Shitou Huoshi zupu 石頭霍氏族譜 [The genealogy of the Huo surname in Shitou village]. N.d. Held in the Guangdong Provincial Library.

Shitou ji 石頭記 [The story of the stone]. Courtesy of Shanghai tushu guan cang 上海圖書館藏 (collection of the Shanghai Library).

Shoseki meihin sōkan 書跡名品叢刊 [Compendium of famous calligraphy]. 1965. Vol. 2, no. 22. Tokyo: Nigensha 二玄社.

Shouyi guangxun 授衣廣訓 [Expanded instructions on procuring clothing]. 1808. Revised ed. of the *Mianhua tu* 棉花圖, by Fang Guancheng 方觀承. Reprinted in *Zhongguo gudai banhua congkan* 中國古代版畫叢刊. Beijing: Zhonghua chubanshe 中華出版社, 1960, vol. 4.

Sickman, Lawrence. 1978. *Chinese Classic Furniture*. London: Oriental Ceramics Society.

Silber, Cathy. 1994. "From Daughter to Daughter-in-Law in the Women's Script of Southern Hunan." In Christina K. Gilmartin, Gail Hershatter, Lisa Rofel, and Tyrene Whites, eds. *Engendering China: Women, Culture, and the State*, pp. 47–68. Cambridge, Mass.: Harvard University Press.

Simoons, Frederick J. *Food in China: A Cultural and Historical Inquiry*. Boca Raton, Fla.: CRC Press.

Skinner, R. T. F. 1958. "Chinese Domestic Architecture." *Journal of the Royal Institute of British Architects* 65:430–431.

Smith, Arthur H. 1894. *Chinese Characteristics*. New York: Fleming H. Revell Company.

———. 1899. *Village Life in China: A Study in Sociology*. New York: Fleming H. Revell Company.

Smith, Richard J. 1991. *Fortune-Tellers and Philosophers: Divination in Traditional Chinese Society*. Boulder: Westview Press.

———. 1992. *Chinese Almanacs*. Hong Kong and New York: Oxford University Press.

Sommer, Matthew. 2000. *Sex, Law, and Society in Late Imperial China*. Stanford: Stanford University Press.

Song Kun 宋昆, chief ed. 2000. *Pingyao gucheng yu minju* 平遙古城与民居 [The ancient city and local-style houses in Pingyao]. Tianjin: Tianjin daxue chubanshe 天津大学出版社.

Spence, Jonathan D. 1990. *The Search for Modern China*. New York: W. W. Norton.

Stein, Rolf. 1990. *The World in Miniature: Container Gardens and Dwellings in Far Eastern Thought*. Stanford: Stanford University Press.

Steinhardt, Nancy Shatzman. 1984. *Chinese Traditional Architecture*. New York: China Institute in America.

———. 1990. *Chinese Imperial City Planning*. Honolulu: University of Hawai'i Press.

———. 1997. *Liao Architecture*. Honolulu: University of Hawai'i Press.

Steinhardt, Nancy Shatzman, Fu Xinian 傅熹年, Liu Xujie 刘叙杰, Pan Guxi 潘谷西, Guo Daiheng 郭黛姮, Qiao Yun 乔匀, and Sun Dazhang 孙大章. 2002. *A History of Chinese Architecture*. New Haven: Yale University Press.

Stockard, Janice E. 1989. *Daughters of the Canton Delta: Marriage Patterns and Economic Strategies in South China, 1860–1930*. Stanford: Stanford University Press.

Su Bai 宿白, ed. 1989. *Zhongguo meishu quanji* 中国美術全集 [Universal history of Chinese art]. *Huihua bian* 繪畫編 [Painting series] 12: *Mushi bihua* 墓室壁畫 [Tomb wall painting]. Beijing: Wenwu chubanshe 文物出版社.

Sullivan, Michael. 1996. *Art and Artists of Twentieth-Century China*. Berkeley: University of California Press.

Summerson, John. 1963. "The Mischievous Analogy." Reprinted in John Summerson, *Heavenly Mansions: And other Essays on Architecture*, pp. 195–218. New York: W. W. Norton. Originally published 1949.

Sun Jianai 孫家鼐 et al. 1905. *Qinding Shujing tushuo* 欽定書經圖說 [Imperially approved illustrations and notes to the Shujing]. Beijing: Daxuetang bianshuju 大學堂編書局.

Sun Xiaoxiang 孫曉翔. 1982. "Jiangsu wenren xieyi shanshui pai yuanlin" 江蘇文人寫意山水派園林 [Scholar landscape gardens of Jiangsu province]. In *Linye shi yuanlin shi lunwen ji* 林業史園林史論文集 [Essays on the history of forestry and gardens]. Beijing: Linyexueyuan 林業學院.

Sun Zongwen 孙宗文. 1957. "Huanghe Lou" 黄鶴樓. Wenwu 文物 [Cultural relics] 11:49–51.

Szonyi, Michael. 1997. "The Illusion of Standardizing the Gods: The Cult of the Five Emperors in Late Imperial China." *Journal of Asian Studies* 56 (1): 113–135.

———. 2002. *Practicing Kinship: Lineage and Descent in Late Imperial China.* Stanford: Stanford University Press.

Tanaka Issei 田仲一成. 1985. "The Social and Historical Context of Ming-Ch'ing Local Drama." In David Johnson, Andrew J. Nathan, and Evelyn S. Rawski, eds. *Popular Culture in Late Imperial China,* pp. 143–160. Berkeley: University of California Press.

Tang Mei-chun. 1978. *Urban Chinese Families: An Anthropological Field Study in Taipei City,* Taiwan. Taipei: National Taiwan University Press.

Tianjin daxue jianzhuxi 天津大学建筑系 and Chengde shi wenwuju 承德市文物局, eds. 1982. *Chengde gu jianzhu* 承德古建築 [Chengde's ancient architecture]. Beijing: Zhongguo jianzhu gongye chubanshe 中国建筑工业出版社.

T'ien, Ju-k'ang 田汝康. 1988. *Male Anxiety and Female Chastity: A Comparative Study of Ethical Values in Ming-Ch'ing Times.* Leiden: Brill.

Tong Jun 童寯. 1984. *Jiangnan yuanlin zhi* 江南園林志 [Gardens of the southern Yangzi River Delta]. Beijing: Zhongguo jianzhu gongye chubanshe 中國建築工業出版社.

Topley, Marjorie. 1978. "Marriage Resistance in Rural Kwangtung." In Arthur Wolf, ed. *Studies in Chinese Society,* pp. 247–268. Stanford: Stanford University Press.

Tuan, Yi-fu. 1969. *China.* Chicago: Aldine.

———. 1989. "Traditional: What Does It Mean?" In Jean-Paul Bourdier and Nezar Alsayyad, eds. *Dwellings, Settlements, and Tradition: Cross-Cultural Perspectives,* pp. 27–34. Lanham, Md.: University Press of America.

Valder, Peter. 2003. *Gardens in China.* Portland, Ore.: Timber Press.

Waley, Arthur. 1937. *The Book of Songs.* Boston and New York: Houghton Mifflin.

Wan Yi 萬依, Wang Shuqing 王樹卿, and Lu Yanzhen 陸燕貞, chief compilers. 1988. *Daily Life in the Forbidden City: The Qing Dynasty, 1644–1912.* Translated by Rosemary Scott and Erica Shipley. Harmondsworth and New York: Viking. Originally published as *Qingdai gongting shenghuo* 清代宮庭生活. Hong Kong: Commercial Press 商務印書館香港分館, 1985.

Wang Jie 王杰 et al., comps. 1971. *Shiqu bao ji xubian* 石渠寶笈續編 [Catalog of the Qing imperial painting and calligraphy collection, 2d series]. Facsimile reprint, Taibei: National Palace Museum. Originally issued 1793.

Wang, Joseph C. 1998. *The Chinese Garden.* Hong Kong and New York: Oxford University Press.

Wang Naigong 王乃弓. 1981. "Jianzhu tingyuan kongjian de minzu tezheng" 建築庭院空間的民族特性 [National characteristics of garden spaces]. *Jianzhushi* 建築師 [The architect] 8:132.

Wang Qijun 王其鈞. 1991. *Zhongguo minju* 中国民居 [China's vernacular dwellings]. Shanghai: Shanghai renmin meishu chubanshe 上海人民美術出版社.

———. 2000. *Zhongguo gu jianzhu daxi minjian zhuzhai jianzhu* 民间住宅建築

[Ancient Chinese architecture vernacular dwellings]. Bilingual Chinese-English edition. Vienna and New York: Springer.

———. 2003. *Zhongguo minjian zhuzhai jianzhu* 中国民间住宅建筑 [The architecture of China's folk dwellings]. Beijing: Jixie gongye chubanshe 机械工业出版社.

Wang Shixiang 王世襄. 1986. *Classic Chinese Furniture: Ming and Early Qing Dynasties.* London: Hanshan Tang 寒山堂.

———. 1990. *Connoisseurship of Chinese Furniture: Ming and Early Qing Dynasties.* Hong Kong: Joint Publishing Company.

Wang Shucun 王树村, comp. 1985. *Minjian nianhua* 民間年畫 [Popular New Year's prints]. Vol. 21 of *Zhongguo meishu quanji: Huihua bian* 中國美術全集，繪畫編 [Complete series on Chinese art: Painting section]. Beijing: Renmin meishu chubanshe 人民美術出版社.

———. 1992a. *Paper Joss: Deity Worship through Folk Print.* Beijing: New World Press.

———. 1992b. *Zhongguo jixiangtu ji cheng* 中国吉祥图集成 [Collection of Chinese auspicious images]. Shijiazhuang: Hebei renmin chubanshe 河北人民出版社.

———. 1997. *Zhongguo minjian nianhua* 中国民间年画 [Chinese New Year's prints]. Jinan: Shandong meishu chubanshe 山东美术出版社.

Wang Tianxing 望天星 and Shi Yongnan 施永南. 1997. *Ming Qing di houling* 明清帝后陵 [Imperial tombs of the Ming and Qing dynasties]. Beijing: China Esperanto Press 中國世界語出版社.

Wang Xingbang 王興邦. 1999. "Ji Baoding guban de xin faxian" 记保定古板新发现 [Notes on the discovery of ancient wood-blocks in Baoding]. *Third World Symposium on Chinese Popular Prints,* pp. 59–62. Tokyo. Japan Folk Crafts Museum.

Wang Yalin 王雅林 and Zhang Ruli 张汝立. 1995. "Nongcun jiating gongneng yu jiating xingshi" 农村家庭功能与家庭形式 [The function and form of the rural family]. *Shehuixue yanjiu* 社会学研究 [Sociological studies] 1:76–85.

Wang Zhili 汪之力 and Zhang Zugang 张祖刚, eds. 1994. *Zhongguo chuantong minju jianzhu* 中国传统民居建筑 [Chinese traditional architecture of residence *(sic)*]. Jinan: Shandong kexue jishu chubanshe 山东科学技术出版社.

Warren, Carol, and Barbara Laslett. 1977. "Privacy and Secrecy: A Conceptual Comparison." *Journal of Social Issues* 33 (3): 43–51.

Watson, James L. 1985. "Standardizing the Gods: The Promotion of T'ien Hou 'Empress of Heaven' along the South China Coast, 960–1960." In David Johnson et al. *Popular Culture in Late Imperial China,* pp. 292–324. Berkeley: University of California Press.

Watson, Rubie. 1985. *Inequality among Brothers: Class and Kinship in South China.* Cambridge: Cambridge University Press.

Watt, James, and Anne Wardwell. 1997. *When Silk Was Gold.* New York: Metropolitan Museum of Art.

Webb, Richard. 1995. "The Village Landscape." In P. H. Hase and Elizabeth Sinn, eds. *Beyond the Metropolis: Villages in Hong Kong,* pp. 35–47. Hong Kong: Joint Publishing Company.

Wen Zhenheng 文震亨. 1615–1620. *Treatise on Superfluous Things, Zhangwu zhi* 長物誌,

12 *juan*. Annotated edition by Chen Zhi 陳植. 1984. Nanjing: Jiangsu kexue jishu chubanshe 江蘇科學技術出版社.

Wenyuan Ge, ed. 1983–1986. *Wenyuan Ge Siku quanshu* 文淵閣四庫全書 [Wenyuan Ge Library Hall copy of the Comprehensive Library of the Four Treasuries]. Taibei: Shangwu yinshuguan 臺灣商務印書館.

Whitfield, Roderick. 1998. "Material Culture in the Northern Song Dynasty: The World of Zhang Zeduan." In Kai-Yin Lo, ed., *Bright as Silver, White as Snow: Chinese White Ceramics from late Tang to Yuan Dynasty* 如銀似雪—中國晚唐至元代白瓷賞析. Hong Kong: Yungmingtang 雍明堂.

Wilhelm, Richard, and Cary F. Baynes. 1967. *The I Ching or Book of Changes*. 3d ed. Princeton: Princeton University Press.

Wittkower, Rudolf. 1971. "The Problem of Harmonic Proportion in Architecture." Reprinted in Rudolf Wittkower, *Architectural Principles in the Age of Humanism*. New York: W. W. Norton. Originally published 1962.

Wolf, Margery. 1968. *The House of Lim*. New York: Appleton-Century-Crofts.

———. 1972. *Women and the Family in Rural Taiwan*. Stanford: Stanford University Press.

Wong, Young-tsu 汪榮祖. 2001. *A Paradise Lost: The Imperial Garden Yuanming Yuan*. Honolulu: University of Hawai'i Press.

Wu Liangyong 吳良鏞. 1999. *Rehabilitating the Old City of Beijing: A Project in the Ju'er Hutong Neighbourhood*. Vancouver: University of British Columbia Press.

Wu, Nelson [Wu Nosun 吳納孫]. 1963. *Chinese and Indian Architecture: The City of Man, the Mountain of God, and the Realm of the Immortals*. New York: George Braziller.

Wu Youru 吳友如. 1983. *Wu Youru huabao* 吳友如畫寶 [Treasury of Wu Youru's drawings]. Shanghai: Shanghai guji shudian 上海古籍书店.

Wu Zhaozhao 吳肇釗. 1992. *Duo tian gong* 奪天工 [For the art-excelling nature *(sic)*]. Beijing: Zhongguo jianzhu gongye chubanshe 中國建築工業出版社.

Wuqiang xianzhi 武强县志 [Wuqiang local annals]. 1996. Beijing: Fangzhi chubanshe 方志出版社.

Xia Cangshi 夏昌世. 1995. *Yuanlin shu yao* 園林述要 [Critical essays on gardens]. Guangzhou: Huanan ligong daxue chubanshe 華南理工大學出版社.

Xixi jiacheng 西溪家乘 [The family genealogy of the Western Stream]. 1913(?). *Historical Literature of Sham Chun* 深圳, vol. 1: 53b. Available in Hong Kong University Library 香港大学图书馆.

Xu Anqi 徐安琪, ed. 1997. *Shiji zhe jiao Zhongguoren de aiqing he hunyin* 世纪之交中国人的爱情和婚姻 [Love and marriage among Chinese at the turn of the century]. Beijing: Zhongguo shehui kexue chubanshe 中国社会科学出版社.

Xu Ke 徐珂. 1917. *Qing bai lei chao* 清稗類鈔 (preface dated 1916). Shanghai: Shangwu yinshuguan 商務印書館.

Xu, Ping. 1990. *Feng-shui: A Model for Landscape Analysis*. Unpublished Doctor of Design dissertation, Graduate School of Design, Harvard University.

———. 1998. "*Feng-shui* Models Structured Traditional Beijing Courtyard Houses." *Journal of Architectural and Planning Research* 15 (4): 271–282.

Xu, Yinong 许亦农. 2000. *The Chinese City in Space and Time: The Development of Urban Form in Suzhou.* Honolulu: University of Hawai'i Press.

Yan, Yunxiang 阎云翔. 1992. "The Impact of Rural Reform on Economic and Social Stratification in a Chinese Village." *Australian Journal of Chinese Affairs* 27:1–23.

———. 1996. *The Flow of Gifts: Reciprocity and Social Networks in a Chinese Village.* Stanford: Stanford University Press.

———. 1997. "The Triumph of Conjugality: Structural Transformation of Family Relations in a Chinese Village." *Ethnology* 36 (3): 191–212.

———. 2003. *Private Life under Socialism: Love, Intimacy, and Family Change in a Chinese Village, 1949–1999.* Stanford: Stanford University Press.

Yang Bo 杨博. 1998. *Zui'e de yidianyuan* 罪恶的伊甸园 [The sinful Eden]. Beijing: Zhongguo shehui chubanshe 中国社会出版社.

Yang Hongxun 楊鴻勛. 1988. "Lue lun Zhongguo jiangnan gudian zaoyuan yishu" 略論中國江南古典造園藝術 [A brief discussion on the art of gardening in China's Southern Yangzi River Delta]. In *Jianzhu shi lunwen ji* 建築史論文集 [Essays on the history of architecture] 10. Beijing: Qinghua daxue chubanshe 清華大學出版社.

Yang, Martin 楊懋春. 1945. *A Chinese Village: Taitou, Shantung Province* 一个中国村庄：山东台头. New York: Columbia University Press.

Yang Yunfu 楊允孚. 1368. *Luan jing za yong* 灤京雜詠 [Songs of the (Yuan) capital city]. *Zhibuzu zhai congshu* 知不足齋叢書. *Congshu jicheng* 叢書集成, no. 3180.

Yangjiabu cunzhi 杨家埠村志 [Yangjiabu local annals]. 1993. Jinan: Qilu chushe.

Yu Hongwen. 1994. *Yangjiabu muban nianhua jingpin xinshang* 楊家埠年画精品欣赏 [The appreciation of Yangjiabu *nianhua*]. Hangzhou: Zhongguo meishu xueyuan chubanshe 中国美术学院山版社.

Yu, Weichao. 1997. *A Journey into Chinese Antiquity.* Beijing: Morning Glory Publishers.

Yu Zhuoyun 于倬雲, comp. 1984. *Palaces of the Forbidden City.* New York: Viking Press.

Zeng Dexin 曾德馨. 1981. "Zengjia dawu cangsang shi" 曾家大屋滄桑史 [A history of the ups and downs of the Big House of the Zeng family]. Manuscript.

Zhang Dianying 张殿英. 1990. *Yangjiabu muban nianhua* 杨家埠年画 [Yangjiabu woodblock *nianhua*]. Beijing: Renmin meishu chubanshe 人民美术出版社.

Zhang Hong 张宏. 2002. *Xing, jiating, jianzhu, chengshi: cong jiating dao chengshi de zhuju xue yanjiu* 性，家庭，建筑，城市：从家庭到城市的住居学研究 [Sex, family, architecture, city: Research on inhabitation from families to cities]. Nanjing: Dongnan daxue chubanshe 东南大学出版社.

Zhang Xiaoping 张小平. 2002. 徽州古祠堂 *Huizhou gu citing* [Ancient ancestral halls of Huizhou]. Shenyang: Liaoning renmin chubanshe 辽宁人民出版社.

Zhang Zhongyi 張仲一 et al. 1957. *Huizhou Mingdai zhuzhai* 徽州明代住宅 [Ming dynasty houses of Huizhou]. Beijing: Jianzhu gongcheng chubanshe 建筑工程出版社.

Zhao Feng 赵丰. 1999. *Treasures in Silk: An Illustrated History of Chinese Textiles.* Hong Kong: ISAT/Costume Squad.

Zhao Mengfu 趙孟頫. 1970. *Songxue Zhai wen ji* 松雪齋文集 [Collected works of the Songxue Studio]. Taibei: Taiwan xuesheng shuju 臺灣學生書局.

Zhao, Qingquan 赵庆泉. 1997. *Penjing: Worlds of Wonderment*. Athens, Ga.: Venus Communications.

Zhao Xinggen 赵杏根. 1996. *Zhonghua jieri fengsu quanshu* 中国节日风俗全书 [Comprehensive account of Chinese festival customs]. Hefei 合肥市: Huangshan shushe 黄山书社.

Zheng Zhenman 郑振满. 2001. *Family Lineage Organization and Social Change in Ming and Qing Fujian*. Honolulu: University of Hawai'i Press

Zhong Baoxian 鍾寶賢 (Stephanie Chung). 1999. "Faren yu zuchan: Huanan zhengqing yu Xianggang zaoqi de huazi gongsi" 法人與祖嘗：華南政情與香港早期的華資公司 [Corporation and ancestral property: South China politics and Chinese-financed companies in early Hong Kong]. In Xianggang keji daxue Huanan yanjiu zhongxin 香港科技大学华南研究中心 and Huanan yanjiu hui 华南研究会. *Jingying wenhua: Zhongguo shehui danyuan de guanli yu yunzuo* 经营文化，中国社会单元的管理与运作 [Management culture: The management and operation of the social unit in China], pp. 154–158. Hong Kong: Xianggang jiaoyu tushu gongsi 香港教育图书公司.

Zhongguo Shehui Kexue Yuan Kaogu Yanjiu Suo 中国社会科学院考古研究所 [Institute of Archaeology], Ding Ling Bowuguan 定陵博物馆 [Ding Ling Museum], and Beijing Shi Wenwu Gongzuo Dui 北京市文物工作队 [Beijing Municipality Cultural Relics Work Team]. 1990. *Ding Ling* 定陵 [The imperial tomb of the Ming dynasty]. In the series: *Zhongguo tianye baogao ji* 中國天野報告集 [Chinese fieldwork report collection]: *Kaoguxue juan kan* 考古學專刊 [Archaeology monographs], *dingzhong* 丁 no. 360. Beijing: Wenwu chubanshe 文物出版社.

Zhou Luanshu 周鸾书, ed. 2000. *Qiangu yicun: Liukeng lishi wenhua de kaocha* 千古一村：流坑历史文化的考察 [A 1000-year-old village: A study of Liukeng's historical culture]. Nanchang: Jiangxi renmin chubanshe 江西人民出版社.

Zhou Shaoquan 周紹泉 and Zhao Yaguang 趙亞光, eds. 1993. *Doushan gong jiayi jiaozhu* 竇山公家議校注 [The family comments of the venerable Doushan]. Hefei: Huangshan shushe 黃山書社.

Zhou Wu 周蕪, comp. 1993. *Jinling gu banhua* 金陵古版畫 [Old woodblock prints from Nanjing]. Nanjing: Jiangsu meishu chubanshe 江蘇美術出版社.

Zhou yi Zheng Kangcheng zhu 周易鄭康成注 [The Book of Changes, with commentary, by Zheng Xuan 鄭玄]. 1983–1986. Reduced-size facsimile reproduction of Wenyuan Ge Siku quanshu 文淵閣四庫全書. Taibei: Shangwu yinshuguan 臺灣商務印書館.

Zhu Jiajin 朱家晉. 1986. *Treasures of the Forbidden City*. English edition, Graham Hutt, consultant ed. Harmondsworth: Viking. Originally published as *Guobao* 國寶, 1983.

Zi Jun 紫君 and Xue Mei 雪梅. 1998. *Feichang yinsi* 非常阴私 [Unusually private]. Lanzhou: Qinghai renmin chubanshe 青海人民出版社.

Contributors

Nancy Berliner is Curator of Chinese Art at the Peabody Essex Museum (PEM), Salem, Mass., where she has played a central role in the acquisition, movement, re-erection, preservation, and interpretation of Yin Yu Tang, a Qing dynasty house, as part of PEM's commitment to Asian art and architecture. Her publications include *Yin Yu Tang: The Lives of a Chinese House* (2003); editor of *Beyond the Screen: Chinese Furniture of the 16th and 17th Centuries* (1996); *Friends of the House: Furniture from China's Towns and Villages*, with Sarah Handler (1996); and *Chinese Folk Art: The Small Skills of Carving Insects* (1986).

Maggie Bickford is Professor and Chair of the Department of the History of Art and Architecture and Professor of East Asian Studies at Brown University. Her books include *Ink Plum: The Making of a Chinese Scholar-Painting Genre* (1996), which won the Association for Asian Studies Levenson Book Prize (China before the twentieth century), and *Bones of Jade, Soul of Ice: The Flowering Plum in Chinese Art* (1985). Recently, her research has focused on imperial Song initiatives in painting; the first phase of the research appeared as "Emperor Huizong and the Aesthetic of Agency" in *Archives of Asian Art* (2002–2003). She is working on two book manuscripts: "The Shape of Good Fortune: Auspicious Visuality in China" and "Zhao Mengjian, Qian Xuan, and the Late Song Literati Avant-Garde."

Francesca Bray is Professor of Anthropology at the University of California, Santa Barbara. She has written on the history of agriculture, science, technology, and medicine in China, including *Technology and Gender: Fabrics of Power in Late Imperial China* (1997); *The Rice Economies: Technology and Development in Asian Societies* (1986); and *Science and Civilisation in China,* vol. 2: *Agriculture* (1984). Projects in the pipeline include "The Technics of the Modern American Home" and "Stuff Studies: A Reader."

Myron L. Cohen is Professor of Anthropology and affiliated with the Weatherhead East Asian Institute at Columbia University. Among his books are *House United, House Divided: The Chinese Family in Taiwan* (1976) and *Kinship, Contract, Community and State: Anthropological Perspectives on China* (2004), and he is the editor of *Asia Case Studies in the Social Sciences: A Guide for Teaching* (1992). He has done fieldwork in southern Taiwan and in the Hebei, Shanghai county, and Sichuan regions of China. His current research interests include social and cultural change in China and Taiwan; Chinese family organization, religion, and economic culture; and the historical anthropology of late imperial China.

David Faure is University Lecturer in Modern Chinese History and Fellow, St Antony's College, at the University of Oxford. He has published *The Structure of Chinese Rural Society:*

Lineage and Village in the Eastern New Territories of Hong Kong (1986); *Down to Earth: The Territorial Bond in South China,* co-edited with Helen Siu (1995); *Town and Country in China: Identity and Perception,* co-edited with Tao Tao Liu (2001); *A Documentary History of Hong Kong: Society* (1997); and *A Documentary History of Hong Kong: Economy,* co-edited with Pui-tak Lee (2004). His most recent book is *Colonialism and the Hong Kong Mentality* (2003).

James Flath graduated from the University of British Columbia in 2000 and is now Assistant Professor in History at the University of Western Ontario. He has published *The Cult of Happiness:* Nianhua, *Art and History in Rural North China* (2004), using the popular print form of New Year's pictures *(nianhua)* to explore the culture of rural China. In addition to ongoing research on popular print, his current interests include the historical development and uses of Chinese monuments and museums.

Wen Fong is Emeritus Professor at Princeton University, where he taught Chinese art history from 1954 to 1999. Concurrently, he served for nearly thirty years as a consultant to the Metropolitan Museum of Art, retiring in 2000 as its first Consultative Chairman of the Department of Asian Art. Among his books are *Between Two Cultures: Late-Nineteenth- and Twentieth-Century Chinese Paintings from the Robert H. Ellsworth Collection in the Metropolitan Museum of Art* (2001); *The Embodied Image: Chinese Calligraphy from the John B. Elliott Collection,* co-edited with Robert E. Harrist (1999); *Possessing the Past: Treasures from the National Palace Museum,* with James Watt (1996); and *Beyond Representation: Chinese Painting and Calligraphy 8th–14th Century* (1992).

Puay-peng Ho is Professor of Architecture at the Chinese University of Hong Kong. He was trained and worked as an architect for a number of years and received his Ph.D. from the School of Oriental and African Studies, London University, working on Tang dynasty Buddhist architecture. His books include *Temples of the Empress of Heaven,* with Joseph Bosco (1999); *In the Footsteps of the Buddha,* with Rajeshwari Ghose (1999); *Living Heritage: Vernacular Environment in China,* co-edited with Kai-Yin Lo (1999); and a CD ROM set, *The Tianhou Temple Ritual and Architecture,* with Joseph Bosco (2001). His current research focuses on Chinese vernacular culture and architecture, Chinese Buddhist architecture, and folk religion and architecture.

Nancy Jervis is an anthropologist and Vice President of China Institute in New York City. Her study of a village in Henan spans three decades. Dr. Jervis was a co-organizer of the *House Home Family: Living and Being Chinese* symposium, on which this volume is based.

Ronald G. Knapp is SUNY Distinguished Professor Emeritus in the Department of Geography at the State University of New York at New Paltz, where he taught from 1968 to 2001. Among his books are *Chinese Houses,* with photographs by A. Chester Ong (2005); *China's Old Dwellings* (2000); *China's Walled Cities* (2000); and *China's Living Houses: Folk Beliefs, Symbols, and Household Ornamentation* (1999); he is the editor of *Asia's Old Dwellings: Tradition, Resilience, and Change* (2003). *China's Traditional Rural Architecture: A Cultural Geography of the Common House* (1986) was the first book in English on the subject.

Cary Y. Liu is Curator of Asian Art at the Princeton University Art Museum. A licensed architect and specialist in Chinese art and architectural history, he has publications on architecture and architectural aesthetics, including contributions to *T'oung Pao* (1992), *The Embodied Image: Chinese Calligraphy from the John B. Elliott Collection* (1999), *Arts of the Sung and Yüan: Ritual, Ethnicity, and Style in Painting* (1999), *Oriental Art* (2000), and *Hong Kong University Museum Journal* (2002). He is currently directing the research project and exhibition, "Recarving China's Past: The Art, Archeology, and Architecture of the 'Wu Family Shrines,'" which focuses on a reevaluation of Han dynasty funerary architecture.

Kai-Yin Lo, an independent scholar and designer living in Hong Kong, is a collector of Chinese furniture, Song dynasty white ceramics, and the decorative arts. She organized the landmark exhibition on modern Chinese painter Wu Guanzhong at the British Museum (1992) and a retrospective of twentieth-century Chinese painting (1995–1997), and she guest curated "Living Heritage: Vernacular Environment in China" at the China Institute, New York (2001). She has edited *Classical and Vernacular Furniture in the Living Environment* (1998); *Bright as Silver, White as Snow: Chinese White Ceramics from Late Tang to Song* (1998); and *Living Heritage: Vernacular Environment in China,* co-edited with Puay-peng Ho (1999).

Nancy Shatzman Steinhardt is Professor of East Asian Art at the University of Pennsylvania and Curator of Chinese Art at the University Museum of Archaeology and Anthropology. She received her Ph.D. in Fine Arts at Harvard in 1981. Steinhardt is author of *Chinese Traditional Architecture* (1984); *Chinese Imperial City Planning* (1990); and *Liao Architecture* (1997); editor of *Chinese Architecture* (2002); and co-editor with Victor H. Mair and Paul R. Goldin of *Hawai'i Reader in Traditional Chinese Culture* (2005). She has written more than fifty scholarly articles on the subjects of East Asian art, architecture, and city planning.

Joseph Chuo Wang was educated on three continents and is now Professor of Architecture at Virginia Tech. A native of Suzhou, he has traveled extensively in China and writes about its architecture, gardens, people, and places. His publications include *The Chinese Garden* (1998); *Chinese Classical Gardens of Suzhou* (1993); and articles in professional books and journals.

Yunxiang Yan is Professor of Anthropology at the University of California, Los Angeles. He is the author of *The Flow of Gifts: Reciprocity and Social Networks in a Chinese Village* (1996) and *Private Life under Socialism: Love, Intimacy, and Family Change in a Chinese Village, 1949–1999* (2003). His current research interests include urban consumerism and the impact of cultural globalization on Chinese society.

Index

Wen ("words" and "writing"), xii, **xiv**, 14, 71, 73, 75, 112, 130, **141**, 146, 149, 223

Wen Zhengming (Ming dynasty painter, 1470–1559), 84

Wen Zhenheng (author of *Zhangwuji* [Treatise on superfluous things], 1585–1645), 78, 188

Wenyuan Ge (imperial library hall), Beijing, 143–145, **145**

Wolf, Margery, 226, 273, 278

Women and household space. *See* Gendered space

Woodblock prints, 325–327, 349, 351, 353

Words. See *Wen*

Wu, Nelson, xiii

Wudu (five noxious or poisonous creatures), 134, 340, **340**

Wushi tongtang ("five generations under one roof"), 281

Wuxing (the Five Agents or Five Phases: wood, fire, earth, metal, and water), 105, **106**

Xianqing ouji (*A Temporary Lodge for My Leisure Thoughts* by Li Liweng), 80, 188

Xiao (filial piety), 300–301

Xiao kang zhi jia (contemporary well-off family), 202–203

Xinfang (new room, as well as a newly married couple), 243–244

Xingshi Zong (Configurations School, also called Forms School, of *fengshui*), 102–103, 104–109, **106, 107**

Xinjiang, tent dwellings, **43**

Xiu jiu ru jiu ("repairing old like old"), 216

Yan Yunxiang, 225, 233

Yang, male principle, 101–102. See also *Yin-yang*

Yangzhai (dwelling for the living), 102

Yi Yuan, Suzhou, Jiangsu, 95

Yijing (Book of Change), 146–148, **146**

Yin, female principle, 101–102. See also *Yin-yang*

Yin-yang (complementary opposites), interaction of, 101–102, 356

Yin Yu Tang (restored Huizhou dwelling at Peabody Essex Museum), 220

Yingbi, also *zhaobi* (protective screens), 124, **125**

Yingzao fashi, 189

Yinsi (trendy term for privacy), 390, 394

Yinzhai (an abode for the dead), 102. *See also* Tombs

Yu Lei and Shen Tu. *See* Door Gods

Yuan (inner courts or courtyards formed by adjacent buildings and walls), 47–53

Yuan Cai (Song dynasty author and literatus, fl. 1140–1195), 8–9, 260

Yuan dynasty, **33**

Yuan ye (*Manual of Garden Design* by Ji Cheng), 81–82, 84

Yuanzhai (garden-house), 75

Yuanzi (inner courts or courtyards formed by adjacent buildings and walls), 41–53

Yuchi Gong and Qin Qiong. *See* Door Gods

Yue Fei (hero general of the Southern Song dynasty), 132

Yungmingtang Collection, **182, 184, 186, 198**

Yunnan: houses, **29**, 53; tombs, **23**

Zaojun. *See* Stove God

Zhan Yuan (Ming garden in Nanjing), 89–90

Zhang Tianshi (Heavenly Master, 34–156), **118**, 339–340, **340**

Zhang Zhongyi, 39, **41**

Zhejiang: amulets, **128, 130, 131, 134, 135**; ancestral halls, 313, **313, 314**; furniture, **187, 190**; houses, **45, 46, 65**; lattice, **65, 190**; monasteries, **17**; pagodas, **152**; Stove God, **230**; Tianyi Ge, **145**; villages, **62, 119**

Zhen (calligraphic charms used "to stabilize" a bed, stove, well, chicken coop, etc.), 122–124

Production Notes for Knapp / HOUSE HOME FAMILY
Cover and interior designed by Barbara Pope Book Design
Text in Minion Multiple Master and display type in Frutiger
Printing and binding by SNP Leefung Printers Limited
Printed on 115 gsm matte art paper